The Wild Card of Reading

The Wild Card of Reading
On Paul de Man

Rodolphe Gasché

HARVARD UNIVERSITY PRESS

Cambridge, Massachusetts

London, England

1998

Library of Congress Cataloging-in-Publication Data

Gasché, Rodolphe.
  The wild card of reading : on Paul de Man / Rodolphe Gasché.
   p. cm.
  Includes bibliographical references and index.
  ISBN 0-674-95295-2 (cloth).
  ISBN 0-674-95296-0 (pbk.)
  1. De Man, Paul—Contributions in criticism.
 2. Criticism—History—20th century. I. Title.
 PN75.D45G37 1998
 801'.95'092—dc21 97-42400

Acknowledgments

Some of the chapters of this book, or parts of them, were published previously. "'Setzung' and 'Übersetzung'" first appeared in *diacritics* (Winter 1981). I thank the Johns Hopkins University Press for permission to reproduce this essay. I am also grateful to have permission to reprint "In-Difference to Philosophy," from *Reading de Man Reading*, ed. Lindsay Waters and Wlad Godzich (Minneapolis: The University of Minnesota Press, 1989). A part of Chapter 4 appeared in *Poststrukturalismus: Herausforderung an die Literaturwissenschaft, DFG-Symposium 1995*, ed. Gerhard Neumann (Stuttgart: Verlag J. B. Metzler, 1997, pp. 376–398). I thank Verlag J. B. Metzler for permission to republish this section. A part of the Appendix is reprinted from *Responses: On Paul de Man's Wartime Journalism*, ed. Werner Hamacher, Neil Hertz, and Thomas Keenan, by permission of the University of Nebraska Press, copyright 1989 the University of Nebraska Press.

I am grateful to use materials from *The Rhetoric of Romanticism* by Paul de Man, copyright 1984 by Columbia University Press, reprinted with permission of the publisher. I also thank Yale University Press for granting me permission to quote from Chapters 8 and 9 of *Allegories of Reading* by Paul de Man (New Haven: Yale University Press, 1979). My thanks go to the University of Minnesota Press for permission to use material from Paul de Man, *Aesthetic Ideology*, copyright 1996 by the Regents of the University of Minnesota, as well as from Paul de Man, "Reading and History," which before having been included in Paul de Man, *The Resistance to Theory* (Minneapolis: University of Minnesota Press, 1986), first appeared as the introduction to Hans Robert Jauss, *Toward an Aesthetic of Reception*, copyright 1982 by the University of Minnesota. Many thanks also to *Yale French Studies* for permission to use materials from Paul de Man, "The Resistance to Theory," which first appeared in *Yale French Studies*, 63 (1982). I am grateful to the University of Nebraska

Press as well for permission to use material from Paul de Man, *Wartime Journalism: 1939–1943* (Lincoln, Neb.: University of Nebraska Press, 1989). Acknowledgment is also made to the University of Chicago Press for lines quoted from Jacques Derrida, *Dissemination*, trans. Barbara Johnson, copyright 1981 by the University of Chicago. Finally, I am grateful to Jacques Derrida's English publisher of *Dissemination*, The Athlone Press, for permission to quote from that same work.

I also wish to name Lutz Ellrich, Werner Hamacher, Anselm Haverkamp, and David Wellbery. I am indebted to them for comments, criticism, and suggestions from which this book has benefited greatly. My special thanks go to Michele Sharp for her editorial help in turning the manuscript into a publishable book.

Contents

Abbreviations

AI   *Aesthetic Ideology,* ed. and with an Introduction by A. Warminski (Minneapolis: University of Minnesota Press, 1996)

AR   *Allegories of Reading: Figural Language in Rousseau, Nietzsche, Rilke, and Proust* (New Haven: Yale University Press, 1979)

BI   *Blindness and Insight: Essays in the Rhetoric of Contemporary Criticism,* Introduction by W. Godzich (Minneapolis: University of Minnesota Press, 1983)

D   Jacques Derrida, *Dissemination,* trans. and Introduction by B. Johnson (Chicago: University of Chicago Press, 1981)

RR   *The Rhetoric of Romanticism* (New York: Columbia University Press, 1984)

RT   *The Resistance to Theory,* Foreword by W. Godzich (Minneapolis: University of Minnesota Press, 1986)

The Wild Card of Reading

Introduction

Confessing the inability to understand a subject matter or critical approach that, in principle, concerns one's own field of competence is not exactly an academic virtue. Yet only few, if any, of those who have tried to read the writings of Paul de Man have been spared the experience, at least at first, of near total incomprehension. His prose is dense, opaque to the point of obscurity; the sequence of the arguments is unfathomable; and the relevance of the points made, if one is able to discern them at all, is far from being clear. However, given de Man's prestige in North American academia, few have felt they could actually admit their failure to gain a toehold in de Man's work. And many, to maintain an appearance of authority, have felt obliged to cast judgment on it. However, and not surprisingly, these judgments were rarely made on theoretical grounds, for theoretically questioning the well-foundedness of de Man's position would have required arguments based on some minimal familiarity with de Man's writings. Rather, de Man has been called "morally wrong," "nihilistic," even "outlandish." The 1987 discovery of de Man's wartime writings then provided an unexpected confirmation of what the critics had always already suspected and sanctioned, after the fact, for their intellectually more than dishonest kind of exercise. But whatever this discovery may have proved to those who failed in their first effort to come to grips with de Man's difficult writings, the task to read him remains. In their opaqueness and defying difficulty, de Man's texts precisely call to be read, to be checked for exactly what they advance or perform.[1] However, no mere skimming, no first reading, nor even a second reading, will suffice here.

The difficulty of reading de Man's work stems in part from his singular way of using terminologies that originate in the history of philosophy or literary criticism. These technical terms are often employed without regard for their established definitions and procedural rules, or they

1

become terminologically attached in what Frederic Jameson has called "strategic transcoding" to a whole range of other, utterly unrelated, objects or materials.[2] One is left with a sense of confusion and the suspicion that de Man's language is a private language, exclusively intelligible to its author alone. A second profound difficulty stems from the movement of de Man's arguments, once they have been identified. For, instead of recognized argumentative strategies—be they propositional or not—the reader, more often than not, is faced with elliptical, oddly unelaborated assertions, often in the total absence of even a semblance of development. More often than not, de Man's text seems to string together a number of declarations. The scant reference, if any, to conventional argumentative modes (in even the broadest sense) further disorients the reader and reinforces the suspicion of inconsistency. One is tempted to conclude that de Man's texts are merely the hasty exposition not of clear and distinct insights but of (possibly weighty) intuitions. Finally, an attempt to situate de Man's writings with respect to the problematics and methodologies of the philosophical or critical schools he mentions leads equally to confusion, for one quickly realizes that if these schools and their representatives are mentioned at all, it is merely to put their problematical horizons and methodologies radically into question. One gains little by linking de Man's thought to any particular school or thinker (including Derrida). Even his references to *rhetoric* are of little help in making his work readable for de Man's use of the term deviates considerably from that of the tradition. Indeed, the singular way in which de Man understands *rhetoric,* or, for that matter, *language,* is precisely one of the issues to be elucidated in reading his work. Small wonder, then, if we suspect de Man of wanting to situate his work outside any tradition, of being intent on establishing his own school of thought, a kind of discourse, moreover, that would be the sole representative of its genre.

I first met de Man in Berlin in the early seventies when, at the behest of Peter Szondi, he directed a seminar at the *Institut für Allgemeine und Vergleichende Literaturwissenschaft* on the literary, linguistic, and political aspects of Rousseau's writings. While I immediately came to respect him for his tremendous erudition, as well as for his intellectual and personal generosity—I like to think that the amiable relationship we had from the beginning was due partially to our mutual ties to the Flemish region of Belgium—I began to study his work only much later and out of a sense of perplexity stemming from the fact that many of my friends and colleagues persistently showed great admiration for this body of work whose pertinence escaped me and whose interest diminished in the torture of reading what seemed merely incomprehensible. This book, gathering some essays written in the late seventies and early eighties, but whose main, and interrelated, parts were completed in the summer 1995, represents a continued attempt to come to grips with what I would like to call "de Man's critical idiolect."[3] While some may deem this effort to understand inappropriate, perhaps futile, given what they believe to be the thoroughly unintelligible nature of de Man's writings, or just one more instance of what Friedrich Schleiermacher (before he became the founder of hermeneutics) disparagingly called "the rage, or furor, to understand (*die Wut des Verstehens*)" suffered by those who sought to make sense of religion,[4] I will advance the following remarks in its favor. At the very least, the singular event represented by de Man and his writing compels some response. But, more importantly, I suggest that this work merits a responsible, critical engagement, for any other denies de Man the gift of intelligibility and hence precludes the recognition of just what it is that makes his work so peculiar. Therefore, I argue as well that to demand, because of an unsurpassable radicality of de Man's teaching, a merely mimetic, or quasi-religious, faithfulness to it is a no less irresponsible way of responding to its undeniable singularity. Since the singular nature of de Man's work almost "naturally" invites either wholesale rejection or uncritical celebration, the central thrust of my work has been to determine what precisely sets de Man apart from established terminologies, strategies of argumentation, and critical traditions. Neither philosophical, nor linguistic, nor literary critical in a strict sense, de Man's writings incessantly cross the frontiers of these disciplines, mixing themes and methods originating in them in the oddest way. Therefore, a second concern has been to figure out the principle according to which de Man combined seemingly philosophical, linguistic, and literary motives. In the pursuit of these tasks, it became clear to me that both on the level of strategy and the disposition of the moments to form the "argument," de Man left nothing to chance. I soon began to suspect that many eccentricities of the texts and even sometimes revolting philological inaccuracies obeyed a tight logic and could be meticulously accounted for. What seemed arbitrary, artificial, forced, if not simply wrong, began to reveal its place and reason. I have thus come to respect de Man as a thinker and to value his work for its strictness and flawless inner consistency.

Still, I must add, it is a very singular rigor and one that informs an intellectual project that is no less singular, a project, indeed, as I shall hold, that in its own singular way concerns the singular itself.[5] Needless to say, I will have to ask what kind of rigor it is, on what level it occurs, and what its significance is. But were it not for this rigor, one might, perhaps, be able to dispense with the project entirely. Conversely, this project merits being called "singular" precisely because of the rigor that de Man has brought to it. The rigor in question that makes his work so singular, is, first, that of de Man's syncretic combination of philosophy, linguistics, and literary criticism, in the pursuit of his project. As Friedrich Schlegel has remarked, "Syncretism and eclecticism have to take place by way of *laws*, whether laws of art or instinct; otherwise they don't deserve to be called this way."[6] While eclecticism supposedly disdains the art of combination, syncretism is commonly understood to be an artificial union of ideas of entirely disparate origins and that look compatible only because they are ill understood. But in de Man's case it can be shown that the syncretic combinations of literary, philosophical, and linguistic, or rhetorical motives, rest on a number of presuppositions that uphold them by necessity.

Finally, de Man's work is singular in yet another sense, and it is so to the point of bordering on the idiosyncratic. Here I refer, of course, first of all, to the style and ductus of his writing, its terrible density, its cryptic declarations, lack of elaborations, philological inaccuracies, dismissal of other discourses, and so forth. But let me recall that while the term *idiosyncratic* commonly denotes mere eccentricity, it names first and foremost the characteristic habit (or structure) peculiar to one person only, peculiar to the point of being private and thus at the limit, unintelligible. Etymologically speaking, *idiosyncratic* signifies a personal and distinct way of blending or mixing together. It derives, indeed, from *idio,* meaning "one's own," and *sugkrasis,* "commixture, blending, tempering." But, as Émile Benveniste has demonstrated in his investigations of the Indo-European terms that define the free human being (as distinct from the slave) and, in particular, the individual in his or her personal quality *(idiotes),* that is, nonpublic status, the adjective *idios,* while referring to the notion of the private, to that which is particular to one person only, does not denote an absolute particularity, for the particularity of a given individual is the particularity of a social being confined to him or herself. In other words, the possibility of being oneself in all one's particularity is a function of one's belonging to a social unit. Only within this unit is it possible to be *idios,* and an *idiotes.*[7] What this should alert us to is that however eccentric de Man's enterprise may seem, its idiosyncrasies may have to be accounted for on the basis of the specific methodological and philological traditions, especially those of the North American academic context in which de Man has done most of his writing, and to which these idiosyncrasies represent as many allergic reactions. Further, even though it would be impossible to classify de Man's work, since this would require a rubric limited to a single example, the body of de Man's work is not so very private as to defy all intelligibility. Its idiosyncrasy in no way foils the exhibition of the inexorably stringent necessities that shape it. It might not be inappropriate in this context to evoke, briefly at least, Theodor W. Adorno's notion of the idiosyncratic. As Silvia Bovenschen has noted, Adorno admittedly professed "an idiosyncrasy against the word 'synthesis'." In *Negative Dialectic,* he writes that "idiosyncrasy resists proffering the word synthesis." Bovenschen thus wonders whether "any idiosyncrasy is not also an idiosyncrasy against hasty syntheses, as if *each* idiosyncrasy had this idiosyncrasy against forced unifications and reconciliations for its foundation." And she concludes that for the thinker of the nonidentical to express an idiosyncrasy with regard to synthesis is, of course, not surprising.[8] For a thinker such as de Man who, at least from *Allegories of Reading* on, has systematically denounced all figures of totalization, including that which the systematic denunciation itself of totality may effect, "idiosyncrasy" would seem to be an appropriate epithet. One could also expect such a thinker's mode of denunciation, at all moments of its moves, to manifest the allergies to totalization on a formal and discursive level. However, unlike Adorno, de Man is not so much concerned with the nonidentical. His criticism of totality and totalization, I shall try to show, is conducted in the name of what I shall call the "absolutely singular," that is, a singularity so singular as to defy all relationality—a singularity, hence, that would indeed be idiosyncratic in an absolute sense. As we will see, this emphatic notion of the singular represents the foundation of de Man's understanding of language. One point I make in this book is that de Man must be seen as a thinker of the absolutely singular, the singular that at the limit, and unlike Adorno's nonidentical, rebuffs all attempts at intelligibility. In distinction from the *idiotes,* the idiosyncratic in question is no longer a particularity rooted in a relating (to) self, in something that is also a part of an intelligible whole. Not only does this kind of the idiosyncratic cut all relation to other entities, it refuses to relate to itself as well. In de Man's own words, this idiosyncratic singularity is the radically arbitrary. Nothing can be known of it, according to de Man, not even in negative fashion. But even though this absolute singularity makes up the "center" of de Man's analyses, the analyses themselves, however idiosyncratic, are not for that matter unintelligible themselves. As the readings, hereafter, of certain texts by de Man demonstrate, they progress with implacable and uncompromising stringency, to thwart all temptations at totalization in the name of what eludes all possible cognitive appropriation. The logic of de Man's "deconstructions," whatever its difficulties and eccentricities may be, can be reconstructed. Furthermore, the idea of the "absolutely singular," in the name of which these "deconstructions" are performed, can be philosophically situated and accounted for, even though it is the idea of something that refuses any cognitive comprehension.

Against the claims that de Man's writings, either in style or purported content, are thoroughly incomprehensible, and hence ethically or politically culpable, or the evidence itself, and hence no longer in need of interrogation but tirelessly to be imitated, this book seeks to do justice to de Man's writings by concentrating on the immanent logic put to work in the so singular theoretical or philosophical position it represents. Even though de Man's writings aim at exhibiting the workings of something ultimately withstanding all intelligibility, the difficulties and idiosyncrasies of his texts are not an obstacle to accounting for this singular project. But exhibiting the implacable close reasoning of de Man's readings, and the sternness with which the extreme conception of an absolutely absolute singularity orients these readings, does not necessarily condone his practice of reading or the position he takes. Even though his odd notion of an absolutely irreducible singularity can be construed as taking up the venerable philosophical question of singularity, de Man's answer to this question does not have to be taken for granted. To recognize the consistent conception behind all his readings, and the unyielding precision in its pursuit, is the minimal respect one owes to an intellectual project of such stature as de Man's. It is also to recognize that his is a project one cannot ignore. Precisely because of the oddness of its leading conception, the fact that it stages a canonical question and that, moreover, this staging is executed with redoubtable virtuosity demand that it be addressed. But only by first establishing the strengths and the strong points of de Man's work—strengths that largely explain the idiosyncrasies of his writings, including what seem to be blatant, all too blatant mistakes—is it possible, and legitimate, to express some reserves.

The chapters of this book seek to clarify a variety of issues that arise from a confrontation with de Man's work—for example, what he understands by language; the distinction between metaphor and allegory; to what extent his notion of the performative is tributary to Speech Act Theory; how we are to take his notion of materiality and its distinction from phenomenality; and what he means by *deconstruction*. But all these issues—several of which I take up more than one time in an effort to rethink them and thus tighten my grasp of them—are thematized in an effort to elucidate de Man's conception of reading and to elaborate a reading's immanent logic.

At one point, in *The Resistence to Theory*, de Man, after having described literary theory's nonphilosophical origin and its constitutive, but subversive, "pragmatic moment," likens it to "something of a wild card in the serious game of the theoretical disciplines" (*RT*, 8). Let's bear in mind that literary theory, or theory for short, in that essay, but elsewhere as well, is the theory of the rhetorical, or tropological, dimension of language, a dimension that can be adequately coped with only in and through reading. The theory of reading, or simply (rhetorical) reading, is the wild card in question. Yet what is a wild card? In a card game the wild card is the card able to represent any card designated by the holder, or the highest-ranking card. The joker—the descendent of the fool, and one of the twenty-two unnumbered wild cards in the atouts or trumps in the tarot deck—can be a wild card in card games. However, under certain circumstances, the joker is merely an odd card, carrying no value whatsoever, and hence not wild. Let me also note that when more than one card is wild, as in wild-card games, or Joker Wild, the amount of skill required to play diminishes in proportion to the extra jokers added to the standard deck since chance, and not strategy, becomes the determining factor in these games. Because it carries a value to be determined by the player, a wild card is also a device or expedient for getting the better of or tricking another. If only one wild card is played, the tricking occurs within certain rules; yet, if more than one card is wild, only chance prevails.[9] What, then, are the implications of calling literary theory, or reading, for short, a "wild card"? As the context in which the comparison is made suggests, literary theory, or reading, undermines the serious game of the theoretical disciplines, of philosophy first and foremost. As de Man suggests, reading, at the hands of the player who holds its card, can unexpectedly outwit the theoretical disciplines' game. With it in hand, one can override the rules that govern these disciplines. Reading can substitute itself for all these disciplines and, as the highest card, definitely win on all occasions. What this card subverts is nothing less than the seriousness of the game of the disciplines, that is to say, their cognitive, ethical, or theological import. Whoever reads plays the master trump, wins them all. No truth claim holds up to such a card. To play the wild card of reading is to remain irrefutable.

Any attempt to specifically assess what de Man means by reading cannot also forgo a confrontation with "reading" in the writings of Jacques Derrida. It is certainly not insignificant to remark that in the context of one of the few essays that Derrida has devoted to the question of reading—"Plato's Pharmacy," which I discuss at some length in Chapter 5—Derrida also evokes the wild card. However, the wild card is mentioned here with respect to Theuth, the god of writing. Following an exposition of the god of writing's major characteristics and of the relations of this figure to its other, Derrida writes: "He cannot be assigned a fixed spot in the play of differences. Sly, slippery, and masked, an intriguer and a card, like Hermes, he is neither king nor jack, but rather a sort of *joker,* a floating signifier, a wild card, one who puts play into play *(une carte neutre, donnant du jeu au jeu)* (D, 93). Let me briefly card apart the differences between de Man's wild card and Derrida's. The difference is not only that one refers to reading and the other to writing. If Theuth is compared to a wild card, it is because he is seen by Derrida to open up the differential space, and the play of differences. Theuth, Derrida contends, is "a god of the absolute passage between opposites"; in other words, he both radically opens and, at the same time, makes the differences communicate among one another. More precisely, he represents the matrix of undecidability—what Derrrida shall term the *pharmakon*—within which metaphysics decides about its constitutive oppositions. As my analysis of Derrida's text will demonstrate, writing for Derrida does not foil Platonism and its conceptual polarities. If Theuth is a wild card, it is only insofar as he puts play into the play of metaphysics, in other words, insofar as he represents the nonfixable, and undecideable, medium without which no opposition is thinkable. Now, as will be shown in my account of "Plato's Pharmacy," reading, for Derrida, focuses in on Theuth, on writing, the *pharmakon*—on the wild card, in short—not in order to demonstrate that all theoretical disciplines, including philosophy, fail in establishing truth, but to show to what extent the very possibility of their truth is opened by the wild card of writing and its undecideable play. To read, then, for Derrida, is not to debunk truth but to weave another thread into the Platonic text in which truth is established, a thread by means of which he seeks to come to an understanding with Plato. De Man's wild card of reading, on the other hand, gives no understanding at all and makes Derrida look like a real epistemophilist.

Essentially, what this comparison between the two references to a "wild card" suggests is that while the wild card of writing opens the space of decideability and differential opposition, a space that reading, in a Derridean sense, brings into focus in order to render the Platonic text intelligible to begin with, the wild card of reading, as de Man understands it, exhibits the illusory nature of all comprehension. While the Derridean reading also questions understanding to the extent that it shows understanding to depend for its possibility on the medium of undecideability of writing, or the *pharmakon,* de Man's theory of reading is considerably more radical. Its concern is not with the limits of understanding—limits being also that within which, or from which, something becomes possible—but the possibility of understanding altogether. Reading, indeed, is out to prove that any effort to understand is vain, illusory, self-defeating. But, does such intransigency not come with a stiff price? At what cost can such ultraskeptical radicality be achieved? At what expense is the proclaimed irrefutability of this position to be gained? Does it not meet a delusion of its own? These are some of the questions that cannot be avoided, precisely in the wake of an analysis of the immanent logic of de Man's notion of reading as exemplified by his treatment of philosophical and literary texts. They impose themselves inevitably as a result of a first series of problems that come to the fore at the very moment one inquires into the linguistic and philosophical presuppositions of what de Man terms "reading," and again as one tracks down, step by step, the logic that governs a concrete reading performance. What, indeed, is the plane on which a rhetorical reading proceeds? If language is separated as radically from the phenomenal as de Man contends, the language he speaks about, has, of course, little resemblance to the language of linguistics or philosophy.[10] Might the level of this something called "language" be so abstract as to border on the irrelevant? Bluntly put, if language does not relate to the phenomenal—or even to itself, as we shall see—why be concerned with it all? Finally, given that for de Man language disrupts understanding in that it interrupts the correspondence between the linguistic and the phenomenal, one cannot but wonder whether the kind of subtle, and often infinitesimal, contradictions, disruptions, and dissymmetries that reading discerns in texts to which de Man ascribes an epistemological intention affects epistemology at all. Does the assumption that the dissymmetries in question effectively subvert all effort at understanding not also reveal an inadequate, extremely exaggerated, expectation of what, indeed, epistemology is to achieve? Hence, if it should be the case that de Man's radicality can be upheld only on condition that what he calls "language" is, in principle, entirely severed from the phenomenal, including language's own phenomenality, and is hence a domain entirely of its own, immanent to itself without, however, relating to itself, the disruptions that it performs in the world and in worldly language would be without consequence. The price tag for an ultraradicality such as de Man's would then possibly imply forgoing any intervention in the world and its language.

But let me not hasten to a conclusion. To provoke questions such as those just formulated speaks to an intellectual enterprise of an undoubtedly very peculiar nature. Wlad Godzich, recalling his first reading experiences of de Man, evokes his impression at the time "of a thought in search of itself, so much at odds with the prevalent self-satisfaction of most traditional criticism and with the incipient dogmatism of the newer one."[11] It has been, and has remained, a thought so uncompromising in its demands and its own inner consistency, that it has systematically endured in setting itself apart, thus achieving a singularity that has no like. If de Man's work is odd, it is so because it is at odds with all critical disciplines past and present. De Man undertook it to carve out for himself a "position" that not only resembled no other but that even dared renouncing the semblance of a position. Undoubtedly, the price paid for establishing a radicality of questioning as is found in de Man's work has been high. But to have played the wild card of reading and, indeed, to successfully have won the game of finding, if not founding, a singularity entirely apart, one so peculiar as to put to risk any bearing on the prevailing discourses of the disciplines, cannot but disturb those discourses. What kind of certainty—that is, of course, the sort of certainty that is answerable and that alone merits the name—can claim not to be worried by such an achievement?

"Setzung" and "Übersetzung"

The Total Speech Act

Why is it that literary criticism in recent years has been increasingly taken with Speech Act Theory? What explains this paradoxical fascination with a philosophical doctrine that, in the elaboration of its theory since J. L. Austin, has excluded literary discourse as a nonserious and parasitical use of language? The question is all the more pertinent because this exclusion has never been revoked by the leading figures of this doctrine, least of all by John R. Searle who concludes his essay "The Logical Status of Fictional Discourse" by admitting that "there is as yet no general theory of the mechanisms by which . . . serious illocutionary intentions are conveyed by pretended illocutions."[1] But, if literary theory's flirtation with Speech Act Theory is here put into question, it is especially because Speech Act Theory de jure pertains only to so-called normal acts of speech, i.e., to the ordinary ritual, ceremonial, and conventional uses of language. Since the exclusion of everything "which falls under the *etiolations* of language," as Austin most forcefully expressed himself, is constitutive of the very object of Speech Act Theory—ordinary language—as well as of the content of this theory, the results of this doctrine cannot simply be applied again to what first had to be excluded in order to make that theory possible. Speech Act Theory as it stands applies only to normal acts of speech and not to a use of language that "is parasitic upon its normal use" and in which the healthy, active, male vigor of language is drained or etiolated.[2] Because of the nature of what has to be excluded from the object of Speech Act Theory, its inapplicability to literary language is not simply provisional or a temporary defect that could one day successfully be overcome. They are ills "which infect *all* utterances," which Austin keeps isolated from the thus idealized and normative object of his theory, from ordinary language.[3] However, since these ills that can affect all utterances are consequently *structurally* necessary *possibilities* without which utterances would not be what they are, one cannot, as Derrida has argued, legitimately exclude them from their study.[4] Once one has excluded them, one has created an aberrant object to which nothing corresponds and from which not only no way leads to what was eliminated but which also excludes the possibility of such a return as a senseless undertaking. The only possible return to the rejected, say, to literary language, implies a radical critique of the very idea of "ordinary" language, of the "normal" use of speech, and, thus, of the Speech Act Theory developed upon that fictive object.

Has literary criticism, then, once more been led by its own notorious philosophical naïveté to accommodate within its domain a doctrine fundamentally alien to the object of literary studies? In order to draft the outline of an answer to this question, it will be necessary, in what follows, to determine first what that "revolution in philosophy" consists of—"the greatest and most salutary in its history," of which Austin pretends to be the decisive instigator.[5] It is undoubtedly a revolution that is supposed to affect analytical philosophy, i.e., a philosophy which, according to Austin, is characterized by its logical aberrations. Austin's revolution in philosophy consists in restoring, through a gesture reminiscent of an empiricist inversion of Platonism, the priority of real life over the abstract logical situation, and in demonstrating that the assumption by analytical philosophers that the business of language is to make statements upon facts depends on an illicit abstraction of the constative function of language from the total speech act situation. With this insight, Austin is able to show that a constative utterance is subject to more outrages than mere logical contradiction and that considerations of felicity and infelicity also affect the criteria governing the truth or falsity of statements. Since from the perspective of the total speech act, a statement, an intentional act, and an act of referring are all acts of issuing utterances in speech situations, they are liable to every kind of infelicity to which other acts are also liable. The revolution in question is thus an attempt to reinscribe the linguistic functions of stating, denominating, describing, referring, etc., within the situation of the performance of those functions. This total situation of the speech act determines itself as a performative act, itself no longer referential but which can include within itself, as part of itself, an act of reference. The emphasis on the performative, on the locutionary act as no longer referential, but as possibly inscribing a referential act within itself—an emphasis that undoubtedly attracted the literary critic's attention to the theory of speech acts—is, however, only the first characteristic of the Austinean revolution. It is a revolution in the logical representationalism of analytical philosophy that now becomes reinscribed and determined by the more fundamental pragmatics of the linguistic act itself. The new analysis that begins with Austin has thus become conscious of the difference between what is *stated* and is *implied,* between the function of stating and showing in the utterance of sentences.

The second aspect of Austin's revolution is intimately connected with the first since it is linked to the introduction of the idea of what is called the "*total* speech act." "The total speech act in the total speech situation is the *only actual* phenomenon, which, in the last resort, we are engaged in elucidating," writes Austin.[6] Two characteristics of the total speech act require our attention here, as follows.

(a) Toward the end of the first half of *How to Do Things with Words,* Austin (still trying to find a criterion that would rigorously distinguish constatives from performatives) explains why he favored examples of performatives in the first-person singular, present indicative active: "The 'I' who is doing the action does thus come essentially into the picture. An advantage of the original first person singular active form . . . is that this implicit feature of the speech-situation is made *explicit.*"[7]

This feature is thus constitutive of the speech act as such. A speech act is characterized by its utterance by a subject in the first-person singular and in the form of the present indicative active. This implicit feature of all speech acts possesses, as Austin stresses, a very peculiar and special status: "In particular we must notice that there is an asymmetry of a systematic kind between it and other persons and tenses of the *very same* verb. The fact is, *this* asymmetry is precisely the mark of the performative verb."[8] In short, then, the mark of a total speech act is that it is being enacted by a subject fully present to itself. That what constitutes the *act* of the speech act, what makes this act a *total* act, is its utterance by a self-present, although not necessarily explicit, 'I'.

Austin opposes these explicit performatives to the primary performatives. Austin calls them "primary" rather than "implicit" because his ontological determination of the speech act is immediately paralleled by a historical determination. "Historically, from the point of view of the evolution of language, the explicit performative must be a later development than certain more primary utterances, many of which at least are already implicity performatives."[9]

For Austin, then, the evolution of language represents the development, the unfolding, of what is already implicitly contained in the original primary performatives but which still "preserves the 'ambiguity' or 'equivocation' or 'vagueness' of primitive language."[10] The history of language is in effect the process of making explicit what one was in fact doing when uttering a speech act. It is "to make plain how the action is to be taken or understood, what action it is."[11] This takes place by explicitly distinguishing the different *forces* already contained in the primary utterance. Austin develops this theory of the history of language in order to confront what he terms the "dangerous and erroneous view of the (analytical) philosophers," according to whom, "the primary or primitive use of sentences must be, because it ought to be, statemental or constative." And he adds: "It seems much more likely that the 'pure' statement is a goal, an ideal, toward which the gradual development of science has given the impetus, as it has likewise also toward the goal of precision."[12]

According to this ontological and, moreover, historical determination of the total speech act, the explicit performative formula, i.e., the formula in which the utterance of the speech act is named in the first-person singular present indicative active, is likewise "only the last and most successful of numerous speech-devices."[13] The becoming explicit of the 'I' as the utterer of a speech act is indeed the telos of Austin's history of language.

This ontological and historical determination of the total speech act says a great deal about how the total act of speech, the performative, is to be understood. Insofar as it is the act of a structurally asymmetric person, voice, and tense, of a subject consequently that, unlike other subjects, is determined by absolute presence to itself, it is an *absolute act* or *pure doing*. Before this act comes to mean anything particular, before this act becomes subject to rules that will lay out what the action is, it is meaningful as such, as the act itself. Austin remarks that though an utterance may be void or without effect, "this does not mean, of course, to say that we won't have done anything: lots of things will have been done."[14] What the act communicates is, first of all, itself as act. It is a fully present act of a self-asserting subject that is fully present to itself. For language in general this means that all its achievements (like stating, communicating, meaning, etc.) are only secondary and hinge on the active performance of the speech act by a self-present, and historically prior, subject.

(b) The second half of *How to Do Things with Words* proceeds to determine the full act of speech as an illocutionary act. Indeed, although Austin distinguishes three ways in which a speech act is an act (the locutionary, the illocutionary, and the perlocutionary), he attributes a special privilege to the illocutionary in his determination of the very action of the speech act. The reason that Austin favors the illocutionary over the two other modes of speech acts is first historical and contextual in nature: "There is a constant tendency in philosophy to elide this in favor of one or other of the other two," he writes.[15] But there are systematic reasons as well for this priority. Understanding these last reasons means coming to grips with Austin's revolution in philosophy. Let us first of all remark that the exclusion of the perlocutionary from the center of Austin's investigation of the real nature of the speech act stresses the exclusively verbal nature of the act of the speech act. It follows from this that the primary preoccupation with illocutionary acts serves to determine the speech act as an act *within spoken language* since the illocutionary is said to perform an act *in* saying something. The illocutionary is a speech act *within* the act of language and is thus supposed to be representative of the total speech act.

Austin admits that the notion of act as it appears in the three acts of speech is still unclear and has to be met "by the general doctrine about action." Austin will not deliver such a general theory about action in *How to Do Things with Words*. Yet, by privileging, in his analysis, the illocutionary act as an act *within* language, Austin implicitly reveals the fundamentals of such a general theory. Not only does Austin favor the illocutionary act in his attempt to define the nature of the total speech act, he also recognizes a *"natural break"* between the illocutionary act and its consequences, a break that is missing in the case of physical acts which are *"in pari materia* with at least many of . . . [their] immediate and natural consequences."[16] All this only adds to the consolidation of the speech act as essentially a nonphysical act of language affecting itself. To perform an illocutionary act is to perform an act *in* saying something.

The illocutionary force indicators that make a speech act an act are indicators that come to reflect within the act of speech the conditions, implications, presuppositions, circumstances, etc., of this very act. If the illocutionary act is to be representative of the total speech act, then it must be said that Austin understands the act as essentially an involuted one, an act of language folding back upon itself.

If in saying what I was doing is saying something, I perform an illocutionary act, then that act is basically an act by which language comes to reflect upon itself. Austin's revolution thus consists of the reintroduction of the notion of self-reflection and self-referentiality into the analytical discourse that had completely eliminated this dimension of language from its considerations. From the perspective of analytical philosophy, Austin's move is undoubtedly a revolution. To the contemporary reader, however, or to a reader familiar with the development of continental philosophy, this revolution must be suspect for many reasons, not only because it is, interestingly enough, a revolution in terms of self-reflection, but also because of the amazing lack of historical comprehension, a lack that ordinary language philosophy shows when it speaks of a "revolution."[17] That Austin does not employ the philosophical terminology of reflexivity to describe his so-called revolution is only one sign of this lack. However, literary critics, who in the aftermath of New Criticism have rediscovered the romantic idea of the self-reflexivity of the inner form of the work of art, have immediately recognized the relation of the Speech Act Theory to the problematics of reflexivity. This, then, also explains why the Speech Act Theory could exert the influence on literary criticism we have referred to. Linguistics conscious of philosophical traditions like Émile Benveniste, or more recently philosophers like François Récanati, have never doubted that what Austin's revolution reintroduces into the philosophy of language was nothing more and nothing less than the classical problem of the reflexivity of language.

Benveniste, in his article entitled "La philosophie analytique et le language," after having identified the performative utterance as an act that has the property of always being a unique event, since it is an act of authority by a subject possessing that qualification, writes:

> Since the performative is effectively uttered within conditions that make it an act, this leads to recognizing that the performative possesses the particular property of being *self-referential,* or referring to a reality

which it constitutes itself. This implies that it is simultaneously a linguistic manifestation, since it needs to be uttered, and a fact of reality insofar as it is the accomplishment of an act. The act is thus identical to the utterance of the act. . . . An utterance which becomes its own referent is self-referential.[18]

Indeed, the two moments that contribute to Austin's revolution in philosophy, the subject-character of the speech act and its determination as an act within the act of language, determine the performative as a self-reflexive or self-referential act. "An utterance is performative," writes Benveniste, "insofar as it *denominates* the performed act . . . A performative utterance must name the performance of speech as well as the performer."[19] Both conditions are fulfilled by the speech act's self-reflexivity.

Récanati in *La transparence et l'énonciation*, after having retraced the Austinean problematics back to the determination of the linguistic sign in the philosophy of Port-Royal, and ultimately to Descartes, has been able to demonstrate that Austin's revolution is in fact a return to the problems of enunciation debated in classical philosophy. Indeed, if in the total speech act the illocutionary force indicator, i.e., the reflexive indicator, signifies that an utterance signifies, before signifying what it signifies, and if this recognition of the *factum* of signification is the condition of possibility for the recognition of the *dictum* of the utterance, then the performative prefix of the utterance is analogous to the cartesian *cogito* that must accompany all *cogitationes*. The reflection that an utterance makes upon itself is the very condition of that utterance's possibility of referring. Moreover:

> An idea is only a sign of its object if it represents this object as an object of representation different from representation itself. The idea must represent its object as different from the idea, and, consequently, the idea must be reflected in the representation which it undertakes of the object. It must be different from the object represented in this way. The necessary difference between what serves to represent and what is represented must be reflected in representation itself.[20]

An utterance achieves the difference necessary to its referring function by reflecting upon the *factum* of its utterance. Since there is no referring function without such a self-reflection of the act of enunciation, this self-reflexivity appears to be the very essence of the total speech act. And it is indeed Austin's achievement to have reminded the logicians of analytical philosophy of the classical problem of the sign, and thus of the conditions of possibility, of enunciation. The generalization of the performative in the second part of *How to Do Things with Words* is, then, a generalization of reflexivity, a generalization which intrinsically determines what Austin understood by his notion of a total speech act, as well as by his notion of the act as such.

Literary criticism's temptation for Speech Act Theory must thus be explained by this theory's concern with reinscribing operations like stating, referring, or describing back into the total speech act and depriving them, in this manner, of their hitherto "unique position over the matter of being related to facts in a unique way called being true or false."[21] But above all, literary criticism has been fascinated with Speech Act Theory because of the role it lends to the voice of the utterer and because of its recognition of the necessarily self-reflexive nature of the linguistic act as a whole. But what literary criticism forgets is that the particular rules set up by this theory pertain only to the analysis of ordinary language, i.e., to a purely theoretical construct and ideal object that precludes all fictional use of language—and that this exclusion can be canceled only at the price of annulling the rules and distinctions set forth by this theory.

Detotalizing Translations

But what about a work like Paul de Man's *Allegories of Reading* that seems to rely heavily on the terminology developed by Austin? Is it an attempt to apply the categories of Speech Act Theory to the literary text? And is de Man's work then prey to the same philosophical naïveté of which literary criticism was accused in the previous section? To answer these questions, it will be necessary first to try to assess the project of *Allegories of Reading*. From the outset let us, however, underline some of the difficulties that any reading of this work encounters. Apart from the complex and involuted movements of the essays collected in *Allegories of Reading*, any attempt, like this one, to outline the theoretical parameters they have in common not only encounters the difficulty and the richness of these essays but finds obstacles of a more fundamental nature. These obstacles are consequent upon the status of the leading concepts of de Man's critical enterprise because the way in which they regulate his analysis excludes a rigorous development of a *unified* theory that would underlie all the essays of de Man's work. Indeed, the rigor of de Man's critical endeavor manifests itself in precisely the subversion of what may be misunderstood as a series of key terms. How does this blurring of the theoretical concepts of *Allegories of Reading* come into effect? As will soon become clear, de Man subjects his theoretical apparatus to the results of his analyses so that all his leading concepts become temporalized in a narrative scheme. Or, to put it differently, all of de Man's concepts are allegorized, the concept of allegory being no exception. For this reason it appears structurally impossible to make de Man's theoretical enterprise close upon itself.

Allegories of Reading sets out as an attempt to overcome the traditional antithesis characteristic of the business of literary criticism, the antithesis of referentialism and formalism, as it figures, in particular, in the opposition between traditional criticism and New Criticism. "Rhetorical reading" is the name for an approach intended to unlock the rigid opposition between referentialism and formalism, between realism and criticism centered around the self-reflexivity of the literary form, between thematic and aesthetic criticism. What is a rhetorical reading? It certainly is not an attempt to classify the tropes distinguished by classical rhetoric, which are to be found in literary works. Nor is it simply a reading of the effects of persuasion produced by literary language as an active performance touching the reader. What de Man names "rhetoric" "is precisely the gap that becomes apparent in the pedagogical and philosophical history of the term," i.e., between rhetoric as a system of tropes and rhetoric as persuasion (*AR*, p. 131). "Rhetoric is a disruptive intertwining of trope and persuasion or—which is not quite the same thing—of cognitive and performative language," writes de Man (*AR*, p. ix). In this section, we will try to carefully determine rhetoric as such a disruptive intertwining of trope and persuasion, leaving the discussion of rhetoric as a disruptive, intertwining of cognitive and performative language to the next.

The essay "Semiology and Rhetoric" first determines the rhetorical as that figural potentiality of language that in a text suspends the possibility of deciding whether its grammatical structure conveys literal or figural meaning, proper meaning or the improper meaning of the tropes of classical or semiological rhetoric. In other words, the rhetorical on which a rhetorical reading of texts rests is what causes a text to remain suspended between the claim to univocity, referentiality, truth, logicality, etc., and *what* from the perspective of traditional philosophy and literary criticism appears secondary and derived, i.e., the tropes and figures of speech as classified by traditional rhetoric. Since the rhetorical is what simultaneously invalidates a grammatical or logical reading of texts *and* a reading according to which a text would feature only a figural meaning, a rhetorical reading necessarily presupposes a "rhetorical model of the trope" as much as the subjection of both the grammatical or logical and the figural dimensions of texts to rhetorical structures. How is the rhetorical model of the trope different from the trope of classical rhetoric and from the concept regulating philosophical discourse or the discourse of literary criticism? Because a rhetorical reading of a text proceeds by demonstrating that (a) the figural potential of language is disruptive of grammatical univocity and conversely that (b) the grammatical or conceptual rigor of texts is disruptive of what de Man calls "rhetorical mystifications," the rhetorical model of the trope appears as the figure of disruption of both the classical trope and the concept of logic. It is this gap, "the aporia between trope and persuasion," between trope and concept, that the rhetorical model of the trope comes to "bridge." Yet, before investigating the precise nature of this "bridging," we must clarify first *what* the rhetorical model of the trope disrupts, or, more accurately, *why* the trope of traditional rhetoric and the concept of logic *can* be disrupted. Rhetorical mystifications, as well as the effects of the concept, are the result of the totalizing function of these instances. The trope of rhetoric and the concept both serve to totalize, to subjugate, to synthesize. Both grammatical univocity (the concept, the referent, the value, etc.) and the trope of rhetoric (the figure of speech, the image, etc.) are constitutive of the same metaphysical valorizations. A rhetorical reading, then, sets out to explore the mechanics of grammar as well as of traditional rhetoric, the machinery that produces the effects of univocity and totality. In the case of the trope of rhetoric, its totalizing effect is dependent on the mechanics of the impersonal imprecision of grammar. On the other hand, the trope of rhetoric appears to be constitutive of grammatical univocity, of the subsuming and totalizing function of the concept of logic. Three things can already be established at this point: (a) Since a rhetorical reading is an investigation into the mechanics of totalization of both the image and the concept, it will try to account for both the possibility and the ultimate impossibility of the effect of totalization; (b) since it tries to determine "the rhetorical patterns that organize the distribution and the movement of key terms [in literary texts] . . . contending that questions of valorization can be relevantly considered only after the rhetorical status of the text has been clarified," a rhetorical reading leaves the fallacies of traditional oppositions (for example, the "literary," the "philosophical," the "political") behind "by accounting, at least to some degree, for their predictable occurrence" (*AR*, p. 258); (c) since the rhetorical reading aims at debunking the totalizing function of trope and concept, far from having the pretension of being itself a totalizing reading, it is also systematically suspicious of everything that would turn it again into a totalizing approach, such as thematic or aesthetic readings.

It would be too time-consuming to review the mechanics of totalization in all the various instances specified by de Man: the concept, judgment, the self, identity, genetic totality, images of self-reflection, specular figures, etc. In contesting what he calls "the authority of metaphorical systems" (*AR*, p. 239), de Man demonstrates that by bridging oppositions, by setting up "seductive similarities where they do not exist" (*AR*, p. 239), by performing "analogical, metaphorical substitutions" (*AR*, p. 122), etc., all these instances produce rhetorical mystifications or "aberrant totalizations" (*AR*, p. 237). All these operations share something that is characteristic of the metaphoric process. And, indeed, metaphor, for de Man, is the totalizing instance *par excellence*.[22] Metaphor is to be understood here according to its classical definition, as it appears in theories of rhetoric from Aristotle to Roman Jakobson, as "an exchange or substitution of properties on the basis of resemblance" (*AR*, p. 146). Yet the resemblance that seems to have been "made possible by a proximity or an analogy so close and intimate that it allows the one to substitute for the other without revealing the difference necessarily introduced by the substitution" (*AR*, p. 62) is not only a foreclosure of this ineluctable difference, it is in addition and, in particular, a "way to disguise difference" (*AR*, p. 16) between the poles of the metaphoric exchange. In this leveling of differences, metaphor proceeds by subjugation of difference as such—hence the totalizing—and in fact conceptualizing—power characteristic of "the totalizing stability of metaphorical processes" (*AR*, p. 63). Metaphor, by instauring totalities in this manner, "can be thought of as a language of desire and as a means to recover what is absent" (*AR*, p. 47). This definition of *metaphor,* according to which the exchange or substitution of properties on the basis of resemblance takes place in order to secure totalizations, syntheses, conceptual subjections, etc., implies an understanding of metaphor in terms of "metaphorical synechdo-che." Indeed, a metaphor presupposes, when it substitutes one property for another on the basis of resemblance, a "necessary link," or an "or-ganic link," between the poles of exchange. Because they are thought to be similar, all the interchangeable terms become parts of one whole. All metaphorical systems are totalities precisely because the positing of re-semblance between the terms erases their difference and thus raises them to the status of exchangeable parts of a whole. Since the relationship that exists between parts is one of mutual resemblance and since this resem-blance binds them necessarily into a whole, the relation in question is organic, a link, as de Man argues, that is endowed with attributes of naturalness. This, consequently, allows the principle of metaphorical to-talization itself to be equated with a natural process—hence the alleged superiority of metaphor over metonymy, of the grammatical over the rhetorical, of the philosophical over the literary, etc.

The rhetorical reading that de Man presents is thus a reading which traces the numerous totalizing mystifications of philosophy and literary criticism, of thematic and aesthetic criticism, back to their ultimate source: the figure of metaphor.[23] But how does a rhetorical reading itself avoid falling prey to the gesture and the temptation of totalization? Let us recall that a rhetorical reading is *first and foremost* a reading that shows how the grammatical, conceptual, thematic totalizations of a text are being *deconstructed* by the images, the tropes, the rhetoric of the text.

Before pursuing this point, it is necessary to remark from the outset that while de Man admits in the preface to *Allegories of Reading* to have borrowed the term "deconstruction" from the work of Derrida, he uses this term in an altogether different way than Derrida. Indeed, if one does not pay attention to this difference, one runs the risk of missing the originality of de Man's use of this term, as well as those moments where Derrida's and de Man's work border upon each other. For the moment, suffice it to say that de Man differs from Derrida where he applies the notion of deconstruction and that his work is perhaps closer to Derrida where this philosopher's name is not mentioned at all. In order to clarify some of these seemingly enigmatic points, let us also focus in what follows on the technicalities of the procedure of deconstruction as used by de Man.

A rhetorical reading provides an insight into the mechanics of the the-matic strata of a text and thus deconstructs, as de Man says, the totalizations characteristic of those strata. With this deconstruction, texts become, in de Man's words, "unreadable." If *to read* is to understand a text and if *to understand* means thematically, aesthetically, or conceptually to totalize a text, then the production of insights into the mechanics of the text will certainly render that text opaque and unreadable. But the answer to the question of whether such a rhetorical reading that folds the text back upon itself is not just another totalizing gesture through which the unreadability of a text becomes readable again shows that a rhetorical reading does not yet come to a rest with the demystification of the thematic and conceptual metaphorizations. Undoubtedly, as soon as the rhetorical structure of a poem or piece of literature has served to debunk the mystifications specific to the thematic level of the text, it turns immediately into a new unifying principle. The totality that it confers upon the text is no longer one rooted in *logos* but a totality rooted in *lexis* (*AR*, p. 45). Consequently, *to deconstruct* does not simply mean to escape the possibility of error and illusion distinctive of literature in general. Discussing the deconstruction of self in *On Lie and Truth*, de Man argues that to prove that the self is a metaphor only raises the lie to "a new figural power, but it is nonetheless a lie. By asserting in the mode of truth that the self is a lie, we have not escaped from deception. We have merely reversed the usual scheme which derives truth from the convergence of self and the other by showing that the fiction of such a convergence is used to allow for the illusion of self-hood to originate" (*AR*, p. 112). Through the deconstruction of a rhetorical mode like the self, "we may have changed the rhetorical mode, but we certainly have not escaped from rhetoric" (*AR*, p. 113). Not only does the deconstruction of the self remain deceptive, it may even become the very recuperation of subjectivity and of self-affirmation. "Within the epistemological labyrinth of figural structures, the recuperation of self-hood . . . [can] be accomplished by the rigor with which the discourse deconstructs the very notion of the self" (*AR*, p. 173). Through a dialectical reversal, the authority of the self may be transferred to the authority of interpretation or of deconstruction. When de Man notes that the transformation by the hermeneutical process of "the total insignificance, the nothingness of the self into a new center of meaning is a very familiar gesture in contemporary thought, the ground of what is abusively called modernity," it is obvious that he has as much the performances of so-called deconstructive criticism in mind as the hermeneutics of Heidegger and Ricoeur, which are referred to in the context (*AR*, pp. 173–174). The very rigor with which the rhetorical is opposed to the grammatical, and by means of which the thematic levels of a text are being deconstructed, leads to a reassertion of values that are as deceptive as those deconstructed. Thus, for instance, the debunked referentiality of a text reappears as the self-referentiality of the deconstructive reading. The reason that this return cannot be prevented is that "the notion of a language entirely freed of referential constraints is properly inconceivable." Consequently, a "relapse from a rhetoric of figuration into a rhetoric of signification," is inevitable (*AR*, p. 49). Yet, such a "failure of figuration," the failure to dislodge all the referential constraints from a text, is not simply a failure. Indeed, the relapse of the rhetoric of figuration, or of rhetorical reading into the referential, into meaning and truth, represents the deconstruction of the totality rooted in *lexis*, to which all rhetorical reading is prone. De Man notes: "The failure of figuration thus appears as the undoing of the unity it claimed to establish between the semantic function and the formal structure of language" (*AR*, p. 54). Thanks to this "deconstruction to the second degree" which demystifies the totality to which even a rhetorical reading falls prey, it becomes manifest that, for de Man, literary or poetic language is a language which denounces and disrupts all possible totalizations, those of figurative language included. A rhetorical reading is then, *secondly*, a reading that also *deconstructs* the totalizing effects of the rhetorical dimension of a text. By virtue of this "denunciation of the ultimate figure," of the totalizing figure that a rhetorical reading projects onto a text, poetical language, at the very moment "it asserts itself in the plentitude of its promise," circumvents all possible recuperation in the form of thematic or aesthetic statements about itself, in the form of any knowledge it may confer about itself. Poetical language is, indeed, nothing "but the advent of the disruption" of its self (*AR*, p. 56).

The two readings: grammatical or rhetorical, logical or poetic, etc., are two equally valid readings, although they are entirely incompatible. This is so because a literary text is always both thematic and the simultaneous deconstruction of that thematism, since in producing those thematic effects it is dependent on rhetorical and syntactical devices: "The deconstruction is not something we have added to the text but it constituted the text in the first place. A literary text simultaneously asserts and denies the authority of its own rhetorical mode" (*AR*, p. 17). However, this process, characteristic of the literary text, does not come to a halt with the simultaneous assertion and denial of its own rhetorical mode, with the deconstruction of its own deconstruction or, more accurately, with the deconstruction of the totalizing effects of the deconstruction to the first degree:

> The wisdom of the text is self-deconstructive . . ., but this self-deconstruction is infinitely displaced in a series of successive rhetorical reversals which, by the endless repetition of the same figure, keep it suspended between truth and the death of this truth. A threat of immediate destruction, stating itself as a figure of speech, thus becomes the permanent repetition of this threat. Since this repetition is a temporal event, it can be narrated sequentially, but what it narrates, the subject matter of the story, is itself a mere figure. A non-referential, repetitive text narrates the story of a literally destructive but non-tragic linguistic event. (*AR*, pp. 115–116)

In other words, the process of self-deconstruction constitutive of the literary text is an endless process in which all deconstructions turn into retotalizations which consequently need to be deconstructed again. Such deconstructions to the second degree, deconstructions of the unifying effects of the prior deconstructions, take place through precisely these retotalizations.

This may be the appropriate moment to clarify de Man's notion of deconstruction. From everything we have sought to establish, it should be obvious by now that deconstruction is for de Man primarily an undoing of logical and figural totalizations of all sorts, totalizations that are characteristic of both the thematic and aesthetic strata of texts and on which the respective approaches to the text are based. The deconstructions of these various totalizations take place either by those textual strata on which the logical and figural totalizations have to rely in order to come into being or through the relapse of the equally totalizing deconstructive readings into what they were supposed to overcome. Such a conception of deconstruction hinges on an understanding of the text as deconstructing its own metaphors, i.e., its own totalizing images, for instance, scenes or reading or writing (*AR*, p. 72). Deconstruction, then, is essentially the undoing of all thematic readings that dismiss the structure of the text and fall into the trap of the text's totalizing images. It is as well the undoing of all aesthetic readings of texts, since "aesthetic generality is the precondition for resemblance which also means that it is constitutive of metaphor," i.e., of totality (*AR*, p. 183). This deconstruction takes place as an endless process—there are deconstructions to the second, third, and so forth, degree—paradoxically, because of their constant (deconstructive) relapse into the thematic.

As we have seen, deconstruction proceeds by playing out the mechanics constitutive of the logical, figural, thematic, and aesthetic totalizations against these totalizing effects. In his discussion of Rousseau's *Social Contract*, de Man remarks:

> The deconstruction of a system of relationships, always reveals a more fragmented stage that can be called natural with regard to the system that is being undone. Because it also functions as the negative truth of the deconstructive process, the "natural" pattern authoritatively substitutes its relational system for the one it helped to dissolve. In doing so it conceals the fact that it is itself one system of relations among others, and it presents itself as the sole and true order of things, as nature and not as structure. But since a deconstruction always has for its target to reveal the existence of hidden articulations and fragmentations within assumedly monadic totalities, nature turns out to be a self-deconstructive term. It engenders endless other "nature" in an eternally repeated pattern of regression. Nature deconstructs nature . . . Far from denoting a homogeneous mode of being, "nature" connotes a process of deconstruction redoubled by its own fallacious retotalization.   (*AR*, p. 249)

Hence, the direction of deconstruction is that of a regression along and in total conformity to the hierarchical priorities of metaphysics. By analogy with a Nietzschean reversal, deconstruction turns the priorities of the philosophical discourse upside down while keeping the relation that exists between these hierarchical terms entirely intact. This is why it can be said to be a regression. By restoring in a negative manner the values of metaphysics, by retotalizing that by means of which it has deconstructed metaphysics, deconstruction becomes endowed with attributes of naturalness. It appears as a return to the primitive, the original, the archaic. But even these fallacious retotalizations of deconstruction will not withstand the final negative thrust of deconstruction that will lay bare the hidden articulations and fragmentations that preceded its own retotalization.

Such an endless process in which deconstructions are critical of textual totalizations, totalizations that yield deconstructions to the second (or third) degree since they turn again into new totalizations, corresponds to the process of the endless (self-) reflection characteristic of the literary text. It is a reflection by means of which the literary text unremittingly undoes the threat of being a self, a totality. But in order to achieve this goal, the text has to constantly become its own referent, the very object of its own reflection. A text like Rousseau's *Julie,* for instance, although it disclaims all referentiality, is a portrait of its own deconstruction of referentiality and thus restores, although in a negative way, its referentiality. The pathos of desire, i.e., of figural language (of language without an outside referent), "stabilizes the semantics of the figure by making it 'mean' the pathos of its undoing" (*AR,* p. 199). The text becomes self-referential—that is, it comes to know itself as the object of its own cognition. It is self-reflexive. What does this then imply for the concept of deconstruction? What does a deconstruction achieve when it undoes, say, self-hood as metaphor? It replaces, says de Man, self-hood "by the knowledge of its figural and epistemologically unreliable structure" (*AR,* p. 187). This negative knowledge *is* deconstruction. In other words, deconstruction is, according to de Man, "the negative insight" into the misleading assumptions and effects of metaphor and concept. Deconstruction amounts to the epistemological gesture of falsifying the pretensions to truth and completeness of all totalizing principles and the approaches rooted in these principles. Deconstruction *utters* these negative insights *about* the unifying instances. Therefore, it is an act of understanding, of judging (and, as such, an operation of totalization). Consequently, deconstruction belongs to the cognitive strata of a text, and it is part of its cognitive rhetoric. In other words, deconstruction is a knowledge about a text's referential constraints and belongs to the text's referential mode. It is a knowledge about the mechanics of knowledge, a knowledge destructive of knowledge, but a knowledge nonetheless. What makes this negative knowledge different from knowledge in the first place is, however, that it is an invitation to endlessly and in an infinite process debunk the totalizations of knowledge, its own included. Since "deconstructive labor" has to start all over again as soon as the deconstructive operation has taken place, instead of closing upon itself as upon a final negative insight, it turns into a boundless process precisely because it is still an insight.

To sum up, let us say, that for de Man deconstruction amounts to negative cognition. The referent of this negative knowledge is the text itself, i.e., the text's rhetorical and syntactical structures, its form, etc., as the mechanics that invalidate its referential mode. The negative object to which deconstruction as a mode of cognition regresses confers "attributes of (natural) existence" upon that object (*AR*, p. 240). Yet, what already distinguishes this definition of deconstruction from that used by most of the so-called deconstructive criticism—Derrida's work being, of course, excluded from this newest brand of literary criticism—which it seems so well to describe, is not only its rigor but, especially, the fact that deconstruction for de Man is bound to endlessly question its relapse into referentiality, into meaning, into the authority of its own hermeneutical performance, into the illusions of subjectivity which it confers, and so forth; whereas so-called deconstructive criticism is comfortably installed within the absolute security and certainty of its (negative) insights. But the differences between de Man's notion of deconstruction and that of deconstructive literary criticism are even more decisive.

In order to emphasize these differences, and hence the originality of de Man's approach, let us first ask the question whether a thematic and a nonthematic or rhetorical reading, both of which are equally valid through incompatible readings, can be rejoined in a unity, "into a single totality" in which the differences of the two approaches could be sublated (*AR*, p. 13). What could such a totality be? Could it be the result of the reversals that take place in a text between thematic and nonthematic, between "constructive" and deconstructive strata? Since "all rhetorical structures . . . are based on substitutive reversals," a deconstruction in a text, as "one more such reversal that repeats the self-same rhetorical structure," may be thought to be united with what it undoes in "the cross-shaped reversal of properties that rhetoricians call chiasmus" (*AR*, p. 113). Is this figure that crosses all the orders of a text—this "chiasmus, the crossing that reverses the attributes of words and things" (*AR*, p. 38), the chiasm of the figural potential of language— is this the center of the text? Can "a poetics of chiasmus" (*AR*, p. 49) hope to retotalize the disjunctive readings as well as the different strata of the text? A certain deconstructive criticism certainly tries to do so, all the more as it does not question (nor further deconstruct) the implications of its notion of deconstruction as a negative knowing, a mode of understanding, i.e., of totalizing the negative. But immediately the following question arises. If, as de Man has argued, the process of reversals that characterizes the text is an endless process, if rhetorical readings challenge without end their own inevitable relapse into totalization, how then could "the original chiasmus" (*AR*, p. 43) and the intricacy and wealth of the movements triggered by it, make the text close upon itself? The chiasmus, for de Man, despite being the figure of exchange *par excellence*, the figure of all totalizing figures, is itself no instance of totalization.

Apart from this infinite process of deconstruction that prevents the figure of chiasmus from transforming itself into a totalizing device, it has to be noticed that the cross-shaped figure of rhetorical reversal is not a symmetric figure. De Man writes: "The reversal from denial to assertion implicit in the deconstructive discourse never reaches the symmetrical counterpart of what it denies . . . The negative thrust of the deconstruction remains unimpaired" (*AR*, pp. 125–126).

This explains then why a deconstruction does not come to rest with the inversion of values that it undertakes. Since the negative knowledge conferred by deconstruction "fails to achieve a concluding exchange that would resolve the tension of the original dejection" (*AR*, p. 187) by the deconstruction of metaphysical values, "the totalizing symmetry of the substitutive pattern is thrown out of balance" (*AR*, p. 185). Indeed, as soon as a totalizing identification of the text is about to occur, as soon as more embracing concepts seem to sublate the disjunctive terms and approach a new higher totality, the negative thrust of the reversal comes into effect again. The play of the text is without end.

Thus, although any reading of the text, as far as it is a text, must "start out by undoing the simple antithetical relationship between referent and figure, this does not mean however that it can stop there" (*AR*, p. 200). A rhetorical reading has to go beyond this pseudosymmetry, and to explore the asymmetrical thrust of the text. It has to go beyond the play of reversal between "construction" and deconstruction toward a thinking of the unflaggingly negative and disruptive thrust of detotalization characteristic of deconstruction. But before doing so, another question arises. Considering the asymmetrical nature of the text and the endless process of deconstruction that distinguishes it, one may wonder if a text is "the allegorical narrative of its own deconstruction?" With this question de Man aims at "the possibility of including the contradictions of reading in a narrative that would be able to contain them. Such a narrative would have the universal significance of an allegory of reading" (*AR*, p. 72). The unity de Man refers to cannot be a unity provided by metaphorical synechdoche. On the contrary, from everything seen, it must be a unity due to the undoing of metaphor. Since this process is itself an infinite one, the unity in question must be temporal, a narrative that would include the mutually deconstructive play of the two readings distinguished, as well as the totalizing principles which structure these readings. Needless to say, in order to understand the nature of this temporal totality, it is imperative to come to grips with de Man's use of the term *allegorical*.

It may be difficult to demarcate allegory from the structure of metaphor, "of which it is in fact the most general version." But precisely "by generalizing itself in its own allegory, the metaphor seems to have displaced its proper meaning" in the figure allegory (*AR*, p. 73). This is what de Man proceeds to demonstrate in the chapter entitled "Reading." The displacement of the proper meaning of metaphor in its generalized figure of allegory becomes manifest in the allegorical stress on details that deflect the allegory's potential resemblance:

> In a metaphor, the substitution of a figural for a literal designation engenders, by synthesis, a proper meaning that can remain implicit since it is constituted by the figure itself. But in allegory . . . it seems that the author has lost confidence in the effectiveness of the substitutive power generated by the resemblance: he states a proper meaning, directly or by way of an intra-textual code or tradition, by using a literal sign which bears no resemblance to that meaning and which conveys, in its turn, a meaning that is proper to it but does not coincide with the proper meaning of the allegory.   (*AR*, p. 74)

Consequently, *allegoresis* is a process in which signification does not happen via substitutions along the line of resemblances; i.e., it is not a metaphorical process. The proper meaning of the allegory is linked to a literal sign "which bears no resemblance to that meaning." This literal sign, in turn, has a proper meaning that differs completely from that of its allegorical meaning. "The allegorical representation leads toward a meaning that diverges from the initial to the point of foreclosing its manifestation" (*AR*, p. 75). It follows from this that allegorical representation deflects the reader's or the beholder's attention from the proper meaning of the allegory to the proper meaning of the details that support the first meaning. Such a sidetracking is made possible by the fact that a detail in an allegory has no resemblance to what it is supposed to mean. De Man remarks that "the relationship between the proper and the literal meaning of the allegory . . . is not merely a relationship of non-coincidence. The semantic dissonance goes further" (*AR*, p. 74). Indeed, as de Man demonstrates in an argument too complex to summarize, "the two meanings fight each other with the blind power of stupidity" (*AR*, p. 76). The endless repetition of this struggle turns the allegory into an open figure, into a figure of nonclosure, i.e., into a figure that is no longer a figure. Since the allegory is characterized by such a repetition "of a potential confusion between figural and referential statement—potential, because the confusion never quite takes place," since the potential confusion is only displaced in the temporal process of the fight of the two meanings, allegory is a figure of an endless displacement of its potential closing effect as figure (*AR*, p. 118). It is a totality displaced in time, the narration of a totality that never quite takes place. It is a totality propelled toward an impossible closure. Therefore, de Man calls it "ironic allegory." Allegory determined along these lines is always the allegory of a figure, this figure being the totalizing figure of metaphor. Allegory, then, is a disfigured metaphor whose totalizing potential is metonymically laid out (and, thus, subverted) in an endless process of narrative. The allegory is what permanently disrupts the totality specific of the figure of metaphor. This disruption, or irony, "is no longer a trope but the undoing of the deconstructive allegory of all tropological cognitions, the systematic undoing, in other words, of understanding" (*AR*, p. 301).

No wonder then if de Man will take advantage of the "supplementary figural superposition" of the nonfigure of allegory to account for the complex structures of literary texts, in which the movement between deconstruction and restauration, between the referential constraints and the narrative, between reading and writing, etc., produces a fundamental unreadability. Precisely because the deconstruction of metaphorical figures remains a necessary moment in the production of these intricate textual structures, their rhetorical mode "can no longer be summarized by the single term of metaphor or of any substitutive trope or figure in general" (*AR*, p. 205). It is the allegory of figure that stands for this impossible totalization of the structures of what is called a "text":

> The paradigm for all texts consists of a figure (or a system of figures) and its deconstruction. But since this model cannot be closed off by a final reading, it engenders in its turn, a supplementary figural superpo-

sition which narrates the unreadability of the prior narration. As distinguished from primary deconstructive narratives centered on figures and ultimately always on metaphor, we call such narratives to the second (or third) degree allegories. Allegorical narratives tell the story of the failure to read whereas tropological narratives . . . tell the story of the failure to denominate. The difference is only a difference of degree and the allegory does not erase the figure. Allegories are always allegories of metaphor, and, as such, they are always allegories of the impossibility of reading.   (*AR*, p. 205)

Because the allegory is an ironic figure, a figure of nonclosure, of temporal displacement of a would-be totality, it can come to summarize (yet without summarizing) the movement and the structure characteristic of a text. Since the tropological deconstruction is a process that never comes to a stop, because of the relapse of deconstruction into figure, it is a narrative. The allegorical narrative narrates the impossibility of totalizing the narrative of deconstruction. Since deconstruction is a process of negative insight into the impossibility of understanding, the allegory becomes the narrative of this subverted operation, supposing that it is an operation of totalization. Allegorical narrative, consequently, escapes all epistemological grip.

"Textual coherence" (*AR*, p. 77), that is, "the stability of the text" (*AR*, p. 72), grounds itself in the nonfigure of allegory as the narrative of the text's deconstructions. The allegory is both what holds together the two readings that we distinguished and what prevents them from merging in the permanent displacement of their potential synthesis. But this allegory is only the allegory of "the crossing, or chiasmus, of the two modes of reading." But what about "Reading itself," what about "the allegorical representation of Reading which we . . . understand to be the irreducible component of any text?" If a text is always as a narrative the allegory of its own reading (or, rather, of necessarily incompatible readings), a text also, necessarily, contains a "statement" about Reading itself. From the nature of the text as the narrative of its mutually exclusive readings, it follows that this statement can take the form only of an allegory of Reading. It is a figure that states the unreadability, i.e., the impossibility to conceptualize Reading as such. The allegory of Reading is thus a "statement" about the structural obstacles that a text mounts against all attempts to comprehend it as a whole: "All that will be represented in such an allegory will deflect from the act of reading and block access to its understanding. The allegory of reading narrates the impossibility of reading. But this impossibility necessarily extends to the word 'reading' which is thus deprived of any referential meaning whatsoever" (*AR*, p. 77).

It is "forever impossible to read Reading," asserts de Man (*AR*, p. 77). This impossibility is not only the outcome of the temporal dimension of the allegory of Reading but also of the logic of allegory, which deflects from its proper meaning as a figure to its literal meaning, i.e., to the irreducibly opposed readings. But, more importantly, this impossibility of comprehending Reading itself, an impossibility that entails the allegorization of the concept of allegory, the becoming narrative of the concept of narrative, is what makes Reading appear as the deflection of the deflection characteristic of allegory. Reading cannot be read because it is deflection itself. The allegory of Reading, consequently, stands for the impossibility of reading that which makes reading forever possible. It stands for the impossibility of understanding what forever subverts understanding as an act of totalization.

At this point it should become obvious that all of de Man's concepts are drawn without exception into a maelstrom of temporalization. A concept, in de Man's work, becomes the narrative of its own impossible closure upon what it subsumes. Time prevents the conceptual atoms from exercising their epistemological grip, their totalizing work, by preventing them from closing upon themselves. But something else can be brought to attention here: the fact that the detotalized figure of the allegory grounds the stability of a text in the temporal succession of its moments alone. The allegory, the figure of nonclosure, summarizes the moments of a text solely *as* their temporal unrolling. What does this imply? It implies that the allegory does not bridge the gap between successive and repetitive moments, as little as it bridges the gap between the terms of any opposition. This refusal to bridge the gap between dyadic poles, or successive moments of a text, characterizes allegory as the most radical dislodging of metaphor. Could one say that metonymic deconstruction is thus linked in a systematic manner to a metaleptic deconstruction of temporal categories such as those of anteriority and posteriority? In any case, this refusal to bridge gaps is a refusal of translation. In a development concerning Nietzsche's *Birth of Tragedy*, de Man reminds us that the operation of bridging dyadic oppositions, or opposition in which one term is temporally or logically prior to the other, is an act of translation. Nietzsche, indeed, speaks of *übersetzen* and *über-brücken* (*AR*, p. 101). The act of translating corresponds to the seminal act of *epiphora*, constitutive of the totalizing figure of metaphor. To refuse translation is to reassert the difference of the terms caught in opposi-tions, as well as the difference of terms in sequential unfoldings. Need-less to say, this reassertion of difference in the temporality of narrative thoroughly affects the notion of narrative itself. Consequently, what does it mean for de Man in the various readings of *Allegories of Reading* to retranslate metaphorical illustrations and conceptual theories into lin-guistic facts, totalizations of all kinds into rhetorical potentialities of the signifier, psychological constructions into the absolute randomness of language, and so on? These retranslations are detranslations, i.e., opera-tions by means of which the static and closed off instances of totality are referred back to the "original" mechanics of the text. These detransla-tions are attempts at ungrounding the instances of totality by tying them up with the "original" deflection of the text. A text from this perspective represents the temporal process of detotalizing operations, of detransla-tions of totalizing translations or metaphorical substitutions. Within a text there is no translation from one moment to another. A text is consti-tuted by the repetitive deferral of its translation.

Acts of Disruption

Within traditional epistemology, *to know* is a nonpositional and transi-tive operation. "It cannot be called a speech *act*" (*AR*, p. 122). But in his analysis of a posthumous fragment by Nietzsche, de Man argues that since such a concept of knowing presupposes the prior existence and the identity of the entity to be known, "the claim to know is just an unwar-ranted totalization of the claim to perceive and to feel" (*AR*, p. 123). Indeed, for Nietzsche, the identity of entities is grounded in "an analogi-cal, metaphorical substitution of the sensation of things for the knowl-edge of entities" (*AR*, p. 122). It follows from this that the entity of knowing, characterized by the identity of its being, is the result of "the positional power of language in general," that it is "linguistically *gesetzt*, a correlative of speech acts." Knowing depends on the substitution of a semiotic, metonymic mode of reference for a substantialist, metaphorical one. It is a function of a substitutional linguistic act. And de Man con-cludes his analysis by saying that "since the language of identity and of logic asserts itself in the imperative mode . . . [it] recognizes its own activity as the positing of entities. Logic consists of positional speech acts" (*AR*, p. 123). Is this to say that de Man simply takes over and translates the theoretical parameters of Speech Act Theory into his readings? Are his analyses mere applications of Austin's theory to philosophical and literary texts? But de Man asks: "Is language an act, a "sollen" or a "tun," and now that we know that there is no longer such an illusion as that of knowledge by only feigned truths, can we replace knowledge by performance?" (*AR*, p. 124). This question alone is already sufficient reason to resist any temptation to assimilate and consequently to blur the distinctions between de Man's readings and Speech Act Theory.

The retranslation of knowing into a linguistic act represents an operation that in de Man's terminology is called "deconstruction." But Nietzsche's text does not itself enact what it preaches, objects de Man. "The text deconstructs the authority of the principle of contradiction by showing that this principle is an act, but when it acts out this act, it fails to perform the deed to which the text owed its status as an act" (*AR*, p. 127). By failing to act out the fact that a text springs forth from an act, the text deconstructs what in the first deconstruction had been opposed to knowing, that is to say, acting. Thus "the possibility of 'doing' is as manifestly being deconstructed as the identity principle" (*AR*, p. 126), and "the assertion that language is an act . . . cannot be taken as final" (*AR*, p. 125).

Although Nietzsche, in particular, in *The Genealogy of Morals,* seems to affirm the idea of action, one should not be blind to the fact that as a whole Nietzsche's work is an attack "upon the more fundamental notion of 'act'" (*AR*, p. 128). de Man develops this point by showing that Nietzsche refuses to conceive of thinking as an act: "The illusion of thought as action is the result of an . . . illegitimate totalization from part to whole." But in that case, the affirmation by the first deconstruction that knowing is caused by an illegitimate substitution of a linguistic model again becomes questionable. de Man writes:

> The text on the principle of identity established the universality of the linguistic model as speech act, albeit by voiding it of epistemological authority and by demonstrating its inability to perform this very act. But [a] . . . later text . . . voids even this dubious assurance, for it puts in question not only that language can act rightly, but that it can be said to

act at all. The first passage . . . on identity showed that constative language is in fact performative, but the second passage . . . asserts that the
possibility for language to perform is just as fictional as the possibility
for language to assert.   (*AR*, p. 129)

Consequently, "what seems to lead to an established priority of '*setzen*'
over '*erkennen*' of language as action over language as truth, never quite
reaches its mark." There cannot be a new totalization on the basis of the
concept of language as action, a concept that came to deconstruct the
idea of language as truth. As a result, "the differentiation between performative and constative language (which Nietzsche anticipates) is undecidable" (*AR*, p. 130). Thus, Nietzsche's deconstruction of knowing by
positing a deconstruction that forestalls Austin's reinscription of the constative within the performative, leads, via the rigor of his deconstruction,
to a critique of the very notion of act that is constitutive of the Austinean
concept of speech act. What Nietzsche recognizes is that to use the
notion of act as a conceptualizing and totalizing tool to understand
language is as deceitful as the traditional view, according to which language is knowing. This refusal by de Man to endow the concept of act
with the totalizing explicative power it has in Speech Act Theory is his
first critique of this doctrine.

de Man's entire analysis of Rousseau's *Essay on the Origin of Language*,
as well as of the passages from the *Second Discourse* concerning language,
is testimony to the fact that Austin's revolution can already be found in
Rousseau. In the same way that "the intersubjective, reflective situation
of self-encounter, as in the specular self-fascination of Narcissus, is indeed for Rousseau the paradigmatic experience from which all other
experiences are derived" (*AR*, p. 152), so the congnitive, referential function of denomination is rooted in the self-referential function of the
linguistic event. de Man seems here to accept uncritically the validity of
the theoretical presuppositions of Speech Act Theory.

But to paraphrase de Man, this is not yet the end of the parable since
the self-reflexivity of language as act that he has been speaking about
corresponds to a sort of "original blindness." "A blind metaphorization"
(*AR*, p. 156) constitutes all literal reference and all subsequent figural
connotation. The literal reference is only a *substitute* for a first "wild,
spontaneous metaphor" (*AR*, p. 153). With this it becomes, literally
speaking, impossible to distinguish any longer between literal reference

and figural. And, instead of being the condition of possibility of literal reference, the original self-referentiality of language becomes precisely its impossibility since literal reference appears to be only just one more aberrant metaphor. Thus, although de Man conceives of conceptual language as preceding denominative language, of the self-referentiality preceding the referentiality of language, the blindness of that origin, instead of being the secure origin of referential awareness, is only the condition of possibility of the original aberration. In other words, the self-reflexivity of language, of the act of the speech act, is *not* as in Speech Act Theory the condition of possibility of the representationalism of language; it is on the contrary on the *impossible condition of possibility* (or the *condition of the impossibility*) of referentialism since it is true that "the loss of faith in the reliability of referential meaning does not free language [altogether] from referential and tropological coercion" (*AR,* p. 208). The self-referentiality of language as act is the condition of possibility for the referential illusion of language, for an illusory effect that has all the aspects of reality. With this reinterpretation of the relation between the self-reflexive and the referential function of language, in terms of an impossible condition of possibility, we face de Man's second critique of Speech Act Theory.

But with what has been outlined here as the "self-destructive epistemology of conceptual language" preceding referential, intentional language (*AR,* p. 158), we have not yet reached de Man's major critique of Speech Act Theory. This doctrine, having been subjected to a critique concerning the explicative power of its notion of act, as well as to a critique of the relation between the act and what it is supposed to make possible, will next become exposed to a most thorough critique of the very notion of reflexivity. This happens in the chapters entitled "Self (*Pygmalion*)" and "Excuses (*Confessions*)," in which de Man proceeds to a deconstruction of the totalizing figure of self(-reflexivity) and to a dismantling of totalizing specular configurations.

Precisely because "the pressure towards meaning and the pressure towards its undoing can never cancel each other out," language, by always being only about concepts substituting originally blind metaphors, "can never know whether it is about anything at all including itself, since it is precisely the *aboutness,* the referentiality, that is in question" (*AR,* p. 161). Indeed, if for structural reasons it cannot be decided whether language is about anything including itself, the very distinction between referential and self-referential becomes suspect. This asymmetry is so fundamental, says de Man, that the very possibility of self-reflexivity and self-referentiality of language becomes questionable. de Man's argument in "Self" is indeed that the loss of the epistemological stability of the figure of the self in *Pygmalion* is never recuperated in the text. On the contrary, "a surplus (or deficiency)" (*AR*, p. 184) in the text of *Pygmalion* prevents that play from coming under the authority of an epistemology of self. With this the totalizing symmetry of reflexivity is once and for all thrown out of balance.

Before scrutinizing this "surplus (or deficiency)" that comes to disrupt the possible closure of the figure of self or of specularity, as in "Excuses (*Confessions*)," let us remark that the threefold critique of Speech Act Theory outlined here does not represent a simple rejection of it. Taking de Man's definition of *allegory* into account, one can say that it has been allegorized only as a figure. It has been undermined as a means of theoretical imperialism, as an all-explicatory device. But it is precisely as such an aborted machine of totalization that the allegorical, narrational version of Speech Act Theory can appear again as a model for the totalities in displacement that are texts.

Yet, before being able to fully evaluate the scope of such an allegorization of the speech act, it is imperative to bring to the fore at least some of the philosophical implications of this critique. Philosophically speaking, what does it mean to subject the notion of act to a critique like de Man's? And what does the notion of act in speech act have to be retraced back to? If language is an act, a doing, a performance, then language is positional. Fichte's development of the notion of positing in *Science of Knowledge* is then naturally one of the basic sources that Speech Act Theory must be retraced back to, although no explicit traces of such a filiation can be discovered in the corpus of that doctrine.

Positing (*Setzen*) as a concept means in Kant the affirmation of being in judgment. Yet, in trying to overcome the circularity of all theory of self-consciousness by continuing to develop what in Kant already pointed toward a dialectical philosophy, Fichte proceeds to endow the notion of positing with active meaning. Contrary to Kant for whom being is posited in a passive way by all judgments, being is actively posited (or set forth) according to Fichte's interpretation of this concept. An active positing of being, however, implies that all objective positing presupposes a self-positing, not of a subject since the subject is determined by the posited object that is opposed to it, but of a self *(Ich)*. The self as the absolute presupposition of the subject-object relation is absolutely active and merely active. This pure activity of the self "has no sort of object, but returns upon itself."[24] The infinite activity of the self-positing self secures the self's being through its reflection of itself into itself. It can be envisaged as "that of a self-constituting mathematical point, in which we can distinguish no direction or anything else whatever."[25] The self *must* posit itself in such a manner, if it is to posit anything else. The self before it can as a subject posit an object, before it can limit itself in its infinity by the finitude of a nonself, must have posited itself in an absolutely unconditioned manner as itself. It is thus important to realize that self and subject or ego are not the same. The subject or ego is determined by an opposed object, and vice versa. The self, however, is not opposed to anything before it has constituted itself in the act of self-positing. The pure activity of it is the condition of possibility of the objective activity of a subject, of "the self given in actual consciousness."[26] Fichte writes: "Insofar as no object can be posited without an activity of the self, opposed to that of the object, and insofar as this activity must necessarily exist in the subject prior to any object whatsoever, and simply through the subject itself (so that it is the pure activity thereof), the pure activity of the self is, as such, a condition of any activity that posits an object."[27]

This genuinely speculative theory of the identity of self determines the nonempirical *Act (Thathandlung)* which as the unity of consciousness lies at the basis of all consciousness and all self-consciousness and makes it possible. Now, if this reversion into itself is the condition of possibility of all intentional and objective consciousness, and even of the consciousness of self, it becomes obvious that the status of the performative act, constitutive of the speech act, has its roots in Fichte's idea of a self-positing self. The notion of the identity of the self in Fichte indeed expresses the recognition "that everything that is to be *my* representation *(Vorstellung)* has got to be related to myself" as intelligence:[28]

> The intellect as such *observes* itself; and this self-observation is directed immediately upon its every feature. The nature of intelligence consists in this *immediate* unity of being and seeing . . . I think of this or that object: What, then, does this involve, and how, then, do I appear to myself in this thinking? In no other way than this: When the object is a merely imaginary one, I create certain determinations in myself; when the object is to be something real, these determinations are present

without my aid: *and I observe that creation and this being.* They are in me only insofar as I observe them: seeing and being are inseparably united.[29]

The analogy between Fichte's principle of the unconditioned identity of the self and the act of Speech Act Theory cannot be overlooked: In both cases it is by means of the purity of an "act upon an act itself, which specific act is preceded by no other whatever,"[30] that a subject becomes objective or that a speech act turns into an intentional act. Nor can it be overlooked that Austin's concept of the act as a pure doing is, like the Fichtean *Thathandlung,* linked to the notion of presence. The Fichtean *Act* is an inversion of the self upon itself, a reflection of the self upon itself (prior to all subject-object separation) by means of which it acquires (itself) its present being.[31] Before this inversion of the self there is no self. As seen, Austin's notion of the performative is also linked to the idea of a present act that is constitutive of its very presence. The reason for this similarity is that Fichte's and Austin's philosophy is tributary to the metaphysics of subjectivity (which, by the way, cannot be escaped in any way by opting for a philosophy of the social, the communal, the collective, etc.). At least insofar as the Fichtean principle of self=self is understood as the principle of identity of consciousness and of subjectivity, Fichte's philosophy is a philosophy in which spirit is understood as subject.[32] On the other hand, Austin's speech acts are undoubtedly acts of subjects, and, in fact, of subjects before all social mediation. Positing, then, as the act through which the self asserts itself in its being before all intentionality, or as the act that precedes the speech act's becoming an act of denomination or of communication, is dependent on the conception of spirit as a subject or of language as the predominant manifestation of the subject's subjectivity. Such a notion of positing is, however, the positing of metaphysics. Heidegger has argued in the following way: "According to the tenets of modern idealism, the labor of the spirit is a positing, a setting (thesis). Because the spirit is conceived as subject, and is accordingly represented within the subject-object model, the positing (thesis) must be the synthesis between the subject and its objects."[33]

Positing in Fichte is *the* activity of the self, which is just another name for spirit: "All positing in general, and absolute positing in particular, is attributable to the self."[34] The self in Fichte in virtue of its self-positing nature corresponds to reason (*Vernunft*), which although it inscribes within itself the Kantian oppositions of understanding, particularly that of subject and object, is nevertheless, to be understood basically in terms of subjectivity. Although the self-positing of the self is the condition of possibility of the subject and its positing of an object, it is a synthesis of subject and object under the aegis of subjectivity. Obviously enough, this does not mean that the self would be identical to human subjectivity since it is precisely the subjectivity of the spirit that comes to ground the human opposition of subject and object. However one interprets positing in Fichte, its *Setzen* is not simply human. Nor is it to be mistaken for human law, for *Gesetz*. It is important to be aware of this, particularly because both Fichte's philosophy of positing and Austin's Speech Act Theory (which because of its notion of act is not to be mistaken simply for the act of speaking human beings) have been "humanized" in order to become applicable to a certain analysis of literature. Without mentioning here the conversion of Fichte's philosophy in to the philosophy of early Romanticism, all we want to evoke for the moment is Schleiermacher's romantic hermeneutics. Schleiermacher's notion of free deed (*freie Tat*)—this "immense, almost infinite expression of force"[35]—which is the starting point of any "discourse as a closed off whole," that is to say of all works of art, particularly of literary works of art, is a psychological variation of Fichte's notion of *act (Thathandlung)*. For Schleiermacher it can be understood only with reference to the life of the individual, and by means of what he called the *divinatory*. The applications of Speech Act Theory to literary texts remain within the psychological horizon of this romantic hermeneutics. After everything has been taken into account, positing is thus reduced to the act of subjectivity of empirical selves, be they geniuses or not.

Far from continuing the metaphysics of transcendental subjectivity of Fichte's and Austin's theories of the act, and even less the humanized versions of this philosophy, de Man's critique of Speech Act Theory reaches toward an interrogation of the fundamental assumptions of idealist philosophy and of its application to the interpretation of literature. Far from accepting a concept of positing, or of the performative, which would possess the totalizing explicatory power of a principle associated with values such as presence and subjectivity, de Man's critique aims at a determination of the performative and of positing, which abandons the horizon of metaphysics. Although metaphysics still raises the notion of act to the status of a transcendental concept, by endowing this concept with the attributes of subjectivity, it demonstrates that it still thinks too little of it. Yet, before clarifying the direction in which de Man develops his concept of the performative, it will be useful to mediate on how Heidegger determines the original meaning of positing.

The self-positing of the self is, as absolute positing, the essence of reason. As Hegel has shown, positing sublates the positing specific of understanding *(Verstand)* which still proceeds by oppositions.[36] Yet, since this sublation is conceived in terms of subjectivity, i.e., of creation, production, generation, etc., it is an essentially metaphysical concept of positing. But *positing* originally draws its sense from the Greek notion of *thesis,* which means a doing that is not only not predominantly human but that above all does not signify an activity in the sense of action and agency. The Greek sense of *thesis* is, as Heidegger has argued in "The Origin of the Work of Art," "to let lie forth in its radiance and presence." It has "the sense of bringing *here* into the unconcealed, bringing *forth* into what is present *(Anwesendes),* that is, letting or causing to lie forth."[37] In other words, *thesis* is a mode of *aletheia,* of truth as unconcealing. While discussing Hegel's interpretation of *thesis* as the positing of being without mediation, Heidegger, in his essay *"Hegel and the Greeks,"* shows how Hegel's dialectical critique of the apparent abstraction of this Greek concept of positing and being is the result of his indebtedness to a philosophy of subjectivity. "Hegel when conceiving of being as undetermined immediacy, experiences being as posited by the determining and conceiving subject."[38] This then allows Heidegger to raise the following question:

> When Hegel characterizes being as the first coming forth and the first manifestation of the spirit, it remains to be questioned whether unconcealing must not already be implicated in this coming forth and in this self-manifestation. . . . If Hegel lets the original position of his system culminate in the absolute idea, in the complete self-appearance of the spirit, then one is forced to ask whether unconcealing is not at stake even in this appearing, i.e., in the phenomenology of the spirit, and, consequently in absolute self-knowledge. And immediately one more question must be raised, whether unconcealing has its place in the spirit as absolute subject, or whether unconcealing is itself the place, and points toward the place, in which something like a representing subject can first come to "be" what it is.[39]

In other words, Heidegger suggests that the metaphysical concept of positing (and even more so the empirical, humanized version of it) is in the last resort dependent on the original meaning of positing, that is to say, on the Greek sense of *thesis* as a setting up in the unconcealed. What is true of Hegel is not less true of Fichte. For Fichte the positing of being is identical to that of self. But the original meaning of *positing* is, as Heidegger specifies, donation. All concepts of positing, according to which the act of positing is a present act constitutive of presence, hinge on positing as the letting to come forth into what is present. In order that an act may be the present act of a self engendering itself as spirit, a self presupposed by all real subjects, an original *thesis* must already have taken place: a *thesis* through which the clearing is freed in which a self can come to posit itself.

Like *physis*, which, as the holding-sway (*Walten*) of nature, is *thesis par excellence*, so *poesis* is *thesis*, a mode of *aletheia* as unconcealing.

But to say that *poesis* is *thesis*, a mode of unconcealing, is also to say that *poesis* is a mode of concealing, according to Heidegger's translation and interpretation of *aletheia*. *Thesis* as a bringing into the open of the unconcealed is the concealing of what comes forth, precisely because what comes forth in this manner appears as something present. *Thesis* as a mode of *aletheia* is thus a simultaneous bringing forth into what is present, and a withholding of what is allowed to appear. Or, to put it differently, positing (*Setzen*) is a translation (*Übersetzung*) of the concealed into what is present, the distorting gesture of the revelation of which is at once reversed again by a foreclosing retranslation (*Übersetzung*) into what is concealed. It is this double movement of positing as *thesis* that we will now have to keep in mind as we are circling back to de Man in order to determine in a more precise way the status of the notion of the performative in his analyses of literary work.

That concept of positing, which according to Heidegger is more original than the metaphysical concept of positing, is a concept that stresses the movement of the return into concealment of what is revealed in, or as, what is. It is a concept that accounts for both the disclosure and its interruption since what reveals itself in the mode of *aletheia* appears only as concealed. It is a concept that makes unconcealing hinge on the interruption of presence, i.e., of the mode in which that which reveals itself also conceals itself. A similar movement also characterizes de Man's notion of the performative.

The question we had left pending concerned the nature of the "surplus (or deficiency)," which was said to disrupt totalizing figures, such as the self or specularity. At present it remains to show that such a disruption also impedes a text (in general) from closing upon itself. Like the legal text, all texts are distinguished by "an unavoidable estrangement" (*AR*, p. 266) between the generality of their functioning and the particularity of their meaning, says de Man. This estrangement is one between the system of relationships that generates a text and that functions independently of its referential meaning (i.e., its grammar) and its referentiality; between the text as "a logical code or machine" and considerations of its applicability or interpretability. This relation of estrangement between the text as a machine and the particularity of its meaning is one of constitution and deconstitution. "The logic of grammar generates texts only in the absence of referential meaning, but every text generates a referent that subverts the grammatical principle to which it owed its constitution" (*AR*, p. 269). However, such a determination of the text, as an agonistic field opposing the machine of its grammar to the particular meanings that come to restrict the text's generality, bears witness to an allegorized notion of text. "The divergence between grammar and referential meaning is what we call the figural dimension of language . . . We call text any entity that can be considered from such a double perspective; as a generative, open-ended, non referential grammatical system and as a figural system closed off by a transcendental signification that subverts the grammatical code to which the text owes its existence. The 'definition' of text also states the impossibility of its existence and prefigures the allegorical narratives of this impossibility' (*AR*, p. 270).

This allegorized concept of text, which clearly distinguishes de Man's use of the notion of text from its colloquial use (as well as the possible range of its applications), leads to the notion that a text is the narrative (the temporal and metonymic display) of its impossible closure, that is to say, of the impossibility of what one calls (metaphorically) a "self-reflexive text." To determine a text as the narration of its impossibility to become a whole, however, does not mean that the text would be *about* this impossibility, for narrative is here to be understood primarily in a structural fashion. An allegorized concept of text is not the present performance of the text presenting *itself* as the display of the impossibility of its possible closure.

For de Man, then, a text is the impossible unity of the performative and the constative functions of language since the performative is associated with the generating grammar, with the text as machine, whereas the constative is linked to the referential level of the text. After what we have seen concerning de Man's deconstruction of the totalizing explicative power of both the cognitive and performative function, this should no longer surprise us. But, we also already know that these reciprocal deconstructions are not symmetrical—hence, the narrative layout of the text. The thrust of the performative, however deconstructed, remains unimpaired. Yet, what kind of performative is it that structures in this manner the allegorized concept of text? The irreducible performative constitutive of the text is manifest in the "quantitative economy of loss," in the textual thermodynamics governed by a "debilitating entropy" of the linguistic structure of the text, "in which grammar and figure, statement and speech act do not converge" (*AR*, p. 272), or which is the same thing, in the production of textual excess. It is visible as surplus or as deficiency. It becomes manifest in the displacement of the paired but incompatible functions of the text, such as the cognitive and the performative. The performative constitutive of texts enacts both the performative and cognitive *functions* of language in their reciprocal incompatibility. de Man argues: "Language itself dissociates the cognition from the act. *Die Sprache verspricht (sich)*; to the extent that is necessarily misleading, language just as necessarily conveys the promise of its own truth" (*AR*, p. 277).

The performative constitutive of texts as displaced totalities of paired but incompatible functions, far from permitting texts to close upon themselves (from becoming selves, reflexive and autonomous entities) temporalizes, historizes them. The performative, then, is characterized by its power of dissociation. In particular, by the dissociation of the cognitive from the act within what Austin called "the total speech act." This allegorized notion of the performative, as a disjunctive that generates time and history, is the major topic of the last chapter of *Allegories of Reading*. In "Excuses *(Confessions)*" de Man demonstrates how in Rousseau's *Confessions* "performative rhetoric and cognitive rhetoric, the rhetoric of tropes, fail to converge" (*AR*, p. 300). Yet, these disruptions are no longer part of the representational logic of rhetoric. For in being located at the disrupting intersection of the two rhetorical codes, they are anterior to these codes and generate the sets of their particular figures. For the same reason they cannot become the object of an understanding that would make the mastering of the tropological displacement the very burden of understanding because these nonfigures are the very condition of possibility of intelligibility. They remain "exterior" to understanding. These disruptive figures at the intersection of the two rhetorical functions of the text, which generate the narrative displacement of the text by preventing the two functions from merging in a totality, are no isolated events in a text. On the contrary, they are extended, says de Man "over all the points of the figural line or allegory; in a slight extension of Friedrich Schlegel's formulation . . . [the text] becomes the permanent parabasis of an allegory (of figure), that is to say irony" (*AR,* pp. 300–301). In other words, the text, in the last resort, is constituted (but is this still a *constitution?*) by a notion of performative, of positing, which makes it unconceal itself only as the displaced totality of paired, but incompatible, textual functions. But to speak of unconcealing here, and thus of concealing, is slightly misleading since it may suggest wrongly that the bringing to the fore of the text could still be the task of any hermeneutics whatsoever.

To conclude then, let us try to assess in as succinct a manner as possible the scope of de Man's critical enterprise. Considering the threefold critique of Speech Act Theory, de Man's readings certainly cannot be said to be an application of this theory. This does not, however, mean that this critique is merely negative. On the contrary, it represents an attempt at developing a more fundamental notion of the performative than the notion of self-positing on which Austin's Speech Act Theory rests and which keeps it locked within the boundaries of philosophical idealism and the metaphysics of subjectivity. Similar to that notion of positing, which according to Heidegger is more original than Fichte's or Hegel's dialectical concept of it, de Man's notion of it is more "original" than the concept of positing characteristic of a certain Romanticism, of Schleiermacher, for example, for whom "everything which is represented as a leap (*Sprung*) and as a turning point" unavoidably "leads back again to what is bound."[40] de Man's notion of positing is critical of all Romantic aspiration toward totality, including, albeit negatively, that of the fragment.

If de Man's developments upon the notion of positing and totality show him to be critical of a certain Romanticism, this does not mean, however, that he would reject Romanticism in general. Already to believe in an eventual and definitive separation from Romanticism is indeed illusory and naive, since it would imply that one already knew what Romanticism is. Contrary to those seemingly radical bounds beyond

Romanticism, bounds that invariably only lead one back deeper into what one was trying to escape, slight deviations carry the promise of some fundamental displacements. Such a deviation is "the slight extension," that is to say, the generalization, of Schlegel's notion of parabasis, a generalization that displaces the proper meaning of this rhetorical figure to make it the nonfigure of the performative of the text. This being said, one may take a further step in trying to evaluate the shift in *Allegories of Reading* from Speech Act Theory as a set of rules about ordinary language to its founding concept of act. The critique to which de Man subjects this notion throughout his writing is a critique oriented toward an exploration of a more radical notion of positing. Positing understood as a *disruptive thesis* becomes in this manner the founding principle of a new *poesis*. Instead of being merely studies in poetry or in literary texts, de Man's allegories of reading are attempts at developing a *poetics,* a poetics no longer grounded, however, in the mimesis of nature and of ideas or, as in Romantic aesthetics—reinterpreting Fichte's philosophical problems of self-foundation and self-reflection in terms of a philosophy of language—in the *form* of the activity of the human mind. On the contrary, the poetics envisioned by de Man is the poetics of "act" as disruptive and productive of both form and content. It is a poetics of a process of *poesis* which as *Setzung* translates *(über-setzen)* itself as the disruption of the presence of its own necessarily doubled appearance.

2

In-Difference to Philosophy

Since its incipiency in Greece, philosophy has found itself in rivalry with rhetoric. Yet, as rivals, philosophy and rhetoric also have something in common and make similar claims. What they share, and what thoroughly distinguishes them from the mode of discourse characteristic of the individual sciences, is their title to speak about everything, about all there is. Philosophy and rhetoric feel their competence to be excluded from no subject. But in spite of their common interest, rhetoric and philosophy are separated by an abyss. As Socrates' attempt to demarcate both discourses in the episode in the *Theaetetus* regarding the difference between the rhetorician and the philosopher clearly demonstrates, the difference between rhetoric and philosophy is rooted in incommensurable modes of object-perception. Rhetoric is a type of discourse that services the self-affirming mortal human nature, and it is indeed its highest tool. Therefore, the rhetorician must perceive his or her object in the manner it presents itself to him or her in ordinary sense perception, that is, as a singular and concrete object. Yet, whereas rhetoric's activity takes place within anthropologically determined limits, philosophy relinquishes rhetoric's all-dominating motive of self-affirmation, and, *eo ipso,* rhetorical linguistic competence. In thus surrendering rhetorical and linguistic competence, philosophy, in distinction from rhetoric, acquires the chance to conceive objects in general, objects, consequently, that lack all common base with those of human life. Philosophy, as understood by Plato, is dependent on such a radical break with the necessities of life—a break based, as can be seen from the episode in the *Theaetetus,* and even better from the *Phaedo,* on the assumption that there is something worse than corporeal death. This distance from life radically distinguishes philosophy from rhetoric.[1]

According to a remark made by Plato in the *Theaetetus*—as well as by Aristotle at the beginning of *Metaphysics*—philosophical questioning starts in *thaumazein*, i.e., in wonder and marvel. In wonder, indeed, the human being stands back from the immediate and from his or her most elementary and purely practical relation to it, as Hegel explains at one point in the *Aesthetics*. In wonder, he or she is torn free "from nature and his own singularity and now seeks and sees in things a universal, implicit, and permanent element."[2] In other words, in the wondering retreat, difference irrupts into the world. It is a difference that not only opens up the world *as* world, viz., the world as a *whole,* but one that also constitutes that particular being who in the world, and in distinction from it, is capable of cognition. Because only through this difference does meaning come into a previously indifferent world of immediacy, and it is a difference that cannot be explained by what is. As the opening itself of what exists in a meaningful manner, it is an absolutely irreducible difference. Because of its origin in wonder, in that sort of retreat from the immediate by which the immediate *as such,* in its totality, comes into view, philosophy has, from the start, been concerned with all there is, with the entirety of being, with being in general, as opposed to empirical particulars. This "all," however, is very different from all that rhetoric purports to speak about. It is not everything, each single item that exists, but the totality as such of what exists—in short, the whole of being, being *itself.* Philosophy, from the outset, has been concerned with the enigma that within being there is one such heterogeneous being for whom that which is can turn into an object of cognition. Such a being is clearly entirely different from the self-affirming mortal human being in whose survival rhetoric invests. The object of philosophy is a function of a cognizing subject, of a subject whose possibility presupposes difference and whose object is the whole in its difference to what it is the whole of.

Philosophy must be radically distinguished from rhetoric not only on the basis of its objects and purpose, for philosophy is different from rhetoric insofar as it is a *discourse of difference.* It is rooted in difference and reflects on that difference. It interrogates the difference that the thought of the *as such* (thought *as such*), or of the *whole* makes, in distinction from what is allowed to appear within its opening. Most generally speaking, philosophy, seen independently of its historical modifications, must be said to be concerned with the enigma of difference—with the *essential* difference that is the general, the universal—in short, with an irreducible difference that cannot be explained by what is since the empirically given is as to its meaning dependent on that difference. Philosophy is about a difference that makes all the difference, a difference that can be accounted for only in and by itself, in short, in difference from all other modes of existence.

Philosophy, in contradistinction from rhetoric, acquires the possibility of its object's generality by relinquishing the exigencies of mortal life, as well as the linguistic competence that survival requires. The philosopher gains this position through his or her retreat from language and speech as particular attributes of a mortal human being. (If he or she happens to be a powerful orator, it is certainly not *qua* philosopher.) But what does such a retreat from language and speech consist of, and what does it imply? Precisely because philosophy is concerned with the *as such,* with what as *thought* is in irreducible distinction from what it is the thought of, language in its concrete empirical reality an obstacle, not by accident as may be the case in the particular sciences or in rhetoric too, but *kath'auto,* in and by itself. Philosophy's relation to its objects is therefore always bent by the problematic of linguistic expression. This explains also why from its incipiency, philosophy has been concerned with the possibilities and limits of language. Reflection on language is an integral part of the self-understanding of philosophy. It characterizes the philosophical enterprise as one that cannot be subsumed to any of the possible types of discourse that rhetoric may have distinguished. Concerned with the fact that the expression of a thought of general bearing is immediately and intimately linked to a problematization of language, the philosophical mode of discourse is characterized by a *know-how-to-speak-well—eu legein.*[3] This desire to speak well—contrary to the desire for efficient speech in rhetoric—prescribes that the objective problems arising from linguistic expression of general matters are made an integral part of these matters themselves and radically distinguishes philosophical discourse from the use of language in the individual sciences and in rhetoric as well. This desire represents the attempt to achieve, on the level of expression, the very difference itself that the subject matter of philosophy implies, and is, thus, in principle, irreducible to any empirical usage of language. Philosophical speech achieves the required transparency in language—its transempirical use—through a rigorous methodological practice of distinction. Indeed, philosophy is not only a discourse on the enigma of difference and, therefore, distinguished from all other modes of employing speech, it is also a discourse in which distinction becomes the major organon. As a strictly argumentative and reasoning practice that achieves cognition of what is as such and in its totality through a stating of grounds, philosophy hinges entirely on its sharp distinctions of levels and conceptual differences. Indeed, the considerable conceptual effort that philosophy demands of its reader and interpreter amounts to nothing less than an invitation to face not only its difference from other discourses and their objects, as a difference rooted in the difference that thought itself makes, but also, just as essentially, to a discourse that secures the difference of thought by a rigorous practice of linguistic and conceptual differentiation.

Philosophy comes into its own thus by separating itself from that other (anthropological, empirical) type of discourse—namely, rhetoric—that also claims for itself the right to speak about everything. Yet, at the very moment when philosophy reaches a certain fulfillment of its goal in a type of philosophy in which perhaps the most systematic layout of the totality of all thinkable differences is achieved—in Hegel's philosophy—early German Romanticism, paradoxically enough, is becoming engaged in sketching a retrogression toward rhetoric. Not only did Friedrich Schlegel conceive of rhetoric as the reuniting of in an exclusively formal point of view but also as the annihilation of the differences between what he understood to be merely separate species of "literature"—poetry and philosophy. Despite some major differences to be emphasized hereafter, Paul de Man's linguistic or rhetorical reading of literature and philosophy continues, in a certain manner, that romantic project of dissolving the difference constitutive of both philosophy and literature, philosophy and rhetoric. In the following analysis devoted to de Man's reading of the philosophical texts of Nietzsche, Kant, and Hegel, we will attempt to make this point. As already indicated, de Man's reading differs from the manner in which the romantics aimed at bringing about an original indifference—the indifference of the *menstruum universale*. de Man does not reach back to a point of unity and presence that because it makes all the difference, remains intrinsically linked up with the philosophical *desideratum*. On the contrary, as we will try to demonstrate, it is the unheard-of attempt to think an indifference that makes no difference at all. A rhetorical reading, for de Man, is, indeed, a reading that seeks the transgression of philosophical difference in an indifference that is so radical as to become entirely indifferent—devoid of *all* relation—to the philosophical.

The Wild Card of Rhetorical Reading

Before establishing what a rhetorical reading means for de Man and what it seeks to achieve, it may well be appropriate to first determine, as succinctly as possible, what he understands by *philosophy*. The distinctive feature of a philosophical text is, according to de Man, its proclaimed property of unity. As his essays on Nietzsche reveal, such unity is a function of philosophy's conceptual, argumentational, and above all, developmental nature. A philosophical text, or discourse, is said to unfold in a process, built up from a beginning and proceeding toward a conclusive end. And because de Man considers all these characteristics meaningful only to the extent that they are supposed to demarcate philosophy from literature, they also establish what he calls "philosophy's authority and centrality." de Man's rhetorical reading of philosophy purports to tackle "the perennial question of the distinction between philosophy and literature" (*AR*, p. 119)—a philosophical question *par excellence*, serving philosophy's attempt to establish its own authorial and authoritative difference—yet aims at nothing less than a questioning of the every possibility of such a difference. At stake in a rhetorical reading is philosophy's irreducible difference, the thought of difference and difference as thought.

A rhetorical or linguistic reading or, for that matter, a literary, nonphenomenal reading, as it is also called, is a purely formal reading (see *AI*, p. 77). Although the essay "The Resistance to Theory" seems to link such a reading with the application of Saussurian linguistics to literary and philosophical texts, the Nietzsche essays in *Allegories of Reading* clearly suggest that purely formal linguistics is primarily indebted to certain romantic speculations on language. The linguistic theory of Friedrich Schlegel and Jean Paul, which is still "largely obscured by our lack of understanding," has demonstrated, according to de Man, "that the paradigmatic structure of language is rhetorical rather than representational or expressive of a referential, proper meaning" (*AR*, p. 106). In romantic linguistics, the trope is the linguistic paradigm, *par excellence*, and such privileging of figure over persuasion is said to correspond to the most typical romantic gesture (see *AR*, p. 106 and 130). In short, a purely formal reading of philosophical or literary texts is in essence a tropological reading since tropes are understood to characterize language in depth. Yet, when de Man refers to rhetoric and tropes, he does not think of mere stylistics and the linguistic art of representation. A linguistic or rhetorical reading, as de Man understands it, is essentially a nonphenomenal reading.

To understand what is meant by "nonphenomenal" and, thus, by "nonphenomenal linguistics," it is indispensable to first clarify what *phenomenal* means. Although de Man makes frequent use of the terms *phenomenalism, phenomenality, phenomenalization,* etc., without clearly demarcating them, it is not difficult to see that these terms imply a meaning of *phenomenon* that stresses, in analogy (but in analogy only) to Kant's use of that notion, the object of cognition's appearing to the senses. Phenomenality for de Man denotes accessibility to the senses. A phenomenon is characterized by the fact that it is intuitable *(anschaulich),* imagelike *(bildhaft).* It contains an "iconic factor" and takes place through extension since it is constituted by the aesthetic forms of space and time (*RR,* pp. 115, 127). Figures and tropes are phenomenal in that they appeal to the senses and privilege a certain mode of cognition, that of the experience of the phenomenal world. A nonphenomenal linguistic reading is, thus, first, a nonperceptual or nonaesthetic reading. It centers not on images and tropes but on what de Man calls at one point the "para-figural" (*RT,* p. 15). For de Man, however, the phenomenal "implies the possibility of a determined totalization, of a contour," as well (*RR,* p. 127). It captures the meaning of texts not only as tangible figures but also as totalizing figures. A nonphenomenal reading, consequently, is a reading that reaches beyond the imposition—by a mode of experience in which the perceptual modes of cognition prevail—of unity upon the text. It extends beyond the totalizing function of figures or tropes. Yet, since intuition as *Anschaung* is that type of cognition that causes all experiences to be the experience of phenomena and also implies, to quote de Man, "perception, consciousness, experience, and leads at once into the world of logic and of understanding with all its correlatives, among which aesthetics occupies a prominent place" (*RT,* p. 8), a nonphenomenal reading is also, necessarily, a noncognitive, or nonspecular (nonreflexive) reading.

Now, in Kant, *phenomenon* is used in contrast to what does not appear to the senses. But the nonphenomenal reading that we are here dealing with is not for that matter a noumenal reading. Although it aims at something nonperceptual, to "factors or functions that cannot be reduced to intuition" (*RT*, p. 13), phenomena, for de Man, are not in opposition to noumena. Until we are able to clearly pinpoint the exact nature of the "object" of a nonphenomenal or rhetorical reading, let us only say that it aims at "the modalities of production and of reception of meaning and of value prior to their establishment," or at "reference prior to designating the referent" (*RT*, pp. 7–8). More simply put, a nonphenomenal reading centers on what de Man terms the "autonomous potential of language," on what foregrounds in language, and is prior to, the figural and the logical, in short, on "literariness" (*RT*, p. 10).

A reading that focuses on what is prior to the production and reception of meaning in a text is geared toward overcoming what de Man considers "the unwarranted separation between the way of reading and interpreting 'literary' as opposed to 'philosophical' or discursive texts" (*AR*, p. 226). In "The Resistance to Theory," he notes: "By considering language as a system of signs and of signification rather than as an established pattern of meanings, one displaces or even suspends the traditional barriers between literary and presumably non-literary uses of language and liberates the corpus from the secular weight of textual canonization" (*RT*, p. 9). A reading based on a nonphenomenal linguistics not only erases the difference between literary and nonliterary texts or between two types of critical reading that would take discursive differences into account, it also frees these discourses within themselves from all other "naive oppositions" (*RT*, p. 11). Such a reading intends to break down all differences as unwarranted distinctions and barriers. In thus subjecting philosophy to what the reading of its texts had until now been deprived of, namely, the "elementary refinements that are taken for granted in literary interpretation" (*AR*, p. 226), aim is taken at philosophical difference itself, i.e., at the possibility of a universal or general discourse. As we will see, the claim to such difference, and all it implies, is, for de Man, a sheer aberration, if not even a sort of *hybris*. Rhetorical reading sets out to demonstrate that difference cannot be made, that opposites remain undecidable and levels blend into one another—in short, that texts contain only a "potential confusion" (*AR*, p. 116). de Man's nonphenomenal linguistic reading, a reading that works at bringing about a systematic and generalized annulment of difference, would, consequently, seem to favor a "philosophy" of the same. Yet, whether or not this critique of philosophy (and of literature as well) really ends up in what Schelling called "indifference" remains to be seen.

In order to be able to reach beyond the difference that philosophy as such presupposes, a rhetorical or nonphenomenal reading of philosophy must necessarily transcend the literal meaning of the philosophical text as well as its canonized interpretations. Indeed, the work of differentiation in which philosophy is engaged becomes superimposed, in de Man's eyes, on the text as text by the philosopher's desire for meaning as well as by the tradition of canonized interpretation. de Man's manner of reading philosophical writings pretends to being a reading "prior to the substance that such reading reveals" (*AI,* p. 186). It is an approach to the *texte brut,* to the text before it starts to signify and prior to the established meanings that the community of interpreters has inflicted upon it. It would seem, at first, that the possibility of such an approach to the text in its material and empirical immediacy is entirely unproblematic for de Man. But his repeated insistence that the necessity of such a highly prosaic reading—a reading "by rote," as he also calls it, that is, a reading that proceeds mechanically and unthinkingly—is inscribed in the philosophical text itself, considerably complicates the issue. When de Man remarks that "the necessity to revise the canon arises from resistances encountered in the text itself (extensively conceived) and not from preconceptions imported from elsewhere" (*AI,* p. 186) or that it springs forth from the disarticulating representation by the text itself of its own figuration, it becomes obvious that de Man is consistent in his attempt to debunk *all* differences. Indeed, if the necessity for a linguistic reading is prefigured in the text, it becomes eventually impossible to radically demarcate it from, say, philosophical models of reading. If the necessity of a nonphenomenal reading—one that centers on the text in its immediacy—"is itself phenomenally represented in the dramatic tension of the text," then the difference between such a reading and one centered on meaning fades away. Textual immediacy, consequently, cannot clearly be separated from the mediation owing to the philosopher's desire for meaning or the cumulative interpretative work of the tradition. To "choose to hear," in a nonphenomenal reading, what a text or a philosophical sentence "actually says," in contrast to what it wishes to say, is not to choose between two absolutely distinct approaches. But, as will become evident hereafter, although both types of reading blend into one another, the necessity for reading in a nonphenomenal manner has a clear priority over the other and thus displaces the indifference into which both models of reading seemed to have mingled.

The nonsymmetric priority of rhetorical reading can already be recognized by its claims to truth. It pretends to be a reading that allows for an adequate understanding of the text, as opposed to the inadequate understanding that thematic reading provides (*RR*, p. 112). A reading such as de Man's aims at teaching what is true (*RT*, p. 4). It claims to be doing justice to the text under investigation. de Man contends that what he asserts about Hegel, for instance, is true in the sense of *adequatio* because it "corresponds to an inexorable and altogether Hegelian move of the text" (*AI*, p. 189). Of the method of rhetorical reading in general, he writes that if it is technically correct, it is irrefutable (*RT*, p. 20). Yet, since he also asserts that the deconstruction of the aberrations of philosophy is not meant to "recover a measure of truth" (*AR*, p. 110), the truth yielded by rhetorical reading must be demarcated from philosophical truth. The deconstruction of philosophy as error takes place, indeed, in the name of the "higher" truth of "the untruth, the lie that metaphor was in the first place," as de Man puts it on one occasion. It takes place, in short, in the name of "the rhetorical, symbolic quality of all language" (*AR*, p. 111). Certainly, the truths revealed about the aberrations of philosophy eventually appear indistinguishable from these aberrations themselves. Still, the thrust of rhetorical reading and of its claims to truth remain unimpaired.

Contrary to readings within the confined polemical space of canonical interpretation and centered on what a philosopher actually said or proclaimed, a rhetorical reading is interested in what the philosopher qua philosopher could never have admitted. The philosopher, writes de Man, could almost never be expected to be candid about the "threatening paradox at the core of his system against which his thought has to develop a defense" without stopping to be a philosopher (*AI*, p. 191). Such a rhetorical reading must necessarily be bold. It cannot indulge in "misplaced timidity" and the literalism of canonical reading. It should not shrink from tampering with the canon because the problems that it points at cannot be resolved by the canonical system itself (*AI*, pp. 190–191). But as de Man also insists, the rhetorical commentator "should persist as long as possible in the canonical reading and should begin to swerve away from it only when he encounters difficulties which the methodological and substantial assertions of the system are no longer able to master" (*AI*, p. 186). Such a rhetorical reading must, therefore, at least up to a certain point, remain accountable to the tradition of interpretation. It must measure up to the philosopher's intentions, the exigencies of philosophy as philosophy, and the demands of the history of canonical exegesis. In short, a rhetorical reading claims to be faithful to the texts it reads: It pretends an adequate understanding of the text itself. The production of such understanding must remain, at least to some degree, in touch with what traditional scholarship has established about the texts to be read. This is an indispensable rule securing a minimal intelligibility of the understanding that nonphenomenal reading is to produce.

But does de Man honor this self-imposed demand in his readings of the philosophical texts of Kant, Hegel, and Nietzsche? His constancy to this demand is indeed difficult to prove not so much because a rhetorical reading (i.e., one that reaches beyond all canonized readings) would focus on "neglected corners in the Hegel canon," for instance, or because it would listen "to what is being said obliquely, figurally, and implicitly (though not less compellingly) in a less conspicuous part of the corpus" (*AI*, p. 104; *AI*, p. 192). The difficulty in question first arises from a systematic estrangement to which the philosophical texts are subjected in rhetorical reading. Indeed, from a traditional philosophical perspective, it is altogether incomprehensible why certain passages to which de Man refers in his readings are supposed to be "baffling," "surprising," "bewildering," or "startling," and thus taken as key passages. The philosopher has also difficulty realizing why certain philosophical movements are said to occur "somewhat abruptly" or why the introduction of certain specific statements is judged "unexpected" or "sudden." From an intraphilosophical perspective, all these statements can easily be accounted for, as can the specific moment of their occurrence in the argumentative context. To give just one example: In "Phenomenality and Materiality in Kant," de Man contends that contrary to the illusion of clarity and control that seems to characterize the section on the beautiful in the *Third Critique*, the section that deals with the sublime is "one of the most difficult and unresolved passages in the entire corpus of Kant's works" (*AI*, p. 73). Yet, historically speaking, the "Analytic of the Sublime," however important its place may be in the total architecture of the *Third Critique*, is a concession to eighteenth-century aesthetics. In the "Analytic of the Beautiful," by contrast, Kant strikes new ground, and this section therefore reveals, as Ernst Cassirer, among others, has pointed out, a certain foreign quality as far as the subject is concerned, in spite of all the rigor and conceptual refinement invested in its developments. According to Cassirer, Kant moves "once again on terrain that is personally and genuinely his" when broaching the problematics of the sublime as the supreme synthesis between the basic principles of his ethics and his aesthetics. In contrast to the section on the beautiful, that dealing with the sublime is, from a theoretical perspective, excessively clear—indeed, it is of spotless transparency. It displays, says Cassirer, "all the moments of the Kantian spirit and all those properties indicative of the man as well as of the writer in genuine fulfillment and in the most felicitous mutual interpretation. Hence the trenchancy of the analysis of pure concepts is found united with the moral sensitivity that forms the core of Kant's personality; here the eye for psychological detail that Kant had already evidenced in the precritical *Observations on the Feeling of the Beautiful and the Sublime* is allied with the encompassing transcendental perspectives, which he had achieved since that time over the whole domain of consciousness."[4]

But, however disconcerting the affirmation of obscurity in the place of clarity may be, however incomprehensible it may be to the philosopher that certain statements made with full regard to the requirements of philosophical argumentation are called "bewildering," the philosophically trained reader is certainly floored when he or she realizes that the rhetorical reading of philosophical texts not only completely disregards the literal meaning of texts but proceeds by means of a *total leveling* of everything constitutive of the text's specificity. The nonphenomenal reading collapses all differences that serve as barriers between concepts and discursive levels, as well as between the premises and conclusions of the separate steps of argumentation, differences on which the whole argument and its movements are dependent. Such a reading pays no respect to the architecture of a work of philosophy or to the differences between different works in the corpus of a philosopher.

That such an annulment of difference orients de Man's linguistic approach to philosophy can perhaps best be shown in the case of his readings of Hegel. Of the many examples that one could summon to make a point in case, we choose de Man's interpretation of the symbolic in Hegel's *Aesthetics*.

For Hegel, according to de Man, art "belongs unreservedly to the order of the symbol" (*AI*, p. 95). "The theory of the aesthetic, as a historical as well as a philosophical notion, is predicated, in Hegel, on a theory of art as symbolic" (*AI*, p. 93). In his "Critical Response: Reply to Raymond Geuss," after having repeated that "the aesthetic sign is symbolic," he insists that this "is *the* canonical sentence of Hegel's Aesthetic, and any attempt to make it say something else is either false or, as I suspect is the case here [in Raymond Geuss's objections], says the same thing but in less precise terms" (*AI*, p. 188).

de Man's contention that, for Hegel, all art is in essence symbolic is based on his interpretation of the following passage from the *Aesthetics* that we quote here in his own translation: "In the case of art, we cannot consider, in the symbol, the arbitrariness between meaning and signification [which characterizes the sign], since art itself consists precisely in the connection, the affinity and the concrete interpenetration of meaning and form (*AI*, p. 93). Read in its proper context, the passage in question establishes that because all art qua art presupposes at least some form of connection and affinity between meaning and form, the symbolic—if it happens to occur in art—cannot have the structure of the sign. The fact that all art rests on a minimal relation between form and content does not, according to the terminology of the *Aesthetics,* make all art symbolic. Indeed, the symbolic is only one of the three possible relations between form and content in art, the other two being the classical and the romantic. Throughout the *Aesthetics,* the term *symbolic* designates that particular form of art in which the content, because it is still entirely abstract, stands in a relation of total inadequacy to its material form. It is certainly the case, as Peter Szondi (to whom de Man refers in his essays on Hegel with respect to other issues) has amply made clear, that this use by Hegel of *symbolic* is most unusual. Indeed, rather than stressing its etymological meaning as falling into one, or as throwing together, Hegel emphasizes the content's inadequacy to its form and thus reduces the relation on which the symbol is based to that of a mere search for a mutual affinity between meaning and form.[5] Yet, this is the sense in which Hegel understands *symbol* in the *Aesthetics*. Instead of signifying the traditionally recognized natural kinship between its two parts, *symbol* in the *Aesthetics* only indicates the minimal relation between these two inadequate parts which thus can be said to be in search of adequation. As soon as full adequacy is achieved, the relation in question can no longer be termed "symbolic." This is also true of the subsequent reseparation of form and content in the aftermath of classical art. In short, Hegel uses *symbolic* in his *Aesthetics* to indicate a form of art prior to both the classical—where the concept of art is fully realized in a perfect harmony between form and content—and the romantic, a reseparation of these two elements following the classical. The symbolic is not only one form of art among others but is, in comparison to the classical, merely a preart *(Vorkunst)*.

In his response to Geuss, de Man admits that his reading of Hegel never referred to that "more precise sense of the term [symbolic]" as "a historical term in a system of periodization" but rather to a purely linguistic sense of *symbolic* (*AI*, pp. 187–188). Although de Man's essay did not demarcate his linguistic sense of *symbolic* from the technical sense in Hegel, he justifies his move in the "Response" by asserting that "the term 'symbolic' appears conspicuously in the *Aesthetics,* though it is not always used in the same sense." Hegel is said to also gloss "[symbolic] in purely linguistic terms, by setting up a distinction between sign and symbol. This differentiation belongs to all language in general," de Man remarks, concluding that: "The term 'symbolic' thus functions in a linguistic as well as historical register" (*AI*, p. 187).

In the following we must verify whether there is indeed another use of *symbolic* in the *Aesthetics.* As a matter of fact, one sees Hegel at times speaking of a "symbolic manner of representation and sensuous perception."[6] What Hegel means by this sense of "symbolic" is made explicit in the same part of the *Encyclopaedia* to which de Man turns in his essay— not, as one would expect, to substantiate his interpretation of *symbolic* in purely linguistic terms but to prove that *symbolic* implies reference to a linguistic *subject*. This part of the *Encyclopaedia* is entitled *The Philosophy of Mind* and is engaged in an analysis of the spirit's self-intuition, wherein the spirit is shown to inquire into its own being alone and to relate exclusively to its own determinations. Hegel determines symbolic imagination to be that form of imagination *(Vorstellung)* which allows the self-intuiting spirit to appropriate, that is, to universalize, not the world (as de Man puts it) but the immediate datum in itself *(das in sich gefundene Unmittelbare)* by giving it the existence of an image, a *bildliches Dasein*. Imagination as symbol producing synthesizes the intellect's self-intuited immediacy with what it has found in perception. Because imagination, in order to achieve such representation, must choose material "whose *independent* meaning *corresponds* to the determined content of the universal that is to be rendered as image," Hegel can equate it with what is formal in art, for art, he writes, "represents the truly universal or the *idea* in the form of *sensuous existence,* of the *image.*"[7] From this perspective, then, art in general can be called "symbolic" since it may choose only such material for its sensuous rendering of the idea that has some sort of natural relation to the content of the idea. Throughout the *Aesthetics,* however, Hegel insists that he is not concerned with this sense of *symbolic* but only and exclusively with the symbolic as one among three *forms of art.* After having criticized the Romantic attempt to extend symbolism to every sphere of mythology and art, he notes: "Our task must therefore consist, not in accepting diffusion of the symbolic over the entire field of art, but conversely expressly limiting the range of what in itself is presented to us as a symbol proper and therefore is to be treated as symbolical."[8]

It has become clear that de Man considers all art symbolic because it implies a minimal (natural) relation between meaning and material form. In what comes closest to a definition, he writes that "the symbol is the mediation between the mind and the physical world of which art manifestedly partakes" (*AI,* p. 93). Such a traditional understanding of *symbolic* also explains why de Man, in flagrant disregard of what Hegel wrote, can assert that because Hegel considers "the symbolic by way of an increasing proximity between sign and meaning, a proximity which, by principles of resemblance, analogy, filiation, interpenetration, and so forth, tightens the link between both to the ultimate point of identity," this identity would reach its climax in classical art: "Far from being nonsymbolic, classical art is the moment at which the semiotic function of language, which is, in principle, arbitrary and detached from meaning, is entirely transformed into a symbolic function" (*AI,* p. 188). Now although this sense of symbolic seems to correspond to what Hegel developed under the rubric of symbolic imagination, it is certainly not *the* canonical sentence of Hegel's *Aesthetics.* If there is such a sentence with respect to the symbolic in Hegel's work, it is one that stresses the relation of inadequacy between idea and natural form.

In addition to what has already been developed, it must be pointed out that *symbolic* in the sense of the universal images produced by imagination, is not, in essence, linguistic. To call it linguistic by arguing, as does de Man, that "we now associate [the term 'symbolic'] with linguistic structures" is merely to import a problematic into Hegel's text that reflects present theoretical concerns (*AI,* p. 93). The move is capital to de Man's whole argument, for it serves to suggest that an essentially Cratylian definition of language as symbolic sustains the whole of Hegel's *Aesthetics.* But, because of its imagelike products, symbolic imagination is still prelinguistic for Hegel. In symbols, the intellect only *looks at itself* in sensuous representations that are very distinct from the signs and words with which language begins. Hegel notes in the *Aesthetics* that "the symbol is *prima facie* a sign" only because it *designates* something however inarticulately.[9] But such designation is not yet linguistic, and certainly not in the modern sense of that term. A full demonstration of this would require long detours through the *Encyclopaedia.* Therefore, we will confine ourselves here to a number of points that indicate the direction that such a demonstration would have to take: (1) It must be recalled that *within* the sphere of art, a movement takes place from the symbolic, which is essentially mute, to the sign and word in the last form of Romantic art—poetry—which also brings about a passage to the higher spheres of the spirit. (2) As a whole, the sphere of art belongs to prelinguistic symbol-producing imagination. As soon as productive imagination turns into sign-producing imagination, that is, as soon as it becomes potentially capable of being linguistically expressed, the self-intuiting spirit leaves the realm of art behind itself. (3) As Hegel argues in the *Encyclopaedia,* imagination becomes sign-producing imagination when it gains greater freedom in the use of its interiorized perceptions for designating itself in its own immediate universality, or as *idea.* Such passage occurs where the spirit's perceptions *as* perceptions (perceptions belonging to the spirit alone) are put into relation with the spirit's *own* independent representations. Whereas the symbol's own content "corresponds, essentially and conceptually, to the content it expresses," signs have an arbitrary relation to what they refer to because, in them, the intellect has annuled the immediate and proper content of the perceptions, giving them a meaning derived completely from itself.[10] Yet, what is true of the symbol is also true of the sign: It is not linguistic *per se* for Hegel. Not only are linguistic signs, or *words,* merely one, however important, form of signs but signs in general function at first only as mute representations of the spirit. Their linguistic articulation is still excluded. Signs, for Hegel, are only the mute foundation, or if one prefers, the condition of possibility of speech and language. (4) de Man refers to these parts of the *Encyclopaedia* in order to prove that the problematic of the symbol, and especially of the sign, implies reference to a subject. It surely does, but the subject is here the self-knowing spirit, not a linguistic subject engaged in speech acts directed upon the world. If the foregoing points are carefully developed, they lead to the conclusion that the minimal relation between form and content that art generally presupposes cannot be called "symbolic" as referring to linguistic structures. If, however, de Man does so, if he subreptitiously turns Hegel's *Aesthetics* into a text based on and held together by a symbolic understanding of language, it is because for de Man, *all* "aesthetic theory, including its most systematic formulation in Hegel," is to be considered "as the complete unfolding of the model of which the Cratylian conception of language is a version" (*RT*, p. 10).

Rather than discussing the intriguing point of de Man's argument—an argument that extends Gérard Genette's contention that a "spontaneous belief in the resemblance of words and things, which is illustrated by a kind of eternal Cratylism . . . has always functioned as the ideology, or the 'indigenous theory' of poetic language," to the philosophical discipline of aesthetics in general—we would like to take de Man to task for his systematic leveling of conceptual differences and strata of argumentation in his own text.[11] Indeed, to argue that art in general is symbolic in Hegel's *Aesthetics,* de Man must disregard the difference between the symbolic as a *form* of art and art as a function of symbolic *representation,* as well as confound symbolic representation with *linguistic* representation or acts of speech. Only by ignoring the difference in status between the developments in the *Aesthetics* and what takes place in the *Encyclopaedia,* as well as the difference between certain parts of the *Encyclopaedia* itself, can de Man's rhetorical reading arrive at the conclusion that the *Aesthetics,* as an aesthetic, is based on a metaphysical conception of language.

What is further revealed by this short analysis of an important segment of de Man's approach to a philosophical text is that the leveling of differences—the subversion of all possible development through an annulment of differences—is itself only one prominent effect of de Man's more general "methodological" procedure of analogizing. More precisely, his "method" is based on positive analogy, i.e., one that emphasizes the likeness among instances and moments of a text, or different parts of a work, while neglecting the differences. Such analogical inference allows for comparisons between truly incommensurable elements, or more precisely, between two incompatible types of relationships, or proportions. As a result of this procedure, de Man does not only indefatigably point out mirror effects, close proximities, allusions, equivalences, resemblances, etc., between elements and movements in, or even outside texts, he also, and especially, draws similarities between relationships that because they are situated on completely different planes or in entirely different corpora are, in fact, uncomparable. Let us limit ourselves to two examples. In "Hegel on the Sublime," he notes: "The relationship between pantheism and monotheism in the history of art and religion . . . is like the relationship between natural sciences and epistemology" (*AI,* p. 111). Or, in "Phenomenality and Materiality in Kant": "If critical philosophy and metaphysics (including ideologies) are causally linked to each other, their relationship is similar to the relationship . . . between bodies and their transformations or motions" (*AI,* p. 72).

Such analogies, according to de Man, do not operate solely on the semantic level of the text but are also to be found on the level of enunciation, as well as between that level and the semantic level. In his essays on Nietzsche, he argues that one can draw similarities in *The Birth of Tragedy* between the theses stated there and the enunciatory text's level, between statement and what he calls, in one instance, "the *history* of the text," between its statements and its rhetorical praxis, between its semantic assertions and its rhetorical mode (*AR,* p. 116). He emphasizes that an analogy is to be found in *The Birth of Tragedy* "between genetic movements in history and semiological relationships in language" (*AR,* p. 102). Because such analogy produces "a potential confusion between figural and referential statement" and makes it impossible to distinguish the philosophical statements from the rhetorical figures on which they hinge, de Man concludes in these essays that the "textual authority" of the philosophical text is without all ground (*AR,* pp. 116, 99).

Generally speaking, one can say that for de Man the very possibility of such analogy prohibits all clear and distinct establishment of levels and conceptual differences. As far as his own texts are concerned, this analogical reasoning also explains and accounts for the onionskin structure of his texts (especially his later texts), as well as for the relation of chiasmic inversion through which the various skins mirror each other into a certain identify or, rather, sameness.

Is one not, in light of the results produced by this truly systematic leveling of difference and positive analogization—a leveling that is clearly deliberate, and not attributable to mere oversight or philosophical naïveté in general—immediately reminded of Hegel's famous dictum concerning those philosophers for whom thought is a night in which all cows are black? Because of de Man's claim that his treatment of philosophical texts can at least up to a certain point be measured against the standards of the canon and the rules of interpretation, the philosopher's scorn about such a handling of philosophical difference is fully justified. Still, to become merely outraged at de Man's activity may well mean to become trapped and ensnared. A step-by-step refutation of all the gross, and almost too blatant, errors that de Man seems to entertain in his readings of philosophy may blind the critic, and disable him from grasping the uncannily coherent, if not cogent "theoretical" project underlying all these flagrant violations. As said, de Man's work is involved in a rhetorical, nonphenomenal, literary, or linguistic reading of philosophical texts. Yet such a reading focuses on the "autonomous potential of language," and not, as a philosophical reading, on the transparent meaning that language purports to convey. The shift in focus to the autonomous potential of language, free of all relation to what is signified, causes language to turn opaque. Together with all the discursive differences of meaning, language, if thematized as such, loses all its previous semi-invisibility; it becomes objectified and acquires an unpenetrable opacity. Ultimately such analysis of the autonomous potential of language has no relation whatsoever to the meaning that this language appears to transport. Indeed, a rhetorical reading of a text is not geared toward revealing anything regarding the meaning of that text. It is not *about* a text, and thus cannot be measured against it. For such a reading, all the distinctive discursive moments and levels blend into one undifferentiated and nontransparent mass. But does this mass, therefore, correspond to that night of abstraction in which all cows are black? Although it is clear that such a reading does not contribute to the understanding of the text it deals with, de Man claims that precisely because such a reading is not *on* the texts it reads, it is *truer* to those texts (see *RR*, p. 123). De Man's readings make truth claims, but these claims do not concern the meaningful distinctions that literary criticism or philosophical canonical interpretation are concerned with. As far as philosophy is concerned, the truth that interests a linguistic reading of texts is not of the order of generality or universality. As seen, a linguistic reading is suspicious of the difference that philosophy makes and of all the differences that it must set up to unfold and account for its own status. But such a reading remains concerned with a certain truth, and, because this truth goes as far as to question the very possibility of abstraction, it does not seem to be a function of the black-on-black painting to which Hegel refers. But is it for that matter comparable to the gray on gray in which, according to Hegel, philosophy paints all things? Undoubtedly, de Man's enterprise presupposes, as does philosophy in general, a certain dusk—a "glimmering," in de Man's words—of meaning and difference. It also takes its flight with the oncoming of night, but it does not do so in order to reveal the thought of the world, the ideal, or the concept. The truth it summons is not one of difference, and its use of language in articulating that truth no longer yields to the philosophical imperative of speaking well.

Toward a Formal Materialism

In order to better circumscribe the sort of truth that a rhetorical reading is interested in, it is imperative to analyze in greater detail rhetorical reading's razing of philosophical difference. We return, therefore, to a discussion of de Man's essays on Nietzsche. As in his treatment of Hegel's *Aesthetics,* he sets out arguing that the illusion of coherence and of genetic development, which *The Birth of Tragedy* displays in spite of its obvious patchwork character of disconnected fragments, is an illusion rooted in a metaphysical assumption underlying that work. This assumption implies that all statements are grounded "in ontology and in a metaphyics of presence," thus securing "the possibility of language to reach full and substantial meaning." It is not without importance to mention that de Man neglects to actually prove that such "a deep-seated generative conception" controls all the levels of discourse in Nietzsche's early work (*AR*, p. 88). While de Man underpinned his assertion of the symbolic nature of Hegel's *Aesthetics* as a whole by reading "symbolic" in a nontechnical sense and according to the meaning that it has *now,* for us, the same assertion with respect to Nietzsche's text is taken for granted as having been proved by *recent* criticism on Nietzsche.[12] This assertion by de Man can be construed as one facet of a double strategy that organizes his readings of texts; this first movement consists of stating that the seemingly coherent and continuous nature of texts, as well as their referential properties, hinges on the symbolic and genetic model of language that sustains them. The second facet of the strategy of a rhetorical reading attempts to prove that a text inscribes reference to its nonphenomenal figuration. This reference is shown to take place in a twofold manner: through the text's thematic self-destruction of its own illusionary continuity, on the one hand, and through thematic representation of the nonphenomenal and autonomous potential of language within the text, on the other hand. Such double reference, according to de Man, not only destroys the genetic continuity of the text, it also reveals the metaphysical assumption regarding language at the base of the text to be thoroughly erroneous.

It is certainly not insignificant that de Man does not find this inscription of the nonphenomenal power of language in the text of *The Birth of Tragedy* itself but rather—already emphasizing in this manner the lack of phenomenal unity of Nietzsche's work—in the "discontinuous aphoristic formulations" not included in that work and which feature Nietzsche's "main theoretical speculations on language and art at the time of *The Birth of Tragedy*" (AR, pp. 101, 88). Yet what do these fragments, which are said to found the whole of Nietzsche's work on tragedy, establish? After having argued that in *The Birth of Tragedy,* unity and genetic unfolding hinge on the possibility of Dionysius's appearance as Apollo, on a will representing itself as music, on the authority of a human voice as the origin of the narrative, etc.—possibilities that, according to de Man, are all grounded in a genetic and symbolic model of language—de Man asserts that these fragments put the *possibility of such a passage or transition*—say, from the literal to the figural, from essence to appearance, from origin to representation, etc.—radically into question. de Man contends that these fragments contest "the will as the ontological category by means of which beginning and end, origin and purpose are united in one genetic pattern." By totally separating these instances, "all possible claim at genetic totalization" becomes undermined: "No bridge, as metaphor or as representation, can ever connect the natural realm of essences with the textual realm of forms and values" (AR, pp. 99–100). The thrust of the second facet of the strategy constitutive of rhetorical and nonphenomenal reading thus serves to establish the complete impossibility of development, continuous construction, and unfolding of a philosophical argument.

As the essay "The Rhetoric of Tropes" holds, this impossibility of processlike development is a function of a structural aspect of language.

In analyzing one passage from the *Will to Power,* de Man attempts to show that here the logical priority of one of the terms of the binary conceptual polarities in the history of metaphysics—the example is the priority of cause over effect—is always based on a "cumulative error" resulting from a linguistic event of erroneous substitutions, that is, without regard for truth, made possible by the rhetorical essence of language "as the play of reversals and substitutions." The logical priority of cause over effect thus appears to be a function of the rhetorical figure of metonymy or metalepsis by which cause and effect become interchangeable. But since, according to that very figure, "the priority status of the two poles can be reversed," as well, there is, from a linguistic point of view, absolutely no intrinsic reason why one option would have to be privileged over the other (*AR,* pp. 107, 108). As a consequence, all philosophical truth and *a fortiori* all philosophical distinctions are considered nothing but erroneous assumptions rooted in the figurative power of language. In the same essay, de Man also claims that although a philosophical text such as Nietzsche's may be critical of the category of self-hood, the critical discourse's own centrality and alleged self-identity is nothing but a metaphor of self, a displaced self never questioned and based on an exchange made possible by the figural essence of language. In the same way as self-hood is an illusion, philosophy's centrality and authority are a lie, as a matter of fact, a cumulative lie because they are the lie of a lie, grounded in what de Man calls "language's positional power" (see *AR,* pp. 111–112). All of philosophy's ontological claims as well are based on the linguistic "possibility of unwarranted substitutions" and on "misinterpreted systems of relationships." They are said to be, without exception, rooted in "the rhetorical substratum" of language (*AR,* p. 123). Yet, if this is the case, if, indeed, all philosophical truths and ontological claims are but the result of erroneously fixed exchanges or substitutions on the rhetorical level of language, then, instead of following from insight or genuine development, philosophical statements do nothing but *repeat* the figural properties of language as such. All philosophical cognition and its claims to truth stem from misinterpretations of the relations made possible by figures of exchange and substitution, figures that thoroughly undermine the very possibility of an unequivocal and continuous passage from one pole to another because the relations between them can always be inverted. From the perspective of de Man's linguistic or literary reading of philosophy, there can be no such thing as development, a continuous and articulated unfolding of an argument from a premise to a conclusion or of a discourse from a beginning to an end. Indeed, in such a reading, the philosophical text *separates* into absolutely *unrelating* agencies, instances, levels, acts. The philosophical text becomes atomized in an out-and-out fragmentization against the backdrop of its rhetorical substratum.

In order to refine our analysis of rhetorical reading's dismantling of relations between terms, planes, and parts of a text, we now turn briefly to de Man's analysis of Shelley's *The Triumph of Life*. In this essay, de Man, following his double strategy of reading, first concentrates on what he calls a "thematic" or, rather, "specular understanding of the text." Such an understanding that coincides with a cognitive approach to the text—"in which the text serves as a mirror of our own knowledge and our own knowledge mirrors in its turn the text's signification"—is rooted, according to de Man, "in the illusion of doubleness" or of a split between self-contained unities that would make self-reflexive closure possible (*RR,* p. 112). A speculative reading bent on achieving self-reflective closure presupposes difference, more precisely, a difference in which the differents stand in a relation of duplication to one another. On the whole, "Shelley Disfigured" wants to demonstrate that such self-reflexivity is never attained because the text—in this case, Shelley's poem—does not produce the doubles required to achieve specular closure. de Man insists that all specular understanding becomes blocked already at its thematic level. Indeed, instead of providing answers to questions that punctuate the poem, answers that, as the doubles of these questions, would permit cognition, Shelley's poem only features further questions. de Man writes: "The structure of the text is not one of question and answer, but of a question whose meaning, as question, is effaced from the moment it is asked. The answer to the question is another question" (*RR,* p. 98). In the question that answers the first question, the initial question becomes forgotten because there is no answer that would still refer to it. In other words, with the mere occurrence of the second question, all relation to the first question is cut off—it is literally forgotten. After having evoked the Platonic and Neo-Platonic definition of forgetting as anamnesis, de Man notes that in contrast to the latter, "what one forgets here is not the previous condition, for the line of demarcation between the two conditions is so unclear, the distinction between the forgotten and the remembered so unlike the distinction between two well-defined areas, that we have no assurance whatever that the forgotten ever existed" (*RR*, p. 104). This is a radical forgetting that makes it impossible to distinguish something as preceding or following something else since all relations are disconnected. Yet, if that is so, it is already impossible on the thematic level itself to relate anything to anything, to tell the difference between one thing and another. Instead of giving way to symmetrical differents that could be related in a specular manner to one another, the text, already from a thematic perspective, appears to have a pulverizing structure that leads to hovering, or glimmering, ambivalence, to use de Man's own terms. None of the images of Shelley's poem can be clearly determined with respect to (their) opposites, and hence the symmetry required by cognitive reflection is never attained. The poem's text is thematically disarticulated—nothing relates to anything—and this pointedly prevents the gathering of some unifying and totalizing meaning from the poem.

To understand adequately and truly why such a text as Shelley's poem allows understanding itself "to wane away, layer by layer, until it is entirely forgotten and remains present only in the guise of an edifice that serves to celebrate and perpetuate its oblivion," however, it is necessary to proceed with de Man to the second facet of rhetorical reading's strategy, that is, to its nonphenomenal phase. The necessity of such a reading is thematically, phenomenally, inscribed in a text. In the case of Shelley's poem, de Man locates it in the text's reference to "measure"—here understood as the figuration of "articulated sound, that is language," and not music, since "its determining property is an articulation distinctive of verbal sound prior to its signifying function." Indeed, if "'measure' separates from the phenomenal aspects of signification as a specular *representation,* and stresses instead the literal and material aspects of language," then, "measure," in the text of the poem, corresponds to a "thematization of language" (*RR*, pp. 112, 113). With the term *measure,* the text refers to its own linguistic figuration, to "the nonsignifying, material properties of language," signification, and figuration itself. de Man distinguishes at least three aspects of the literal and material properties of language. The characteristics of all of these have a disruptive effect on the illusionary continuity of the text and its meaning: (1) referring to the classical theories of the sign, he determines these properties to be relatively *independent;* (2) their "free play in relation to . . . (their) signifying function" shows them to be characterized by *randomness* and *arbitrariness;* (3) their representation or figuration in the text "disrupts the symmetry of cognition as representation," or to use more colorful terms, it extinguishes and buries all "poetic and philosophical light" (*RR*, pp. 114, 113). These literal and material qualities of language are a first cornerstone of the very particular and extremely idiosyncratic philosophy that animates the nonphenomenal reading phase of texts. de Man calls it "formal materialism." As remains to be seen, it is a philosophy whose gaze traverses the substance of texts attending neither to the objectivity of its structures nor to the spiritual activity at its base but to qualities of the text that, as can already be seen from the nature of the material and literal properties of language, stand in no relation whatsoever to the texts' figural and conceptual constructs amenable to aesthetic and nonaesthetic experience. Considering the sheer arbitrariness and intrinsic senselessness of the material and signifying agencies of language, the randomness of their individual occurrences, the relative independence of their play, and the opacity of their literal materiality, all experiencable meaning appears *superimposed* on them. But since these properties cannot because, of their material opacity and lack of meaning, relate to one another in any significant manner, all objective intelligibility, that is, the texts' latent armature—its structure—seems to be the result of an imposition as well. As these literal instances become thematized in the text's inscribed reference to its own figuration, they tend to exhibit a sphere of irreducible heterogeneity characterized by the absolute impenetrability and material singularity of the linguistic sounds or letters that, therefore, do not lend themselves to any meaningful interaction. These instances form a chaotic sphere of radically fragmented material agencies between which no text can ever be woven.

In his readings of Kant and Hegel, de Man has made the attempt to conceptualize, so to speak, what must be viewed as the first element of the "ontological" base not only of all texts but of de Man's own highly disturbing practice of reading. Indeed, all his transgressions, whether related to the commensurability of concepts, levels of argumentation, parts of works, or works among each other, in short, all of his infractions against the philosophical law *par excellence,* the law prohibiting all *metabasis eis allo genos* find their "ontological" justification in de Man's theory concerning the absolute heterogeneity and intrinsic meaninglessness of the linguistic signifier. This theory alone explains the coherent, if not cogent, nature of his infractions against the law of interpretation.

In order to situate and assess the nature of those literal and material properties of language, it is certainly appropriate to turn to de Man's essay "Phenomenality and Materiality in Kant" as well as to the article "Kant's Materialism." In the latter essay, de Man claims that "a materialism much more radical than what can be conveyed by such terms as "realism" or "empiricism" inhabits Kantian idealism. What this materialism amounts to can best be grasped in "Phenomenality and Materiality in Kant." After having asserted that ideologies and metaphysics depend on transcendental philosophy and that metaphysics and critical philosophy are interdependent as well, de Man raises the question of how transcendental philosophy can be said to be dependent on something metaphysical or empirical. In a more than questionable operation of analogy, that relation of dependence becomes conceptualized in terms of a causal link. The place where such causal relation can best be established, according to de Man, is the *Critique of Judgement,* which itself "corresponds to the necessity of establishing the causal link between critical philosophy, between a purely conceptual and an empirically determined discourse," that is, between the *Critique of Pure Reason* (in de Man's terms, a transcendental *philosophy*) and *The Critique of Practical Reason* (in short, "an empirically determined discourse," or what, for de Man, amounts to the same, an ideological or metaphysical *philosophy*) (*AI,* p. 73). In total oblivion of the fact that the *Second Critique* is a critique and not a dogmatic philosophy and that the category of causality is applicable to the realm of objects of nature alone, de Man turns the aesthetic—and above all one of its forms, the sublime—into the "phenomenalized, empirically manifest principle of cognition on whose existence the possibility of such an articulation" of the transcendental and the metaphysical depends. The privilege accorded to the sublime in this respect rests on Reasons's involvement in the latter. In the sublime, the "noumenal entity" of Reason becomes phenomenally represented. Whereas "the beautiful is a metaphysical and ideological principle, the sublime aspires to being a transcendental one," writes de Man (*AI,* p. 73). Yet, the task of finding a phenomenal equivalent for a conceptually infinite notion turns out to be the real crux of the analytics of the sublime. Indeed, de Man notes, the model that Kant advances in answer to this problem, a model whose paradigmatic totalization leads to comprehension's discovery of its limitations regarding the noumenal entity of Reason, is, because of its economic pattern of loss and gain, "no longer, properly speaking, philosophical, but linguistic." Thus, instead of allowing for a transcendental determination, the sublime can be only formally determined. The model that Kant uses to phenomenalize Reason "describes, not a faculty of the mind, be it as consciousness or as cognition, but a potentiality inherent in language. For such a system of substitution, set up along a paradigmatic and a syntagmatic axis, generating partial totalizations within an economy of profit and loss, is a very familiar model indeed . . . It is the model of discourse as ˄ tropological system. The desired articulation of the sublime takes place, with suitable reservations and restriction, within such a purely formal system" (*AI*, p. 73). This purely formal system that animates aesthetic judgment in the dynamics of the sublime and that under the guise of a philosophical argument produces a causal determination and a paradigmatic totalization of infinite Reason is formal to the extent that it refers to language independently of all semantic depth, that is, to language in its purely material properties devoid as yet "of any reflexive or intellectual complication" (*AI*, p. 83). Yet the causal determination of Reason in the sublime thus brought to light—a determination of the transcendental by something metaphysical, that is, empirical and ideological in de Man's own terms—is based on a causation by something that, in the last resort, is accessible neither to the powers of transcendental philosophy nor, for that matter, to metaphysics or ideology. Hence, the materiality of the linguistic signifier radically disrupts the economy of interdependence and of cognitive reflection in the play between transcendental philosophy and metaphysics since the materiality in question, a materiality that does not illustrate or represent the infinite, is no longer of the order of metaphysics; rather, it stands in a relation of asymmetry to all of the forms of cognition referred to, and their reflexive interplay.

This, then, is the status of the materiality of language in its unwrought, or native, state: It is a cause devoid of all meaning, of all semantic depth, that stands in a relation of eccentricity to what it appears to effect.[13] Because of its ultimate meaninglessness and its exorbitant situation, because of the absence of a (meaningful) relation between it and what becomes superimposed on it as its effect, this irreducibly formal materiality functions as "a break or discontinuity" at the heart not only of the *Third Critique* but, more generally, of thought itself (*AI*, p. 79). It disarticulates what it effectuates, says de Man. On the last pages of "Phenomenality and Materiality in Kant," he seeks this materialism "that Kant's posterity has not yet begun to face up to" in the very "dismemberment of language," in meaning's dependence on "the fragmentation of sentences and propositions into discrete words, or the fragmentation of words into syllables or finally letters" (*AI*, p. 89). de Man goes as far as to ascertain that the very success of certain Kantian arguments, rather than resulting from philosophical development, is decisively dependent on "the play of the letter and of the syllable," in short, on elements that are in themselves without any meaning whatsoever. He writes:

> Is not the persuasiveness of the entire passage on the recovery of the imagination's tranquility after the shock of the sublime surprise based, not so much on the little play acted out by the senses, but on the proximity between German words for surprise and admiration, *Verwunderung* and *Bewunderung*? And are we not made to assent to the more than paradoxical but truly aporetic incompatibility between the failure of the imagination to grasp magnitude with what becomes, in the experience of the sublime, the success of this same imagination as an agent of reason, are we not made to assent to this because of a constant, and finally bewildering alternation of the two terms, *Angemessen(heit)* and *Unangemessen(heit)*, to the point where one can no longer tell them apart? The bottom line, in Kant as well as in Hegel, is the prosaic materiality of the letter and no degree of obfuscation or ideology can transform this materiality into the phenomenal cognition of aesthetic judgement.   (*AI*, pp. 89–90)

But, although the prosaic materiality of the letter, the arbitrary element of the nonsignifying properties of linguistic articulation, undoes "the representational and iconic function of figuration," as de Man argues in his analysis of Shelley's *The Triumph of Life*, it "does not by itself have the power to break down the specular structure which the text erects" (*RR*, pp. 114). The materiality in question disrupts only the figural, the sensory cognitive aspect of the iconic function. But figure, de Man adds, is not essential to figuration: "The iconic, sensory or, if one wishes, the aesthetic moment is not constitutive of figuration." Figuration creates the illusion of meaning neither merely nor primarily through sensory pleasure but through signification rooted in the semiological possibility of substituting reiteration (*RR*, pp. 114–115). We are told that this latter possibility is a function of the irreducibly mechanical rules of grammar and syntax. Functioning "on the level of the letter without the intervention of an iconic factor," these mechanical rules, whose repetitive senselessness constitutes the signifying function of language, are, because of their exorbitant position, disfigurative of figuration as the meaning-creating process itself. There is, however, a last nonsignifying aspect to language that serves as another essential disruptive ground of all linguistic figuration in that it concerns the act of the signifying function as such. If what we developed under the category of the literal and material dimension of language could be considered to be the "ontological" foundation of rhetorical reading, this last, and complementary linguistic function, bears on its "epistemological" foundation. Together these two aspects of formal materialism seem to represent a miniature philosophical system, one that combines an ontology with a theory of cognition. The formal materialism at the base of de Man's rhetorical reading is a philosophy, consequently, that in its own way lives up to the major standards and requirements of classical philosophy. But, as remains to be seen, this is not yet all. It is indeed a philosophy similar to all others in that it also submits to the aegis of *theoria*. Yet, before engaging in a discussion of what thus appears to be *in nuce,* at least, a comprehensive system of foundation, let us first establish the nature of that aspect of language that, according to de Man, radically disrupts figuration as a meaningful act.

What radically disfigures figure is nothing less than the fact that "the figure is not naturally given or produced but that it is posited by an arbitrary act," as de Man notes in his analysis of *The Triumph of Life.* In other words, de Man asserts that between the linguistic act constitutive of signification and meaning itself, there is no relation of any sort. It is an arbitrary act that, by virtue of the total absence of continuity between itself and what it causes, is itself absolutely meaningless. But this blind, and in itself senseless, act is not only separated from what follows it as its effects, it is also preceded by nothing. We read that it "relates to nothing that comes before or after." It is "detached from all antecedents," and, consequently, it is an act in "its own right," absolutely singular and pointlike, "brusque and unmotivated." Or, to cite again: It is "a single, and therefore violent, act of power achieved by the positional power of language considered by and in itself" (*RR,* pp. 116–117). This positing power of language, as de Man understands it, whose performative properties differ "considerably from conventional as well as from 'creatively' (or, in the technical sense, intentionally) constitutive" performance elaborated by speech act theories, "is both entirely arbitrary, in having a strength that cannot be reduced to necessity, and entirely inexorable in that there is no alternative to it. It stands beyond the polarities of chance and determination," de Man remarks (*RT*, p. 19; *RR*, p. 116). In the same way as the sun, which in the poem is said to spring forth of "its own unrelated power," free from all dependence on the agonistic pathos of the dialectical battle between the doubles or differents, the speculative play of cognition and the self-reflexivity of the text—the *act* of linguistic figuration—is irreducibly singular and, because it relates to nothing, is instantly forgotten. A text is punctuated by its myriad positing acts. In a manner similar to the literal and material properties of the linguistic signifier, these acts form a chaos of opaque (since they are always unique and unrelated) linguistic events that in principle "cannot be made part" of the text (*RR*, p. 116). But, without these meaningless events of positing, there would be, of course, no text.

A rhetorical reading, one that focuses on the nonphenomenal and autonomous potential of language, rather than producing noumena, exhibits a fragmentary chaos of meaningless linguistic matter, repetitive mechanical rules, and absolutely opaque linguistic events. The radically irreducible empiricalness of all these agencies and instances represents the truth about texts. It is the truth by which a rhetorical reading must abide. But one question remains: How can this truth be beheld? In short, it is the question of how the "ontological" and "epistemological" substratum of texts comes into view at all. We recall that a nonphenomenal, nonaesthetic linguistic reading is a reading that reaches not only beyond the aesthetic and sensuous categories but beyond the intuitable as such. In this sense it is necessarily nonperceptual. What sort of gaze, then, animates a nonphenomenal reading? How is one to look at texts in order to bring that "ontological" and "epistemological" substratum to the fore, in whose light they revert into an uncanny opaqueness? To circumscribe this opacifying glance that stares at the incomprehensibility or chaos, which Friedrich Schlegel considered the origin left in darkness out of which the intellect constructed the entire unending world, to circumscribe this, it is necessary to return once again to de Man's reading of the *Critique of Judgement*.[14]

The problem facing the *Third Critique* is, according to de Man, one of finding a representation for what in principle is unrepresentable—reason and the ideas. As we have already pointed out, de Man finds Kant's solution to this problem, in the part of the *Critique of Judgement* devoted to the mathematical sublime, unsatisfactory, obscure, and ridden by difficulties. He explains these difficulties by the constraints forced upon Kant to seek recourse under the guise of rigorous philosophical argumentation to something which is not philosophical at all, namely, to a linguistic and formal structure of substitution void of all content. Neglecting the fact that the two parts of the sublime—the mathematical and the dynamical sublime—represent symmetric possibilities of the sublime as such, de Man notes that rather than further developing, let alone solving, the difficulties apparent in the mathematical sublime, the chapter on the dynamics of the sublime only repeats, restates, and refines those difficulties. The obscurity and difficulty to which de Man refers especially in the second chapter on the sublime, lie with Kant's reminder that, if nature is to produce sublime effects, it must be experienced in an entirely disinterested manner, free of all teleological judgment. The starry heaven and the vast ocean are sublime only if we regard them "as poets do, merely by what strikes the eye *(was der Augenschein zeigt)*," in short, as "a distant, all-embracing, vault" or, respectively, as "a clear mirror of water only bounded by the heaven."[15] Yet, what is, according to de Man, so difficult and obscure about Kant's demand? Seemingly, it is the fact that the sublime as a representation of ideas is dependent on what de Man perceives as an irreducibly mindless act of ocular vision, a purely *material* vision, as he translates *Augenschein*. Now, before further analysis of what de Man means by such a vision, it needs first to be clarified whether or not one can, indeed, equate disinterested vision of objects of nature, that is, a vision free of all particular judgments of sense, of logically determinate, and of teleological judgment, with mere (mindless) vision.

The question, first, is whether, in Kant, there can be a thing such as mere vision at all? Is regarding nature "just as we see it" really free of everything intellectual? Although de Man recalls that Kant speaks in his *Logic* of mere intuition *(blosse Anschauung)* as an intuition devoid of concepts, it is questionable whether mere intuition can be equated with mere vision in de Man's sense. One certainly remembers Kant's famous sentence from *The Critique of Pure Reason* that concepts without intuitions are empty, and intuitions without concepts, blind. The savage's observation of an object whose purpose he does not know—Kant's example is a house—is a blind perception, for sure, since from a formal point of view, it lacks all relation to consciousness. But Kant's limitation of the savage's perception to the matter *(Materie)* of perception alone is meaningful only insofar as the lack of determination of the matter of cognition immediately calls upon cognition's other facet, its relation to the subject. Even if the savage perceives without concepts, this very lack implies a negative relation to the formal aspect of cognition. The faculties never operate alone, absolutely independent of one another, in the last resort, because of the transcendental unity of apperception. The mere vision de Man speaks of cannot be identified with the mere intuition in question. By right, it is asymmetrical to the amorph sensation of the savage (which is not even, strictly speaking, visual) whose lack of concepts is meaningful for Kant because it is counterposed to the formal categories.[16]

The aesthetic judgment on the beautiful is excellent proof of this essential interdependence of the faculties since it exhibits, in what is called the "play of the faculties," the minimal agreement between imagination as the highest sensible faculty and understanding as the intelligible faculty of the concepts.[17] By contrast, the judgment of the sublime is witness to a play that implies a minimal relation between imagination and the faculty of the ideas, i.e., Reason. In the same way as the aesthetic judgment on the beautiful can be constructed as the formal condition of possibility, or the minimal interplay of the faculties required for there to be a cognition of nature, the aesthetic judgment on the sublime must be understood as the minimal interplay needed for there to be a mediation between concepts of nature and concepts of freedom. The sublime is, by definition, this relation *sine qua non,* without which no application of Reason to imagination could ever be envisioned. The sublime, then, is at first a relation. Kant writes in the *Third Critique:* "The *Sublime* consists merely in the *relation* by which the sensible in the representation of nature is judged available for a possible supersensible use."[18] Yet, what sort of relation can the sublime be if one remembers that it is a relation between a sensible faculty (however elevated) and a supersensible faculty, the "faculty expressing the interdependence of absolute totality?"[19] Imagination is the faculty of *Darstellung,* that is, of the sensible presentation of the spontaneity of understanding and Reason. Contrary to the beautiful, which must be understood as the direct presentation of the possibility of schematizing presentable concepts, the sublime takes it upon itself to present what by right is unpresentable. Thus, the task that seems to be devolved upon it seems to be a variation of what Kant calls in Chapter 59 "symbolic hypotyposis," a variation because Kant distinguishes only two types of hypotyposis, schematical and symbolic hypotyposis.[20] Indeed, in the same way as symbolic presentation presents only indirectly, the sublime renders the intelligible in an indirect manner. It does so by what can best be designated as a *negative* hypotyposis. As is well known, the relation established between imagination and Reason in the judgment on the sublime is not a harmonious relation but one of conflict. It is a relation, nevertheless and, as such a relation, the conflict *(Widerstreit)* staged between the two faculties does not exclude totality. On the contrary, totality is presupposed by the conflict of the faculties: Their severing takes place within it. Yet, how does this negative presentation of the unpresentable take place in that play of the faculties of imagination and Reason properly called "sublime"? It is brought about, Kant tells us, by imagination's extension *(Erweiterung)*. Imagination becomes extended as soon as it gives up its primary bias toward sensibility—in short, as soon as it brings its presenting function to a stop. This interruption occurs in an act of freedom and of self-determination. The extension of imagination, as Kant stresses, is the result of a self-violation and self-dispossession by which imagination sacrifices its sensible nature, i.e., its destiny as a faculty of mere presentation. Yet, in doing so, imagination submits to the rule of Reason, or what is the same, to the law of freedom as the law of absolute totality. Thus, in extending itself in an act of freedom, imagination turns *itself* into the subjective-purposive presentation of the unpresentable. In the context of Kant's treatment of the sublime, the reference to the Jewish commandment "Thou shalt not make thyself any graven image, nor the likeness of anything which is in heaven or in the earth or under the earth" as a command of Reason, leaves no doubt as to the necessity of imagination to give up its attempt to visualize Reason, to make an image of it.[21]

But, by following this reasonable demand, imagination attains itself a nonsensuous resemblance to Reason, that is, of the unpresentable totality itself. In short, then: In the sublime a minimal (and negative) presentation of the unpresentable, of the faculty of ideas that is Reason, takes place, which, by the way, is, in its very negativity, the matrix of all sensible actualization of these ideas in the ethical realm.

Let us now circle back to the problematics of the *Augenschein*. The philosophers immediately preceding Kant (those from Wolff to Baumgarten) make a strong link between the sensible faculty of imagination and eyesight. The specificity of the images of imagination consists, apart from their reproductive function, in conferring a sensible unity (individuality) upon appearances. What Kant calls "immediate intuition" or the "mere sight" or "what merely strikes the eye" is akin to Baumgarten's "dispositio naturalis ad perspecaciam," through which nature is perceived in its totality, not in a conceptual mode, however, but in a mode immanent to the being of nature.[22] The *Augenschein* is a synthesis of phenomenality in a minimally phenomenal manner. In Kant, this synthesis is made possible by the fact that the *Augenschein,* as soon as it enters into the service of the sublime, no longer sees anything determinate, but the unseeable itself. What does the *Augenschein* refer to if not to nature *as a whole*—the sky "as a distant, all-embracing, vault" (an example of the mathematically sublime), and the ocean as a similar totality— or to nature as a negative presentation of our incommensurable faculty of Reason in the image of the "abyss threatening to overwhelm everything" natural (an example of the dynamically sublime)? In seeing nothing determinate but the unseeable *par excellence,* the *Augenschein,* thus, yields to the law of freedom and Reason. Free from concepts of understanding and a sensuous presentation only to the extent that it is the faculty of eyesight itself, the *Augenschein,* because it does not see anything particular but the whole of nature or Reason, is itself an imageless image of Reason. But, ultimately, the unseeable revealed by the *Augenschein* as the *one* glance that embraces center and periphery at once, fails to show what it shows. It is, for Kant, an impossible endeavor to try to present the intelligible totality *as* the totality of nature not only because that totality is by right unpresentable but also because no totalization of nature can be achieved. The *Augenschein,* however, while failing to present the intelligible, offers it to thought. Although the synthesis by imagination of the whole of nature fails, the *Augenschein* is sublime because it reveals "imagination in its greatest extension," that is, imagination as yielding to "the principles of the schematism of the judgement (being so far, therefore, ranked under freedom)."[23] The *Augenschein,* thus, shows imagination yielding to Reason; it is witness to imagination's minimal relation to that faculty. This conclusion springs forth, last but not least, from Kant's rather intricate statement that despite what the *Augenschein* shows, the ocean must (nonetheless) be judged sublime (*man muss den Ozean bloss, wie die Dichter es tun, nach dem, was der Augenschein zeigt . . . dennoch erhaben finden können*)."[24] Rather than being mere ocular vision, the "immediate intuition" of the *Augenschein* is immediate in a negative fashion through which it negatively presents the very faculty of the ideas. Instead of being an obstacle to the presentation of ideas, the *Augenschein* thus seems to be another name for the extended imagination itself and, consequently, the very presentation, however negative, of the faculty of absolute totalization.

But reading Kant by rote, de Man is compelled to understand the *Augenschein,* which confers sublimity on nature, as entirely destitute of all intervention by the intellect. He writes: "No mind is involved in the Kantian vision of ocean and heaven" (*AI*, p. 82). It is a "purely material" vision, "devoid of any reflexive or intellectual complication; it is also purely formal, devoid of any semantic depth and reducible to the formal mathematization or geometrization of pure optics." "In this mode of seeing, the eye is its own agent and not the specular echo of the sun" (*AI*, p. 83). According to de Man, this act of perception is absolutely unrelated, unique, entirely unintelligible in its singularity. Therefore, he can also hold that the perceptions of heaven and ocean as vault or floor are not themselves of the order of trope or figuration: "Heaven and ocean as buildings are a priori, previous to any understanding," and unseparable from the material vision itself which knows no duality (*AI*, p. 82). Now, in "Kant's Materialism," de Man speaks of the unity of *Augenschein* and Kant's architectonic world, as a "stony gaze" (*AI*, p. 127). This stony gaze is, for de Man, a moment of "absolute, radical formalism, that entertains no notion of reference or semiosis" and that lies forgotten at the heart of the *Third Critique's* attempt to bridge Reason and the empirical (*AI*, p. 128). More precisely, the *Third Critique* is itself the result of a forgetting of its source in a purely formal, material, and mindless stare.[25]

But this stony gaze of material vision, a vision in which the materiality of the letter and of the linguistic acts of positing are still one, in which no difference, and hence no substituting exchange between differents, is possible, this stony gaze is also what provides de Man's rhetorical reading with its theoretical thrust. In the nonperceptual perception of its frozen gaze, one indeed recognizes a formal and material act of synthesis—a transcendental apperception, of sorts—in which both sides of de Man's enterprise, his "ontology" and "epistemology," appear still undifferentiated, one, and thus, absolutely impenetrable. But, obviously, this monstrous synthesis is also indistinguishable from the fragmentary chaos of the irreducibly singular material instances and purely formal acts of language.

At this point, one can no longer overlook the fact that de Man's destruction of philosophical difference, of the difference that philosophy makes by virtue of its claims to generality and universality, takes place in the name of a singularity so radical that it cannot be termed "empirical" anymore, a singularity that, in its irreducible idiosyncrasy, seeks to thoroughly foreground the possibility of intelligibility. But this extreme singularity that defies all comprehensibility also, by virtue of its fragmentary nature, appears to be a function of a very particular type of philosophy that can be construed as a "materialist" variation of the still idealist romantic project, namely, that of the fragmentary chaos of progressive universal poetry. However, the elimination of all *differentiae* in the romantic medium of reflection takes on, in de Man's rhetorical reading, unheard of proportions. Instead of opening up to *one* universe of seed-like fragments susceptible of engendering worlds, de Man's philosophy emphasizes a much darker picture. His is a world of unrelated singulars, each so idiosyncratic that in it everything universal becomes extinguished; it is a world of heterogeneous fragments forming a whole only insofar as, by their mutual indifference and lack of generative power, they are all the same, endlessly repeating the punctuality of their lone meaninglessness. De Man's philosophy thus seems to invoke Schelling's originary indifference of the One, yet the connotations of indifference resonate here in a manner very different from that of the romantic philosopher.

Must we conclude, at this point, that the annulment of philosophical difference in nonphenomenal reading is a function of just another philosophy—of a philosophy that, in contradistinction to classical philosophy, would *not speak well* and that would be resisting the difference that philosophy makes, would relinquish universality for the sake of the absolutely singular? One might be inclined to think so and explain the naïvetés to which such a philosophy would have to give in, as well as the insurmountable difficulties that it presents, by recalling the objections Sartre aimed at Bataille, who, as one knows, was involved in a similar enterprise of recuperating a radical singularity, namely, that the neglect of philosophical difference and its exigencies inevitably results in philosophy's revenge: a philosophy of indifference as outlined suffers, indeed, from irreparable philosophical naïveté! But, rather than embarking on a discussion of the problems that such a variation on romantic thought may pose, we prefer to consider a variety of issues that, in the case of de Man, may severely limit the possibility of such criticism in the first place. Undoubtedly, the philosophy of formal materialism that we have shown to animate the nonphenomenal phase of de Man's reading of philosophy is one of this critic's major and consistent concerns. In literary theory it is the "necessarily pragmatic moment that certainly weakens it as theory but that adds a subversive element of unpredictability and makes it something of a wild card in the serious game of the theoretical disciplines," and upon this pragmatic moment de Man focuses his interest (*RT,* p. 8). When dealing with the philosophy of Kant, for instance, de Man brings a material vision into view that is said to remain external to the concept, while his readings of Hegel focus on the alleged dependence of thought as such on a material inscription and on the mechanical function of memory as *Gedächtnis.* de Man's reproaches to the tradition of Kant and Hegel exegesis to have "entirely overlooked what we call the material aspect," clearly demonstrate that his formal materialism comes closest to what could be considered his own "positive" philosophy (*AI,* p. 83). But the fact that this formal materialism is indeed a correlate of reading specific texts and also primarily of rhetorical reading's second facet of nonphenomenal reading should already be ample reason for caution against overhasty conclusions. Indeed, formal materialism as a philosophy is not de Man's last word.

Beyond the Pathos of Difference

By considerably simplifying the complex organization of de Man's critical operations, we were able to determine two major, and juxtaposed, moments of this operation: one that invalidates a thematic reading of texts by thematic means, another that reaches toward the text's inscription of its own figuration. As remains to be seen, these two approaches are superseded, so to speak, by a "third" facet of rhetorical reading.

Before we begin to develop this "third" overarching approach that supersedes the two facets of rhetorical reading, we must recall that de Man, in his nonphenomenal phase of reading texts, unearthed a formal materiality punctuating the texts that makes figuration as such possible. But since this materiality is without relation to the meaning that becomes superimposed on it, it is also immediately forgotten and cannot be made part of the text. Yet, this meaningless cause of the text, precisely because the text cannot take in such a cause, also undoes the text's figuration, its meaning-producing activity. Although there would be no text without such a cause, the possibility of a meaningful text requires that the material and formal cause of the text recede into oblivion. Such constituting forgetting is achieved by imposing the authority of sense and meaning on the material and formal linguistic event and on the senseless power of positing language.

In what precedes, we insisted with de Man that the material and formal base of texts is absolutely indifferent to what comes before it and what follows it. It is irreducibly singular, destitute of all possible relations. But the following objections can be easily anticipated regarding the status of such singularity: If the material linguistic event has as such no relation whatsoever to a meaning intention, how then can it be said to make such intention possible or to subvert it? We have already stressed that meaning is the result of a forgetting of imposition. What this means is that the act of sense creation itself corresponds to an act of positing, that is, to an arbitrary intervention that has no relation to the preceding linguistic act and that is thus also immediately forgotten. The production of meaning occurs through an act of imposition, that is, through an act uncalled for by the material and linguistic stratum of an utterance or text. It is as singular, as devoid of all relations as the act of linguistic positing itself. de Man writes: "Considered performatively, figuration . . . performs the erasure of the positing power of language"; yet, since it has itself, as a positing act, no relation to the act that precedes it, "the initial violence of position can only be half erased, since the erasure is accomplished by a device of language that never ceases to partake of the very violence against which it is directed" (*RR*, pp. 118–119). In other words, the act by which the event performed by language becomes forgotten and by which meaning and cognition come into life is itself a senseless act. It partakes in the very violence of mindless and absolutely singular positing of the "preceding" linguistic act. Thus, the production of meaning, or figuration, rather than being a beginning is nothing but a repetition of the material and formal linguistic act itself. It remains as punctual, as sterile, as the "first" cause.

For de Man, the semantic levels of a text, its strata of aesthetic or conceptual figuration, are nothing but the always already aborted attempts to cover up, or recuperate, the total lack of meaning at the base of the irretrievably singular linguistic events, by exactly repeating the orginary act of violence. In his essay "Sign and Symbol in Hegel's *Aesthetics*," after having stated that Hegel's aesthetics is in essence an aesthetic of the symbol, he argues that the symbol and, *mutatis mutandis,* the whole of Hegel's science of the beautiful, is "an ideological and not a theoretical construct, a defense against the logical necessity inherent in a theoretical disclosure" (*AI*, p. 100). Referring in that same essay to Hegel's *Science of Logic,* he also claims that "an inescapable obstacle threatens the entire construction" of the logic from its very beginning and that as a whole it represents the attempt to recuperate a "logical difficulty devoid of any phenomenal or experiential dimension" by staging that difficulty as if it were "an event in time, a narrative, or a history" (*AI*, pp. 98–99). In short, the literary and the philosophical discourse, are, for de Man, meaningful enterprises involved in forgetting or recuperating the non-phenomenal properties of the material and formal act of figuration, properties that come into view, as he insists, through figuration itself, precisely to the extent in which figuration is itself a repetition of the originary violence of positing. All there can be, consequently, is an endless series of acts of imposition that, because they lack all continuity with what precedes them, repeat, without ever lending themselves to any real discrimination, the "original" arbitrary act of linguistic positing. Ultimately, there is no difference between that act and the authority of meaning.

An additional consequence follows from the preceding developments, and this is of particular interest to us. As de Man has pointed out in his essays on Nietzsche, a philosophy geared toward spelling out the originary violence and arbitrariness of the irreducibly singular linguistic acts of positing—a violence that threatens, as we have seen, the closure and reflexive totalization of all meaning creation—remains as philosophy tangled up in what it denounces. To state philosophical aberration, says de Man, is deceiving, since by merely stating error and thus failing to apply those insights to itself, a critical philosophy as Nietzsche's is ultimately indistinguishable from what it criticizes. It does not itself enact what it teaches. Yet this is a complication that is not attributable to some negligence of the thinker. It is not intentional but rather "co-extensive with any use of language," as de Man holds (*AR*, p. 125). The knowledge that a text gains of itself, of its own figuration—the link that it establishes with itself lifting its total arbitrariness in a remotivating act of self-reflection—is, as de Man asserts in "Shelly Disfigured," "a figure in its own right, as such, bound to repeat the disfiguration of metaphor"

(*RR*, p. 120). In the same way as such a figure is deconstructed by the fact that it is itself a repetition of the singular and senseless act that it seeks to overcome through reflexive remotivation, a critical philosophy, which, as in the case of Nietzsche states the rhetorical origin of all truth, must let itself be deconstructed by the fact that such stating is, in essence, a repetition of the senseless act of linguistic positing. But since such deconstruction is, according to de Man, itself an act of cognition—that is, an act that pretends to speak *about* something, and to thus entertain a nonarbitrary relation to something—it always stages only a figure in need of further deconstruction.

Such endless deconstruction is indeed, for de Man, the fate of all theory. Because theory is, as theory, a totalizing operation rooted in an all-embracing gaze and, ultimately, in the originary synthesis of transcendental apperception, it is, in de Man's own words, a figure. But as a figure, that is, as a totalizing and thus motivating device of everything arbitrary in language, it is put into question by the universals of the "consistently defective models of language's impossibility to be a model of language" (*RT*, p. 20). As he writes in "The Resistance to Theory," all theory, de Man's included, is a theory and not a theory; in short, it is the "universal theory of the impossibility of theory" (*RT*, p. 20). What follows from this is that no "positive" philosophy can emerge from a rhetorical reading. Such a reading cannot come to a final stop in what has been called the "philosophy of formal materialism" based on a disfiguring and disarticulating gaze that, however stony, constituted it into the figure of a theory. Precisely, to the extent that such a theory or philosophy would be "positive," it would have failed to enact what it points out, and would have forgotten what it tries to recall: the irreducibly singular positing power of language. If a rhetorical reading proceeds by demonstrating first that a text on its thematic and semantic level already undoes what it weaves and, second, by showing that the inscription of figuration in the text itself points to the positing powers of language, disfiguring all meaning production, then the third facet of rhetorical reading will consist of deconstructing the latter's figural status—the illusion of having come to grips with the arbitrariness and the senselessness of the materiality of language and its acts of positing. Yet, such a debunking is not final. There is no end to it since all deconstruction, as de Man understands it, forgets what it is about. The third facet of rhetorical reading does not, therefore, supersede the first two. All it effectuates is thoroughly to strip the first and second phase of rhetorical reading of all their generalizing power and to bring them to their status of hopelessly singular and unrelated acts in which the "originary" arbitrariness of linguistic positing becomes reenacted. Only by deconstructing the philosophy of formal materialism that emerges from the second phase of rhetorical reading, and thus enacting the rhetorical substratum of theory, can such a theory be faithful to what it is "about." Only by achieving idiosyncratic singularity, in short, by undercutting all motivating relation, does a theory concerning the formal and material substratum of discourses or texts achieve its goal.

Only by constantly offering itself to a singularizing deconstruction does a rhetorical reading live up to its task. The rhetorical substratum to which theories point becomes realized in the infinite series of deconstructed theories. But that series of repeated deconstructions, by which the conceptualization of the rhetorical substratum is endlessly deferred, has as such no generality or universality either. The endless repetition of the same figure or theory is for de Man a figure as well. In reference to Friedrich Schlegel, he calls it "ironic allegory," that is, a figure in constant displacement. It is a figure in deconstruction. Hence, the series of theories in which the impossibility of theory becomes enacted also remains, in its totality, irreducibly singular. The thrust of idiosyncratic individuality or singularity remains unimpaired. It is, so to speak, the last word.

To draw some conclusions from these developments, we must circle back again to the theoretical movements characterized earlier—the one concerning figuration's repetition of the senseless act of positing, and theory's need for (self-)deconstruction. As we recalled, Nietzsche's criticism of philosophy is a criticism that can never come to a halt. It is, therefore, in de Man's sense of that term, literary. But de Man says, as well, that the deconstruction of metaphysics, or philosophy, is an impossibility precisely to the extent that they are already literary (*AR*, p. 131). What follows from the crisscross of these two parallel arguments is that Nietzsche's critique of metaphysics and metaphysics itself are ultimately indistinguishable and, moreover, that there is no difference in principle between literature and philosophy. This conclusion is emphasized in the following passage: "The critical deconstruction that leads to the discovery of the literary, rhetorical nature of the philosophical claim to truth is genuine enough and cannot be refuted: literature turns out to be the main topic of philosophy and the model for the kind of truth to which it aspires. But when literature seduces us with the freedom of its figural combinations, so much airier and lighter than the labored constructs of concepts, it is not the less deceitful because it asserts its own deceitful properties (*AR*, p. 115). Although "philosophy turns out to be an endless reflection on its own destruction at the hands of literature," literature itself, to the extent that it "asserts its own deceitful properties," is philosophical, indistinguishable from philosophy, and also in need of a destruction (*AR*, p. 115). Or, more precisely, in the same way as philosophy as aberration is put into question by the literary dimension of the linguistic signifier, literature as philosophy is constantly challenged by its own literary qualities. Philosophy and literature, the critique of metaphysics and metaphysics itself, are the same. For the same reason, distinctions such as linguistic and semantic, transcendental and empirical, distinctions that play a significant strategical role in de Man's analyses, finally blur into total indifference, incapable of difference and, hence, of generality. But that blurring does not reside in a symmetrical canceling out. The conceptual oppositions, the sides of the arguments, the onionskin layers of de Man's text, are not abolished into one universal indifference, into the figure of the all-embracing essence of the medium of reflexivity. Since that stratum of a text that destructs its symmetrical opposite cannot itself escape destruction by what it points at, the thrust of deconstruction remains unimpaired. And since the series of the successive rhetorical reversals of the theories establishing the priority of formal materialism does not itself escape disfiguration, the negativity of the senselessness of the material dimension of language and its positing power remain unaffected. Yet, does such an insight justify the conclusion that these properties of language are truly universal? de Man seems to say so at the end of "The Resistance to Theory." His radical empiricism—his stress on the arbitrariness, extreme singularity, and impenetrable materiality of the linguistic acts and signifier—appears to have gained such momentum here that its own generality and universality turn into a radical challenge to the generality of philosophical difference.

It must, however, be remarked that it is a longstanding philosophical truth that empiricism is capable of explaining everything except explication itself, that is, the difference that explication makes. Are the nonphenomenal material and formal properties really capable of putting into question—that is, accounting for—philosophical difference, the difference that thought makes with respect to what it is the thought of? If they are empirical qualities, pragmatic properties, they will never be able to elevate themselves to the thought of difference. If they are universal and general properties, then they are properties that make *the* difference, and all that has been achieved is a, perhaps, more sophisticated philosophical questioning of philosophical difference.

But must one not recall that de Man does not write *on* philosophy? His texts do not pretend to clarify philosophical problems or to contribute to philosophical scholarship. Hence, de Man cannot be concerned with the *philosophical* problem of difference as such. His is not an approach that would recognize the legitimacy of such a distinction. Consequently, if the material and positional properties of language that de Man refers to were, indeed, capable of generality, it would be possible to *truly speak badly* from an empirical and pragmatic point of view and thus to challenge from a however negative *philosophical* viewpoint, and in the name of another difference (that of the universal singular), philosophical difference itself. But the rhetorical substratum de Man speaks of is so destructive of generality that the theory of the universality of this substratum cannot but yield to its own singularizing effects. If one follows de Man's text to its logical conclusion, all there remains in the end of the rhetorical substratum's generality is the idiosyncratic singularity of such a contention. If the formal and linguistic properties to which de Man's texts have been referring have an assertable generality, it is a generality so particular that, ultimately, it must remain utterly incomprehensible. It is a generality that confounds with the unique and punctual proposition in which it becomes cast by de Man himself. It is a generality, then, that, paradoxically, makes no difference to philosophical difference and that challenges it precisely by not challenging it.

What de Man has established as the lesson of his reading of Shelly's *The Triumph of Life* must thus be seen to apply to his own reading of philosophy as well: "Nothing, whether deed, word, thought, or text, ever happens in relation, positive or negative, to anything that precedes, follows, or exists elsewhere, but only as a random event whose power, like the power of death, is due to the randomness of its occurrence" (*RR*, p. 122).

de Man's reading of philosophy is not *about* philosophy. It tries to show little or no concern about philosophy. It is a reading that challenges philosophical difference by not being about it, by not referring to it, by making no difference with respect to it. In contrast to philosophy, de Man's readings do not attempt to make any difference. In this sense they are "different," idiosyncratic to a point where, by making no point, they will have made their point—so singular as to make no difference but, perhaps, in that total apathy a formidable challenge to philosophical difference.

3

Apathetic Formalism

The conflict between philosophy and rhetoric, a conflict that dates back to their mutual origin in Greece, has not only determined the form and content of philosophy; it has determined the form and content of rhetoric as well. This has become evident once again since a certain rehabilitation of rhetoric has taken place, say, in the last thirty or forty years, well after its fall into discredit and disrepute at the end of the eighteenth century. Indeed, the positions taken in the present wave of interest in rhetoric are far from being homogeneous. It is as if the conflict between philosophy and rhetoric could not but reproduce itself in rehabilitated rhetoric itself. Among the scholars who have significantly contributed to the contemporary interest in this disputed discipline are Ernst Robert Curtius and Paul de Man. As I intend to show in what is to follow, at least up to a certain point, their contrary evaluations of rhetoric divides along lines that have been staked out in antiquity—namely, between Plato and Isocrates, whose prestigious school of rhetoric stood in the very proximity of Plato's academy.

In *European Literature and the Latin Middle Ages,* Curtius deplores the industrial and literary revolution that, starting in the middle of the eighteenth century, shattered the continuity of what until then had constituted 'Europe'—"the spell of the antique tradition."[1] The crisis in question starts with English Pre-Romanticism and peaks in the philosophical rationalism and the social theories of Rousseau. Rationalism, with its idea of an innate human rationality, and Romanticism, with its focus on the inherently good nature of the natural self, have one thing in common—the autonomomy of the individual—and hence contest any other authority except that of reason or the heart. But the implicit rejection of all mediation and, hence of universality based on a unifying tradition of such a faith in the individual's faculties alone, is what has led, since the end of the eighteenth century, to the breakdown of Europe as an ideal unifying totality, to an explosion of that unity into the different nationalities in which "the 'voices of the people' can ring out."[2] National Socialism is, one can easily infer, the natural inheritor of this break with the antique heritage and the Romantic or Enlightenment discovery of individuality. It is in order to counter the catastrophic effects of this interruption of European culture, as they manifest themselves in German Nazism and World War II, that Curtius writes *European Literature and the Latin Middle Ages*. What Curtius argues throughout this work is that what gave Europe up to the middle of the eighteenth century a unity, an intelligible, historical, and cultural (not merely geographic) unity, is its literature. To understand what Curtius is after with such a statement, it is important to note that the historical unity of Europe does not begin for Curtius in 1500 but in Greece (and Rome) and that the literature that constitutes it as an intelligible unit of sense is one that not only ranges from Homer to the present but whose very substance is based on its uninterrupted participation in the classical past. Yet the specificity of Curtius's contention comes into view only if one follows him in the determination of this "substance of antique culture [that] was never destroyed," whose more or less uninterrupted *translation* secured the unity and universality of Europe throughout the centuries.[3] Indeed, what makes literature so special is that since "the Greeks found their past, their essential nature, and their world of deities ideally reflected in a poet," "literature has been a school subject, and the continuity of Europe is bound up with the schools. Education becomes the medium of the literary tradition." In short, what characterizes Europe for Curtius is that its system of education is based "upon the liberal (*freie*) arts."[4] Not that there would be an essential necessity for such an identity. It is a factual relation characteristic of Europe, and Europe alone, Curtius insists. "It could well have been otherwise. In Judaism the pupil learns the 'Law'; and the Mosaic books are not a poem. But what the Greeks had done, the Romans imitated . . . The Middle Ages took over from Antiquity the traditional connection between epic and school . . . Later, the classics of the modern nations became school reading, even though they might be as little suitable for the purpose as Shakespeare or Goethe's *Faust*."[5] The first implication of this crucial role that literature plays within the European system of education is that Isocrates' point of view, and not Plato's, prevails in Europe's pedagogical system. Not the standpoint of Plato, whose negative views on the literary arts are well known from the *Republic*, but that of Isocrates, laid the foundation for the Greek 'paideia,' and the ensuing European culture according to Curtius. In other words, the educational model that was to become the model for Europe's educational system in general is a model based on the teaching of those arts that Seneca termed "worthy of a free man" but that are also called "liberal arts" because, in contradistinction to Plato, they were not subservient to philosophy. In short, then, what unifies Europe is that within its educational system, the liberal arts are being taught—and in particular, literature, which as Curtius notes, "has [not only] an autonomous structure, which is essentially different from that of the visual arts" but also "possesses a freedom which is denied to art."[6] It is thus a system of education whose goal is to foster freedom; and this, its goal, is what provides the unity and continuity of Europe as a historical entity. But this is not yet all. Indeed, what such a stress on literature in the educational system of Europe ultimately implies is that rather than philosophy, rhetoric is the foundation and the "integrating factor of all education."[7] This is, indeed, the fine point of Curtius's thesis on what makes the unity of Europe.

It is important to remark here that the art of oratory, although originating in the Greeks' delight in discourse and its artistic elaboration, is intimately tied up with the development of the Greek polis, and especially the development of democracy under Pericles and the "Greek Enlightenment." With the birth of the state as a public space of competition—it is also significant to mention here that the Sophists were the first to discuss the nature of the state—with every citizen being drawn into public life, the ability to speak becomes an absolute requirement for winning a place in the polis. This is also the moment when schools of rhetoric arise where one could learn to recite and speak in public. But the rhetoricians—Isocrates first and foremost—understood themselves not only to be teachers of techniques for conducting pleas but also as serving "*paideia* through the power of the word." The rhetor and the "sophist also desired to be [a] molder(s) of men, [and] educator(s) of the nation," Curtius remarks.[8] As a consequence, rhetoric entered upon new fields of activity, and in particular, poetry. Thus, when the very place and function of political and legal eloquence foundered after the fall of the Roman

Empire, rhetoric did not only continue in school eloquence for centuries to come, but, having penetrated into all literary genres, "its elaborately developed system became the common denominator of literature in general."[9] Out of this movement begun in Greece by Gorgias arose authors like Cicero, Ovid, Livy, and Virgil. But rhetoric's educational mission became formulated perhaps most powerfully by Quintillian, whose influence on European literature is paramount. Curtius notes that "rhetoric, through Quintillian, claims to be able of itself to satisfy all the needs for which philosophy and general education were held to be competent." Indeed, it becomes intrinsically linked up here with the aim of education and, to such a degree, that it allows Curtius to conclude that in Quintillian the subject of rhetoric is transformed "into the humanistic recognition of literary studies as the highest good in life."[10] For centuries to come, rhetoric stands in Europe for the educational and intellectual values of antiquity. Rather than suggesting the use of deceit and fraud, rhetoric is understood as the prime guarantor of freedom. Freedom, however, is not thought to be here as rooted in some inner sentiment of the self or in reason as a property of the individual; such freedom does nothing more than hypostatize the natural singularity, if not idiosyncrasy, of the individual. The freedom that rhetoric stands for is a public freedom that is enacted in the public sphere of mediation and debate (constitutive of the polis) and that owes its universality to the fact that such public debate is governed by established rules, public standards, and constant forms that are essentially communicable. These forms are the *koinoi topoi,* the *loci communes;* in short, all those stereotyped intellectual themes or arguments that are usable on diverse occasions because they are suitable for development and modification. By drawing on the thesaurus of the *topoi,* on "the storehouses of trains of thought," as Quintillian labeled them, the arguing, praising, justifying subject acquires his or her own publicly constituted freedom. Because this universal fund of commonplaces, or identical forms of expression, is linked to the constitution of self in public discourse, it is not a collection of neutral forms. "Forms are configurations and systems of configurations in which the incorporeal things of the mind *(Geistiges)* can manifest themselves and become apprehensible," Curtius writes.[11] Rhetorical forms such as the *topoi,* serve as a lattice *(Gitter)* in which spirit exists in its freedom. They serve as a code through which freedom can manifest itself in a public and universal fashion. Freedom and spirit, Curtius suggests, crystallize into "configurational schemas [*Gestaltschema*] (Platonically: *eidos*)."[12] The commonplaces in question could thus be called (in a certain sense) "schemata for the spirit's coming into its proper freedom." Now, in the aftermath of the extinction of the Greek city states and the Roman republic, the universally usable clichés that had initially served in political and juridical oration enter literature—in a transition from the political to the aesthetic that is not arbitrary since the spirit, although it "speaks its own language," "only in words," is "in its perfect freedom" "only in the creative word"—as its treasure of forms (*Formenlehre und Formenschatz*).[13] With this the lasting, durable *topoi* become "the common denominator of literature in general," "the cellars—and foundations!—of European literature."[14] This stockroom, from which European literature has been drawing and which cannot be replaced by anything lest the spirit be given up, is what has given European literature its continuity and universality, according to Curtius. This same historical substance, which provides the continuity of Europe as a historical and intelligible unit up to the decline of this entity in the eighteenth century, is thus the totality of the irreplaceable discursive schemata, or forms, through which freedom and universality crystallize. The idea of Europe, as based on publicly established freedom, as well as its model of education for such freedom, draws its possibility from the universally applicable rhetorical forms in which spirit can manifest itself. They are its alphabet, as it were.

What Paul de Man has developed as a method for reading texts rhetorically seems, in many ways, to have been conceived to undo a concept of rhetoric such as Curtius's. First, and in most general terms, one can say that de Man's rhetorical readings resist the unifying and universalizing pathos of Curtius's notion of rhetoric, a pathos that flows from the sovereign rule that rhetoric acquires when raised to the status of a theoretical explicatory device. Second, one can also imagine that de Man would have been strongly suspicious of all the references by Curtius to "Europe," the "West," "Geistiges," etc. (as well as of the history of decline of these values as outlined by Curtius), references that often have undemocratic overtones but that, if they do not, are nonetheless mobilized for a quite conservative and elitist conception of history or, more specifically, for a conception of history from the liberal right. Third, de Man's recasting of rhetoric aims at dismantling what I would call the categorial axioms of Curtius's discourse, namely, of the notions of "translation," "continuity," "unity," "universality," and so forth. Finally, de Man's own notion of rhetoric is on guard against the humanistic celebration of rhetoric. Indeed, I will argue that although de Man does not simply give in to Plato's condemnation of oratory art as conveying opinions *(doxa)* and fostering the illusory, his conception of rhetoric pits, up to a certain point, Plato against Isocrates. In order to make the argument that de Man's rehabilitation of rhetoric serves, at first, philosophical purposes, I shall turn to the analysis of "Kant's Materialism," and in that essay to one notion in particular, that of "apathetic formalism."[15]

Although this essay overlaps to some degree with the one entitled "Phenomenality and Materiality in Kant" and is in the same way as the latter (and most of the later work of de Man) engaged in a debate with aesthetics, it pursues a question not addressed in that essay. Its debate centers on the issue of the affects and affectivity in the *Third Critique.* Of course, it is not fortuitous that in the *Third Critique,* de Man chooses to limit himself to the chapters on the sublime, since, as is well known, it is in the *genus sublime* that the main center of the area of application of pathos is to be found.[16] In my summary and ensuing discussion of de Man's essay, however, I shall not be concerned with comparing de Man's analysis to what Kant himself establishes about the sublime; I shall be interested only in de Man's own moves and in what the implications of his moves are.

The essay is framed by a discussion of attempts, at the time of writing, to draw a direct lineage between Kant ("by ways of Schiller and Coleridge") (p. 119) and decadent formalism and aestheticism. Such filiation, de Man argues, is based on a profound misunderstanding of Kant's aesthetic. It assumes, indeed, that the realm of the aesthetic is "'free from cognitive and ethical consequences'," and that aesthetic experience is "'barred from the truth of the phenomenal world'," as Frank Lentricchia has claimed (p. 119). But according to de Man, to construct a genealogy of this kind is to overestimate the apparent frivolity of Kantean aesthetics, to underestimate its complicity with the phenomenalist epistemology of realism and above all, to pay no attention to what in Kant's idealism reaches beyond the categories of cognition and morality toward "a materialism much more radical than what can be conveyed by such terms as 'realism' and 'empiricism'"(p. 121). de Man will construe this materialism in terms of a "radical formalism" much more outrageous, if you wish, than what theoreticians of literature have been worrying about. de Man sets out to explore this radical formalism and materialism, that ultimately will run counter to all possibility of establishing a lineage, a continuity, between the *Third Critique* and later trends in literature and aesthetics. He will do so by focusing in Kant's discourse on something that according to de Man has "the triviality of the particular," that is imbued with "ostensible silliness," and that is responsible for the "blandness" (p. 123) and "flatness of the discourse" (p. 127) at crucial moments in Kant's text. In light of what I have shown to be the importance of the *koinoi topoi* in Curtius's understanding of rhetoric, let me remark immediately that the question of this radical formalism will be debated in the space of the "vocabulary in the *Wortschatz* (or Thesaurus)" (p. 124).

The section on the sublime in *Critique of Judgement* is a privileged place to look for the radical formalism in question, de Man argues, the reason being that "the sublime is indeed where the congruity *(Angemessenheit)* of the aesthetic to the order of pure reason is being established" (p. 121). de Man refers to the fact that the sublime connects with reason *(Vernunft)*—as opposed to the beautiful, in which imagination and understanding *(Verstand)* are linked in the freeplay of the faculties. As a reference to Foucault's treatment of Kant in *The Order of Things* reveals, de Man is interested in the sublime because it would be the space where the tension between Kant's critique from a transcendentalist perspective of representation and the methodology of empiricism on the one hand and the singularity of the empirical world on the other can best be beheld. If the sublime is, according to the interpretation and translation of a specific Kant passage by de Man, "the source of pure aesthetic judgment" (p. 126),[17] of a judgment based on the congruity of the aesthetics to the order of reason, then to show "a return of the empirical" (p. 121) in all its singularity in what would represent the thinking of the infinite, the transcendental, would amount to demonstrating that pure aesthetic judgment, in all its so-called formalism, is haunted by something that breaches the congruity that it is supposed to establish, and that is by far more empirical and singular than what is usually called so. That this is the point de Man wishes to make becomes clear from a rather allusive reference to Hegel's observation that the sublime would imply a loss of the symbolic—that is, of all "congruence between formal structure and intellectual content," "sign and meaning" (p. 121). As de Man's insinuates, Hegel's criticism of Kant's treatment of the sublime fails to do justice to the status of this "necessary negative moment" (p. 121), which Hegel views only in the perspective of its inscription in the dialectical process of cognition. de Man's own discussion of the loss of the symbolic in Kant's presentation of the sublime is thus to both set straight Kant's record and correct what he deems to be a distortion, by the tradition, of that very record.

Whereas "the section on the mathematical sublime establishes the loss of the symbolic in the failure to represent, by sensory means, the infinite powers of inventive articulation of which the mind is capable" (p. 122), the congruence, the homogeneity between aesthetics and reason, is reinstated in the section entitled "Of the dynamic sublimity of nature," according to de Man. Kant, he says, reaches this objective "by ways of the affectivity of the subject" (p. 122). The continuity between sign and meaning is restored in that the judgment concerning the sublime, rather than being a rational judgment, is an affective judgment. Indeed, the power "of one emotion (admiration, respect, etc.) over another emotion, such as fear" (p. 123), in front of the natural sublime, becomes *indicative* of man's rational and infinite powers. The affects, their mutually overpowering play, would thus defeat and overcome the loss of congruity between sign and meaning that Kant had elaborated on when dealing with the mathematical sublime. "But what exactly is affectivity in Kant?" de Man asks (p. 123). Affectivity, he suggests, has to be demarcated in Kant from all associations with inwardness (whether Romantic or Pre-Romantic). This can be beheld, for instance in the "ostensible silliness" of his discourse when it speaks the "language of the affections" (p. 123). de Man claims, indeed, that Kant's discussion of the affects does not start out from the inner experience of a subject but, as his precritical text entitled *Observations on the Sentiment of the Beautiful and the Sublime* would show, takes its starting point in the dictionary. The typology of distinctive states of mind listed in this text—a text "which reads at times like a collection of eighteenth-century provincial platitudes" (p. 123)— "is never based on actual observation but entirely on words. Kant starts out from the verbal fund of the ordinary German language to set up elaborate classifications that need no further justification than their existence in the vocabulary, in the *Wortschatz* (or Thesaurus), of common speech. Page after page consists of the listing, as mere *langue*, of terms which, in the realm of affect, are separated from each other by slight but decisive distinctions" (p. 124). The symbolism of language, in this contrastive typology of affects, has entirely disappeared because, as de Man notes, "the words are considered in themselves, without any concern for connotation, etymology or figurative and symbolic overtone" (p. 124). Kant's discussion of the affect is hence entirely without affect; it is apathetic. de Man concludes: "Such a reduction from symbolic feeling to mere words, such a loss of pathos, of theatricality, and of self-reflection, is not easy to interpret and very easy to misjudge" (p. 123). But let us nonetheless risk an interpretation in the spirit of what de Man has set out to demonstrate in this essay. What de Man is saying is that, when Kant, in the chapter on the dynamic sublime, sets out to suture the aesthetic and reason, the sensory and the intelligible, he does so by taking recourse to something—the affects—that has absolutely no suturing power. What he has recourse to at that crucial juncture of his development is not so much the difference between the linguistic materiality of signifiers (which de Man has shown to have been the sole ground on which Kant distinguished such important states of emotion as *Verwunderung* and *Bewunderung*)[18] but, rather, differences between lexicological entries void of all connotations. Not *koinoi topoi* serve to make the argument but a set of words reduced to a differentially articulated classification of entirely empty—that is, merely formal—verbal distinctions. These empty forms of affects are entirely without affect, which means that they do not possess any connecting and unifying potential. Their apathy connotes, if they connote at all, only the punctuality and singularity of these forms. The conclusion to be drawn, then, is that if such apathetic forms are to heal the loss of the symbolic in the Kantian sublime, this sublime is thoroughly nonsymbolical.

But let us follow de Man through the next step of his argument, in which he shows the loss of the symbolic to be coupled with a thematic emphasis on a very specific type of temperament or humor, in both the precritical *Observations* and the *Critique of Judgement*. The emphasis on the type of humor in question is enhanced, moreover, by the fact that it receives contrasting evaluations in both texts. Whereas Kant "disposes contemptuously of the phlegmatic in one brief paragraph" (p. 124) in the text from 1764, because it could never be either beautiful or sublime, "the phlegmatic as loss or absence of affect *(Affektlosigkeit)*" (p. 125) turns out to be associated with the highest form of the sublime in the *Third Critique*. de Man refers here to a passage from the *Critique of Judgement* where Kant, having spoken of the sublimity of enthusiasm—a sublimity based on this affections' tension of forces produced by ideas—writes as follows: "But (which seems strange) the *absence of affection* (*apatheia, phlegma in significatu bono*) in a mind that vigorously follows its unalterable principles is sublime, and in a far preferable way, because it has also on its side the satisfaction of pure reason. A mental state of this kind is alone called noble; and this expression is subsequently applied to things, e.g., a building. . . ."[19] Let us pause again to take stock of what we have just read. In order to demonstrate the compatibility of the sublime and reason, Kant takes recourse on a *formal* level to the thesaurus of verbally distinguished affects in order to bridge the gap opened by the failure of all sensory means to represent the infinite powers of the mind. On a *thematic* level of Kant's text, this same goal is achieved by calling the absence of all affections the most excellent, or most admirable, form of the sublime. de Man is, of course, aware of the fact that for Kant, such privileging of *apatheia* is based on this state of mind's analogy with reason, with reason's nonsensuous but intelligible essence. Yet, as the final pages of de Man's essay, to which we now turn, show, de Man believes such privileging of apatheia on the thematic level of Kant's text to have still another reason.

Returning to the passage from Kant just quoted, de Man points out that although the sublime is constituted by its reference to the supersensory, this does in no way "isolates the sublime in an otherworldly realm" (p. 125). As the example shows, the sublime applies to a variety of things—to buildings such as the pyramids of Egypt and Saint Peter's Basilica in Rome, among others—to which Kant refers in Paragraph 26 on the estimation of magnitude of natural things in the mathematically sublime. Now, although the sublime can be found, in its pure form, only in nature in the raw, the fact that one of the examples of sublimity is a building implies, de Man concludes in a most elliptical fashion—whose logic could perhaps be reconstructed through a careful reading of Paragraph 26 as well as of Derrida's "Le colossal" to which de Man alludes in this context—that, therefore, "the *techne* of art is architectonic" (p. 125). I assume this to mean that on a technical, or artistic level, art conforms to rules similar to those of the art of building. Now from this Paragraph 26, we also learn that if an aesthetical judgment is to be *pure*, that is, "*mingled with no teleological judgment* or judgment of reason," the sublime must not be exhibited "in products of art (e.g., buildings, pillars, etc.) where human purpose determines the form as well as the size."[20] Consequently, the architectonic, which de Man has said to be is at the heart of artistic *techne* and which he subsequently links to questions of virility and erection in Kant, cannot be purposeful as architecture normally is; just as "erection" is, then, something other than what one usually thinks it to be. To determine the specific sense in which he wants *architectonic* to be understood here, de Man centers in on a passage from the "General Remark upon the Exposition of the Aesthetical Reflective Judgment," a passage that he will also comment on in "Phenomenality and Materiality in Kant" but that he puts to use here in his attempt to demonstrate an essential apathy not only on the formal and thematic but also on the technical level of Kant's reflections on the sublime, on aesthetic and the work of art in general. I should quote this passage in its entirety (not, however, from de Man's own translation of it, but from Barnard's translation):

> If, then, we call the sight of the starry heaven *sublime,* we must not place at the basis of our judgment concepts of worlds inhabited by rational beings and regard the bright points, with which we see the space above us filled, as their suns moving in circles purposively fixed with reference to them; but we must regard it, just as we see it *(bloss wie man ihn sieht),* as a distant, all-embracing, vault. Only under such a representation can we range that sublimity which a pure aesthetical judgment ascribes to this object [and not as de Man translates: "This is the only way to conceive of the sublime as the source of pure aesthetic judgment." RG] And in the same way, if we are to call the sight of the ocean sublime, we must not *think* of it as we [ordinarily] do, as implying all kinds of knowledge (that are not contained in immediate intuition). For example, we sometimes think of the ocean as a vast kingdom of aquatic creatures, or as the great source of those vapors that fill the air with clouds for the benefit of the land, or again as an element which, though dividing continents from each other, yet promotes the greatest communication between them; but these furnish merely teleological judgments. To call the ocean sublime we must regard it as poets do, merely by what strikes the eye *(nach dem was der Augenschein zeigt)*—if it is at rest, as a clear mirror of water only bounded by the heaven; if it is restless, as an abyss threatening to overwhelm everything.[21]

This passage, de Man remarks, is not to be read from a romantic perspective as if it were Wordsworth, Shelley, Baudelaire, or even Mallarmé who had written it. It does not, de Man claims, talk about nature, about nature "in its most all-encompassing magnitude"; "in fact, it does not see nature as nature at all, but as a construction, as a house. The sky is seen as a vault or a roof, and the horizon as the enclosure by this roof of the surface on which we dwell" (p. 126). More precisely, in this passage, Kant would speak of a vision, not so much of the sky *as* a roof, as of a gigantic roof all by itself. This is obvious from de Man's repeated insistence that this perceived roof does not say anything about nature, that it does not relate to it as an inside to an outside, or vice versa, and that, in particular, no judgment is present in this perception. Nor is it a sensation, he continues: "The eye, left to itself, entirely ignores understanding; it only notices appearance (it is *Augenschein*) without any awareness of a dichotomy between illusion and reality—a dichotomy which belongs to teleological and not to aesthetic judgment" (p. 127). Thus, because no "substitutive exchange," no "negotiated economy, between nature and mind" takes place here, this perception of the sky and the ocean as buildings "is not a trope," de Man asserts (p. 127). No tropological "facing or defacing of the natural world" (p. 127) is hinted at in the passage in question. On these grounds, de Man concludes that "Kant's architectonic vision here appears in its purest form" (p. 126). It is pure because, at the heart of the perception of sublimity that, as seen, is construed by de Man as "the source of pure aesthetic judgment," that is, as the source of all aesthetic judgment (on the beautiful as on the sublime)—there lies a "stony gaze" through which "the infinite is frozen into the materiality of stone" (p. 127). This architectonizing gaze is pure in that it is impossible to think of it "as an address or an apostrophe" (p. 127). It does not relate, face—it is absolutely phlegmatic to the point of being petrified. At the heart of all aesthetic experience is to be found a moment, consequently, "when no pathos, anxiety, or sympathy is conceivable; it is, indeed, the moment of a-pathos, or apathy, as the complete loss of the symbolic" (p. 127). Before all facing, all exchange—before all substitution, that is, also before all rhetoric of figures and tropes—there lies, according to de Man, a moment of absolute singularity that is thematized here in terms of a complete lack of pathos. It is a moment so singular that it has the emotional passivity of stone, or architectonics. But before further commenting on the status of such a radical *apatheia*, that de Man has now shown to be constitutive of the formal, the thematic, and also the technical level of aesthetic experience, let me hasten to finish reading de Man's text to the end.

If the passage commented upon does not operate tropologically, if, in this text, Kant does not transform or metamorphose the sea into the abyssal foundation of a house—a transformation that would depend "on the opposition between mirror and abyss"—but merely produces a "mere sequence of two random [that is, unrelated, absolutely singular] events," it is because all "depth perception is entirely absent from the flatness of the discourse" (p. 127). It is so flat that in it no reflection is possible. It is flat to such a degree that it becomes reduced to the singularity of a mere point. This flatness is also, as Kant remarked when he referred to the poet's glance, characteristic of the latter's vision, of aesthetic vision. From this de Man infers that "the language of the poets . . . in no way partakes of mimesis, reflection, or even perception, in the sense which would allow a link between sense experience and understanding, between perception and apperception" (p. 128). Now this look, Kant's and the poet's—because it entertains no relation (to something that it would transform, or metamorphose)—is entirely singular, a merely formal look.[22] It is "an absolute, radical formalism that entertains no notion of reference or semiosis" (p. 128), not even negatively, as formalism would in Hegel. This formalism, at the heart of the *Third Critique,* at the core of aesthetic experience, is an "entirely a-referential, a-phenomenal, a-pathetic formalism" (p. 128), a formalism that de Man, in what is supposedly to be a parody of Kantian definition, calls "materialism." This is a formalism much more formal and formidable than the one that certain theoreticians alluded to at the beginning of de Man's text had been worrying about, a formalism that, because of its lack of depth, and hence of the possibility of entering relations, remains forever cut off from all lineage, tradition, translation.

Now this radical formalism, that de Man has shown to be constitutive of both Kant's and the poet's glance—similar in many ways to the state of mind of *ennui* of Valéry's *Monsieur Teste,* as analyzed by Jean-Luc Marion in *Dieu sans l'être*[23]—is also what makes up de Man's own approach to texts in what he has called a "rhetorical reading." As he has acknowledged in *Allegories of Reading,* such a rhetorical reading is indebted to the Romantic theory of language that views language as essentially rhetorical. Within the framework of Romantic linguistic theory, de Man claims, *rhetoric* refers not only to language's nonrepresentational and nonreferential nature but also to its privileging of figure (or trope) over persuasion, that is, over all "actual action [by language] upon others"

(*AR*, p. 8). As de Man conceives of it, a rhetorical reading by concentrating on figure or trope focuses in on what he calls "the autonomous potential of language" (*RT*, p. 10), language's positional powers. This positional power is analyzed by de Man on principally three distinct levels—the material, literal properties of language, the mechanical rules of grammar, and the linguistic acts themselves. As I have tried to show in the preceding essay, a rhetorical reading—and the text "Kant's Materialism" is a good example of it—emphasizes the arbitrariness of what is produced on each of these levels, and at on occasion on which a linguistic act takes place.[24] Arbitrariness, however, means for de Man, absence of the symbolic; that is, absence of *all* natural, but also conventional, relation. Absence of relation, in turn, implies the singularity, punctuality, and ultimately idiosyncrasy of anything that occurs in language. Indeed, a rhetorical reading explodes texts into the linguistic atoms, into the mechanical grammatical rules, and into the singular acts by which it is constituted, all of which are so singular as not to relate to one another and thus to be ultimately meaningless. Based on extreme singularity, all of a text's instances are immediately forgotten as soon as they occur, and thus they do not lend themselves to any dialectics of universality by which they could be sublated and made to work as moments in a meaning that could be shared and communicated. It therefore comes as no surprise if this linguistic atomism at the core of rhetorical reading also understands itself as an entirely apathetic formalism. Indeed, ancient atomistic theories—the materialism of Democritus, for instance—conceived of the atoms as *apathe,* as impassive, or lacking all affection. Democritus, according to Galen, conceived of the atoms as producing by means of their associations all possible combinations, "including our own bodies, as well as their affections and sensations *(ta pathemata auton kai tas aistheseis).* The atomists formulate [he continues] the hypothesis of the absence of quality of the primordial corpuscles *(apathe th hupotithentai ta somata einai ta pronta)* . . . and assume that they are unable to experience alterations. . . ."[25] But in contradistinction from the early materialists, for whom the totally apathetic atoms are *capable* not only of forming worlds through their combinations but affects *(pathe)* as well—in the sense either of the body's experiencing of change, of incidents in things, or of emotions and passions by the soul—here the linguistic atoms are so inflexible that they *cannot lend themselves* to forming or entering meaningful, orderly relations. They are impassive to the point of excluding the very possibility of their becoming elements of worlds or bodies, a becoming that would in a very elemental manner imply some form of incidence. The linguistic corpuscles of de Man forfeit all possibility of anything happening to them, the possibility of being possible elements of possible worlds as well. Cut loose from meaning and universality, remaining on this side of affection, and hence allowing for no change or alteration, let alone development, passage, transition, to occur, the apathetic linguistic elements and acts turn into something so punctual that they become incomprehensible, unreal, meaningless. In taking up this same issue in the next chapter, it will be shown that the rhetorical elements of language, though *they do not lend themselves* to forming meaningful worlds, can be usurped for (cognitive) purposes. But such appropriations remain impositions on language, and its elements, that "in themselves" resist meaningful relations.

On account of what rhetorical reading thus exhibits as cut off, absolute in an absolute sense, fully idiosyncratic linguistic form or matter, void of all pathetic potential, it will be necessary to examine this rhetoric recast by de Man, which at first sight seems to have a philosophical thrust, opposed as it is to all the values and concepts that we have seen to organize Curtius's appraisal of rhetoric. Let us therefore inquire in some detail, what the implications of an apathetical rhetorical reading must be.

What are the main associations that the very idea of an apathetic rhetoric carries with it and that inevitably come to mind? The first and foremost association is that an apathetic rhetoric is not rhetoric anymore but, by rights, philosophy undisturbed in the clarity of its rational thinking by all pathetic, that is, emotional, influences. Indeed, philosophy ever since Plato is supposed to speak in a manner devoid of passion and emotion.[26] It is believed to be a dispassionate game of thought play based on the concepts alone.[27] The problem of the pathos is that of rhetoric and of everything that belongs to rhetorical speech and thus has pathetic character. In his *Rhetoric,* Aristotle, after having hinted at the limits of what the most accurate scientific information can achieve, adds that such information based on scientific arguments is of no avail when a speaker is to make a case in front of nonphilosophically trained auditors (whether in court, or elsewhere, such as in the classroom). "Argument based on knowledge implies instruction, and there are people whom one cannot instruct. Here, then, [when dealing with a popular audience] we must use, as our modes of persuasion and argument, notions possessed by everybody."[28] *Rhetoric,* then, defined by Aristotle "as the faculty of observing in any given case the available means of persuasion,"[29] is the art of producing a semblance of demonstration where scientific demonstration is not possible. Such proof, however, proceeds through persuasion. Among the means by which persuasion is effected, Aristotle cites the *ethos* of the speaker, the argument proper, and the emotions in the hearer. Aristotle notes that persuasion takes effect in the listeners when "the speech stirs their emotions. Our judgements when we are pleased and friendly are not the same as when we are pained and hostile."[30] Indeed, the passions, or emotions, "are all those feelings that so change men as to affect their judgements, and that are also attended by pain or pleasure," Aristotle remarks.[31] He discusses this particular instrument of persuasion, which is an essential ingredient of rhetoric, without which there would be no art of oratory, in Book Two of his treatise. But it must also be noted that Aristotle, who adopts the doctrine of the passions elaborated by other theoreticians of rhetoric, in the perspective of the *techne* of persuasion as protases of argumentative chains, considers them only according to what they are said to be in public opinion. All the traits that serve in the second part of *Rhetoric* to define the various passions are givens taken from public opinion. They are *hendoxa.*[32] Barthes puts this very poignantly when he writes that for Aristotle, "public opinion is the first and last given . . . for him passions are ready made pieces of language, that the orator simply needs to know well."[33] Indeed, Aristotle's goal in *Rhetoric* is not to properly describe passions—this is the object of *Nichomachean Ethics*—but to discover those traits that can be used in oratory to influence the audience's predisposition to judge. Since the domain of rhetoric is the verisimilar, all the traits that serve to determine the passions can be of the same order. Yet, however flat these popular opinions are, they are an essential ingredient of rhetoric as such since it is precisely a nontheoretically trained audience that has to be persuaded and convinced. To eliminate them from persuasive speech would mean to purge it of the *doxa* constitutive of the art of rhetoric. An apathetic rhetoric, or for that matter, rhetorical reading, would thus represent a form of what Plato refers to in *Phaidros* as "good rhetoric," a rhetoric in the name of philosophical truth. An apathetic rhetoric would then be a rhetoric free of all charm or violence, using rhetorical figure beyond rhetorical abuse. It would make a philosophical use of it, and hence it would amount to being a philosophical or dialectical rhetoric. Its disenchanted prose would ultimately turn this rhetoric into philosophy it-self.[34] Does this mean that de Man's reenactment of rhetoric is geared toward theoretical knowledge? Has Plato gotten the upper hand in de Man's rehabilitation of rhetoric? Not only Plato but Aristotle as well, who canonized logic's priority over against rhetoric? Rather than turning this hierarchy upside down by extending the sovereignty of logic to the do-main of rhetoric, does not de Man show himself here as a champion of logic itself? As expected, the answer can only be: yes and no.

But before hastening to give even such a double answer, let us first consider the following: Although rhetoric and philosophy have been warring since their inception in Greece, rhetoric belongs by full right to the very content of philosophical (speculative) discourse. It is in philoso-phy that rhetoric is given its status as the other of philosophy, opening thus the space for the agonistic exchange that has characterized the history of Western thought and in which philosophy retains in principle the upper hand, having determined in advance the nature and the out-come of the conflict. That such is the case is evident, for instance, from Book VI of *Republic*. Indeed, Socrates after having established the very qualities that make up the philosophical nature—courage, sobriety, gran-deur of soul, aptness to learn, memory, etc.—tells Adeimantes that these gifts of nature, precisely because they are so noble, can backslide and turn into their exact opposite if they are forced to grow "in the wrong environment" of the "opinions of the multitude" and if they are not properly nurtured but, instead, corrupted.[35] "The best endowed souls become worse than the others under a bad education," Socrates holds.[36] Thus corrupted souls, souls in which the seeds of philosophy, rather than attaining to consummate excellence, have grown into "quite the contrary unless some god comes to the rescue," become as bad as they can be since their wickedness springs from the corruption of a vigorous na-ture.[37] The gifts of nature for the perfect philosopher not only "tend to corrupt the soul of its possessor and divert it from philosophy" but make this soul the champion of the other of philosophy—the opinions of the multitude.[38] In short, it is precisely the philosophically inclined who have a tendency to become corrupt, to turn into corrupt philosophers—that is, sophists or private teachers. In contrast to the uncorrupted or honest philosopher, the wicked philosophers, the sophist and rhetori-cian, use thinking only to stir the most powerful emotions. Of their teaching, and of what they call "wisdom," Plato writes:

It is as if a man were acquiring the knowledge of the humors and desires of a great strong beast which he had in his keeping, how it is to be approached and touched, and when and by what things it is made most savage or gentle, yes, and the several sounds it is wont to utter on the occasion of each, and again what sounds uttered by another make it tame or fierce, and after mastering this knowledge by living with the creature and by lapse of time should call it wisdom, and should construct thereof a system and art and turn to the teaching of it, knowing nothing in reality about which of these opinions and desires is honorable or base, good or evil, just or unjust, but should apply all these terms to the judgments of the great beast, calling the things that pleased it good, but should call what is necessary just and honorable, never having observed how great is the real difference between the necessary and the good, and being incapable of explaining it to another.[39]

Consequently, the sophist or rhetorician, as a *corrupted* philosopher, as one "who does the greatest harm to communities and individuals," and as one whose crimes and unmixed wickedness are sublimely great, is intelligible not in him or herself and on his or her own merit but only to the extent that he or she is a corrupted *philosopher.*[40] He or she can be what he or she is, a great demagogue or seducer, because in essence, he or she had all the qualities to become a sober philosopher.

On the other hand, rhetoric itself has never been able to escape its own fascination with philosophy—Plato's rival is a good example of this fascination since he considered his rhetoric as *philosophia.* Consequently, although de Man's apathetic rhetoric seems to drift toward philosophy by definition, as well as by its concern with the idiosyncratic linguistic atoms—which on a problematic level, are at first sight much closer to Plato's ideas (however different they may be) than to the *koinoi topoi* that make up rhetoric for Curtius—its emphasis on absence of affect and the loss of the symbolic may well be geared toward removing—*abstracting*—rhetoric entirely from its domination by philosophy. Such an operation requires, of course, that rhetoric be dismantled by ridding it of persuasion. Whether such a dismantling is a high price to pay for rhetoric's liberation from philosophy is difficult to say. Is a rhetoric subtracted from the influence of philosophy still a rhetoric? In any case, the conception of rhetoric to which such a dismantling gives birth—beyond philosophy, beyond good and/or bad rhetoric—cannot easily be dismissed, if only because of the boundary phenomenon that this conception as conception represents, at the boundaries of thinking.

Let us then sharpen our ears for whatever the concept "apathetic rhetoric" may imply. As our reading of "Kant's Materialism" has demonstrated, an apathetic rhetorical reading centers in texts on those elements and acts that, despite their constitutive function (for the text), remain entirely punctual and that de Man calls "formal" or "material." Whereas de Man has shown these formal atoms to be a-referential, a-phenomenal, non-symbolical, etc., in other essays, "Kant's Materialism" stresses their apathy. This means at first that they do not have any emotional value effect attached to them, that they do not prompt any affective reaction but also, as seen, that they do not lend themselves to change (development, passage, transition, etc.). They are irreducibly passive and thus absolutely dead. The philosophical thrust of apathetic rhetoric thus seems to be evident. It is a search for what precedes all exchange, substitution, relation, development, and so forth, in what could be called a "materialist theory of language, discourse-, and text-formation." But what de Man shows is that these constituting elements, rules, or acts are so singular as to never lend themselves to any meaning intention. Whatever they may possibly come to mean, will always have been the result of an imposition as arbitrary in the end as the linguistic atoms and acts themselves. Yet if this is the case, then these elements cannot, in the last resort, be thematized under the rubric of singularity. From a classical perspective, to which I limit myself here,[41] the category of singularity is indeed, as is the particular, a conceptual stage, a moment, on the way to the universal. The singular makes sense only with respect to the universal, from which it can be deduced. It is true that "philosophy cannot deduce the concrete content of the multiplicity of the singular or the dispersion of the contingent, but it can and must deduce and comprehend the occurrence of this factuality and its unclarity as something necessary," Adriaan Perperzak has noted.[42] The singular is intrinsic to philosophy and, at the same time, as far as its content is concerned, entirely outside it. The factuality of the singular or the contingent partakes of the universal, while its content is ultimately entirely insignificant. This insignificance, also characterized as irrationality, is, however, an insignificance from the standpoint of reason and, thus, as Perperzak puts it, the "dark inner lining" of it.[43] As a result, even the content of the singular has a signification, however negative, with regard to the universal. Indeed, the Aristotelean topos constitutive of the universality of rational cognition—namely, that all nomination and designation of a singularity *as* an atom or a simple element is necessarily universal (and thus incapable of isolating such singularity in its singularity), because it can be achieved only with the help of a singular word or name, a word or name that is always already a universal since it can also serve to name and designate another singularity—this topos can, in principle, and without contradiction, be accompanied by the complementary topos, "that universal cognition of reason must recognize a general and universal unsayable and unknowable."[44] Rather than being a price to pay, such a complementary topos merely extends the realm of rationality to the unknowable. If reason recognizes the universality of what it misses because of the necessarily universal essence of language, then, as Hegel has convincingly argued, the unknowable and unsayable is (at least minimally) known. But the singular that apathetic rhetoric centers on is so left to itself, is so insoluble and absolute, that it escapes the dialectic of the universal altogether. For the same reason, it cannot be called "irrational" either. Or to put it differently, the apathetic linguistic atoms are singular to such a degree that their singularity no longer expresses singularity.[45] Nor does it, in its very apathy, convey any negative pathos. There cannot be any pathos of apathy. In contradistinction from glossolalia, in which the total breakdown of language into mere verbal materiality is expressive of passion—at least as far as its theological origin, in the pentecostal events celebrated on Whitsunday in commemoration of the descent of the Holy Spirit, is concerned—the radical atomization of language in an apathetic rhetorical reading aborts, from the start, the becoming meaningful of the meaningless. For all these reasons, I prefer to characterize these instances of irreducible punctuality as idiosyncratic. The term *idiosyncrasy* denotes, according to its etymology, the mixing, or tempering, of the characteristic properties pertaining to only one individual. It is originally an antique medical term. It names the specific combination of the elementary components that constitute the body, temperament, and character of an individual (and that hence serves also to explain its distinctive sensitiveness, reactiveness, or allergy). The notion of idiosyncrasy that is now more commonly used—to refer to the individual bent of mind or inclination of a person, to the view or feeling peculiar to one single individual, to the characteristic peculiarity of the mode or style of expression of a particular author—with its emphasis on the peculiarity and severance of what is unique to just one person thus seems a more appropriate term than *singularity,* for describing the irreducible singleness of the instances in question at least for the time being.[46] But as already indicated, such singleness, into which a materialist theory of language would inquire, is entirely insignificant from a philosophical viewpoint. To investigate these literally meaningless instances that escape all philosophical categorization and possible universalization is, strictly speaking, vain research. Inquiry into what is irrelevant because it is punctual and single to a degree that it does not even lend itself to a dialectic of universalization cannot, therefore, be called a "theory" or "philosophy" anymore.

The apathetic rhetoric that I have shown de Man to be interested in, a rhetoric that reaches beyond the rhetoric of tropes with its "logic" of substitution and reversal and that is still the main object of *Allegories of Reading,* has at first, all the appearance of a positive theory or philosophy. By abstracting the linguistic atoms and arbitrary acts of positing from the texts that it reads, apathetic rhetoric has all the allures of a theoretical enterprise. Indeed, by pointing at elements and instances that foreground the rhetoric of tropes, that are no longer of the order of the trope, de Man seems to be engaged in a type of inquiry concerned with ultimate elements of constitution. Does this then mean that the notion of an apathetic rhetoric no longer yields to the movement of inversion and reversal? Is there nothing anymore that comes to challenge its authority, to undo, to unposit, what such an apathetic rhetoric proposes or posits as the ultimate elements of the linguistic universe? Since the gesture of apathetic criticism is "foundationalist," "transcendental," and so forth, its discourse is, in principle, the metadiscourse *par excellence* that cannot be challenged by any counterdiscourse. And yet, the very concept of apathetic rhetoric, or for that matter, of a materialist philosophy of ultimate idiosyncrasy, is an impossible endeavor, strictly speaking, and could at best be achieved only in an idiosyncratic fashion. A rhetoric that sacrifices persuasion, a philosophy of what escapes all universality, a philosophy of the irrelevant, and the meaningless—these are contradictions in terms. Such enterprises are autodestructive. Thus, although nothing comes to undo from outside the transcendental gesture of apathetic criticism, its very concept undoes itself from within and thus surrenders its authority to make claims. Apathetic rhetoric, or the philosophy of the single, turns upon itself in itself. It erases itself in itself. Its concept crosses itself out.[47]

The idea of apathetic rhetorical reading therefore invokes additional meanings that must be mentioned here. As a rhetoric that renounces affections, it is first a rhetoric that does not display any pathos.[48] But, more importantly, as such an affect-free discourse, it renounces appeal to emotions in its addressee. Even though the affects are only one instrument by which persuasion becomes effected, it is rather obvious from everything developed until now that such a rhetoric no longer seeks to persuade in the first place. Since apathetic rhetoric is not engaged in theoretical cognition either, the refusal to play on the feelings of any possible addressee implies that ultimately, it is without an addressee. Remember de Man's saying that the stony gaze at the heart of the poet's vision cannot be understood as an address or an apostrophe. In other words, it is not directed at any present or absent recipient, the subject of apathetic criticism included. It is absolutely for no one, not even for its author himself.[49] It is, if you will, a type of discourse so objective that it is entirely idiosyncratic.

Such a rhetoric, cut off from any possible addressee, remains absolutely singular to the extent that it reenacts the positional power of language. It is thus impossible that it could seek imitation, let alone become an integrating factor in a humanistically inspired *paideia*. Apathetic rhetorical reading achieves a singularity so radical that it defies all communication, all mediation, and thus, all universality. Or, to put it once again in paradoxical terms, the apathetic formalism of rhetorical reading is universal to such a degree, that its very absoluteness prevents it from serving as a common denominator upon which a unifying pedagogical system could be based. Such surrendering of the possibility of a unifying *Bildung* is a necessary consequence of apathetic rhetoric's *simultaneous* refusal of philosophy and rhetoric—of a *paideia* in which either philosophy is the dominating force or in which literature reigns supreme. de Man's apathetic formalism has thus moved beyond the Platonic or Isocratic alternatives, beyond the founding fathers of Europe and its conception of pedagogy.

What then, one will ask, are the political implications of apathetic formalism? The conclusion that to think extreme singularity would represent a nihilistic abandonment of the idea of community, as well as of pedagogy as such, is premature, to say the least. Indeed, the thrust of de Man's apathetic formalism is directed against determinations of community and pedagogy that are a function of a *mediating* effort between the individual and the whole and that conceive of community as the *higher totality* of which the individual can become a member only on the basis of a sacrifice of his or her particularity. What the apathetic formalism seems to undermine is a community based on the *relations* of individuals exiting from their particularity. Yet precisely because the de Manean questioning of the unifying and continuity-producing values of education based on either the Platonic or the Isocratic conceptions is limited to an interrogation of the traditional concepts of community, the legacy of his endeavors consists in attempting to think a notion of community that would not represent a higher whole of relations, whose public stature would not be grounded in universal forms of mediation, and that would escape altogether the dialectic of universality and individuality. It is a formidable task, undoubtedly, at the limit of the possible perhaps, but therefore an assignment for thinking . . .

In conclusion: Apathetic rhetoric attempts the impossible, but it does so in and as an adventure of thinking. All great thinkers, Heidegger contends, have only *one* thought that gives unity to their thinking and to which they return in the repeated attempts to think it. If such a thought informs de Man's thinking, it is one that is so singular as to destroy its oneness and with it, the unifying power that thought must be able to exercise to be the one thought in the first place. It is therefore a thought so singular that it risks incomprehensibility. Yet in that very risk it appeals to thinking, which must face the challenge of the uniqueness of such an idea. Uniqueness on the level of thought, however, is not only exceptional, as is often believed in total disregard of the essence of thinking. Uniqueness, ultimately, is what thought *itself* makes impossible. Although absence of uniqueness does in no way exclude the independence or autonomy of a thinking enterprise, thinking begins with the fallout of all uniqueness. Yet to have tried to think the impossible singularity, uniqueness of thinking in its universality, is what, forever, will make de Man's 'impossible' thinking *incontournable* for anyone who claims to be in the business of thinking.

4

The Fallout of Reading

Is it not self-evident that literary critics read the texts on which they critically speak? Paul de Man, however, has argued that this presumption is a delusion. Although de Man's contention that the study of literary texts is not necessarily based on reading seems, at first glance, to state an idiosyncratic and irritating paradox, it merits a closer investigation. In the first place, in "the by no means self-evident necessity of reading" (RT, p. 15), the reading in question—the reading that it is not obvious that literary critics do—must imply something other than the reading that literary critics obviously do. For the latter, de Man contends, "the sole purpose is to do away with reading entirely" (RT, p. 31). Second, such a statement must presuppose a different notion of literary text and of the function of reading in relation to the text. Whatever literary critics may read, they do not read literary *texts*. Further, reading, as they understand it, though it intervenes in the text, "is a means toward an end, a means that should finally become transparent and superfluous" (RT, p. 56), de Man writes. In contradistinction to a reading that effaces itself before the textual structures that it actualizes, or the educational values whose transfer it guarantees, reading, for de Man, has its own rules. It is an independent quantity, as it were. Finally, one can assume that reading in de Man's sense has a distinct finality that stands in sharp contrast to the outcome of traditional criticism.

The reading that literary studies (be they historical, hermeneutical, or formalistic) avoid is what de Man calls "mere reading." But what is "mere reading"? Is it *only* reading, reading that is pure, undiluted, and un-mixed? A reading that is what it is only in the full sense of the term

114

reading, absolutely and exclusively, and nothing else? Or is it only reading, that is just reading, bare reading? An immediate response to these
questions is to take *mere reading* as a silent reading. Hegel, for one, uses
the term *mere reading* to describe a silent reading, a *lectio tacita.* But has
the distinction between reading aloud and reading silently any bearing
whatsoever on what de Man means by *mere reading?* Is it simply too
farfetched to entertain the possibility that a discussion of mere reading in
de Man's sense could benefit at all from such contextualization? Given
that customarily mere reading is, indeed, understood as silent reading, it
is certainly not entirely inappropriate to briefly, at least, engage the question. A succinct discussion of the inventions of silent reading in Greece,
respectively, in the Middle Ages, as well as of the ways in which it has
been experienced, might provide a good framework for this. But, first,
back to Hegel.

When we read poetry, Hegel writes, we are "accustomed" and "satis-
fied with reading merely *(blosses Lesen).*" Although such a reading is
legitimate, Hegel maintains in his dialectical account of mere reading,
because "of the readiness with which we imagine as spoken what is seen
. . . [and] because poetry alone of all the arts is in its essential aspects
already completely at home in the spiritual element and does not bring
the chief thing to our minds through either the ear or eye," poetry as art
must not strip itself entirely of what makes it an actual external *(wirk-
liche)* expression of the spiritual content. Further, as the "*material* basis"
in which the spiritual content of a work of poetry finds its expression is
language, in order to fully emerge as art and to avoid imperfection, works
of poetry "must be spoken, sung, declaimed, presented by living persons," since language "does not exist . . . on its own account apart from
the artist." In short, although poetry's borderline situation with religion
and philosophy predisposes it for a *lectio tacita,* as long as it is to be
recognized as art, loud reading alone will do justice to it. "It is the living
man himself, the individual speaker, who alone is the support for the
perceptible presence and actuality of a poetic production," Hegel adds.[1]
Mere reading in Hegel's sense is thus a reading that reads exclusively for
the spiritual content of a work of poetry, oblivious to its art character.
The following remarks can thus be made: Since the essential link between the spiritual content and the material base, the link constitutive of
the work of art according to Hegel and to the aesthetic tradition, is
precisely what mere reading in de Man's understanding seeks to undo,

one might suppose a continuity between the two notions of mere reading. But mere reading in de Man's sense is certainly not a reading that, like the *lectio tacita,* centers on the spiritual content oblivious to the fact that poetry is a manifestation of art. de Man, clearly echoing Derrida's statement in *Of Grammatology* that reading must be aware that in the entire history of texts in the West the specificity of the (philosophical as well as literary) text is determined by "the project of effacing itself in the face of the signified content which it transports and in general teaches," takes task with "*transcendent* reading," a reading in search of the signified.[2] Although de Man's mere reading, like Hegel's, is a reading that reposes on the unhinging of meaning from its material basis—that is, neither is aesthetic—the two now seem very much at odds. But it remains that silent reading is an undoing of the link between meaning and language's material base. Even if, according to de Man, mere reading does not read for the spiritual content but rather for the material base, it is a reading bent on interrupting the link between language and what it supposedly means to say. Moreover, reading for the material basis is, as shall become clear, not only not to read for the sensible basis *of* a linguistic meaning, it is neither to read for an element that has its support in the living voice. Hence my question whether de Man's mere reading is not also a silent reading of sorts. The silence of mere reading, then, might not simply be the opposite of the living voice in reading aloud. It is therefore, perhaps, not completely inappropriate to pursue for a moment one possible affinity between mere reading as de Man understands it and silent reading by lingering on the traditional distinction between reading aloud and reading in silence. Are not de Man's readings, indeed, remarkably atonal? As Christiaan L. Hart Nibbrig has observed, one is surprised "how what Paul de Man offers to read comes out so soundless, unsensual, and flat."[3] Further, as we shall see from our reading of "Anthropomorphism and Trope in Lyric," in Chapter 6, the determination of mere reading as a reading that allows for incomprehensibility takes place in a process of sharp demarcation from a (lyrical) voice's and the song's reading. The voice, de Man suggests, in *Allegory of Reading,* is "a metaphor inferring by analogy the intent of the subject from the structure of the predicate" (*AR*, p. 18). In other words, the voice is that in which a text is made meaningful, and hence intelligible. Singing and understanding being one and the same thing, one can confidently assume that merely reading is closer to a silent reading. But the following passage from

"Autobiography as De-Facement" is perhaps even more significant in that it links language (and reading) not merely to silence but to muteness. After having said, in the context of an analysis of Wordsworth's *Excursion,* that language, inasmuch as it is figural, "is silent, mute as pictures are mute," de Man writes: "To the extent that, in writing, we are dependent on this language we all are, like the Dalesman in the *Excursion,* deaf and mute—not silent, which implies the possible manifestation of sound at our will, but silent as a picture, that is to say eternally deprived of voice and condemned to muteness. No wonder that the Dalesman takes so readily to books" (*RR,* p. 80). Finally, what is one to make of the aside in "The Resistance to Theory" that one of the consequences of the voiding by literature of aesthetic categories "is that, whereas we have traditionally been accustomed to reading literature by analogy with the plastic arts and with music, we now have to recognize the necessity of a non-perceptual linguistic moment in painting and music, and to learn to *read* pictures rather than to *imagine* meaning" (*RT,* p. 10)? This is not the place to take up the Idealist and Romantic gesture of ranking the arts by prioritizing literature, notwithstanding the radical rethinking to which literature has here been exposed. What should interest us, however, is that if reading consisted of making what is written visible and audible, mere reading implies bracketing not only of the visual but of the auditive moment as well. A certain blindness and a certain deafness are required to keep the aesthetic categories from creeping back into the reading of literature.

Since de Man considers his theory of mere reading to be in sync with Derrida's appraisal of the relation between writing and the living voice—and with Derrida's resistance to transcendent reading, a reading which Derrida, as is to be shown in the next chapter, does not at all wish "to annull . . . but to understand . . . within a system to which such a reading is blind"[4]—we should recall that Plato's condemnation of writing in *Phaedrus* derives from the contention that writing cannot speak for, defend, or explain itself. It is a mere (though dangerous) supplement to the living voice, on whose help it is at all times dependent. But Plato's account of writing is perhaps only the distinct philosophical attempt to invert and reappropriate the quite singular mode in which writing was linked to the voice from its first appearance in ancient Greece. On the basis of the discovery that the invention of alphabetical writing was originally linked to the commemoration of the dead, Jesper Svenbro has convincingly shown that if voice is to be added to writing, it is first and foremost to make writing ring, and resound. The voice, in the same way as writing, functions here as a mere signifier. No meaning yet inhabits the voice. Indeed, the inscriptions on grave stelae, where writing makes its first appearance in ancient Greece, are not transpositions of previously oral utterances and already constituted meanings but invitations to produce oral events. The voice that supplements the silent commemorative inscriptions is thus in no way a means to reactivate a living meaning that would represent the interiority of the dead letter. The oral event alone that results from reading aloud an inscription is what is meaningful. Svenbro writes: "Using his own voice, the reader adds a *logos* to what is written. The *logos* allows writing to become an intelligible sonorous trace for the reader become listener, a sonorous trace, however, that, like the written trace itself, lacks all interiority."[5] The reading voice is a necessary part of what is written, its natural prolongation, as it were. It belongs to what is written and is claimed by it. As Svenbro argues, "Greek writing is first and foremost a machine to produce sound." It is, indeed, "a machine to produce *kleos*," that is, renown, fame, reputation, a fundamental value in Greek society which, by definition, is accoustic.[6] By reading the epigrams inscribed on the commemorative stones aloud, and with it the name of the dead, the resounding voice, itself without interiority, allows "every reading to become the audible blossoming of meaning, in short, of the *kleos*."[7] Since the function of the inscription is to trigger the production of *kleos*, and a *kleos* is by necessity sonorous, the inscription must be completed by the reading voice. It needs the voice to be able to resound. This voice ensures that the dead's name endures and continues to resound in the future and be heard far away. By way of the reader's voice, the voice of the deceased him or herself will live on.[8] In this conception of writing, writing thus does not represent the spoken word (and the spoken word does not articulate a meaning confined to the silence of writing). Writing "here, aims only at producing a voice that, one could say, imitates the same by means of the same."[9] It is only when, toward the end of the fourth century B.C., reading begins to become silent that writing acquires a representational function.

This is also the moment when the Platonic problematization of writing becomes the possibility that has dominated the thinking of writing in the West. Indeed, writing, philosophically redefined and interiorized as the inscription of truth in the soul, seems to require only silent reading. The latter is at least not an obstacle to its truth function. In any case, the positive appraisal of a certain kind of writing—of "good writing," as Derrida has called it—and that follows Socrates' second speech in the *Phaedrus,* is not only the foil against which the other (bad) writing, but reading aloud (written speeches in the absence of its author, for instance), as well, is condemned. As Svenbro shows, remarkably following up Derrida's suggestion in "Plato's Pharmacy" that we consider together "the writing *and* the pederasty of a young man named Plato,"[10] the voice in the loud reading of a written speech, like Phaedrus's voice reading the speech of his lover Lysias, is a voice forced upon the reader by the written text and is comparable to what Plato in the *Charmides* calls "incantation." It is a voice drugged by the *pharmakon* of writing. "The *pharmakon* makes one talkative," Svenbro writes. In reading a written speech aloud, one speaks under the constraints *(ananke)* of the *pharmakon.* One's voice is reduced to an instrument, and an object. One does, therefore, not speak in one's own voice. Yet in order to say the truth, one must be free of all constraint.[11] From the moment truth becomes the issue, reading should take place silently, one must assume. In silent reading, where meaning is captured by the eyes alone, the reader and his or her voice are no longer instrumentalized.[12] Only with the establishment of a good writing—preferably to be read silently—can reading tend toward the transcendent reading with which both Derrida and de Man take issue.

As Svenbro has remarked, the advent of silent reading in Greece represented a quite "unnatural" turn for a society entirely based on the production of sound.[13] But the passage in the European Middle Ages from a mode of reading dominated by the primacy of the *phone* to silent reading was equally troublesome and was experienced, as Maria Tasinato has argued, as an outright scandal. Although Saint Ambrosius, the first, according to Saint Augustin, to read with his eyes alone, dispenses with the living voice only to "enter into a silent dialogue with the divine," Saint Augustin, for one, was alarmed and profoundly disoriented by the withdrawal into inaudible reading.[14] Indeed, if reading aloud permitted a dialogue between the reader and his or her listeners, Ambrosius's attitude is plainly asocial. "He makes it understood, by not uttering any sounds, that he does not wish to be interrupted while reading. He shows at that moment that he considers the loud *'causae alienae'* and demands for clarification as chitchat, small talk . . . His *lectio* is a solitary feast *('feriatus')* celebrated to make those who are present absent, mere onlookers."[15] No surprise, then, that the excluded bystanders might won-der about the precise nature of the divinity by which Ambrosius is pos-sessed when he reads. Tasinato writes: "Ambrosius is seen as celebrating a mysterious rite in the face of which those who are present—as non-in-itiates—are reduced to a state of dumbfounded incomprehension. He is in the process of secretly honouring a heretofore unknown deity: the silent demon of reading."[16] For what interests me, however, it is neces-sary to look more carefully at what happens, according to Tasinato, in the passage from reading aloud to the *lectio tacita* of Ambrosius. Faced with the *scripta continua* of ancient writing's compact mass of letters, the ancient reader had interpretatively to shape, with the reassuring help of his voice, that almost fissureless block of letters with separating spaces of silence. In "*tacite legens,* Ambrosius dilates to the highest degree this silence that the reader who reads aloud had to introduce into the *contin-uum* in order to re-form the discontinuous (the discontinuity of the voice itself). At first glance, Ambrosius's attitude might seem to plunge again into the formless. On the contrary, it is a circumspect (*avisée*), entirely visual pursuit, of meaning."[17] Relinquishing in silent reading the voice's power to interrupt the continuum of writing, Ambrosius appears to give away the very possibility of reading itself. But Ambrosius also replaces the interpreting voice with the discriminately interpreting eye. He makes the eye do what the voice did before. Yet substituting in silent reading the eye for the voice also changes the status of writing and of the written itself. Under the primacy of the voice, which "felt itself capable of rees-tablishing, all by itself, its own discontinuous structure," writing was secondary and inessential. Ambrosius's silent reading, Tasinato argues, "breaks this absolute solidarity between reading and the voice that took place at the expense of writing" and returns writing "entirely to the mute realm of the graphic sign," the realm that Plato denounced as incapable of defending itself and hostile to all dialogism.[18] At the same time that silent reading deposes voice and restores writing to itself, it "also restores to the eyes their sovereignty in reading." Yet, it is precisely this privilege accorded to the eye in reading that makes silent reading so threatening to Saint Augustin. For, indeed, "between reading and vision, the vision as much of the demon as of the one who gives way to him, as of the one who opposes the giving-way, there exists an affinity." It is this affinity that prompted Saint Augustin's praise of blindness, even though, as Tasi-nato has demonstrated, "the silent reader may well be better protected against the demons than the one who reads aloud, because reading silently he or she does not present the demons with the possibility of phonic *mimesis*."[19]

To return to the question triggered by Hegel's reference to "mere reading" as to whether any significant link can be made out between de Man's notion of mere reading and silent reading, it would first seem that mere reading is, indeed, a silent reading, in that no voice supplements nor guarantees the eclosion of meaning. Further, mere reading is precisely geared toward disconnecting the voice in its phenomenality (but perhaps not its materiality) from the meaning production of writing, thus endowing this reading with the characteristics of unnaturalness and anomaly that have accompanied the emergence of the *lectio tacita*. Finally, it is a silent reading because its severs the solidarity characteristic of reading aloud, of reading and voice, restoring in this manner the written and the text to itself. But mere reading as conceived by de Man is not a silent reading, if the latter is understood to tend toward writing's ultimate signified. It is not even a reading in which sight replaces voice and hearing in order to achieve silent and undistracted dialogue with meaning. Nor does mere reading directly grasp writing's spiritual content by imagining as spoken the written letters that the eye beholds. But then we might say that mere reading is, indeed, a reading that is more silent than silent reading in that it has silenced the power of the eye to hear as much as its power to see. For mere reading is not to proceed anymore in analogy to the plastic arts and music. Mere reading is a silent reading in that it silences all intuitive, perceptional, sensual approaches to the written text. As if echoing Saint Augustin's denunciation of the seductions of the senses, mere reading practices radical asceticism. It is deliberately mute, and deliberately blind.

Given that theory—from *thea*, sight, contemplation—is in essence a perceptual approach, it comes, therefore, as no surprise that, from the outset, de Man defines *mere reading* as a reading "prior to any theory." *Theory*, here, refers not only to what has come to be known in North America under this title since the sixties—for it includes even theories of reading insofar as they are theories, de Man's as well—but more importantly, the "minimal set of concepts . . . of at least some general import" (*RT*, p. 6) of which all, even intuitive, and explicitly antitheoretical approaches to literature, must make use. Even when minimally present in the critics' approach, theory, for de Man, is linked to preconceptions of the literary, that is, "to the power of a system (philosophical, religious or ideological) that may well remain implicit but that determines an *a priori* conception of what is 'literary' by starting out from the premises of the system rather than from the literary thing itself" (*RT*, p. 5). Although de Man recognizes a manifold of systems that inform traditional ways of treating literature, one system draws de Man's antagonism. The philosophical approach to the literary, which de Man terms "aesthetic speculation," is, for de Man, the fundamental preconception that grounds all the others. Mere reading is thus in particular a reading prior to all aesthetic appropriation of the literary. When de Man calls such a reading "deeply subversive to those who think of teaching literature as a substitute for the teaching of theology, ethics, psychology, or intellectual history" (*RT*, p. 24), we sense that de Man's concept of "mere reading" will bear a debt to what Husserl developed under the title of a phenomenological reduction. However, as we shall see, it is a phenomenological reduction in a literal sense, one that aims at radically foregrounding phenomenality as such. In any event, seeking to read a text in advance of all theoretical recuperation—and, paradoxically, this is the goal of de Man's own theory of reading—mere reading, and its theory, is construed as the exact opposite of speculation. This is a first reason why de Man can say that literary theory "contains a necessarily pragmatic moment that certainly weakens it as theory but that adds a subversive element of unpredictablity and makes it something of a wild card in the serious game of the theoretical disciplines" (*RT*, p. 8).

Reflecting in the essay "The Resistance to Theory" on the development of contemporary literary theory, or the theory of reading, de Man insists that it is not "a by-product of larger philosophical speculations" in contemporary thought. Although a direct link might occasionally exist between how the two disciplines have developed, "contemporary literary theory is a relatively autonomous version of questions that also surface, in a different context, in philosophy, though not necessarily in a clearer and more rigorous form," de Man writes. In short, it "came into being from outside philosophy and sometimes in conscious rebellion against the weight of its tradition." What are the reasons for this sharp contrast? I recall that the theory of reading aims at reading texts prior to all theoretical approaches, and especially, to aesthetic considerations. Indeed, aesthetics, for de Man, is not so much a "specific theory" as "part of a universal system of philosophy." However, it is not just a part, but, though "never dominant," "a constitutive part of its system," de Man holds, the reference being not merely to a historically specific form of philosophy but to philosophy in general. Moreover, when he asserts that Nietzsche's and Heidegger's philosophical critique of metaphysics "includes, or starts out from, the aesthetic" (*RT*, p. 8), it is to demarcate the nonphilosophical—more precisely, empirical—or pragmatic criticism of aesthetics of the theory of reading from the philosophical or, as de Man also says, speculative nature of philosophy's critique. The autonomy of literary theory has an advantage over the philosophical debate with aesthetics in that philosophy qua philosophy contains aesthetics as a constitutive part of its system. It has always been, and is still, intrinsically aesthetic and, therefore, remains necessarily trapped in what it seeks to criticize. By contrast, literary theory's autonomy from philosophy allows for a clearer, more rigorous, more consequential critique of aesthetics.

To understand de Man's contention that philosophy is an inherently aesthetic speculation and that this speculation grounds all other theoretical approaches (theological, hermeneutical, psychological, historical, formalist) to the literary, and further what it is that mere reading leaves behind in its antiaesthetical vista, we must address the question of aesthetics as it is posed by de Man. I should note from the outset that in his attack on aesthetics, de Man does not stand alone. Indeed, most reflections on art in this century have probed the limits of aesthetics to do justice to the artwork. But before taking up the issue of aesthetics, a preliminary, and succinct, outline—to be expanded in due time—of what mere reading is to achieve cannot be avoided.

Reading concentrates "on the way meaning is conveyed rather than on the meaning itself," de Man argues (*RT*, p. 23). All by itself this definition of reading remains ambiguous in that it can also describe a host of critical approaches with which de Man disagrees. What it means, however, is that mere reading, which is a certain kind of close reading, closes in on "structures of language." Yet, "the philological or rhetorical devices" that reading is concerned with are not primarily particularities of a given national language and its literature but, as we will see, structures and linguistic properties of language in general. The aim of mere reading is to bring into view and to reactivate the linguistic structures by which in all cases meaning is conveyed. If the literary critics who entertain an ethical, historical, theological, formalist conception of the literary work have avoided these structures, it is, one can assume, because these structures make it rigorously impossible to link the literary artifact to the pre-supposed or implied meanings and values. Consequently, a mere reading focuses on what in the literary work interrupts or disrupts the presumed relation to meanings and values. As will become more clear, this is not to say that mere reading thematizes the linguistic structures as such, in and for themselves, in complete abstraction from what they are made to mean. Entirely different from "aesthetic appreciation . . . the latter can be a way of access to" (*RT*, p. 24) the philological and rhetorical devices of language itself, de Man acknowledges. Indeed, the object of mere read-ing is not simply to bring into view a pure linguistic substratum that might exist independently of the meaning intentions that are violently bestowed upon it. Such a turn to the structures of language—a turn also strangely qualified as a return to philology (*RT*, p. 24)—makes "the attri-bution of a reliable, or even exemplary, cognitive and, by extension, ethical function to literature . . . much more difficult," de Man says (*RT*, p. 25). What is more, "literary theory raises the unavoidable question whether aesthetic values can be compatible with the linguistic structures that make up the entities from which these values are derived." Thus, while not roundly denying, for reasons to be discusssed later, all relation to the ethical, moral, social, epistemological, etc., the possibility of such relation is obviously at stake. With mere reading, a certain kind of rela-tion, if not relation strictly speaking, between the linguistic structures of the work and meaning becomes problematic. For de Man, it is the aes-thetical as the relation between the sensible and the intelligible, the senses and the spirit, that is thus at issue. The aesthetical is, indeed, synonymous with relation. The question whether or not literature has any relation to the realm of cognition or morality goes back, de Man insists, "to the rise of aesthetics as an independent discipline in the later half of the eighteenth century. The link between literature (as art), epis-temology, and ethics is the burden of aesthetic theory at least since Kant. It is because we teach literature as an aesthetic function that we can move so easily from literature to its apparent prolongations in the sphere of self-knowledge, of religion, and of politics," de Man argues (*RT*, p. 25). However, aesthetic theory, in the historical and theoretical sense that derives from Baumgarten's coining of the term, is itself rooted in Cratylism, de Man contends, that is to say, in a philosophical distortion of the essence of language according to which a natural correctness exists in the names of things. The philosophical conception of language that makes up the core of Cratylism is, according to de Man, an aesthetic conception. He writes: "To the extent that Cratylism assumes a convergence of the phenomenal aspects of language, as sound, with its signifying function as referent, it is an aesthetically oriented conception; one could, in fact, without distortion, consider aesthetic theory, including its most systematic formulation in Hegel, as the complete unfolding of the model of which the Cratylian conception of language is a version" (*RT*, p. 9).[20] This conception is aesthetic in that language is here approached from its sensible side, that is, from what of it is perceivable, and in that this sensible aspect is believed to stand in a natural relation to the order of meaning. Cratylism, with its assumption of a natural, or a symbolic relation between word and thing, is the philosophical matrix of aesthetics. It posits that what is of the order of language entertains a natural relationship to the order of things, in short, that there is a naturally meaningful relation between the two. But Cratylism is not only the model for all aesthetics for de Man; it is also the reason that all philosophy is intrinsically aesthetic. Indeed, Cratylism is only a version of a model for the understanding of language that presupposes the phenomenalizibility of aspects of language that are not yet phenomenal in the way that the sound character of language is. According to this model, language is by nature a specular mirror of the world. If aesthetics, then, is said to be a constitutive part of philosophy, it is because philosophy, for de Man, is essentially Cratylic in a broad sense. It follows that the program pursued in mere reading that puts into question aesthetic considerations in the approach to the literary work ultimately aims at undoing what de Man conceives of as the foundation of philosophy. If, indeed, aesthetics is what makes it possible to tie the literary to the epistemological and the ethical and to assert that it has meaning and value, is it not because its hidden Cratylism posits a natural relationship to begin with? By putting the aesthetic on trial, de Man, then, intends not only to disqualify the more narrow "tradition of aesthetic speculation" (*RT*, p. 22) about the literary but all other, historical, theological, and ethical traditions as well.

Having thus outlined in general terms the basic characteristics and stakes of mere reading, a more systematic exposition of what mere reading assumes about the linguistic and the text becomes possible, as does a discussion of its implications. Let us begin with the following more complex definition of the aims of literary theory, or theory of reading. de Man writes that it "can be said to come into being when the approach to literary texts is no longer based on non-linguistic, that is to say, historical and aesthetic conceptions or . . . when the object of discussion is no longer the meaning or the value but the modalities of production and of reception of meaning and of value prior to their establishement—the implication being that this establishment is problematic enough to require an autonomous discipline of critical investigation to consider its possibility and its status" (*RT*, p. 7). Linguistics would thus make all the difference for a theory of reading. Inquiring into the modalities of the production and reception of meaning and value, the theory of reading opens a domain of investigation prior to what historical and aesthetic interpretations take for granted, as if meaning and value were just natural givens. But even though the theory of reading is historically and theoretically dependent on structural linguistics, it is not assimilable to a linguistic structuralism.[21] Nor is it a theory of linguistics itself. Given its philosophical stakes as a critique of aesthetics, the theory of reading is closer to a philosophy of language, a philosophy, however, that would have freed itself of the aesthetic appraisal of language on which philosophy since Plato rests.

But if literary theory "occurs with the introduction of linguistic terminology in the metalanguage about literature," what precisely does de Man mean by *linguistic terminology?* And, more importantly, what is meant by *language* in the first place? Does he not describe it as the most "self-evasive" word of all words, one that is "disfigured and disfiguring," in short, as the greatest "theoretical enigma," even when used in the most general and familiar way (*RT*, p. 13)? de Man also characterizes literary theory as an approach that makes "use of language about language" (*RT*, p. 12). How are we to take this statement, and does it simply mean that language and literature are self-reflexive, and thus about themselves? de Man explains: "By linguistic terminology is meant a terminology that designates reference prior to designating the referent and takes into account, in the consideration of the world, the referential function of language or, to be somewhat more specific, that considers reference as a function of language and not necessarily as an intuition" (*RT*, p. 8). Linguistic terminology, or language about language, is not just a language-oriented terminology but one that conceptualizes reference as a function of language. By describing reference as a function of language, reference becomes a relation entirely immanent to the order of language itself. de Man does not deny that language refers, as is often asserted—as a matter of fact, language is all referral, and that is precisely where the problem lies—but if such reference, as he argues, is not necessarily of the order of intuition, it means that the essence of reference remains entirely within the linguistic. In other words, the referential function of language is not primarily understandable from the transcendent, and nonlinguistic realm of the world. "Intuition implies perception, consciousness, experience, and leads at once into the world of logic and understanding with all its correlatives, among which aesthetics occupies a prominent place" (*RT*, p. 8). Rather than understanding the referential function of language as providing ancillary services to the world, or as a function that though meaningful in itself, would nevertheless remain within the realm of the cognitive expectation that what language refers to can always be confirmed by an intuition of the intended referent, reference is here understood from language itself. *Per se*, reference does not transcend language toward something nonlinguistic. If reference is not of the order of intuition—not necessarily, that is, not in essence—it remains on this side of sensibility (*Sinnlichkeit*), and *a fortiori* of cognition. The autonomous realm of investigation characteristic to literary theory thus concerns what one might call the "nonreferential referring function of language," a reference prior to the (nonlinguistic) designation of a worldly (or ideal) referent. In addition, the linguistic terminology invoked is one that conceptualizes language in and for itself. It presupposes a nonaesthetic, i.e., a non-Cratyllic, approach to language and is, as shall be seen, a terminology stripped to its linguistic bone, in other words, immanent to language itself.[22]

In the context of an evaluation of the fruitfulness of linguistic and semiotic theories for literary theory, and how it compares to what previous (nonlinguistic) pilot sciences did for literary theory, de Man not only emphasizes the "natural [*sic!*] attraction of literature to a theory of linguistic signs" (*RT*, p. 8), as well as that "the results of the encounter between semiology and literature went considerably further than those of many other theoretical models," but above all that the analyses made from a linguistic or semiotic perspective "revealed patterns that could only be described in terms of their own, specifically linguistic, aspects" (*RT*, p. 9). Whereas other approaches to literary texts produced "observations that could be paraphrased or translated in terms of common language," the natural concordance between linguistics and literature is such that the patterns brought to light do not let themselves be usurped by discourses whose concerns are extrinsic. Rather, they are specific to language to such a degree that they can be described only in an intrinsically linguistic fashion. In the context of "The Resistance to Theory," this argument serves to stress, in particular, the extraordinary affinity of structural linguistics and literature. Even so, it gives us a further hint at the nature of the linguistic on which a mere reading of texts hinges. Indeed, if the patterns of literary texts exhibited by linguistic or semiotic analyses can "only be described in terms of their own, specifically linguistic, aspect," it follows that these patterns are rigorously untranslatable into any other medium than their own. In other words, if the object of a linguistic inquiry concerns language's structures of reference prior to their designating a referent, these same structures are understandable exclusively in terms of themselves, and not in terms of the intuitions of referents that possibly could serve, to use a Husserlian terminology, to fulfill their referring intention. In short, the object of a linguistic investigation of a literary text is autonomous to the point of being thoroughly untranslatable into any idiom, discourse, or medium.

This untranslatable "substratum" is what de Man calls "literariness." He writes: "The linguistics of semiology and of literature apparently have something in common that only their shared perspective can detect and pertains distinctively to them. The definition of this something, often referred to as literariness, has become the object of literary theory" (*RT,* p. 9). Literary theory, or mere reading, closes in on what in literary texts is absolutely irreducible to any other discourse, the what of language qua language that remains forever untranslatable. Since literariness cannot be made intelligible from or through other discourses, particularly not historical or aesthetical ones, its specificity lets it be defined only tautologically. To define it is to restate, or repeat, it in its own, specifically linguistic terms. If I set aside the possible, but simple-minded objection to the effect that such a definition of language is empty, or vacuous, and says nothing about how language really is, it is because the ontological nature of language, as understood by de Man, may well require tautologism as the one single appropriate mode of speaking about it. Indeed, the literariness of language, what is specific about it, is untranslatable since no equivalent of language exists. Language, indeed, is so unique that its very nature is the resistance to all meaningful and propositional commodification. "Itself" has no use value. Yet, if language can be spoken about only tautologically, it is not because language would have to be named and defined as and in *itself*. Unlike Heidegger's claims in his last seminar, the Zähringen seminar, that the thinking of the simple compels phenomenological thought to become tautological, de Man's tautological gesture might no longer be phenomenological. Its aim is not to bring language "itself" into view. Were it still possible to pinpoint a property of language as conceived by de Man, one would have to say that it consists precisely in the power never to be itself, not even to be the same as itself in not being itself. It does not have the simplicity of an "itself," or selfsame, a simplicity that would indeed require tautological reduplication for it to show itself.[23] As I already cautioned, the "autonomous potential of language" (*RT*, p. 10), though it is the object of literary theory and mere reading, cannot be brought to light directly, or *as such*. It cannot be the object of an (sensible or eidetic) intuition. It can be known only negatively through the weave of that which it makes possible and which it immediately annihilates as well.

Before further probing into the autonomous potential of language, it is necessary to return to the question of the aesthetic response and to consider why this response to literary works forces itself upon the reader with an iron clad necessity, as it were. As de Man puts it, "Aesthetics is in fact, ever since its development just before and with Kant, a phenomenalism of a process of meaning and understanding" (*RT*, p. 7). Given de Man's idiosyncratic blending of a concept of phenomenological origin with one that stems from critical philosophy, the meaning of the statement hinges entirely on how the term *phenomenalism* is contextualized. As a starting point, let me consider the following statement: "In its origin and its development, aesthetics has been the province of philosophers of nature and of the self rather than of philosophers of language" (*RT*, p. 25). Rather than intimating that all is text, de Man here acknowledges the existence of nature as an objective world. The common imputation that de Man implies that everything is language is surely without grounds. Still, his recognition of the existence of an objective realm does not, as shall become clear, make things any less strange. But first this: The historical discipline of aesthetics, as a science of art, is said to be modeled after the world of nature, in Kantian terms, of phenomena, and the modes of cognition by which the self appropriates this world. The "phenomenalism of art"—which dominates aesthetics including "Hegel's *Aesthetics,* the canonical bible, still for Heidegger"—is a "world-oriented" approach to art (*RT*, p. 68). If the "phenomenal world" is mastered "by processes that stem from the psychology of perception"—de Man cites Husserl to substantiate his point—the phenomenalism of art consists of seeking to master art "by analogy" to the cognitive process that, by definition, belongs to the world of nature (*RT*, p. 62). Phenomenality, de Man writes, implies "accessibility to intuition or cognition" (*RT*, p. 34). But "natural or phenomenal cognition" (*RT*, p. 11)—i.e., the cognition of nature, or phenomena—a cognition that proceeds by means of processes that themselves belong to the phenomenal world and which de Man characterizes as "specular (that is to say solar and phenomenal)" (*RT*, p. 69), is inappropriate to the realm of art and especially to the literary text. To bring a phenomenal experience to bear on the literary text amounts to nothing less than a "mistranslation" (*RT*, p. 62). In turn, the referential function of language cannot be used to authorize natural or phenomenal cognition. de Man writes: "In a genuine semiology as well as in other linguistically oriented theories, the referential function of language is not being denied—far from it; what is in question is its authority as a model for natural or phenomenal cognition" (*RT*, pp. 10–11). Having said that a "non-phenomenal linguistics . . . frees the discourse on literature from naive oppositions between fiction and reality," de Man adds that "literature is fiction not because it somehow refuses to acknowledge 'reality,' but because it is not *a priori* certain that language functions according to principles which are those, or which are like those, of the phenomenal world. It is therefore not *a priori* certain that literature is a reliable source of information about anything but its own language" (*RT*, p. 11). The principle of language, and hence of literature, is unlike that of the phenomenal world. In language no *legein ta phenomena*, no "saying" of the phenomema, hence no cognition, takes places. Language is only an appropriate model for language itself. But, as we will see, this does mean at all that language would be self-reflexive, in other words "about" itself even though occasionally de Man makes use of such terminology. As a result, an unbridgeable chasm in principle divides the world of phenonema from that of language.[24] Even though de Man resists all conciliatory attempts to bring the two sides of the chasm together and wishes to keep these two worlds rigorously apart—because, as Christoph Menke has pointedly argued, both sides, for de Man, "cannot be thought *together*,"[25]—it is, however, wrong to assume that nothing happens within that Manichean gap, or that it is an empty place. Quite the opposite is true. It is a space of mystification. In Kantian terms one might say that it is the locus of transcendental illusions, of the illusion of being able to transcend the immanence of language or to use essentially nonlinguistic models of phenomenal cognition as a way to the literary text.

Yet the aesthetic mistranslation of a text is not simply the result of an illicit transposition of the perceptive and the cognitive to its realm. The text itself allows "mystified minds" to read it aesthetically, first, by producing a textual *effect* that generates "the seductive temptation" of Cratylism.[26] Citing Gérard Genette as evidence, de Man argues that "the convergence of sound and meaning . . . [is] a mere *effect* which language can perfectly well achieve, but which bears no substantial relationship, by analogy or by ontologically grounded imitation, to anything beyond that particular effect. It is a rhetorical rather than an aesthetic function of language, an identifiable trope (paronomasis) that operates on the level of the signifier and contains no responsible pronouncement on the nature of the world—despite its powerful potential to create the opposite illusion" (*RT,* p. 10). Language itself gives rise to effects that suggest a natural link between sound and meaning (the implication being that such effects cause the generalized Cratylism that underlies the assumption that language is about the world).[27] Cratylism is made possible by a rhetorical figure, and that means, for de Man, by a purely linguistic function named *paronomasis,* which consists of linking within one sentence words of analogous sonority yet of different meanings. As a mere play of the signifier, the natural, or symbolic, transcendence of the sound is an intralinguistic effect that warrants no assumption of a relationship to the world of phenomena and meaning. No extension beyond the linguistic whatsoever occurs here or, in truth, anywhere. de Man writes: "The phenomenality of the signifier, as sound, is unquestionably involved in the correspondence between the name and the thing named, but the link, the relationship between word and thing, is not phenomenal but conventional" (*RT,* p. 10). What is thus emphasized, is, first, that, yes, indeed, language is referential but that reference is a function of tropes, hence entirely intralinguistic. It takes place between signifiers, in other words, between language's own discrete elements. Second, such intralinguistic reference is "conventional," which following Saussure's distinction, implies arbitrariness compared to the alleged naturalness of symbolic relations with an outside of language.[28] Third, to interpret linguistic reference to bear a substantial relation is to create the illusion that language can tell us something about the world. Only with worldly means such as perception can the realm of phenomena be mastered. The belief that language can help master, and understand, phenomena is to indulge in what de Man calls "aesthetic ideology."

A second facet, by virtue of which language itself makes the aesthetic temptation possible, concerns the question of mimesis. Given that language is governed by rules of its own and refers within itself to its own elements, it is not aesthetic; hence, between it and the nonverbal no natural relation obtains. Language, it follows, in that it does not imitate or copy a transcendent reality, is not inherently mimetic. Still, the illusion of mimesis is made possible by language itself. de Man remarks: "If literariness is not an aesthetic quality, it is also not primarily mimetic. Mimesis becomes one trope among others, language choosing to imitate a non-verbal entity just as paronomasis 'imitates' a sound without any claim to identity (or reflection on difference) between the verbal and non-verbal elements" (*RT*, p. 10). While there is no natural affinity between language and the world, autonomous language has the power to choose to mimetically refer to the world. But such referral not only happens solely for intralinguistic reasons—that is, not in view of a possible cognition of the object (by a subject, or by the object itself)—it happens also in terms, and on the terms of language alone, in that "mimesis is itself a [linguistic] figure" (*RT*, p. 48), a trope. The mimetic relation is a function of language, a discrete trope. de Man refers to mimesis as "the Aristotelian rhetorical category par excellence" (*RT*, p. 67).[29] If language imitates a nonverbal entity, it makes no identity claims, occurring for the sheer benefit of language alone. Yet, needless to say, this intralinguistic possibility of a mimetic relation fosters aesthetic mistranslation.

What we have just seen further confirms the claim that language is autonomous. Reference, de Man holds, is a function of language itself and thus remains entirely within its bounds. Moreover, discrete figures or tropes shape all these referential relations. They are intralinguistic including their form. "This gives the language considerable freedom from referential constraints" (*RT*, p. 10), de Man declares. Differently put, since language interconnects only elements within itself, it is shielded from being linked to extralinguistic referents, disconnected from the cognitive process and the value considerations characteristic of the phenomenal world. Following up on de Man's suggestion that "rhetorical categories might lead a life of their own" (*RT*, p. 45), one must conclude that language, whose nature is intrinsically rhetorical, has, indeed, a "life" of its own. However, the "autonomous potential of language" (*RT*, p. 10), a potential whose title is "literariness," is not merely the power to interconnect its own elements within itself but also the potential, or power, not to relate (to something outside itself)—not to be determinable by something else, not to be ancillary to the phenomenal world. More precisely, language is a *dynamis adynamia;* in other words, the power not to proceed to action, to remain pure potentiality, a negative power which, according to Aristotle, constitutes all potentiality as such.[30] In distinction from Aristotle, for whom the power not to proceed to action is the condition of possibility for the passage to action, language, in de Man's understanding, hovers in a state of pure *adynamia.* This conception of language and the ontology that it presupposes—an ontology of de Man's own making—brings an additional meaning of *phenomenalism* into view. Indeed, if language is equipped with a potential not to relate, it can be said to resist not only phenomenalism, in the sense of being understandable in terms of what obtains in the world, but phenomenalization as well, that is, appearance in sensible shape, and hence the becoming accessible to the senses and the certainty that is associated with them.[31] Phenomenalism then also implies the sensible manifestation of something nonsensible, in Kantian terms, noumenal. Now, it should be recalled that a theory of reading, as well the practice of mere reading, is concerned with the production and reception process of meaning prior to its establishment. This process of production has been further specified in terms of language's intralinguistic function of referral. What language resists then is the phenomenalization of this production process, more precisely, of language's immanent referential function. If language in literature can, according to de Man, be said to suspend, at the very least, "the actual aesthetic function" (*RT*, p. 9), it is to suggest that it undercuts the effort to aesthetically reify its referential structures and to transform them into phenomena, into sensibly apprehendable commodities. By phenomenalizing the production process, the process itself is stripped of what is proper to it, made into meaning and understanding. Yet, as should be evident by now, phenomenalization is also an illusion made possible by language itself.

In discussing an objection raised against literary theory, namely, that the insistence on literariness denies "the reality principle in the name of absolute fiction" (*RT,* p. 10), de Man notes that this is absolutely not the case. Fictional narratives, for instance, are "part of the world and of reality; their impact upon the world may well be all too strong for comfort," he claims. Is this to revoke the sharp divide between language and world that we had previously seen? To illustrate how narratives affect the world, de Man mentions how difficult it is not to conceive "the patterns of one's past and future existence as in accordance with temporal and spatial schemes that belong to fictional narratives and not to the world." There is thus an unmistakable impact of what is not of the mundane order, but of the order of language, onto the world, an impact that does not put into question the Manichean chasm alluded to. Speaking of such impacting, de Man remarks: "What we call ideology is precisely the confusion of linguistic with natural reality, of reference with phenomenalism" (*RT,* p. 11). From what we have seen hereto, language resists, but, on occasion, and when it suits it, it is also liable to relating to the world of phenomena. In addition, its own structures lend themselves to a phenomenalization. Yet such mistranslations generate ideology. Ideology is a *metabasis eis allo genos* of sorts, in that it mixes entirely separate orders, realms, or genres. The linguistic and the natural, or phenomenal, worlds ought to be kept distinct. To confuse them is to engage in ideology, say, in aesthetics. de Man, therefore, claims that "the linguistics of literariness is a powerful and indispensable tool in the unmasking of ideological aberrations, as well as a determining factor in accounting for their occurrence." Even though in the context of the essay "The Resistance to Theory" de Man gestures toward Marx's critique of ideology, another sense of ideology might well be at work here. Speaking of ideology, de Man does not primarily think of the false consciousness of ideal superstructures. Although de Man frequently refers to ideology as the belief in certain knowledge, this latter conception presupposes an even more crucial understanding of ideology. Indeed, the referential structures immanent to language can be phenomenalized not only in the sense that they would become applicable to the order of the phenomenal but also in the sense that they themselves are transformed into patterns of meaning and understanding for an order of things that is incompatible with the linguistic. In such phenomenalization of literariness, ideology occurs not simply because two orders are fused into one but because the phenomenalized patterns of language are raised to the status of ideas intent on illuminating natural, phenomenal reality. These ideas function as the philosophical foundation for "natural or phenomenal cognition," in short, for the sciences in general and their respective spheres of knowledge. If ideology is said to be an aberration, it is also in the sense that the confusion of language and the world idealizes intralinguistic referential patterns that as a result begin to scintillate like so many stars in the *topos ouraneos*. As at least a reader of Michel Foucault's *The Order of Things*, de Man must have been familiar with Destutt de Tracy's conception of ideology in *Éléments d'idéologie*, as the science of ideas.[32]

For de Tracy, this rational and scientific discipline coincides with philosophy. One can thus assume that the linguistics of literariness, which, as de Man is quick to point out, "may also reveal the links between ideologies and philosophies" (*RT*, p. 11), has the additional charge of unmasking philosophy as an "ideological mystification" not simply because it is the source of the aesthetics that has dominated literary theory to date but more essentially in so far as it rests on an illegitimate idealization of purely immanent structures of language.

With this I provisionally conclude my exposition of the concept of language as literary theory, of mere reading, as de Man's understanding of these notions presuppose it. Mere reading is a reading of language prior to meaning and understanding. Its object is language's referential function, which as a function of language lacks the thrust of transcendence. In thus reading the autonomous potential of language, mere reading unreads its interweavings with phenomenalism and unmasks the ideologies to which language has been committed. As de Man asserts on more than one occasion, readings in this sense, if "technically correct," are irrefutable (*RT*, p. 19). Their apodictic truth claim is based on the inner consistency of the reading operation, and the ineluctable necessity of each interpretive move.[33] The same apodicticity is valid for the theory of mere reading. In the essay on which I am commenting, de Man claims that "the arguments in favor of the legitimacy of theory are so compelling" that it is unnecessary to even bother refuting possible objections (*RT*, p. 12). Although "the shared reluctance [of literary critics of all shades] to acknowledge the obvious" (*RT*, p. 18) remains a baffling problem, the truths of reading are self-evident, de Man maintains. For de Man, these truths, one might say, are the bloody obvious. The recurring emphasis on the obviousness of reading demonstrates that its insights are immediately intelligible, the object of immediate intuition, as one would say in philosophy. What kind of knowledge can claim such apodicticity, and what sort of intuition is possible of a realm such as language said to be prior to intuition? Are the truths of mere reading always true because the actual truth-values are merely logical and not factual? Or are its truths tautological in a Wittgensteinean sense—in other words, always true because their statements do not yield to any truth conditions? Is the object of mere reading simply something so trivial that it always obtains? What then would be the import of a theory about the obvious? de Man suggests that the truths of mere reading are universal, but the "ontological" status of the order about which these universality claims are made remains a question. One might argue that such questions are not pertinent since reading also undoes all those claims. But this answer begs the question precisely because the universality concerns the undoings of reading itself.[34]

Anyhow, it is clear that the nature of the object of mere reading sets limits to its own theorization. Since I am interested here only in the sense of reading and its linguistic presuppositions, I will forgo a detailed discussion of de Man's main arguments in "The Resistance to Theory" concerning the resistance to theory that arises from literariness itself. Still, we do need to address one consequence of the resistance of literariness to theory since it sheds further light on language itself. If language is constituted by a potential not to relate (except within itself, and with itself), that is, by a *dynamis* that does not extend beyond itself and thus remains pure potentiality, the theory adequate to such a potential must necessarily resist its own possibility. If this exigency of an isomorphism between literary theory and literariness is not to represent a secret return of aesthetics and mimesis in de Man's own theory, it must be understood to mean that literary theory itself must remain a function of language, in other words, a description of language in language's "own, specifically linguistic, aspects" (*RT*, p. 9). Consequently, the metalinguistic discourse on the literariness of language not only fails to totalize language from outside it—since all reference is intralinguistic—but the theory in question falls short of a thematic reflection on language as such. At this point, it is certainly appropriate to recall that at the beginning of "The Resistance to Theory," de Man held that it was impossible to make general claims in theory about literary theory. The reason he gave is, first, that it is impossible to fix the borderlines of the corpus of objects covered by such a theory. But more fundamental is the contention that it is the literariness of the object itself that is the major predicament. It is not certain, de Man writes, "if such a 'thing' [as the literary thing itself] indeed exists" (*RT*, p. 5). The notion of "literature as such," that is, literature as an identifiable object that presents itself *in propria persona,* is precisely what is in question (*RT*, p. 4). What might have sounded like an outrageous statement at the outset of the essay now seems fully justified. If, indeed, literature is constituted by literariness, by language's referentiality prior to the designation of a referent, then literature is of an order other than that of appearing. It does not appear (as) itself. Rather, it is nothing but the potential not to show itself. The theory of literature, or, the object of mere reading, can hence never encounter its object itself, as such, and in totality, nor muster the minimal conditions to reflexively thematize it. Language as an autonomous potential is immanent to a point that it radically undercuts all transcendence, including that to itself. It is never rigorously *about* itself. The difference for which it allows—between its elements (as well as between itself and tropically mediated nonverbal entities) and between itself and itself—is not the difference of the concept. Consequently, it allows for reflection neither, as is still to be established, between its elements nor between itself and itself. The difference of language makes itself—its self—implode without any hope of recovering itself.[35] But the ensuing congenital failure of literary theory—and of mere reading—is not entirely negative. Its inability to arrive at a general theoretical statement about literariness or language testifies uniquely to the uniqueness of its object. The failure to thematize language properly, or as such, to establish in universal terms what it is, allows language—that which is without equivalent—to become *known* in its singleness. It is single to the point, thus, of allowing only for an empirical or pragmatic approach.[36]

In de Man's own words, all these difficulties regarding the object of mere reading and the theory of that object "precipitate out in the problem of reading" itself (*RT*, p. 15). Since the way in which these difficulties manifest themselves is cast in terms linked to what he labels the "the most familiar and general of all linguistic models, the classical *trivium,*" his elaborations on this aspect of the medieval conception of the liberal arts need to be be taken up. At stake in this discussion, and the ensuing reading of the title of a poem by Keats, is de Man's identification of language with rhetoric.[37] Thus understood, language, at all times, undermines all sense of security and certainty in the relation to the world; more precisely, it effectively disrupts phenomenal referentiality. In the deaestheticizing movement of what de Man calls "reading," language is set free from all its extralinguistic associations, and it is restored to its own uniquely nonphenomenal and nonphenomenalizable being.

Following de Man through this additional exploration of the nature of language that precedes his explicit thematization and exemplification of reading, I shall overlook the seemingly blatant historical and theoretical shortcomings of de Man's discussion of this issue. They are so numerous and so prominent—so obvious, one might add—that, clearly, his concerns cannot be with the historical specificity of these medieval disciplines.[38] Rather, it is another concern that guides his approach. de Man writes: "The classical *trivium,* which considers the sciences of language as consisting of grammar, rhetoric, and logic (or dialectics), is a set of unresolved tensions. . . . These difficulties extend to the internal articulation between the constituent parts as well as the articulation of the field of language with the knowledge of the world in general, the link between the *trivium* and the *quadrivium,* which covers the non-verbal sciences" (*RT,* p. 13). Turning first to the link between the two divisions of liberal arts, he notes that "in the history of philosophy, this link is traditionally, as well as substantially, accomplished by way of logic, the area where the rigor of the linguistic discourse about itself matches with the rigor of the mathematical discourse about the world." The ensuing recourse to seventeenth-century epistemology and its language shaped after geometry, that is, after a science of nature, is supposed to demonstrate that logic, in essence, is a conception of language modeled after a nonlinguistic discourse about the phenomenal world.[39] "This articulation of the sciences of language with the mathematical sciences represents a particularly compelling version of a continuity between a theory of language, as logic, and the knowledge of the phenomenal world to which mathematics gives access," de Man writes. Seventeenth-century epistemology, with its "interconnection between a science of the phenomenal world and a science of language conceived as definitional logic," would thus prove that the relation between the *trivium* (the lower division) and the *quadrivium* (the higher division) is one in which language has been colonized by the natural sciences by virtue of a phenomenalization of one of its parts (logic), which is thus promoted to lead the other parts. The relation in question is supposed to be a continuum, but this is an ideological assumption as far as de Man is concerned. "In such a system, the place of aesthetics is preordained and by no means alien, provided the priority of logic, in the model of the *trivium,* is not being questioned" (*RT,* p. 13). What this thoroughly dehistoricized conception of the *trivium* is supposed to reveal is a conception of language that, de Man claims, is general and familiar and in which language is modeled after the "knowledge of the phenomenal world," that is, in terms of intuition and perception. Language, once understood from the phenomenal world, becomes an instrument for the understanding of that world. This way of thinking about language takes for granted a continuity between language and the world that, if not already aesthetic itself, is the ground on which aesthetics can emerge. Up to this point, the discussion of the *trivium* has served to demonstrate that the most familiar and general concept of language is already intrinsically aesthetic. Understanding language to relate to things, whatever the modes of such relating, that is, conceiving of it logically, is to have aestheticized language. This aesthetic conception of language dominates as long as "the priority of logic, in the model of the *trivium,* is not being questioned" (*RT,* p. 13).

I recall de Man's assertion that no word is more self-evasive than the word *language.* Continuing his investigation of what he terms the most general conception of language with an elaboration on the relations between grammar, rhetoric, and logic within the confines of the model under consideration, de Man will show *language* to be itself a "disfigured and disfiguring" word. The relationship between the disciplines that make up the lower division of the liberal arts "is the point at which literariness, the use of language that foregrounds the rhetorical over the grammatical and the logical function, intervenes as a decisive but unsettling element, which, in a variety of modes and aspects, disrupts the inner balance of the model and, consequently, its outward extension to the nonverbal world as well" (*RT,* p. 14). Let me then follow de Man through the various moves in which this disruption is said to occur. He begins, of course, with still another excursion into the seventeenth century to highlight the "natural . . . affinity for each other" of logic and grammar. This "persistent symbiosis between grammar and logic" is said to hold true from the medieval *trivium* to contemporary methods and terminologies however different they may be among one another. "Any theory of language" grounded in grammar—Greimas serves as an example—"does not threaten what we hold to be the underlying principle of all cognitive and aesthetic linguistic systems. Grammar stands in the service of logic, which, in turn, allows for the passage to the knowledge of the world," de Man concludes (*RT,* p. 14). Having thus intimately intertwined grammar and logic, having precipitated them as one sediment—"Grammar is an isotope of logic" (*RT,* p. 14), he writes—allows rhetoric by the same token to be neatly separated, extracted "in purity," and reserved for a special treatment.[40] Difficulties arise in the model of the lower division of the liberal arts "when it is no longer possible to ignore the epistemological thrust of the rhetorical dimension of discourse, that is, when it is no longer possible to keep it in its place as a mere adjunct, a mere ornament within the semantic function" (*RT,* p. 14). The sole instance that de Man mentions and where the instability of the model becomes manifest—the tension between rhetoric and grammar in the *trivium* being only a "latent tension"—concerns the seemingly uncertain status of tropes or figures of speech. de Man writes: "Tropes used to be part of the study of grammar but were also considered to be the semantic agent of the specific function (or effect) that rhetoric performs as persuasion as well as meaning" (*RT,* pp. 14–15).[41] Following up on this statement by declaring that "tropes, unlike grammar, pertain primordially to language," de Man gestures toward what would explain the wavering status of tropes and figures in the *trivium*. Unlike grammar, which stands entirely in the service of the *logike episteme,* that is, of a nonlinguistic conception, tropes and figures are the essence of the linguistic itself. "They are text-producing functions that are not necessarily patterned on a non-verbal entity, whereas grammar is by definition capable of extra-linguistic generalization" (*RT,* p. 15). Tropes produce language's textual quality, in other words, its complex weave of intralinguistic referrals. Tropes and figures are, as we have seen, the shapes under which reference as a function of language, and among its own elements, comes to be. Language, as understood by de Man, is at its most fundamental a fabric of tropical substitutions.

In elaborating the relation between logic and grammar, on the one hand, on the other, rhetoric in the *trivium,* de Man has been able to demonstrate only a latent tension between the two sets of disciplines. In order to make this latency manifest, de Man introduces at this precise point the question of reading.[42] But it is not introduced as a theoretical problem but rather in the form of a reading in practice, a performed reading that exacerbates and brings to light the tension in question. In reading, the latent tension "precipitates out," given that reading is "the process that necessarily partakes of both" (*RT,* p. 15), de Man claims.

Mere or rhetorical reading—*rhetorical* being synonymous with *linguistic* to the extent that it is constituted by tropological reference—causes grammar and rhetoric, which had formerly been in a merely latent condition of tension with each other, to precipitate out. In other words, reading is a chemical process, of sorts, whose fallout is the separation of the extralinguistic from the "purely" linguistic. In reading, the impositions of phenomenalism and ideology come abruptly to an end as they are made to separate from the medium of language, thus breaking up the continuity between the verbal and the nonverbal on whose ground language had been forced into an outward extension in the first place. The fallout of reading thus enables grammar and rhetoric or, more precisely, language "itself," to have an explicit fall out. Yet, the chemical process of separation constitutive of reading does not bring language *as such* to exhibit itself. Language manifests itself in reading only negatively. In "the epistemological thrust of the rhetorical dimension of discourse" (*RT,* p. 14), and through the negative knowledge that it provides, language makes itself present. It manifests itself only in, or as, the reading that unreads grammar's and logic's extralinguistic generalizations. But, recalling that language itself is the origin of the aesthetic temptation, one can conclude by saying that it makes itself manifest in the destruction of what it itself has rendered possible.

What is the fallout of the fall out between grammar and rhetoric that occurs in reading? Taking up the question of the "by no means self-evident necessity" of reading, de Man points to two of its implications: "First of all, it implies that literature is not a transparent message in which it can be taken for granted that the distinction between the message and the means of communication is clearly established. Second, and more problematically, it implies that the grammatical decoding of a text leaves a residue of indetermination that has to be, but cannot be, resolved by grammatical means, however extensively conceived" (*RT,* p. 15). Where does the confusion in the literary text between message and the means of communication stem from? Is it because in literature the constitutive factors of all linguistic processes and of all verbal acts of communication, as distinguished by Roman Jakobson, and with respect to which he would situate the poetic, are not pertinent?[43] If indeed, the message cannot be clearly distinguished from the means of communication, the Jakobsonian distinctions that characterize all linguistic acts,— in particular, the framing distinction of an addresser and an addressee—

seem not to apply. In any case, what counts for de Man is the lack of transparency, a certain constitutive opaqueness, that seems to come with literature and that requires reading not to vaporize it but to do it justice as something specific to the literary. Moreover, the grammatical, that is, logical decoding of literary texts, leaves a residue that does not let itself be dissolved into reference to the outside world. The necessity to read follows, therefore, from the recognition that a literary text is a text, an intralinguistic weave that defies patterning after nonverbal reality. "No grammatical decoding, however refined," can replace or "reach the determining figural dimensions of a text. There are elements in all texts that are by no means ungrammatical, but whose semantic function is not grammatically definable, neither in themselves nor in context" (*RT*, pp. 15–16). Reading, then, is not called for in order to make the indetermination in question meaningful but to give it its due rights since the text's figural, not grammatical, dimension makes it a text determined by literariness.

de Man does not claim texts to be nonreferential in the sense of not having any outside extension whatsoever. His point is rather that the semantic function of such reference is not cognitively definable. Reference, therefore, is a privileged place for a reading to demonstrate that the text itself undoes its referential effects. That the fallout of such a reading would center around the question of a fall is no accident. The essay "The Resistance to Theory" performs an exemplifying reading not, as one would expect, of the linguistic model of the *trivium* but of the title of John Keats's unfinished epic, "The Fall of Hyperion." Keats's inability—an inability rooted in the tension between grammar and rhetoric—to read the referent of his own title explains, according to de Man, why Keats failed ever to conclude the poetic versions he gave of the title. de Man emphasizes that the fall in question is first of all "Hyperion's Fall." But thanks to the double inflection, the title permits the equally correct grammatical reading: "'Hyperion Falling,' the much less specific but more disquieting evocation of an actual process of falling, regardless of its beginning, its end or the identity of the entity to whom it befalls to be falling" (*RT*, p. 16). Philologically speaking, the story told by the first version (simply called "Hyperion") substantiates the first reading; the later fragment, "The Fall of Hyperion" corroborates the second. In the later version, Hyperion is said to have all the character traits of Apollo, a figure who *should* have stood erect in the first version since it is he who causes Hyperion to fall. But by confusing the two characters in the second fragment, and thus having Apollo fall as well, the epic seems to be about falling itself. But, says de Man, the first version refers to the fall of Hyperion only if Apollo has truly stood erect in that poem. Since, however, the poem was never completed, how could he be said to stand and Hyperion to fall? Keats had "been compelled to interrupt, for no apparent reason, the story of Apollo's triumph" (*RT*, p. 16), de Man recalls. Hence, the grammatical reading of the title that attributes the fall to Hyperion loses its certainty. What, then, about the second grammatically possible reading, and its referent? de Man asks: Does the title "tell us that Hyperion and Apollo (and Keats, whom it is hard to distinguish, at times, from Apollo) are interchangeable in that all of them are necessarily and constantly falling?" Undoubtedly, for de Man, the characters' resemblance prevents the context from becoming determinate. The confusion of the characters (and Keats himself) prohibits the second version of the story from pinpointing its heroes, and hence the referents for the falling in question. It is thus quite plausible that the title be read as "Hyperion Falling." But what prevents us from determining this reading to be the correct one?

If, indeed, it seems impossible to make the title "The Fall of Hyperion" refer to a steadfast referent, be it the historical or mythological character, one could "read the word 'Hyperion' in the title *The Fall of Hyperion* figurally, or if one wishes, intertextually, as referring not to the historical or mythological character but as referring to the title of Keats' own earlier text (*Hyperion*)" (*RT*, p. 16). The lack of a proper referent suggests a figural reading. With the second version Keats might well have thematized or reflected on the failure of his first attempt to write the epic in question. Its second version would successfully establish the first as the referent of the title (and the whole poem). But does this figural reference go without complications? Can it be established in all certainty? de Man asks: "But are we then telling the story of the failure of the first text as the success of the second, the Fall of *Hyperion* as the Triumph of *The Fall of Hyperion*? Manifestly, yes, but not quite, since the second text also fails to be concluded" (*RT*, p. 16). Reading the title as referring to its first version, a reading that seems to impose itself once the confusion of characters in the second version has made any proper reference impossible, cannot be sustained as the second text never effects its triumph. I recall that the first reading of the title as meaning "Hyperion's Fall" was put into question by the fact that Keats, for no apparent reason, had to interrupt his poem. For de Man such an interruption will be no mere accident. If the reasons for Keats's failure to complete his text are not apparent, this means that they do not show themselves and that hence they are of the order of nonphenomenal, that is, purely linguistic reasons. Since the second version of the epic also remains a fragment, essential reasons as well must have been responsible for the impossibility to unambiguously decide on whether this poem is on the failed first version.

Given that a single figural referent—the single text of "Hyperion"—failed in securing a firm referent for the title, might it not be possible to replace it by a general referent, and thus to salvage the referentiality in question? Could not "The Fall of Hyperion" be "telling the story of why all texts, as texts, can always be said to be falling? Manifestly yes, but not quite, either, since the story of the fall of the first version, as told in the second, applies to the first version only and could not legitimately be read as meaning also the fall of *The Fall of Hyperion*" (*RT*, p. 16), de Man argues. The second fragment fails to recount the general story as it fails itself to fall. In sum, none of the referents (and ensuing stories) that the double genitive might yield—subjective or objective, proper or figural, single or general—while certainly possible, can attain any certainty. The title cannot be read if reading seeks univocity. de Man writes: "One is tempted to suggest that the fact that Keats was unable to complete either version manifests the impossibility, for him as for us, of reading his own title" (*RT*, p. 16). Reading in the de Manean sense, however, is reading such unreadability. Its fallout are the failed success stories of grammatically correct referential assignings. But it remains to be seen what the rhetorical residue is that prevents grammatical correctness from becoming determinant.

"The undecidability involves the figural or literal status of the proper name Hyperion as well as of the verb falling, and is thus a matter of figuration and not of grammar" (*RT*, p. 16).[44] Although the double (grammatical) inflection operative in the title had at first yielded two proper referents—the mythological character Hyperion and a falling that though qualified as hyperion is, at first, "an actual process of falling"—the figural meanings that are paired with the literal ones, and that are equally present as possibilities in reading the title, make the possibility of grammatical reading entirely dependent on a rhetorical dimension of

language. It follows from this that the undecidability regarding the referent was never a function of grammar, but of rhetoric. de Man continues:
"In 'Hyperion's Fall,' the word 'fall' is plainly figural, the representation of
a figural fall, and we, as readers, read this fall standing up. But in 'Hyperion Falling,' this is not so clearly the case, for if Hyperion can be Apollo
and Apollo can be Keats, then he can also be us and his figural (or
symbolic) fall becomes his and our literal falling as well. The difference
between the two readings is itself structured as a trope. And it matters a
great deal how we read the title, as an exercise not only in semantics, but
in what the text actually does to us" (*RT*, p. 16). Read as referring to
Keats's first draft, "fall" is, of course to be understood, figurally. To read
that the first draft was a failure, that it is falling, implies that the reader
himself stands (literally?) erect. The reader, aware as he is in this case of
a figural falling, must himself occupy the secure position of proper up-
rightness. But when the title is read as referring to a hyperion falling, the
interchangeability of the characters does not stop with the text, and
falling's figural meaning forces him to literally come down. The way in
which readings mutually restrict their legitimacy clearly has all the characteristics of a chiasmatic reversal. By showing how the reader is involved in such a reading, the reader is not only troped but turns out to be
part of a chiasmic structure. What follows from this is not merely a
further deepening of the unreadability of the title but an extension of the
rhetorical to the relation of the reader to the text—and to the author.
"Just as Keats had to break off his narrative, the reader has to break off
his understanding at the very moment when he is most directly engaged
and summoned by the text. One could hardly expect to find solace in this
'fearful symmetry' between the author's and the reader's plight since, at
this point, the symmetry is no longer a formal but an actual trap, and the
question no longer 'merely' theoretical" (*RT*, pp. 16–17). The title under
discussion—a minitext in truth—by its sheer unintelligibility compels
both writer and reader to surrender all possible mastery. It makes the
author interrupt his narratives, and the reader, his understanding (or
reading). This unintelligibility engulfs both author and reader, textual-
izes them in that they become deontologized, mere intralinguistic out-
sides of the text, and yoked through the trope of chiasm. The chiasmic
symmetry, however, is not a formal, that is, aesthetic trap, a trap that, as
a last Cratylian hideout, could still be savored. As de Man's insistence on
the actuality of the trap indicates, the chiasm in question is not symmet-

rical.[45] I close the discussion of this example of a reading, and its abyssal fallout, by stressing that from a reading in de Man's sense, one does not come away with an uplifting truth. But, if the plight of the reader is actual and no longer "merely" theoretical, as de Man argues, we might begin to understand the pragmatic or empirical moment constitutive of a theoretical, or mere reading. If the literary object is encountered only where all understanding breaks off, that is, where all aestheticization has been successfully checked, the encounter itself, with its unintelligibility, escapes intelligibility as well. It is marked by an irreducibly opaque moment, a moment of pragmatism or the empirical.

The reading that we have just followed through its different phases and moves, seeks to locate in a text a point of unintelligibility, associated with figural undecidability, a point, moreover, that sends shock waves throughout the whole text with the effect that on none of its possible strata any certitude whatsoever is allowed to occur. No unfolding takes place either. By contrast, there is only a repetitive reverberation of the text's figural undecidability. Faced with readings of this kind, one might conclude that they are possible only if texts have previously been stripped of all their aesthetic qualities. Hence, the fallout of reading is of no pertinence whatsoever to the texts read insofar as they are texts of art. Such an objection, however, overlooks the fact that the deaestheticization is a constitutive moment of the reading itself and that it is by reading against the grain of possible effects of language, and their aesthetic appropriation, that the fallouts of reading make themselves known. Rather, what is in question is the "obviousness" of mere reading. What is the "ontological" status of the rhetorical that is at odds with the grammatical? Moreover, what is the precise "ontological" relation of the methodological moves to the literariness that is the object of readings? Finally, to what kind of "rationality" do the distinct moments of a reading yield? Could it be that the ground on which these questions are to be answered is only postfactically provided by the readings themselves? In other words, is reading performative to the degree that its fallouts produce the objective evidence—the workings of language—that legitimizes it as a method *après coup?* Is the obviousness of rhetorical reading a function then of its performative structure? Should this be a plausible possibility, what then constitutes the uniqueness of readings. What kind of intelligibility can the inevitably pragmatic readings claim and can secure their recognizability as unique interventions in texts? Are they interventions, to begin with? And, finally, can these rhetorical or tropological analyses of language that intimately combine method and object lay claim, and on what basis, to being recognized as possible, and plausible, if not even necessary projects? These are indeed some of the questions on which a final evaluation of the import of reading depends, even if that import is, as is to be expected, cognitively negative.

I conclude by circling back to the question of the relation between grammar and rhetoric. The reading performed on Keats's title has shown that "rhetoric, by its actively negative relationship to grammar and to logic, certainly undoes the claims of the *trivium* (and by extension, of language) to be an epistemologically stable construct" (*RT*, p. 17) de Man writes. The tension between grammar and rhetoric that could be diagnosed only in a latent state in the *trivium* as the most general and familiar of all models of language has been activated and brought to light in the reading performance. Reading, then, is a way of precipitating out what in common, as well as theoretical models of language, and even in the word *language,* is forced into latency. In the performance of a reading, the tension between grammar and rhetoric is not only made manifest, it is literally acted out. But this exercise in reading has also revealed that reading a text comprises both a grammatical and rhetorical dimension. Rhetoric cannot be isolated "from the generality that grammar and logic have in common" (*RT*, p. 19). de Man remarks: "Since grammar as well as figuration is an integral part of reading, it follows that reading will be a negative process in which the grammatical cognition is undone, at all times, by its rhetorical displacement" (*RT*, p. 17). Just as little as there is a purely grammatical reading—a "phenomenalism of reading," as it is also called (*RT*, p. 18)—just as little is there a rhetorical reading independent of a reading whose thrust is epistemological. Two readings must intertwine to form mere reading. Mere reading takes place as a nonsymmetrical undoing of one (the grammatical) by the other (the rhetorical).[46] It is a "negative process," that is, a process in which nothing is gained, but in whose occurrence the workings of language reveal themselves in so far as they are at work. Not unlike the *via negativa* of negative theology, mere reading destroys, by dint of a reactivation of the rhetorical, all the sediments of meaning by which the grammatical has covered language, to exhibit language in its pristine state of unintelligibility, before all epistemological and aesthetic commodification. Reading is the negative process in which the text is restored, as it were, to the bare facticity of language, to what Husserl called *"das Faktum der Sprachen."*[47] Yet, unlike Husserl's merely empirical understanding of this facticity— Husserl, indeed, refers to the manifold of the different languages, language for de Man "exists with such uniqueness that the plural makes no sense when applied to it," a status that Husserl attributes only to the world-horizon. In the same way as "every plural, and every singular drawn from it, presupposes the world-horizon," in the same way, language for de Man is first and foremost single.[48] Reading is not only the process in which this uniqueness of language is restored, language's facticity has here the sense of the raw workings of language, as they manifest themselves in the unreading of grammar at the hands of rhetoric. Although severing all ties of language with phenomenalization, this process of reading does not bring language itself into view. Nothing presents itself. No phenomenon, however refined, offers itself here as the eidetic object of an intuition. The autonomous potential of language, alone, will have been at work.

5

Giving to Read

From the late sixties de Man has developed his theory of reading in a complex exchange with Derrida's work. Even though, at times, he distinguishes what he terms "reading" from Derridean deconstruction, he also counts Derrida among the practitioners of reading as he understands it. "The only French theoretician who actually *reads* texts, in the full theoretical sense of the term, is Jacques Derrida," de Man writes (*RT*, p. 33). But this claimed proximity to Derrida's work, although real, up to a certain point, not only deepens the confusion regarding the meaning of "mere reading," on the one hand, but of "deconstruction," on the other. Indeed, as Richard Klein has aptly remarked, de Man's programmatic essay on Derrida in *Blindness and Insight* "in many ways marks the most uncanny, the most insane, the most bizzarely interesting critical encounter imaginable."[1] Even the later work, I would hold, is not free of the tensions and contorsions that characterized the encounter at the beginning. But this is not the place to engage a much needed systematic clarification of the difference between the two thinkers,[2] a clarification that, as far as de Man is concerned, would have to begin with how, after the conceptual breakdown noted by Klein in de Man's essay on Derrida's reading of Rousseau,[3] de Man's earlier thinking of the fifties and sixties— indebted to phenomenology, existentialism, and the philosophy of consciousness—continues to inform his thinking from *Allegories of Reading* on. Although Derrida's references to "reading" are relatively sparse, there is one text in which the question is explicitly raised. A reading of this text will both elucidate the significant difference that does exist between the two thinkers, as far as the conception and the practice of reading are concerned, and also further refine what actually occurs in a de Manean reading. This text is "Plato's Pharmacy."[4] The reason for my privileging this text over the section in *Of Grammatology* entitled "Question of Method," for instance, is that in this text Derrida reads Plato's *Phaedrus,* a text on reading. In the first place, Plato's dialogue begins with Phaedrus's reading to Socrates a speech written by Lysias. In the second place, the set-up of Phaedrus, who has been unable to learn Lysias's speech by heart, needing the written text as a *pharmakon,* that is, as a supplement for his lack of live memory, and who is, indeed, unable to come to the defense of the written discourse of his teacher and lover when criticized by Socrates, prefigures the ensuing discussion of the relation of writing to the living voice and to live memory. Derrida's reading this text of Plato in which writing is condemned for its alleged inability to come to its own defense—even when read aloud—writes a new thread into Plato's dialogue. Although the verb for reading in the *Phaedrus* is *anagignoskein,* to know again, or recognize, Derrida's reading adds not a *logos* to the first text, as it would if, in conformity with the verb *epilegesthai,* in the sense of reading—"literally, 'to add a *logos*' [to what is written]"[5]—but a novel line of thought. de Man's readings too add something to the first text and, occcasionally, as is the case in the essay "Anthropomorphism and Trope in Lyric," acknowledge as much. In what follows, I will expound on Derrida's understanding of reading as an addition and on the presuppositions of this understanding. A subsequent close reading of the above-mentioned essay by de Man will allow a more precise circumscription of what a reading does for him.

The multilayered complexity of Derrida's text prevents a full discussion of "Plato's Pharmacy." I shall thus restrict myself to an analysis of Derrida's understanding of reading and its presuppositions. From the outset, let me stress that although reading in Derrida's sense is based on a concept of textuality, this concept of text is not primarily a linguistic concept. Reflecting on the structural constraints weighing about Plato's discourse from "language," Derrida remarks that "the word 'language,' through all that binds it to everything we are putting in question here, is not of any pertinent assistance, and to follow the constraints of a language would not exclude the possibility that Plato is playing with them, even if his game is neither representative nor voluntary. It is in the back room, in the shadows of the pharmacy, prior to the oppositions between conscious and unconscious, freedom and constraint, voluntary and involuntary, speech and language, that these textual 'operations' occur" (*D*, p. 129). Even though Derrida may refer here only to the Saussurian notion of language—to *langue* as opposed to *parole*—and thus to the linguistic assumption that the structural laws of a language form a system and a totality, the reference to the back room of Plato's pharmacy as the locus of the textual operations in question is a warning to not construe them too hastily as linguistic. Yet Derrida does not simply dismiss the assumption that the words of a language compose a system. On the contrary, he puts this aspect of language to good use in his analyses. The distinction is that the level on and the manner in which words interrelate not only restrains the system from ever closing upon itself, but the principle of such relating is not strictly speaking linguistic. Indeed, Derrida's exploration, in his reading of the *Phaedrus,* of all the various ramifications of a single word, attempts, as we shall see, to elicit a structure of differentiation whose constitutive traits are still preconceptual and prelinguistic. Considering what makes words words and concepts concepts, "Plato's Pharmacy" looks toward structural constraints "older" than language and conceptuality. And calling these structural constraints "constraints of language" risks obliterating the play that generates the very array of meaning through which such constraints have, in the first place, come into view. Since structural traits in question are thus intimately linked to the notion of play, it is important to recall that, according to Derrida, "as soon as it comes into being and into language, play *erases itself as such*" (*D*, p. 156). To understand the structural constraints to be constraints of language is not unlike Plato's theological uplifting of play which amounts, as Derrida argues, to the progressive neutralization of the "*singularity* of play" (*D*, p. 157). In any case, confounding these structures of differentiation anterior either to single terms or opposition, or language, overlooks a crucial difference.

Before beginning to read Plato's *Phaedrus*—a text whose texture, according to Derrida, has been dissimulated for centuries since commentators from antiquity on, unable to fathom its organization, considered this dialogue inferior—Derrida makes, in an exordium, some preliminary, and general remarks about the relation of reading to the text (in general). In these opening pages Derrida claims that any criticism that proceeds in the belief that it can "look at the text without touching it, without laying a hand on the 'object,' without risking—which is the only chance of entering into the game, by getting a few fingers caught—the addition of some new thread" (*D*, p. 63) deludes itself. Still, as the whole text, of "Plato's Pharmacy" clearly testifies, not merely in its scholarly apparatus and its argumentative ductus but especially through the filigree of its texture, the assertion that objective criticism is rigorously impossible does not simply obviate the standards or methodology of objectivism. Nor does the inevitable adding of a new thread to the weave of the text imply that anything goes. Indeed, the philological objectivism or licentious subjectivism imputed to Derrida's reading equally fail in the task of reading. They are equally foolish and equally sterile. Derrida writes that "that person would have understood nothing of the game who, at this, would feel himself authorized merely to add on; that is, to add any old thing [*n'importe quoi*]. He would add nothing: the seam wouldn't hold. Reciprocally, he who through 'methodological prudence,' 'norms of objectivity,' or 'safeguards of knowledge' would refrain from committing anything of himself, would not read at all" (*D*, p. 64). Yet add one must if one is to get into the game of the text and to read at all. "Adding, here is nothing other than giving to read," Derrida remarks (*D*, p. 63). While a reading addition must infringe on the philological demand for immanent cognition of the text, it is not free to be anything at all. Demarcating such adding from "embroidering," that is, from embellishing and ornamentalizing enrichment, Derrida suggests that the addition could be called "embroidery" if "one considers that to know how to embroider still means to have the ability to follow the given thread" (*D*, p. 63). In other words, an addition that gives to read, and without which there would be no reading, requires that it follow the thread of the text in question. "The reading or writing supplement must be rigorously prescribed, but by the necessities of a *game,* by the logic of a *play,* signs to which the system of all textual powers must be accorded and attuned" (*D*, p. 64). If the reading supplement must be prescribed, its possibility must lie entirely with the text itself. It must be made possible by the game or play of the signifier. In other words, only structural reasons, reasons that concern the texture of the text to be read—and not contents, themes, signifieds— must prescribe what kind of addition can claim to be a legitimate addition, one that gives the text to read. Moreover, an addition is rigorously prescribed, and effectuates a reading, only if the addition yields to the rule of the text; differently put, only if it reenacts itself the law constitutive of the text. To read a text thus implies adding a thread that obeys the same law as the text itself.[6]

Unquestionably, understanding reading as a prescribed addition to the text that adds to its supposedly immanent weave another thread that obeys the rule of the text presupposes a quite specific conception of the text. The exordium spells these premises out in general terms, but with unmistakable clarity, even though it does not explicitly state its reasons for understanding the text this way: "A text is not a text unless it hides from the first comer, from the first glance, the law of its composition and the rules of its game. A text remains, moreover, forever imperceptible. Its law and its rules are not, however, harbored in the inaccessibility of a secret; it is simply that they can never be booked, in the *present,* into anything that could rigorously be called a perception" (*D,* p. 63). A text must remain forever imperceptible. As he invokes the concept of a rigorous perception, Derrida alludes, of course, to Husserl who defines it as "the primal mode of intuition (*Anschauung),*" in short, as that kind of intuition that "exhibits with primal originality, that is, in the mode of self-presence."[7] If a text, then, does not present itself in *propria persona,* or show itself as such in full presence; if it refuses ever to become a phenomenon, and this not for contingent or hermetic reasons, there must be essential reasons that prevent it from claiming an identity that could become the object of an intuitive exhibition. Never to be booked in the present, a text, therefore, also risks forever being lost. Yet, despite this necessary dissimulation of the text itself and the impossibility of making the law of its composition and the rule of its game appear as such for a perception, they can, in principle, be established in their ideality by a second glance—a glance that is neither that of the first comer, nor that of originary exhibition. Indeed, what this second glance makes out are the specific reasons for which there can be no text itself that can be revealed once and for all in its propriety. The reasons for which the text lacks identity are thus of the order of the text's rules of composition and the laws of the play of the signifier. When we specify these reasons, we will call them "structural."

However, this fundamental uncertainty that necessarily characterizes the text and its laws and that prevents its manifesting itself as such and in totality spells the impossibility of the objectivist approach to texts, an approach assured in its belief that it has "mastered the game, surveyed all the threads at once" (*D,* p. 63). Paradoxically, making an addition to the text in the absence of the totality without which immanent philological understanding cannot do mimics the philological gesture, remaining faithful to some degree to its exigencies. Under these insecure circumstances, adding an extrinsic thread to the text in conformity with the law of the text and the rules of its game "secures" a reading of it in the first place. More precisely, only because there is uncertainty can there be something like a reading to begin with. But, needless to say, this addition that gives the text to read inevitably has the nature of a "cutting trace," of a decision, "the decision of each reading" (D, p. 63). To read is to take a risk. Without the risk of failing, there is no possible chance that the addition could give the text to read. Thus, while readings under these uncertain conditions never have the (illusory) security and legitimacy of transcendent readings, they are achievements. Readings are necessarily performative.

In Derrida's demonstration—a demonstration that not only proceeds according to the strict precepts of philology and its Platonist underpinnings but, in particular, according to Socrates' assumption that a speech must be an organic whole with a head, a middle, and a tail—that the *Phaedrus,* contrary to the venerable tradition of Plato scholarship, is, up to a certain point, a well-crafted and highly integrated text, the word *pharmakon* carries a significant (though not the only) burden. The debate of writing in the so-called second, and mythological part, is undoubtedly dominated by the question of the *pharmakon*. But if this very word, and others related to it, are also present in the so-called first, and philosophical part, the traditional pronouncement that its parts are unrelated might not hold. Derrida concedes, with reference to the evocation, at the dialogue's beginning, of the dangerous nymph Pharmacia (*Pharmakeia*) and to Socrates' comparison of Lysias's written speech to a *pharmakon* that has drugged him into leaving the walls of the city, that this initial association of writing and poison might not have been intentional on Plato's part. Yet, with the same linkage made explicitly in the second half of the dialogue, it may be assumed that the association of writing and poison in the first part is not accidental after all. However, Derrida is quick to point out that the unity underlying the two parts is not, thus, an intentional unity. Speaking about this unity in terms of the voluntary or the involuntary misses the structural reasons that make a link between the grapheme to the *pharmakon* virtually inevitable. These reasons—of the order of the "textual level" (D, p. 73)—are also responsible for the text's unity. But as structural reasons, they inscribe within the text the possibility of the addition that will give the text a chance to be read. If, hereafter, I draw the term *pharmakon* into center stage, it is because its analysis will provide us with the rules of the text's game, and thus also with the conditions for the addition that gives it to read.

Leaving out of account, for the moment, the chain of signification in which the word *pharmakon* is caught in Plato's text, let me look, first, at the word itself. Traditionally, it is rendered as "remedy," "recipe," "poison," "drug," "philter," and so forth. All these quite diverse translations are correct, yet each one, excluding the others, also disperses, and obliterates, what Derrida calls "the malleable unity of this concept, or rather its rules and the strange logic that links it with its signifier" (*D*, p. 71). Indeed, as Derrida argues, the word *pharmakon* in Plato's text is literally untranslatable because while it may, according to context, be justly translated this or that way, it continues to refer to its other meanings. Commenting on the translation of the passage in *Phaedrus* in which Theuth presents his invention—writing—to the King, arguing that now "both memory *(mneme)* and instruction *(sophia)* have found their remedy *(pharmakon),*" Derrida remarks that to render *pharmakon* here with "remedy" is certainly not wrong. He writes: "Not only can *pharmakon* really mean *remedy* and thus erase, on a certain surface of its functioning, the ambiguity of its meaning. But it is even quite obvious here, the stated intention of Theuth being precisely to stress the worth of his product, that he *turns* the word on its strange and invisible pivot, presenting it from a single one, the most reassuring, of its *poles*" (*D*, p. 97). And yet, however plausible, the translation of *pharmakon* as *remedy* "erases, in going outside the Greek language, the other pole reserved in the word *pharmakon*. It cancels out the resources of ambiguity and makes more difficult, if not impossible, an understanding of the context" (*D*, p. 97). In other words, in Plato's text the word *pharmakon* functions ambiguously every time it is used. Each meaning that it can have in addition to the contextually plausible one continues to bear on each of its singular occurrences in a mode still be elucidated. It is a polysemic word, and it can indeed appear as one of its meaning aspects, but only by a turn that hides its other poles. The word *pharmakon* contains, to begin with, the two opposite (but, as remains to be seen, perhaps not yet rigorously opposites) poles of poison and remedy. But it also contains many other meanings that cohabit within it that are not in bipolar opposition. The ambiguity springs from the multitude of possible meanings in the Greek language, and this is one reason why the word is not a *coincidentia oppositorum,* as Derrida maintains. Neither do the meanings that it comprises mutually cancel each other out. If, notwithstanding the polysemy of the word, Derrida highlights the word's meaning of poison and remedy, it is primarily because of his interest in "Plato's Pharmacy" to trace the structural origin of philosophical distinction and the logic of oppositional thinking. In any event, with the reference to the "strange and invisible pivot" on which the word can be made to turn, Derrida points at its structure and its nature as a signifier. Its different meanings are distributed around a pivot, as it were, that produces its various turns, but not without holding all the excluded meanings in reserve at the same time. Translating the word as "remedy," in the passage under consideration, thus obliterates:

> the virtual, dynamic references to the other uses of the same word in Greek. The effect of such a translation is most importantly to destroy . . . Plato's anagrammatic writing, to destroy it by interrupting the relations interwoven among different functions of the same word in different places, relations that are virtually but necessarily 'citational.' When a word inscribes itself as the citation of another sense of the same word, when the textual center-stage of the word *pharmakon,* even while it means *remedy,* cites, re-cites, and makes legible that which *in the same word* signifies, in another spot and on a different level of the stage, *poison* (for example, since that is not the only other thing *pharmakon* means), the choice of only one of these renditions by the translator has as its first effect the neutralization of the citational play, of the 'anagram,' and, in the end, quite simply of the very textuality of the translated text.   (*D*, p. 98)

The word *pharmakon* is not polysemic in the sense that its possible meanings are actually present in the word. It does not simultaneously mean all its other possible meanings. It is rather a cluster of its *virtual* references to all its possible usages in Greek. A word such as *pharmakon* inscribes these citational relations within its identical self (*dans le même mot*). *Pharmakon,* strictly speaking, is not a word in the sense of a semic unity. Rather, despite the meaning fixed into place by a context (or a translator), *pharmakon* remains interwoven structurally with other possible uses in the language to which it belongs. Returning to the question regarding the difficulty of translating the word *pharmakon,* it thus becomes clear that this difficulty is not limited to its translation from Greek into other languages but rests within Greek language itself. Derrida writes: "It is a difficulty inherent in its very principle [*"difficulté de principe"*], situated less in the passage from one language to another, from philosophical language to another, than already . . . in the tradition between Greek and Greek; a violent difficulty in the transference of a nonphilosopheme into a philosopheme. With this problem of translation we will thus be dealing with nothing less than the problem of the very passage into philosophy" (*D*, p. 72).

From the first occurrence of the word in Plato's dialogue, but especially from the moment Theuth appears on the scene and presents his invention to the King as a remedy against memory loss while the King retorts that it is a poison, the *pharmakon*, with its beneficent or maleficent power, is cast in the form of a concept, more precisely, of a substance. Derrida writes: "The *pharmakon* would be a *substance*—with all that the word can connote in terms of matter with occult virtues, cryptic depths refusing to submit their ambivalence to analysis, already paving the way for alchemy—if we didn't have eventually to come to recognize it as antisubstance itself: that which resists any philosopheme, indefinitely exceeding its bounds as nonidentity, nonessence, nonsubstance; granting philosophy by that very fact the inexhaustible adversity of what funds it and the infinite absence of what founds it" (p. 70). In the context of his dicussion of the translation problems posed by the word *pharmakon*, Derrida notes that to render it either as poison, or remedy, a translation by virtue of which the other meanings are violently suppressed, is an effect of Platonism, "the consequence of something already at work in the translated text, in the relation between 'Plato' and his 'language'." The translation proceeds by means of a "blockage (*interruption*) of the passage among opposing values" (*D*, p. 98). Forcing the *pharmakon* into unequivocity makes it a concept, the concept of a beneficial or malevolent substance. In what follows, we will have to analyze in some detail the modalities of the reductive translation that produces a philosophical concept. This analysis will also bring to light how the *pharmakon* exceeds the concepts into which it is forced, and how, by virtue of this excess, it grants philosophy an abyssal foundation.

Before further discussing the reductive and violent Platonic translation of the *pharmakon*, it is necessary to keep in mind that this is not the violation of an unbroached and unbreached semantic innocence. As Derrida holds, "It is part of the rule of this game [the *pharmakon's* ambivalence] that the game should *seem to stop*. Then the *pharmakon*, which is older than either of the opposites, is 'caught' by philosophy, by 'Platonism' which is constituted by this apprehension, as a mixture of two pure, heterogeneous terms" (*D*, p. 128). The philosophical translation of the *pharmakon* is not something arbitrary. It is also part of the the *pharmakon's* game, a game of passage and inversion, to freeze. And this, in fact, is the aspect of its play that makes it possible for philosophy to interpret it as a mix of two definite, two pure, and entirely different meanings. More precisely, the play's play at stopping the game is the exact condition at which philosophy is born as the apprehension of the *pharmakon* as a mix of two already constituted pure terms.

Before further clarifying how "play" is to be understood, I also note that what Derrida calls the "citational play" of a word such as *pharmakon* is constitutive of the "very textuality of the . . . text." Indeed, as we shall see, the structural analysis begun with the discussion of the word *pharmakon* is intended to bring out the textuality of the text and thus to locate the place where a possible addition to the web of the text can be made. The word analysis of the *pharmakon* defines textuality by the differential play of a linguistic entity's virtual references. These virtual references, as we have seen, may relate a word to entirely heterogeneous meanings that it may have within the same language and to which it can always revert. A word's virtual references thus interrupt its identity on a structural level. One same word (or any linguistic entity) always cites *other* virtual uses. Derrida writes: "Textuality being constituted by differences and by differences from differences, it is by nature absolutely heterogeneous and is constantly composing with the forces that tend to annihilate it" (*D*, p. 98). In other words, as a play of virtual and dynamic references, textuality provides itself the means for its own destructive neutralization through, say, conceptualization. More precisely, since textuality itself creates the structural possibility that its own play be arrested in an unequivocal discourse (such as philosophy, for instance), the counterforces with which textuality composes can tend only toward its own annihilation. Should such annihilation ever succeed in abolishing the play of the text, the annihilating discourse would also lose its own ground of possibility and annihilate itself in the same breath.

From what has just been established, it follows that Plato's text must be considerably more complex than its commentators have suspected. Indeed, if the Platonic doctrine is rooted in a gesture intent on limiting the play of the text, such limitation presupposes the "presence" in his work of the textual matrix that enables the forces of restriction to work. If hereto, Derrida's analysis of Plato's text has been of the order of a commentary in strictly observing the precepts of philology and aiming toward the reconstitition of the Platonic system, it is to be expected that in shifting his attention to the matrix that enables Platonism, he will leave behind the questions, models, and methods specific to the genre. This exploration of the textual play that exceeds Platonism, makes an addition to it—but an addition that is still entirely indebted to the Platonic text for all its resources—and moves. This coming "to an understanding with Plato" is already a reading. Derrida writes: "To come to an understanding with Plato, as it is sketched out in this text, is already to slip away from the recognized models of commentary, from the genealogical or structural reconstitution of a system, whether this reconstitution tries to corroborate or refute, confirm or 'overturn,' mark a return-to-Plato or give him a 'send-off' in the quite Platonic manner of the *khairein*. What is going on here is something altogether different. That too, of course, but still completely other" (*D*, p. 104). This is certainly a reading in the sense that reading had been defined in *Of Grammatology,* where we read that "reading must always aim at a certain relationship, unperceived by the writer, between what he commands and what he does not command of the patterns of the language that he uses. This relationship is not a certain quantitative distribution of shadow and light, of weakness or of force, but a signifying structure that critical reading should *produce*."[8] "Production"—in "Plato's Pharmacy" it will be called "writing"—brings forth the infrastructural text making the not-seen *a priori* system of the writing and reading of, in this case, the *Phaedrus* accessible to sight. Such a production, Derrida stresses, "does not leave the text."[9] Even though reading, in the sense of crafting an infrastructural text, breaks with the models and methods of the commentary, it proceeds entirely within the limits of philology. However, reading, in the emphatic sense encountered in the exordium to "Plato's Pharmacy," namely, as an addition that gives to read, is not simply identical with the notion of reading as the production of a signifying structure. Reading as thematized in the text on Plato exceeds the text in a complex a fashion. One could call it, perhaps, reading in an emphatic sense, or reading *cum emphasi*. The differences between the two, and as we shall see, intimately interrelated concepts of reading, will be elucidated hereafter.

Before turning to the reconstruction of the textual matrix "itself" on which Platonism draws, a reconstruction that, despite the break with recognized models and aims of commentary, does not cut all ties to it, I return to the question of the composition of the two forces that compose in the textuality of a text such as the *Phaedrus*. Having defined the *pharmakon* as an untranslatable citational play, Derrida remarks:

> On the one hand Plato decides in favor of a logic that does not tolerate such passages between opposing senses of the same word, all the more so since such a passage would reveal itself to be something quite different from simple confusion, alternation, or the dialectic of opposites. And yet, on the other hand, the *pharmakon* . . . constitutes the original medium of decision, the element that precedes it, comprehends it, goes beyond it, can never be reduced to it, and is not separated from it by a single word (or signifying apparatus), operating within the Greek and Platonic text.   (*D*, pp. 98–99)

The Platonic fixing into place of the *pharmakon* by translating it into the concept of a substance (benevolent or malevolent) is witness to Platonism's option for, and decision according to a logic of identity. Yet this identifying arrestation becomes possible only where there is something to be decided, arrested, and identified in the first place. The *pharmakon* as an element of passage and inversion is, indeed, that medium of decision in which, by "an *effect of analysis*" and interpretation, poles can be made out and defined as "simple elements." But this medium is not annihilated simply because it has been reduced "to one of its simple elements by interpreting it." Referring to the interpretative translation of the word *pharmakon*, Derrida notes that "it destroys the *pharmakon* but at the same time forbids itself access to it, leaving it untouched in its reserve" (*D*, p. 99). The interpretative translation, indeed, depends on the element of passage for its very possibility. Now, the reductive translation not only divides the *pharmakon* into simple, fixed elements, it also arrests its movement by polarizing these simple elements. If the translation of the *pharmakon* can tame its ambiguity by linking its elements into oppositional relations, this is because, as a medium of passage, it lends itself to such an operation. But in "itself," if one could still speak of the *pharmakon* in those terms, it is not structured by binary oppositions.

In his analysis of the depreciation of writing in the *Phaedrus*, Derrida remarks that the King's contention that writing produces "the 'opposite' effect from what one might expect" masters the recognized ambiguity "by inserting its definition into simple, clear-cut oppositions" (*D*,

p. 103). But, as Derrida holds, as far as the *Phaedrus* is concerned, "it is not enough to say that writing is conceived out of this or that series of oppositions. Plato thinks of writing, and tries to comprehend it, to dominate it, on the basis of *opposition* as such" (*D,* p. 103). For contrary values such as good/evil, true/false, inside/outside, etc., to be in opposition, "each of the terms must be simply *external* to the other, which means that one of these oppositions (the opposition between inside and outside) must already be accredited as the matrix of all possible opposition. And one of the elements of the system (or series) must also stand as the very possibility of systematicity or seriality in general" (*D,* p. 103). If, indeed, the characteristic traits of writing are all modalities of exteriority, as Derrida asserts (*D,* p. 101), writing is cast into the simple exteriority of all interiority. By ousting writing on the grounds that it is the outside of all interiority, Plato has not only used one particular item in the system of oppositions to denigrate writing, he has cast it in term of that opposition that represents the constitutive feature of all opposition. But if this is so, Plato implicitly acknowledges that something exceeds the system of oppositions and that this something must exceed opposition as well. By coercing the *pharmakon* into opposition, Plato, unknowingly, but yielding to structural necessities, as it were, throws the *pharmakon* into a position from whence it begins to take on the contours and the characteristics of being the source of opposition itself, and hence of the system of all oppositions. Derrida, consequently, can raise the following questions:

> And if one got to thinking that something like the *pharmakon*—or writing—far from being governed by these oppositions, opens up their very possibility without letting itself be comprehended by them; if one got to thinking that it can only be out of something like writing—or the *pharmakon*—that the strange difference between inside and outside can spring; if, consequently, one got to thinking that writing as a *pharmakon* cannot simply be assigned a site within what it situates, cannot be subsumed under concepts whose contours it draws, leaves only its ghost to a logic that can only seek to govern it insofar as logic arises from it—one would then have to *bend* into strange contortions what could no longer even simply be called logic or discourse.   (*D,* p. 103)

With these questions, Derrida closes the discussion of the translatability of the word *pharmakon* and turns to the construction of the matrix of Platonism that his reading is intent on producing. Even though the difference inside/outside is a "strange" difference, it remains a part of the system of metaphysical differences. If it can serve Plato to dominate the *pharmakon* by denouncing it as exteriority itself, the thus defined *pharmakon* cannot yet be the condition of possibility of opposition but only its metaphysical ghost. Derrida's questions seek, indeed, to bring that condition itself out from behind its ghost. *Pharmakon* remains the name for the matrix in question, but it is understood neither as the concept of a substance nor according to clear-cut oppositional attributes but in terms that are structural in nature and that subtend oppositional thinking.

In the parts of "Plato's Pharmacy" devoted to showing that if the sophists, as Gorgias contends, are magicians or poisoners, Socrates too is a *pharmakeus,* in that he uses a *pharmakon* (the socratic *pharmakon,* socratic irony), and more generally, that for Socrates the "philosophical, epistemic order of *logos* . . . [is] an antidote"—a contention which, as Derrida remarks, is far from being "a daring interpretation of Plato-nism"[10]—Derrida arrives at the conclusion that if philosophy can oppose to its other a drug transmuted into a remedy, this is because the *logos* is "a force *inscribed within the general economy of the pharmakon*" (*D*, p. 124). He writes:

> Such an operation would not be possible if the *pharmako-logos* did not already harbor within itself that complicity of contrary values, and if the *pharmakon* in general were not, prior to any distinction-making, that which, presenting itself as a poison, may turn out to be a cure, may retrospectively reveal itself in the truth of its curative power. The "es-sence" of the *pharmakon* lies in the way in which, having no stable essence, no "proper" characteristics, it is not, in any sense (metaphysi-cal, physical, chemical, alchemical) of the word, a *substance.* The *phar-makon* has no ideal identity; it is aneidetic, firstly because it is not monoeidetic . . . But it is neither a composite, a sensible or empirical *sunthethon* partaking of several simple essences. It is rather the prior medium in which differentiation in general is produced, along with the opposition between the *eidos* and its others; this medium is *analogous* to the one that will, subsequent to and according to the decision of philosophy, be reserved for transcendental imagination, that "art hid-den in the depths of the soul," which belongs neither simply to the sensible nor simply to the intelligible, neither simply to passivity nor simply to activity. The element-medium will always be analogous to a mixed-medium.   (*D*, p. 125)

What transpires from this passage is that the matrix of Platonism to be produced in Derrida's reading occupies an exorbitant position with respect to elementary philosophical distinctions. In this sense it is not unlike transcendental schematism in its relation to the sensible and the intelligible. Just as schematism is to explain how realms as different as the sensible and the conceptual can relate to one another, the *pharmakon* serves "to come to an understanding with Plato" and Platonism. This analogy also commands that the *pharmakon* be neither of the order of a substance nor an empirical composite. It is neither homogeneous nor heterogeneous (in an empirical sense). It has no identity, not even an ideal one. But nor is it an empirical composite. It could be said to partake in both (as does transcendental schematism). Further, the demarcation of the *pharmakon* from substance hints clearly at its structural nature. In addition, the *pharmakon* is portrayed as a play, a differential play. But since it is not *a* play, the *pharmakon* is a structure in which there is play. In order to get a more precise sense of how the *pharmakon* is anterior to the elementary philosophical differences and oppositions, we need to clarify what *play* means in this context. I recall that in Theuth's eyes, writing is a remedy; yet for Thamous it is a poison. Discussing this crossed connection making in Plato's text, Derrida asks whether it is the result of a mere artifice or play. He writes: "There is certainly *play* [il y a surtout *le jeu*] in such a movement, and this chiasmus is authorized, even prescribed, by the ambivalence of the *pharmakon*. Not only by the polarity good/evil, but by the double participation in the distinct regions of the soul and the body, the invisible and the visible. This double participation, once again, does not mix together two previously separate elements; it refers back to a *same* that is not identical, to the common element or medium of any possible dissociation" (*D*, p. 127). Let me tease out what Derrida advances here: As the medium of differentiation, the *pharmakon* prescribes the crisscross inversion of predicates—of the predicates of the *pharmakon* as it surfaces in Plato's text; the *pharmakon* has this power to invert inasmuch as it is the ambivalent medium of differentiation; in its capacity as a medium, the *pharmakon* is said to participate in the distinct, and bipolarly opposed, predicates; and, yet, it is not to be understood as a mix. Let me, then, interpret: As the medium of dissociation, the *pharmakon* is not a mix of what springs from it, of what becomes constituted by it, or of what is carved out within its medium. In the medium nothing is yet constituted. Its ambivalence derives from the fact that in its element no decision has yet occurred, nothing has been been separated. But it is not for that matter a mix of what arises from it through decision, that is, a mix of what, as a result of a separation, are bipolar opposites. The *pharmakon's* ambivalence or ambiguity as a medium implies that it is neither remedy *and* poison, nor their dialectical synthesis, since such synthesis already presupposes that what it unites has arisen from the medium. For the same reason, neither can we say that the opposite values collapse in the *pharmakon.* Its ambiguity is not due to its being rich, or even pregnant, with meaning. The matrix's ambiguity is strictly structural in that it is nothing but the (no)place of an exchange and inversion of the traits that are involved in oppositional distinction and interpretation. It "itself," however, is not yet oppositional and therefore not a *coincidentia oppositorum* or a dialectical synthesis. The *pharmakon* participates in the oppositions that arise from it, as well as in the syntheses to which the constituted may lend itself (to the extent that what has sprung forth from it is bipolarly organized), in that the traits of passage and inversion that make up the medium are distributed through and over the distinct oppositions. At this point, one can also grasp how *play* has to be taken in this context. It is a rigorously structural concept that concerns only the traits of passage and inversion that make up the matrix of Platonism. Moreover, if there is play in the *pharmakon,* it is precisely because its element is not yet that of opposition and contradiction. *Play* designates an unrest of sorts that is not yet qualifiable in terms of binary polarization. As we shall see, the *pharmakon* is the play that "puts play into play" (*D,* p. 93). But first this:

> If the *pharmakon* is 'ambivalent,' it is because it constitutes the medium in which oppositions are opposed, the movement and the play that links them among themselves, reverses them or makes one side cross over into the other . . . It is on the basis of this play or movement that the opposites or differences are stopped by Plato. The *pharmakon* is the movement, the locus, and the play: (the production of) difference. It is the differance of difference. It holds in reserve, in its undecided shadow and vigil, the opposites and the differends that the process of discrimination will come to carve out.   (*D,* p. 127)

Not only is the *pharmakon* the ambivalent reserve of traits whose passing into one another is interrupted by Platonism in order to create opposition and to distribute them to bipolarly opposed identities, it is also the reserve for the movement that exists between simple identities in opposition. It allows one to account for the controlled relations that philosophy admits between the poles of dyadic oppositions, but also for what happens in spite of all control, inadvertently, to what is made to stand against one another. The *pharmakon* is therefore also that which "puts play into play," into the mastered play, if not masterplay of Platonism.

To sustain this point, a digression is in order. It concerns a philosophical opposition, indeed, one that according to Derrida belongs to "the great structural oppositions of Platonism," and the one that also motivates the condemnation of writing in the *Phaedrus*. This opposition is in memory, the difference between *mneme* (live memory) and *hypomnesis* (memory of memory substitutes).[11] As Derrida notes, "What is played out at the boundary line between these two concepts is . . . something like the major decision of philosophy, the one through which it institutes itself, maintains itself, and contains its adverse deeps" (*D*, p. 111). Now, according to the conceptual dyad and to the kind of relation prescribed by oppositional thinking, *hypomnesis* (to whose realm writing belongs) is not only inferior to live memory, it is entirely exterior to it. Yet, however significant this difference may be for the constitution of philosophy, it is not only much more complex than anyone admits, it is also very subtle, fine to the point of being invisible. As Derrida shows, the difference between the concepts of memory concerns two different kinds of repetition. Whereas live memory repeats truth itself, *hypomnesia* repeats only the aids to memory, and it is thus prone to an endless repetition of repetition. Writing stands for such senseless repetition in the absence of the thing itself. In Derrida's words, "writing would indeed be the signifier's capacity to repeat itself by itself, mechanically, without a living soul to sustain or attend it in its repetition, that is to say, without truth's *presenting itself* anywhere. Sophistics, hypomnesia, and writing would thus be separated from philosophy, dialectics, anamnesis, and living speech by the invisible, almost nonexistent, thickness of that *leaf* between the signifier and the signified" (*D*, pp. 111–112). But this leaf— a clear reference to Saussure's comparison of language to a "sheet of paper"[12]—that makes the difference between live memory and memory substitutes not only divides and separates them but also links them (as it does philosophy and sophistics, discussed within the same context). Derrida continues: "But by the same token doesn't the unity of this leaf, of the system of this difference between signified and signifier, also point to the inseparability of sophistics and philosophy? The difference between signifier and signified is no doubt the governing pattern within which Platonism institutes itself and determines its opposition to sophistics. In being inaugurated in this manner, philosophy and dialectics are determined in the act of determining their other" (*D*, p. 112). What does this mean for the distinction of *mneme* and *hypomnesis?* Precisely because a leaf makes a difference between them, this difference does not sever live memory from memory substitutes, or vice versa. However exterior live memory may be to hypomnetic devices such as writing, and however mechanical and senseless these devices may prove to be, there is, for Derrida, a "profound complicity in the break" (*D*, p. 112). There is a point of contact, a point of passage, between the so different poles of metaphysical oppositions. This point of contact is precisely what allows them to mutually determine each other in all their respective differences. Differently put, the link that the opposition institutes between them is what allows them to claim radical exteriority in relation to the other. In the most general terms, philosophical distinction—be it between itself and all its others, or between valorized concepts and their opposite such as *mneme* and the *hypomnema*—presupposes a medium of passage and exchange that enables each particular pole to borrow from the other the traits that sustain its difference. For there to be difference and opposition, there must be communication. Throughout "Plato's Pharmacy," Derrida has shown that such communication between what is (indeed) radically different makes it necessary, but also entirely philosophically legitimate, to have recourse to the excluded to establish the excluding term in distinction from it. Indeed, this is the only way that philosophy can establish itself in difference from its others, the only way that it can draw the line between what is good and what is not. Rather than implying either an absence or impossibility of difference, the fact that the dividing line between Platonism and its closest other—sophistics—allows "the parties and the party lines frequently to exchange their places, imitating the forms and borrowing the paths of the opponent" (*D*, p. 108); the fact that Socrates can conceive of the *logos* as pharmakon to "be opposed to the *pharmakon* of the sophists and to the bewildering fear of death" (*D*, p. 124); the fact that, after having condemned writing as a threat to live memory, Socrates defines *live memory* in terms of a good kind of writing, but a writing nonetheless (*D*, pp. 149f.)—all this proves the existence of a common medium between philosophy and what it casts into opposition, between philosophy and that on the basis of which alone philosophical distinctions can rigorously be made. It also follows that since the exchange in question is a structural necessity, Plato himself might not always have been conscious of what he was doing. In any case, even though, in Derrida's reading, the Platonic text appears considerably more complex than commonly believed and appears to say more than what Plato actually meant, in no way puts Platonism as such into jeopardy. It is rather a reading that renders the structural necessities without which Platonism could not effectively draw its distinctions visible.

Yet, if opposition presupposes a medium for transaction between the opposed terms, a medium in which each pole can negotiate (but also force the other into) its respective difference, this necessary communication can, of course, also provoke the opposite effect: a corruption, for example, of *mneme* by *hyopomnesis,* by writing. Indeed, if *mneme* in itself must communicate with its opposite and thus represent a good form of writing, it is always exposed to the threat (not necessarily its actual occurrence) of that kind of writing condemned by both Thamous and Socrates in the *Phaedrus.* The very condition that allows it to be itself and radically different from its opposite is also what makes it virtually, potentially, corruptible.

To conclude my analysis of the textual matrix that Derrida produces in reading Plato's text and which he develops in order "to come to an understanding of Plato" and Platonism, I remark, in that the *pharmakon* not only represents the element of passage and inversion in which philosophical distinctions are carved out but also explains the conditions under which philosophical difference can be maintained and the intrinsic threats facing it, the *pharmakon* is the matrix in question. Since philosophical distinguishing takes its opposite marks from the ambivalent reserve of the *pharmakon* by interrupting the passage and inversion of the traits, it becomes clear why opposites must refer to each other. The distinguishing mark is lifted from the medium, cut off from other marks to which it referred and into which it can incessantly pass. But because each distinctive mark is such a mark only in distinction from what has become its opposite in the interruptive interpretation, each mark can cause that which it marks to revert into its opposite. This possiblity is the danger ever present to all rigorous distinguishing. The threat to rigorous distiction, distinguishing itself, originates from the same, that is, from the structural nonsite of the *pharmakon.* Not a substance, the *pharmakon* is only "the bottomless fund" (*D,* p. 127) that exceeds the play of difference, and opposites, in that it is the fund from which they draw the traits of predication and in that it puts play into their play.

Reading, as Derrida understands it, consists of producing the matrix of Platonism. "Plato's Pharmacy" articulates this generalized theory of Platonism, its matrix—the *pharmakon*—on the basis, and in terms of one singular text, the *Phaedrus*. The understanding that such a reading adds to Plato's text derives from structural necessities bound up with philosophical difference and shows certain tensions and complications in his text to be rigorously necessary, neither accidents nor unintended effects. Such a reading presupposes that "every model of classical reading is exceeded," precisely insofar as classical reading is indeed informed by that for which it is supposed to account—Platonism, in this case. It is exceeded at the precise point at which such a reading attaches to the inside of Platonism, to the inside that Platonism understands itself to be. Reading, in Derrida's sense, achieves such an excess through "a functional displacement, which concerns differences . . . more than any conceptual identities signified" (*D*, p. 104). Such a reading sheds a bit of light into the shadows of what Derrida calls the "deep backroom of Plato's pharmacy." It brings into view the structural laws to which, wittingly or not, philosophy must yield. Reading, therefore, makes truth claims inasmuch as its ambition is to make Plato understandable. Yet, how can this possibly be for a reading that not only exceeds the classical models of reading but that establishes that "any full intuition of truth, any truth-filled intuition, is impossible" (*D*, p. 166)? I recall that the thrust of Derrida's investigation of the *pharmakon* consists in bringing into view structural imperatives to which philosophical distinction must yield, but which also threaten it from within with a reversion into what it opposes. The *pharmakon* is a condition without which philosophy cannot assert its values. It is an enabling condition. Even though this condition can always cause the constituted to revert into its opposite and thus inscribes an inner limit within what it makes possible, it remains an enabling condition. One could even go so far as to say that only and precisely because it is also a condition of impossibility, can the *pharmakon* serve as a matrix for Platonism. Derrida writes: "Differance, the disappearance of any originary presence, is *at once* the condition of possibility *and* the condition of impossibility of truth" (*D*, p. 168). In Heideggerian terms, the "truth" of truth as presence, as total transparency, as full adequation, is that it must compose with a certain untruth. The limiting condition to which truth in an absolute sense owes its very possibility does not do away with truth. Only on the condition of an uncompromising expectation of total transparency, of one-to-one adequation, could the enabling limiting condition of truth be taken to make truth impossible. For Derrida, on the contrary, the necessity that any identity refer to its other and be inhabited by the virtual possibility of reverting to that other, this opacity within the identical, makes it a positive identity. Thus while it makes no absolute truth claims, a reading like the one that we have witnessed can claim to make Plato understandable. The singular occasion of this attempt to produce the matrix of Platonism—the reading of the singular text that is the *Phaedrus*—not only represents the condition under which such a production will have taken place but it will also have been what inevitably inscribes a limit to and into the illumination in question. Still, the reading's singularity is not simply an obstacle that would prevent the reading to make universal claims—the claim to provide the matrix of Platonism, for one. This singularity allows for such claims to be made in the first place.

But the reading of the *Phaedrus* is not limited to the production of the matrix of Platonism. This matrix is undoubtedly already, in a certain sense, an addition to the text. It adds intelligibility, and inasmuch as its elaboration goes hand in hand with the exhibition of an internal and hidden chain of significations in Plato's text, it sheds an illuminating light on its different layers. However, this matrix and this chain open, in principal, the possibility of an addition in a more emphatic sense and by which the text is given to read. What is it of the matrix that allows for such an addition? For Derrida, a *word*, in addition to its actual meaning in a given context, is a cluster of virtual references to the usages of that same word in other places and contexts. The word *pharmakon* has been shown to be a word in such a sense. Moreover, this word has yielded the minimal structure of passage and inversion—called *pharmakon*—implied by the virtual referentiality that breaks the semantic unity of the word. But, inasmuch as a word is *itself* a cluster of references to other of *its* usages, and thus permanently in the position of citation, it is also in virtual communication with other words that belong to the same family or share the same root. In Plato's text, for example, the word *pharmakon* forms a chain, or series of significations with other "pharmaceutical" words. Derrida writes:

> Like any text, the text of 'Plato' couldn't not [insofar as it is a text, that is, always in virtual reference to the other usages of its words and

familiar words] be involved, at least in a virtual, dynamic, lateral manner, with all the words that composed the system of the Greek language. Certain forces of association unite—at diverse distances, with different strengths and according to disparate paths—the words 'actually present' in a discourse with all the other words in a lexical system, whether or not they appear as 'words,' that is, as relative verbal units in such dicourse. They communicate with the totality of the lexicon through their syntactic play and at least through the subunits that compose what we call a word.   (D, pp. 129–130)

Given the structurally ambivalent, or textual, mode in which communications are established "through the play of language, among diverse functions of the word and, within it, among diverse strata or regions of culture" (D, p. 95), the chains of significations in a text do not let themselves be described *in toto*. But the ultimate impossibility of exhausting a word's referrals, does not mean that nothing could be understood with respect to these chains, that no knowledge whatsoever could be gained about them. After having alluded to the reasons that prevent one from "reconstituting the entire chain of significations of the *pharmakon*" and to "absolutely . . . master its textual system," Derrida insists that "this limitation can and should nevertheless be displaced to a certain extent" (D, p. 96). It is to such a displacement, that is, to a broadening of the possible knowledge about the nontotalizable chain, that Derrida will proceed in the following. This displacement consists of adding, within certain strict limits, one item to the series of "pharmaceutical" terms, an addition by which the text is given to be read, in other words, actively interpreted.

The *pharmakon* that Derrida shows as the locus and the support for the word *pharmakon*'s mutations, its negative or positive valuations, and its varying meanings—such as "painting," "color," "perfume," to name a few—also stands in relation to the words *pharmakeia* and *pharmakeus* in Plato's text and corpus. These words "appear in the text of 'Plato.' Only the chain is concealed . . . Curiously, however, there is another of these words that, to our knowledge, is never used by Plato. If we line it up with the series, *pharmakeia – pharmakon – pharmakeus*, we will no longer be able to content ourselves with reconstituting a chain that, for all its hiddenness, for all it might escape Plato's notice, is nevertheless something that passes through certain discoverable *points of presence* that can be seen in the text" (D, p. 129), Derrida claims. As Derrida adds this other "pharmaceutical" word to the chain, he ceases to reconstitute the hidden chain that links together certain words that "actually make an 'act of presence,' so to speak, in the text of the dialogues" (*D,* p. 129). However, the addition of a word not found in the corpus of Plato's work and hence that exceeds the philological constraint that had both guided and, by claiming the presence of the words in the dialogues as evidence of an actual link, secured Derrida's investigation, is not for that matter arbitrary. Although the chain stops being "simply 'internal' to Plato's lexicon" (*D,* p. 13), the word is added with rigor and prudence, and it both refers to part of the system of Greek language and culture and ties in with the references already interwoven with the textual chain. While the word in question "seems strikingly absent from the 'Platonic' text," it "is present in the language and . . . points to an experience that was present in Greek culture even in Plato's days" (*D,* p. 129). With this addition from outside the text, Derrida begins to read emphatically, that is, at the risk of getting a few fingers caught, and the first casuality is the common conception regarding the identity of the Platonic text itself. Derrida writes:

> In going beyond the bounds of that [Platonic] lexicon, we are less interested in breaking through certain limits, with or without cause, than in putting in doubt the right to posit such limits in the first place. In a word, we do not believe that there exists, in all rigor, a Platonic text, closed upon itself, complete with its inside and its outside. Not that one must then consider that it is leaking on all sides and can be drowned confusedly in the undifferentiated generality of its element. Rather, provided the articulations are rigorously and prudently recognized, one should simply be able to untangle the hidden forces of attraction linking a present word with an absent word in the text of Plato.   (*D,* p. 130)

If it is true that the textual structure is a cluster of virtual traits of referral, how then could there be something like a text purely itself, clearly separated from its outside? How, then, could one possibly pinpoint what is absent and what is present in a text? But to move, on these premises, outside the text is not therefore to deny all relative unity of a text. The prudence and rigor demanded in adding something from the outside to the text is clear testimony of a unity however fragile. The addition, indeed, does not drown the text in a presumed element: Greek culture, Greek language, or language in general. This transgression of the philological norm of immanence does not find significations outside the text or the Platonic corpus that represent the exact opposite of significations within the text or corpus whose inverting effect would thus dissolve the text or corpus together with the addition into what Derrida calls "the undifferentiated generality" of the element, and be it the element of language. On the contrary, the addition fits neatly into the chain of significations already present in the text and sheds an additional light on both the chain and the fragile unity of the text itself.

What then is this word? It is "a word that can, on one of its faces, be considered the synonym, almost the homonym, of a word Plato "actually" used. The word in question is *pharmakos* (wizard, magician, poisoner), a synonym of *pharmakeus* (which Plato uses), but with the unique feature of having been overdetermined, overlaid by Greek culture with another function. Another *role,* and a formidable one" (*D,* p. 130). In addition to wizard, magician, poisoner, the word *pharmakos* designates the annual ritual of purification in ancient Greece (still in force in Plato's time) in which two men representing the outside and the threat of otherness (evil, calamities, etc.) were expulsed from the city and occasionally put to death for the city's proper body to reconstitute its unity. Derrida, summing up his analysis of the rite, underscores that "the ceremony of the *pharmakos* is . . . played out on the boundary line between inside and outside, which it has as its function ceaselessly to trace and retrace . . . The origin of difference and division, the *pharmakos* represents evil both introjected and projected. Beneficial insofar as he cures— and for that, venerated and cared for—harmful insofar as he incarnates the powers of evil—and for that, feared and treated with caution." Like the *pharmakon,* the *pharmakos,* is ambivalent not because he is both good and evil, but because he is the passage between and is thus anterior to them, "the passage to decision or crisis" (*D,* p. 133).

What, then, does the *pharmakos,* once it is lined up with the other significations of the chain, bring to bear on the chain and the text of Plato? What does this addition find in Platonism that was not visible on the basis of the terms internal to Plato's text? For reasons of economy, I will not rehearse how the additional connotation bears on each point made hereto. But let me first recall that the absence of the word *pharmakos* from Plato's text has been labeled a curious absence. Why curious? Consider the following: If the rule of the *pharmakon's* play includes the possibility of stopping the play, such stoppage permits the apprehension of the *pharmakon* "as a mixture of two pure, heterogeneous terms." But even so, "the *pharmakon* also acts like an aggressor or a housebreaker, threatening some internal purity and security." Now, "the purity of the inside can only be restored if the *charges are brought home* against exteriority as a supplement inessential yet harmful to the essence, a surplus that *ought* never to have come to be added to the untouched plenitude of the inside." The purity of the inside has thus to be cured from the *pharmakon,* and that is achieved by putting "the outside back in its place." Keeping "the outside out," Derrida stresses, is "the inaugural gesture of 'logic' itself." But exorcising the excess from the self-identity of what is, being therapeutic in essence, "must call upon the very thing [the *pharmakon*] it is expelling, the very surplus it is *putting out. The pharmaceutical operation must therefore exclude itself from itself*" (*D*, p. 128). Differently put, because the operation of purifying pure self-identity from all exteriority must make recourse to what it seeks to exclude, it itself is an impurity within the purity that it seeks to restore. In order for the restored purity to be pure, and identity be truly self-identical, the operation that expels the outside from the inside must be expelled as well. Platonism as a discourse opting for "logic" and the self-identity of what is cannot but pass over in silence the gesture by which it fixes itself properly within its own borders. The *pharmakos,* being precisely the ritual expulsion in the name of propriety, identity, and unity, can have no place within a discourse bent on restoring interiority to its proper self. No wonder, then, that the word *pharmakos* does not make an act of presence within the Platonic texts. But with this we have outlined the interpretative thread, that with the addition of the word *pharmakos* to the chain of significations in question, is woven into Plato's dialogue and gives it to read.

Recurring to Socrates' condemnation of writing—a condemnation that, in the wake of its depreciation by the mythological figure of Thamous, consists in transforming *mythos* into *logos*—Derrida argues that it is not unrelated to the rite of the *pharmakos.* In this light, Socrates' truth, "the knowledge of the real nature of things," reveals itself to be an antidote to a writing depicted as a "hollow, cast-off repetition" that estranges from the thing itself it purports to imitate. Writing being a *pharmakon,* ontological knowledge, now that the *pharmakos* has been inserted or rather reinserted into the chain, appears in the quality of a counterpoison, another pharmaceutical force needed to counter the corruptive powers of writing. From this Derrida can infer that "the order of knowledge is not the transparent order of forms and ideas as one might be tempted retrospectively to interpret it; it is the antidote. Long before being divided up into occult violence and accurate knowledge, the element of the *pharmakon* is the combat zone between philosophy and its other. An element that is *in itself,* if one can still say so, *undecidable*" (D, p. 138). Even though the Socratic *logos* had already shown itself to be an antidote, a benevolent poison, now that the word *pharmakos* has been woven into the chain exhibited in the first reading, an entirely new face of ontological knowledge, or *logos,* reveals itself. As an antidote, the knowledge of the real nature of things is caught up in the element or medium of the *pharmakon,* which thus also appears as the medium of passage (and possible inversion) of ontological knowledge and its other from which philosophy will be carved out in distinction from and in opposition to the nonphilosophical (the mythological).

At this point we need to remember that Derrida's first reading produced the matrix of Platonism as a purely conceptual, impeccably transparent discourse on eternal truths. The *pharmakon* as the structure of passage and inversion allowed an accounting for the possibility of simple identities (of both words and concepts) and their relations of oppositions. Tying the minimal traits needed both to enable single terms and bring them into a relation of opposition in the play of a single structure, the *pharmakon* demonstrates all the characteristics of a quasi-transcendental structure of intelligibility. It will also be remembered that, as an infrastructural synthesis of such intellectual traits, the *pharmakon* had earlier been compared to the schematism, which in Kant's transcendental philosophy, articulates the conditions under which the sensible and the intelligible enter into a relation. To vouchsafe this communicability, the schema must, in some way, participate in what it is to bring into relation. Yet, as far as the *pharmakon* is concerned, only a participation in the intelligible has been demonstrated hereto. As a medium of passage and inversion of those traits that Platonism must arrest in order to secure its logic of identity and opposition, the matrix accounts indeed for the transparent order of forms and ideas. However, if the analogy with schematism is to remain meaningful, the *pharmakon* must also minimally participate in some realm of the sensible. What does this mean? How could Platonism be said to also have a sensible side?

To answer this question, and to begin the analysis of what the addition of the *pharmakos* to the chain of significations gives to read—in a reading that adds itself to, and adds something to the matrix produced in the first reading—let me return, briefly at least, to Derrida's characterization of the *Phaedrus*. The first point of interest is that the insistance on the dialogue's profound unity—the *symploke* of its so-called philosophical and mythological parts—is the first step in an argument that intimately links philosophy in the shape of the Platonic *logos,* with its other, mythology. Derrida upholds such a unity first because, despite Socrates' declared intention to bar all myth, Plato introduces, in the first, and philosophical, part of the dialogue, no less, the first of the two properly speaking Platonic myths—the myth of the Cicadas, a myth that opens already on the question of writing—before recounting the myth of Theuth in the second part, a myth that Socrates then reappropriates to philosophy. More importantly, by arguing that in developing the two specifically Platonic myths, Plato does not draw on his own spontaneity and fantasy but obeys rigorous necessities deriving from his own work, from Greek language and culture, and from the foreign mythology from which Plato borrowed the figure of Theuth, Derrida discovers the unity in question in a system of constraints that embraces both philosophy and mythology. If "Plato's Pharmacy" lingers on the analogies between Plato's Theuth and other gods of writing such as the Egyptian god Thot, and on the permanent identity traits of the god of writing whatever the pantheon he belongs to, it is primarily to confront "the general problematic of the relations between the mythemes and the philosophemes that lie at the origin of the western *logos.*" Indeed, since Plato is able to accommodate a mythological figure such as Theuth in his philosophical discourse, structural necessities internal to Plato's discourse must make such accommodation feasible, and vice versa. As Derrida remarks, "In the simultaneous insertion, so rigorous and closely fit, of these traits [of the god of writing] into the systematic arrangement of Plato's philosophemes, this meshing of the mythological and the philosophical points to some more deeply buried necessity" (*D,* p. 86). It is one of the main objectives of Derrida's text to show this "deeply buried necessity" that organizes the relations between mythemes and philosophemes in Western thought, that is, "the *philosophical* difference between *mythos* and *logos,*" as well as the exchanges that take place between the two, notwithstanding their profound difference. The point is not to show philosophy to be mythology or mythology, philosophy. As philosophy's other, mythology is rigorously distinct from it, but for the same reason it is intrinsically bound up with it. "Plato's Pharmacy" explores the relations of this difference and complicity with the aim of foregrounding the difference and the commerce between the differents in the matrix that enables the differentiation of *logos* and *mythos*.

Now, let me return to a question left in abeyance. In addition to participating in the realm of intelligibility that Platonism stakes out, the *pharmakon* thus also partakes in the *mythos* from which Platonism must demarcate itself in order to establish its identity but to which it remains inevitably tied. The reading of Plato's text made possible by the insertion of the signification of *pharmakos* into the chain of the other "pharmaceutical" terms is a reading that completes, as it were, the very matrix of Platonism that the first reading had began to produce. Together, the readings accomplish what the reference to transcendental schematism promised, namely, the elaboration of a structure that would allow an understanding of Platonism as a discourse on pure forms and ideas but that achieves this goal only by constantly demarcating itself from its other, from *mythos*. Before clarifying the way in which the additional reading supplements the structure in question, I would like to reintroduce the question of how reading in Derrida differs from mere reading in de Man. The Derridean reading, as we have seen, does not presume that the rhetoricity of Plato's text fatally flaws any attempt to interpret and come to understand it. On the contrary, the way Derrida understands text, that is, as a structure of referral, invites productive readings, readings that not only weave new interpretative threads into it but compose so many rewritings of it as well. Like Derrida, de Man also assumes the referentiality of language, but this referentiality is strictly intralinguistic, and, as I will argue in the following chapter, always saturated by an exact opposite such that only negative knowledge is possible. But even, for de Man, no certainty obtains even to this negative knowledge. For Derrida, by contrast, the very idea of referral excludes its limitation to the play of language itself. In addition, reference is primarily virtual and not restricted to opposite meanings. From the perspective of de Manean mere reading, Derrida's philosophical claim—that is, that an essential, though however subtle, difference obtains between *logos* and *mythos*, concept and metaphor, philosophy and sophistics, even though this difference rests on a constituting commerce between the oppositions—is an aberration. In mere reading, relation to an opposite amounts to undermining all claims to distinctness. Further, in de Man's eyes, the singular sweep of Derrida's reading of the *Phaedrus,* its attempt to construct, in analogy to schematism a matricial grid for Platonism, a reading, therefore, that also demonstrates its philosophical affinities, would be denounced as deeply steeped in aesthetic ideology. For, indeed, the *pharmakon,* as a matrix, must, on the elementary level of the structural passage of traits that polarize *logos* and *mythos,* the intelligible and the sensible, concept and metaphor, etc., presupposes a minimal communication of the differentiated element. The assumption of such a minimal communication, however, is, for de Man, a last hideout of the philosophical illusion of a reconciliation of language and the phenomenal world. Derrida's reading—which is not a transcendental reading but aims at producing a signifying structure—does not illuminate Plato's text by exhibiting novel meanings. But the reading he performs of Plato's text, a reading that consists of producing or writing the matrix of the text—a matrix that furthermore inscribes within itself the possibility of more readings—comes to an understanding, however limited, of Plato.

The *pharmakon,* then, allows for the difference between mythos and logos. However, in its quality as a matrix for both, the *pharmakon* can participate in *mythos* and *logos* only by dint of certain traits that characterize the relation of exclusion between purity and otherness. These traits won't be like the "categorial" or "intellectual" traits that make up the *pharmakon* as a site of passage and inversion. To uphold the analogy with schematism, they must resemble the phenomenal and sensible. In "Plato's Pharmacy," the sensible or phenomenal side of the matrix is shown to be of the order of a scene, or theater. Evoking this other "level of the Platonic reserves," Derrida writes:

> This pharmacy is also . . . a theater. The theatrical cannot here be summed up in speech: it involves forces, space, law, kinship, the human, the divine, death, play, festivity. Hence the new depth that reveals itself to us will necessarily be another scene, on another stage, or rather another tableau in the unfolding of the play of writing. After the presentation of the *pharmakon* to the father, after the put-down of Theuth, Socrates takes the spoken word back to his own account. He seems to want to substitute *logos* for myth, discourse for theater, demonstration for illustration. And yet, within his very explanations, another scene slowly comes to light, less immediately visible than the preceding one, but, in its muffled latency, just as tense, just as violent as the other,

composing with it, within the pharmaceutical enclosure, an artful, living organization of figures, displacements, repetitions. This scene has never been read for what it is, for what is at once sheltered and exposed in its metaphors: its *family* metaphors. It is all about fathers and sons, about bastards unaided by any public assistance, about glorious, legitimate sons, about inheritance, sperm, sterility.   (*D*, pp. 142–143)

In the discursive and argumentative denunciation of writing that follows the mythological scene of Thamous's verdict, Derrida discerns another scene. Derrida's reading first brings into view how the philosophical discourse of Platonism is not simply the transparent discourse of ideas and eternal forms. Having woven one more thread into the chain of significations of Plato's text, Derrida shows that a scene of boundary setting and purification through violent expulsion subtends Socrates' discourse. Although Socrates wishes to replace myth by *logos,* and thus to distinguish the purely conceptual from the mythological, this very attempt in its own way repeats the patterns of myth. Still, this does not say either that philosophy is mythology or that one cannot distinguish between them. The scene exhibited in Derrida's reading is not strictly speaking a myth. But it is formally and structurally similar to the one recounted in the myth of Theuth and Thamous, and, like myth, it is constituted by structural constraints not of the order of the logical. The scene in question consists of a minimal stage or tableau shared between the discourse of philosophy and its other, mythology, in order to be able to make its own decisions, perform its own choices, and thus distinguish itself from its other. This scene—a family scene analyzed by Derrida in great detail—represents the missing link in the *pharmakon* conceived as the matrix of Platonism. It does not consist merely of the simple transparency of a structural law of undecidability. As a matrix of philosophy and its other, it also contains a darker side, a theater scene made up of actions that ensure good reproduction, curb dissemination, and expulse all illegitimate offspring from the family, thus securing its homogeneity with itself. It is a scene in advance of philosophy and mythology as they stand distinct from one another, and in this quality it contains all the traits required that philosophy be philosophy, and in distinction from it, mythology, mythology.

I will not expand on the implications Derrida draws from the presence within the philosophical discourse of a scene that, although not strictly speaking mythological, shares its basic structural constraints. But while this family scene has a constitutive function, it also undermines the status of the self-present father and his *logos,* thus compelling Platonism to constantly seek to master this scene. Further, let me reiterate that Derrida's focus on this scene that Platonism both repeats and represses amounts neither to the dismissal nor the undoing of Platonism. For Derrida, there is no Other to Platonism since only from, and within Platonism arises the thought of the Other.[13] Reading for the matrix of Platonism in the double reading we have witnessed not only comes to grips with Plato but also demonstrates that thinking is thinking only on condition that it sustain the tension between the constituting forces in philosophy and those that tend to annul it. To the question "What does Platonism signify as repetition?" Derrida answers, "Let's repeat: the disappearence of the good-father-capital-sun is . . . the precondition of discourse . . . The disappearance of truth as presence, the withdrawal of the present origin of presence, is the condition of all (manifestation of) truth . . . Differance, the disappearance of any originary presence, is *at once* the condition of possibility *and* the condition of impossibility of truth" (*D,* p. 168). Derrida's reading, a reading that consisted in adding a thread to the web of Plato's text, repeats Platonism by exhibiting the matrix in which the latter is rooted. What this repetition shows is that all being-present, "in its truth, in the presence of its identity and in the identity of its presence, *is doubled* as soon as it appears, as soon as it presents itself. It *appears, in its essence, as* the possibility of its own most proper non-truth." If the absence of any ultimate originary presence is the condition of all identity, presence, truth, etc., it stands to reason that identity, presence, truth, etc., are supplements of, or additions to, what is lacking. Having the structure of supplements, they are prone to being doubled themselves. The being-present, Derrida writes, "is not what it is, identical and identical to itself, unique, unless it *adds to itself* the possibility of being *repeated* as such. And its identity is hollowed out by that addition, withdraws itself in the supplement that presents it" (*D,* p. 168).

Everything that reading Plato's *Phaedrus* has established about identity, presence, and truth also pertains to the text entitled *Phaedrus.* As a discourse, as a linguistic event, and as a unique, seemingly self-identical text, this text in all its positivity rests on the absence of, and ultimate impossibility of a transcendental signified and an authorial, paternal voice. But this absence is a positive chance: Without it there would be no text, discourse, or language. A text must, then, for structural reasons, invite additions to itself and must do this precisely in order to be and remain the self-identical and unique text that it is. It must call readings to be added to it, to interpret and rewrite it. "There is no repetition possible without the *graphics of supplementarity,* which supplies, for the lack of a full unity, another unit that comes to relieve it, being enough the same and enough other so that it can replace by addition" (*D*, p. 168). To read, then, is not only coming to an understanding of the text read by producing, in a double move, its matrix, it is also responding to its call to add a thread to it, and it is thus rewriting it. But this active interpretation, this interpretation that answers the call of the text and that is made for the benefit of the text itself, this interpretation that honors and sustains the identity of the text, can achieve this end only by writing another, and an other text.

6

Adding Oddities

de Man's mere reading is, like reading for Derrida, double. Yet these two brands of double reading differ in important respects: Derrida's analysis of the *Phaedrus* produces the text's infrastructural matrix and hence lays the groundwork for an interpretative supplemental reading of the reasons that, to use de Manean terminology, the text must remain blind to itself. In contrast, de Man's double reading—of the title of Keats's poem, for example—offers no knowledge whatsoever with respect to what it reads. The two proposed readings of the "The Fall of Hyperion" not only conflict with each other by putting both a literal and a figural referent into play but one finds it strictly impossible to decide which of the two referents is correct. This undecidability stems, de Man makes plain, from the fact that the rhetorical mode of the title makes it impossible to establish with any certainty a grammatical referent, and establishing a figural meaning by purely grammatical means is equally out of the question. Reading the title rhetorically—in what de Man refers to as "the rhetorization of grammar"—problematizes any claims that a grammatical reading could possibly make about its referent. But such a reading further prohibits fixing even the figural referent since such fixation is based on a grammatization of rhetoric that overlooks the title's rhetorical mode. In short, then, whatever the mode in which one approaches the title, no referential claim can strictly be made. Clearly, the rhetorization of grammar leaves us empty handed, but the negative knowledge that seems to result from a grammatization of rhetoric is likewise thwarted by the fact that the figural mode of the title cannot be reduced to grammar.[1] Grammar, being an isotope of logic, its claims are referential, and hence cognitive and, even when negative, are inevitably undermined by the rhetorical mode of the title. Mere reading's double reading thus relieves the text of all cognitive function since it is equally impossible to determine any referent, literal or figural, for the title. Mere reading concerns neither a phenomenal referent, nor is it reflexively about itself in that it can neither, with certainty, be said to concern a figural referent. The undecidability against which the double reading of mere reading comes up and which defines it as a rhetorical reading, is final, and it would seem, paralyzing. Indeed, decision is impossible since the double reading of the title has eliminated any possibility of a choice, both referential claims having been definitively voided. All there is, is an oscillation between equally impossible reference claims, which suspends judgment. There is neither escape from, nor solution to, this undecidability lest one take refuge in ideology. *Undecidability* here means the absolute impossibility of decision, for there is nothing to be decided anymore. The options have been voided, and the oscillation precludes the invention of a way out of the dilemma. In contradistinction to Derrida, for whom undecidability is not, finally, a linguistic predicament, de Man's notion of undecidability is rooted in the structures of language, primarily concerning language's referential capability and, consequently, its ability to convey truth. Whereas Derrida conceives the undecidability of the *pharmakon* as a matrix not only of Platonism but of the very possibility of an addition which gives Platonism to read and which thus offers the possibility of coming to an understanding with Plato, undecidability for de Man permits no way out. Whatever might arise from it is irretrievably ideological. If rhetorical reading were understood to yield a negative knowledge and thus to confirm the cognitive and linguistic powerlessness of the human reader, it could then accommodate "an ontology of finite being." But, according to de Man, even a finite subject's negative assurance of blindness is based on an (illegitimate because it is inevitably reductive) grammatization of rhetoric. Any knowledge, even that of the impossibility of knowing, is thus strictly impossible. The unrelieved ignorance caused by the linguistic predicament regarding referentiality thus even subverts conceiving these avatars of language and reading as a function of or appropriate to human finitude.[2] It seems hopeless to expect the play of language to effect any impact on consciousness. Indeed, if language denies all knowledge, including the knowledge of the impossibility of knowing, it is difficult to see in what way, and on what level, it unsettles the subject's security.[3] If, on first sight, the undecidability exhibited in reading amounted to a cognitive paralysis, the fact that such paralysis cannot even be shown to be the proper predicament of a finite consciousness renders its status particularly volatile. As said, this undecidability, unlike Derrida's, is not a medium of decision. It does not set the stage for an interpretative intervention. The complete voiding of all knowledge with respect to the referent of language, including its own (tropological) referentiality, turns language's undecidability, strangely, aloof.

In any event, given that reading provides no certain referential knowledge, a series of questions arises. If a reading in no possible way illuminates the text, what precisely is its relation to the text? Does mere reading's antiaesthetical stand not preempt it from relating to the text in the first place? And further, why read to begin with? And, granted that reading voids all modes of cognition, how do I know that I am performing a reading and not some other activity? Or, in the case that reading could be defined as an objective process, on what basis could a text be said to read itself or another text? Finally, accepting that the pertinence of mere reading cannot be logically justified, why is it more desirable to read than to resist mere reading? Conversely: What must a text be for a mere reading of it, or on its occasion, to get off the ground? What textual qualities necessarily call for a mere reading? And what is a mere reading doing to and for the text when reading? Does it have any significance? In general, for the text, for the reader?

However brief, de Man's reading of the title of Keats's poem has left us an impression of unmistakable rigor and consistency, an impression that will be confirmed by "Anthopomorphism and Trope in the Lyric." Its moves are also rigorously predictable, de Man holds, making predictability a criterion of successful reading.[4] Let us bear in mind that de Man has said a rhetorical reading to be irrefutable if technically correct (*RT*, p. 19). This makes the validity of a mere reading primarily a function of its inner coherence. In other words, if it has been executed in perfect accordance with the technical operations that mere reading as such (according to its concept, one would like to say) demands, its claims are irrefutable. The inner consistency of its predictable operations grounds its correctness, and distinguishes its correctness as entirely technical. As we have seen in Chapter 4, "The Fallout of Reading," mere reading, in all its operations and aspects, derives from de Man's understanding of language. Its technicalities are, in all rigor, nothing but the movements of language itself—as diagnosed by de Man.

But despite this claimed predictability, the reader of de Man's readings of particular texts is often left confused, and even taken aback (at first at least) by the seeming arbitrariness of its single moves and by the textual moments highlighted as evidence. How does this unpredictability square with the claim that rhetorical readings are rigorously predictable? Let me begin by pointing out that the unpredictability in question signals the pragmatism and empiricism of reading. It marks the inevitable arbitrariness of a reading's beginning. I recall that within the context of a notion of deconstruction that attempts to exit from the totality of the logocentric epoch—a notion that *Of Grammatology* still entertained—Derrida remarked that "the first gesture of this departure and this deconstruction, although subject to a certain historical necessity, cannot be given methodological or logical intraorbitary assurances." "Radically empiricist," this departure, he claims, "is affected by nonknowledge as by its future and it *ventures out* deliberately."[5] de Man's readings seem not only to confirm this impossibility of exhaustively accounting for the precise starting point of a reading but to suggest that the totality of its distinct moves are equally arbitrary. And yet in hindsight all the specific operations along with the seemingly arbitrary selection of textual evidence, will have become meaningful. In retrospect, the individual elements and moves appear rigorously predictable, integrated as they now are in the coherent and intricate web of the performed reading. Every element taken from the text and every movemement to which it is subjected will have been assigned a distinctive role in the cohesive fabric of the text read. Differently put, the internal coherence of a reading, the consistency and predictability of what a reading qua reading demands, is what makes the selected textual instances and the particular moves of reading "meaningful."

However, if reading is indeed the independent quality de Man claims it to be, and if its correctness is a function of its internal coherence as a reading, several questions follow. Indeed, given that only retrospectively do all the single reading operations become intelligible, that is, only within the horizon of a technically correct reading, what is the precise relation of such a reading to the texts read? If a reading is correct only if it submits each time to the same predictable operations, in other words, if its validity can be assessed only in its own terms, can it still be shown to relate in a significant manner to what it pretends to read? Does the text's own composition and the internal cohesiveness of its elements and layers make any difference? Does the text not hold any surprises in store for the technically correct reading? Is the singularity of the text of any concern to such a reading? Does a text's dissimulation of its own textuality, and whose principal imperceptibility, according to Derrida, allows for readings that displace, up to a point, this dissimulation, matter at all? Or, on the contrary, does the text embrace such reading with open arms? Is the text transparent to mere reading to the point of offering no resistance to it whatsoever? But if so, is it still possible to distinguish between the text and the text read, that is, the text of a technically correct reading of a particular text? Is the text that is the object of a reading only that text as it is read in a mere reading? In sum, making the correctness of a reading depend on its own immanent rigor imposes a whole host of questions concerning the commensurability of mere reading and the singular text it might reach. Could mere reading in addition to being free of theory not possibly also be free of any preconceptions regarding the specificity of the text? I shall later return to this question.

Granted that readings, if executed in a technically correct fashion, are indeed as irrefutable and obvious as de Man asserts, the next question concerns their specific relation to literature. Is there any intrinsic reason that a conception of reading whose exigencies derive from its own concept and the technicalities of its operation should be, first and foremost, a reading of literature? Can such a reading still afford to prioritize literature, and if so, on what grounds and for what purpose? To outline an answer to this question, let me take up the question in the form de Man has given it in "The Resistance to Theory."

While mere reading is neither a semiological nor a (structural) linguistic reading of text, it is not inappropriate to recall de Man's contention that "the results of the encounter between semiology and literature went considerably further than those of many other theoretical models." Indeed, he even spoke of "the natural attraction of literature to a theory of linguistic signs," and of "the responsiveness of literary texts to semiotic analysis" (*RT,* pp. 8–9). Considering the extent to which the theory of mere reading is indebted to semiology and structural linguistics, de Man's mention of a "natural attraction"—a (symbolist) vocabulary he usually takes pains to avoid—is all the more significant. What this suggests, indeed, is not only the superiority of mere reading over the two linguistic disciplines, not to mention all other approaches, but a flawless compatibility of mere reading and literature. It appears, then, that literature surrenders to mere reading without any reserve. How is this possible? The natural affinity between structural linguistics or semiology and literature stems from the fact that the first are theories of linguistic signs. They consider "language as a system of signs and of signification rather than as an established pattern of meanings" (*RT*, pp. 8–9). One can gather from this that literature is, even more than structural linguistics, exclusively about language, and consequently, that if mere reading is so very compatible with literature, it is because mere reading merely reads the workings of language, and nothing else. But by considering language as a system of signs, structural linguistics and semiology "displace or even suspend the traditional barriers between literary and presumably non-literary uses of language and liberate the corpus from the secular weight of textual canonization" (*RT*, p. 9). In the wake of the structural disciplines, mere reading breaks down the barriers between the literary and the presumably nonliterary, bringing literature down from its traditional height, or what amounts to the same, raising the nonliterary to the status of the literary. From the perspective of structural linguistics and mere reading, literariness, or the workings of language, pertains equally to the literary and the nonliterary. Does it then matter whether or not mere reading takes literature for its object or not? As the following passage reveals, it does, but not absolutely. The literariness of language, or "the rhetorical or tropological dimension of language . . . [is] a dimension which is perhaps more explicitly in the foreground in literature (broadly conceived) than in other verbal manifestations or—to be somewhat less vague—which can be revealed in any verbal event when it is read textually" (*RT*, p. 17). In short, then, the literariness of language is at work in all verbal events. It is not specific to what is traditionally called *literature*. If, nonetheless, literature enjoys a certain privilege for de Man, it is because in it this dimension is (perhaps) more explicitly in the foreground. To bring out the workings of language, it is thus more convenient and economical to read literature rather than so-called nonliterary verbal events. In conclusion, it appears that what counts for mere reading is only reading the workings of language. It is of no essential importance whether literariness is revealed in literary or nonliterary texts, the distinction having been voided beforehand by the linguistic approach. Literature can claim no specificity of any weight (as the modalizer "perhaps" makes more than plain) for what mere reading seeks to achieve.[6] Reading is indeed an independent quantity. Whatever it reads, it is concerned only with the workings of language. But if this can be achieved by reading any linguistic event, is one not to suspect it of performing a suite of operations predicated of language in advance, and which thus become rigorously predictable for all readings? Literature, having been defined as that realm of linguistic events in which language's literality is perhaps more explicitly in the foreground, offers no resistance to such a reading. It is literature and nothing but literature when it gives itself without holding back to a mere reading. But consider this: Precisely because it is nothing but this consenting submission to a rhetorical reading, does not literature "itself" recede at the same time under the web of its reading? Is it not covered up by a reading that inevitably pushes it into unreadability? Successful as the mere reading of literature may be, literature "itself" surrendering in total transparency to such a reading, also resists it infinitely. Like all readings, mere reading fails to read literature "itself." It fails in proportion to its natural affinity with literature and the transparency that it imparts to its object. But what is it of literature that thus resists rhetorical reading, infinitely withdrawing into unreadability, if not literature "itself," that is, the direct and binary correlate of the reading that has dispensed with the specificity of literature itself, the ghost of literature that comes to haunt the lightened premises from which "it" has been expelled?

Let me embark, then, on an analysis of "Anthropomorphism and Trope in the Lyric." Since this text is a model of de Manean reading, I will follow the full course of its progression. The agenda of the essay is triple, at least. de Man's reading of "Correspondances" first seeks to question an interpretation of that poem dominant in literary criticism that makes "transcendental claims . . . for the sonnet" (*RR*, p. 248). Putting the record straight for this one poem is secondly an occasion for de Man to put literary criticism on trial, by showing it to be caught up in a "symbolist ideology of the text" (*RR*, p. 250), that is, to understand the poetic text as a locus of aesthetic and epistemological reconciliation. The last task, but not the least, is to contest not only philosophy's linkage of epistemology with rhetoric but more profoundly, the subtle and surreptitious form such linkage takes where philosophy declares that no such linkage is possible. Since this latter issue frames the preceding ones and provides the distinction between trope and anthropomorphism that will be put to work in the reading of the poem—rather, two poems, "Correspondances" and "Obsession"—it has to be dealt with in some detail beginning with a more precise pinpointing of the stated goal in the discussion of Kant and Nietzsche with which de Man opens the essay.

In spite of their considerable differences, Kant's *Third Critique* and Nietzsche's "On Truth and Lie" are assimilated right from the beginnning as congruous projects on the basis that all critical philosophies including Nietzsche's text—a "late Kantian text," de Man states a bit hastily—and "Romantic" literatures, are involved in the same gesture of linking "epistemology with rhetoric in general." The main tenet of both, he adds, is "the continuity of aesthetic with rational judgment" (*RR*, p. 239), respectively, "their common stake in the recovery of controlled discourse on the far side of even the sharpest denials of intuitive sense-certainties" (*RR*, p. 240). According to de Man, Kant's treaty on aesthetic judgment and Nietzsche's claim in his text that truth is an army of tropes are both examples of the postulated "continuity of aesthetic with rational judgement." It is far from clear what de Man means by the linkage of epistemology and rhetoric, or, respectively, the continuity of aesthetic with rational judgment. It is equally unclear how one is to take the relation between the two gestures. If I understand correctly, linking aesthetic judgments, that is, judgments of taste, with rational judgments, that is, theoretical, or cognitive judgments, asserts a continuity between these two realms and indulges in epistemology. It is de Man's thesis that critical philosophy and Romantic literature achieve this link via language, hence linking epistemology and rhetoric. I recall that in *Critique of Judgement* Kant established that when pure, that is, free of merely sensual, or moral considerations, the estimation that something is beautiful or sublime, an estimation in which nothing is cognized about the object itself, is nonetheless a judgment, one that can make universality claims. In short, even though Kant denies that judgments of taste are cognitive, conceiving them as judgments in the first place, in de Man's eyes, establishes a continuity between the aesthetic and the cognitive, regaining epistemological control over what had been declared immune from all certainty. de Man, however, fails to show where rhetoric comes in in asserting the continuity in question. But what about Nietzsche? Why should, in answer to the question "What is Truth?" Nietzsche's judgment that truth is an army of tropes—a judgment that unmistakably links what have been called "epistemology" and "rhetoric"—also promote a continuity between aesthetic and rational judgment? The judgment that truth is in truth nothing but tropological displacement is a judgment that, while denying certainty to truth, establishes this in truth, and thus reasserts certainty. But where is the continuity between aesthetic and rational judgment in this case? In answer to this question, de Man suggests that since later in the essay, Nietzsche, in order to demonstrate that concept (truth) and figure (trope) are asymmetrical, dramatizes this problematic "in the specular destinies of the artist and the scientist-philosopher" (*RR*, p. 239), trope implies art. Tropological displacement thus comes into line with the aesthetic. In any event, and whatever the remaining vagaries are, let me stress that de Man maintains no interest *per se* in the critical schemes that deny certainty—for his reading of Nietzsche this means that the tropes to which truth is assimilated are not his prime concern—but rather in patterns that disrupt these schemes themselves and that are distinct from the schemes in question. "What interests us primarily in the poetic and philosophical versions of this transaction, in this give-and-take between reason and imagination, is not, at this point, the critical schemes that deny certainty considered in themselves, but their disruption by patterns that cannot be reassimilated to these schemes, but that are nevertheless, if not produced, then at least brought into focus by the distortions the disruption inflicts upon them" (*RR*, pp. 239–240). What are these patterns that interrupt the reappropriation of the denial of certainty, that is, the triumph of reason over the failure of reason?

In Nietzsche's sentence "What therefore is truth? A mobile army of metaphors, metonymies, anthropomorphisms . . .,"[7] "the recovery of knowledge by ways of its devalorization in the deviance of the tropes is challenged, even at this moment of triumph for a critical reason which dares to ask and reply to the question: what is truth?", de Man writes (*RR*, p. 240). To begin with, let me point out that de Man's analysis of the sentence is based on a truncated version of the original. It is particularly remarkable that Nietzsche's long, winding sentence has been cut off at the precise point where he characterizes metaphor, metonymy, and anthropomorphism as "in short a sum of human relations."[8] In severing this significant part of Nietzsche's sentence, de Man also silences the thrust of the whole essay in which Nietzsche explicitly states that truth is "anthropomorphic through and through."[9] With this, the polarization of trope and anthropomorphism so crucial to de Man's attempt to limn a challenge to the recovery of knowledge that takes place despite the devalorization of truth is simply misbegotten. If I do not nonetheless abandon the thread of de Man's argument, it is because I think that this argument operates on a level on which philological faithfulness to the phenomenality of the text must make way for faithfulness to what de Man believes structures of language itself to be.

Where, then, is this challenge to the recovery of knowledge to be located? de Man first makes the point that "the listing of particular tropes is odd, all the more so since it is technically more precise than is often the case in such arguments." Odd, in this rather odd argument, would be the fact that Nietzsche names two (since the third isn't really one) distinct tropes rather than simply writing that truth is an army of tropes! Technical precision (in distinguishing only two, and moreover, the most basic tropes?) of this kind, is unusual, de Man suggests, and could occur only "under the pen of a classical philologist such as Nietzsche." In other words, and this is where the weight of the argument lies, since Nietzsche happened to be a philologist, that is, one who pays attention to the fact of language, a pattern irreducible to philosophy must have crept into his triumphant definition of truth.[10] This also provides the rationale for de Man's statement that because "opportunities to encounter technical tropological terms are so sparse in literary and philosophical writing . . . one can be excused for making the most of it when they occur," even if Nietzsche is "just [being] casual in his terminology" (*RR*, pp. 240–241). Indeed, the more casual Nietzsche the philosopher might have been, the more reason for de Man to pay close attention to chance occurrences prompted by Nietzsche the philologist that have the potential to bring philosophical reason to a fall—casual stems from *casualis, casus*, fall—at the hands of language. Now, the list of tropes is not only odd because it contains precise tropological terms, but especially because "the third term, anthropomorphism, is no longer a philological and neutral term" (*RR*, p. 240). Even though Nietzsche may have been nonchalant in the use of his terminology, the introduction of this third term catches de Man's attention because its presence in an enumeration to which it "adds little," if not nothing at all, seems odd. Neither a tropological term, nor a complement or synthesis of metaphor and metonymy, it comes indeed to interrupt the technically correct enumeration of the two previous terms. But this is not yet all.

Following up on his declared intention to make the most of the technical tropological terms of Nietzsche's sentence, de Man writes: "The definition of truth as a collection . . . of tropes is a purely structural definition, devoid of any normative emphasis; it implies that truth is relational . . . allowing for an answer to a definitional question . . . that is not purely tautological. At this point, to say that truth is a trope is to say that truth is the possibility of stating a proposition . . . truth is the possibility of definition by means of infinitely varied sets of propositions" (*RR*, p. 241). It must be remembered that rather than looking at the schemes themselves that deny certainty, de Man intends to consider only the patterns that thwart the philosophical reappropriation of that loss of certainty. Obviously, by calling truth an "army of tropes," Nietzsche thought to deny it any intrinsic certainty. Abstracting from the critical schemes themselves, de Man shifts to a level of Nietzsche's sentence that can be shown to effect the reappropriation of certainty notwithstanding the declared loss (and which thus in a second move, can be shown to fail). The "purely" grammatical reading of Nietzsche's sentence ignores not only Nietzsche's reference to several tropes—his talk of an army, or collection, of tropes justifies de Man in abstracting from the precise nature of the tropes in question—but the normative connotations of *trope,* in general, not to speak of its possible technical meanings. This grammatical reading is intended to demonstrate that grammar—and, here, a reference to Nietzsche's statement in *Zarathoustra* that grammar is the metaphysics of the people is evident—reasserts and reaffirms certainty even where certainty is most radically negated. Let me then retrace the main moves of this grammatical analysis as concisely as possible. First this: I assume de Man to mean by "a purely structural definition" of truth a definition of only the structure of truth. Truth understood as a swarm of tropes highlights its relationality: It is about something, and it is about this something in a propositional mode, thus allowing for a definition of this something. *Trope,* in such a reading, is merely a predicate in a proposition that satisfies a demand for definition and cognition (of truth, for instance). As something affirmed of a subject (truth), trope is at best an expression of it, hence intrinsically relational. Defined as an army of tropes, truth thus is said to be about something. When read grammatically, this sentence of Nietzsche, which denies certainty to truth, says that truth is the possibility of making propositions about things. It thus reasserts in its grammatical mode the continuity between words and things that it denies on its semantic level. No wonder then that de Man is lead to conclude: "This assertion is purely descriptive of an unchallenged grammatical possibility and, as such, it has no critical thrust, nor does it claim to have one: there is nothing inherently disruptive in the assertion that truth is a trope" (*RR*, p. 241).

On what basis is it possible to proceed to the abstraction requisite to this argument about grammar? How might one evaluate a method of analysis in which a philosophical insight into the status of the copula translates into a seemingly scientific technology of reading? Once isolated in purity, what is the precise relation of the utterly abstract and general truth about grammar, a truth that could have been extrapolated from just any proposition, to Nietzsche's singular sentence? Is its generality different from that of an idea, or conception, of language? And if this unchallengeable affirmation of certainty inscribed in the grammatical articulation of just any sentence is, indeed, an idea of language, and not something at work in precisely this singular Nietzschean sentence, must not what supposedly challenges Nietzsche's affirmation be something equally ideal and conceptual? Is Nietzsche's sentence then merely the stage for a battle between two generalized, if not allegorized aspects of language, a battle of giants indiscriminately fought on the occasion of any linguistic manifestation? If, indeed, the patterns of disruption presuppose and operate on the level of ontologically hypostatized attributes of language itself—I recall again de Man expressed no interest in the critical schemes themselves that would deny certainty—the level of a de Manean deconstructive reading is, one can presume, quite different from the quasi-transcendental order of the cluster of virtual traits of reference that makes up an infrastructure such as the *pharmakon*. In any case, grammar's intrinsic assertion of certainty that not even the claim of truth's tropological nature could challenge, a certainty that operates on a level entirely distinct from what by such a claim affirms, will not go unchallenged. The grammatical certainty reposed on a reading of Nietzsche's sentence that (in a movement of abstraction) understood the "metaphors, metonymies, anthropomorphisms" to be an indiscriminate collection of tropes functioning as the predicate of the subject "truth."

"But 'anthropomorphism' is not just a trope but an identification on the level of substance," de Man goes on. Trope, as the predicate of "a purely structural definition" of truth, had been understood in equally structural terms (as a relating expression). Thinking in polarities, de Man has no choice but to define the distinguishing trait of "anthropomorphism" in terms of substance. Drawing on the binary opposite of the term of *structure,* previously introduced in the characterization of the grammatical understanding of trope, de Man sets the stage for a critical disruption of grammar's unchallenged certainty. Here structure and substance are the first protagonists. Anthropomorphism, de Man explains, "takes one entity for another and thus implies the constitution of specific entities prior to their confusion, the *taking* of something for something else that can then be assumed to be *given.* Anthropomorphism freezes the infinite chain of tropological transformations and propositions into one single assertion or essence which, as such, excludes all others. It is no longer a proposition but a proper name" (*RR*, p. 241). In contradistinction to the in principle infinite substitutability of trope, anthropomorphism arrests substitution by identifying a specific, and final essence, or substance, to which all substitutions refer. In other words, it produces an interpretation of the chain of substitutions and brings substitution to a stop. Anthropomorphism takes substitutability to be evidence for the prior giveness of one single substance. Or, rather, in anthropomorphism, one thing is taken for another in order to be able to assume the giveness of an ultimate referent. The proper name is, for de Man, the linguistic index of an assertion of a (extralinguistic) given that brings substitution to a halt.[11] Whereas tropes lend themselves to infinite transformations and propositions, anthropomorphism suggests the punctuality of a single name. Trope and anthropomorphism relate to one another not only like structure and substance but as proposition and name as well. These being exclusive relations, Nietzsche's "apparent enumeration," his terminology casual or not, shuts itself down. "The apparent enumeration is in fact a foreclosure which acquires, by the same token, considerable power," de Man asserts (*RR,* p. 241). Supposing that the binary grid of structure and substance, proposition and name, is not a simple expedient but can serve to accurately describe the difference between metaphor and metonymy, on the one hand, and anthropomorphisms, on the other, then, indeed, what looked like an enumeration is in truth a division. With this, not only is the certainty concurrent with grammar put into question by the fact that the enumeration is not a homogeneous collection of tropes but the pattern that disrupts it is itself divided in such a way that any assuring synthesis based on reciprocity is no longer possible.

To judge that truth is an army of metaphors, metonymies, and anthropomorphisms is to define it "by two incompatible assertions: either truth is a set of propositions or truth is a proper name." Even though "one reads Nietzsche's sentence without any sense of disruption"—Nietzsche's statement that metaphors and anthropomorphisms alike are human relations, hence anthropomorphic, would then testify to Nietzsche's inability to read his own sentence—de Man will sharpen the difference between them to an extreme. First, he recognizes that, on the one hand, "the tendency to move from tropes to systems of interpretations such as anthropomorphism is built into the very notion of trope." As already seen, "tropes are the producers of ideologies." But de Man reaffirms the difference between tropes and anthropomorphisms when he writes that, on the other hand, "an anthropomorphism is structured like a trope." The difference has thus been deepened since the reciprocal passage between trope and anthropomorphism, rather than promising a sublating synthesis of the difference, exacerbates it. There is an asymmetrical relation between them. de Man writes: "It is easy enough to cross the barrier that leads from trope to name but impossible, once this barrier has been crossed, to return from it to the starting-point in 'truth'" (*RR*, pp. 241–242). Once truth, although a trope, has turned anthropomorphic, the way of return is cut off. From the realm of the nontrue, no way leads back to truth. This pattern, disruptive to the point of nonrecovery of the certainty concomitant with grammar, is a function of a stated asymmetrical distinction between trope and anthropomorphism independent of Nietzsche's determination of both as human relations. On what level does the pattern work? Let it be remembered that the unchallenged certainty that was shown to come with a purely grammatical form of the sentence depended on a radical abstraction of all content. The difference between trope and anthropomorphism that de Man argues for in abstraction from Nietzsche's statement to the contrary is a distinction made on a purely subject (matter)–related level of trope and anthropomorphism. In spite of what Nietzsche means and says, trope and anthropomorphism, properly speaking, are not the same thing. Is the pattern then that disrupts the critical schemes' surreptitious reaffirmation of certainty made up of material differences tied to the "things" listed in Nietzsche's statement, and which remain in force whether or not Nietzsche takes them into account? Does a material difference in effect, whatever the context may be, disrupt the abstract idea of linguistic truth that has been extrapolated from a purely grammatical reading? Trope and/or anthropomorphism do not themselves deconstruct linguistic truth but rather the material difference between the two, and what is deconstructed is not the grammar *of* Nietzsche's singular sentence but the ideal relation that grammar implicitly presupposes as such.[12]

Motivated, undoubtedly, by the hint of a disruption of truth, de Man continues as follows: "Hence the 'army' metaphor. Truth, says Nietzsche, is a mobile *army* of tropes. Mobility is coextensive with any trope, but the connotations introduced by 'army' are not so obvious, for to say that truth is an army (of tropes) is again to say something odd and possibly misleading" (*RR*, p. 242). First, it must be noted that "army" (*Heer*) is here understood figurally. As in "an army of journalists," it has the meaning of swarm, host, large number, multitude, or as de Man already pointed out, of collection. But since *Heer* has the literal meaning of *army*, and since, according to Derrida, for one, a word entertains relations to other possible meanings that it can eventually have, one is, of course, entirely justified in following up on these references. But whereas for Derrida, these references are virtual, for de Man they seem to be actual. Only because the meaning of *army* is thought to be fully present in the word *Heer* can he hold it to be odd to say that truth is an army of tropes. What does this oddity—which as such is symptomatic of a disruption— consist of? Taking it for granted that the meaning of *army* is in act and in fact present in the word *Heer* in Nietzsche's sentence, to what does it add up?[13] De Man writes: "Tropes are neither true nor false. To call them [but Nietzsche also speaks of anthropomorphisms!] an army is however to imply that their effect and their effectiveness is not a matter of judgment but of power" (*RR*, p. 242), of "sheer blind violence," he says later in the text (*RR*, p. 262). Why precisely does de Man single out this one particular connotation of *army*—an *organized* body, a body of *armed* men under *one command*, a *trained* body of men—among the various other possible ones? Certainly, in *Truth and Lie*, Nietzsche refers on one occasion, at least, to war. And yet, de Man's selection of "power" to characterize *army* is not motivated by textual considerations. It is exclusively a function of the logic of binary polarization that propels his argumentation. "Power," indeed, permits the additional division and polarization of truth required to complete an argument that follows its own logic. But why "power"? Why does it do the job? As de Man notes, "one willingly admits that truth has power, including the power to occur." The power in question is that of truth in its epistemological determination. Since one willingly concedes that much, this means that power is an obvious attribute of truth, a natural connotation that, mentioned or not, also accompanies Nietzsche's concept. Yet there is power and power. "What characterizes a good army, as distinct for instance from a good cause, is that its success has little to do with immanent justice and a great deal with the proper economic use of its power," de Man writes. Power, here, is the opposite of the good power of truth. It is not of the order of judgment that requires discerning reason. Devoid of justice, and distinct from the good, its effectiveness proceeds by way of mindless, if not arbitrary, overpowering. Thus de Man can conclude:

> To say that [truth's] power is like that of an army and to say this within the definitional context of the question: what is therefore truth? is truly disruptive. It not only asserts that truth (which was already complicated by having to be a proposition as well as a proper name) is also a power, but a power that exists independently of epistemological determinations, although these determinations are far from being nonexistent: calling truth an army *of tropes* reaffirms its epistemological *as well as* its strategic power. How the two modes of power could exist side by side certainly baffles the mind, if not the grammar, of Nietzsche's tale. (*RR*, pp. 242–243)

In addition to being irreconcilably split between its determinations as proposition and name, truth now appears also to be helplessly divided into two incommensurable powers. The double genitive in "army *of tropes*" not only serves as further evidence for an epistemological and a strategic power but also to argue for the complete independence of the latter from the former. In the position of a subject, the tropes are in control of truth. It has become an army at their service, seeking gains that are entirely different from truth's epistemological goals. The two heterogeneous powers further disrupt the previously unchallenged grammatical certainty that prevailed in even the most thorough devalorization of truth that had already been challenged by the difference of proposition and name. Recovery of the lost certainty is no longer possible. The damage to grammar is irreversible.

Let me pause here to reflect once again on the nature and level of the argument about the two powers as laid out here. It comprises at least three distinct, but interrelated, moments. First, de Man proceeds on the assumption that the literal sense of *Heer* as army is actually present in the word itself and selects among all the possible connotations of *army,* the one connotation of *power.* Second, on the basis that power is an evident, and universal, attribute of truth in its epistemological sense, he opposes to this "good" power the purely strategic power of the tropes. Third, in a grammatical reading of the double genitive, he asserts the complete autonomy of the strategic power from truth's epistemological power, thus suggesting an unbreachable divide between the two powers in question. The first two operations reveal what could be called a "compulsion to polarize": If Nietzsche's sentence contains a figural meaning of *Heer,* a literal meaning must be opposed to it, and if it can be assumed that truth in the epistemological sense is universally recognized as a good power, a power different from it needs to be brought into play. The assumption at work here is not only that each single linguistic entity refers to other possible uses of it but that such referral is actually fulfilled or saturated (and not, merely, virtual) and this, moreover, by its exact opposite. To come up with the bipolar opposites to the meanings that make an act of presence in Nietzsche's text (or are asssumed to do so), de Man draws on the resources of (a) language in general, respectively, on representations about truth taken to be universal. What these assumptions seem to hint at is that de Man's reading of Nietzsche's sentence is not only a function of a conception of language (and representation) in general but that reading it is only a pretext to actualize the general problematic of a language conceived of as a global internet of bipolarly paired linguistic entities that are at all moments actually present. But, as the third moment at work in his analysis demonstrates, the opposites that are joined in these bipolar pairs are thoroughly independent of one another with the effect that the pairs of signifiers that make up language become as many instances of abyssal division. What is thus present in language are bipolarly disjoined entities, or linguistic atoms.

Before further commenting on de Man's triple operation, the last point of its three movements needs further elaboration. Asking how the two modes of power (but the definitions of truth as proposition and name as well) could coexist in Nietzsche's sentence, de Man remarks that such a coexistence baffles the mind. The mind is not only bewildered, confused, confounded by this disrupting coexistence, it is also divided by what does not let itself be gathered into a unity. "To baffle," a word de Man uses frequently, also means "to check or break the force or flow of by or as if by a baffle," a *baffle* being "a device (as a plate, wall, or screen) to deflect, check, or regulate flow (as of a fluid or light)," or a partition "to impede the exchange of sound waves between the front and back of a loudspeaker."[14] As a result of the dominating pressure to binarize, "side-by-side" existence must immediately call upon division. But if the two powers in conflict in Nietzsche's statement about truth also destroy the mind's comprehension by driving partitioning baffles between its mental powers, thus preventing communication between them, they also baffle the mind because their play does not affect it. Solid baffles between it and the powers in question prevent all communication.

Returning to the opening question of the essay regarding critical philosophy's and Romantic literature's marriage of epistemology and rhetoric, de Man now writes: "The sentence that asserts the complicity of epistemology and rhetoric, of truth and trope, also turns this alliance into a battle made all the more dubious by the fact that the adversaries may not even have the opportunity ever to encounter each other" (*RR*, p. 243). de Man's analysis of the fragment of Nietzsche's sentence served to demonstrate that the claimed continuity between truth and trope is hopelessly disrupted by two pairs of incongruous determinations of truth (and trope). But after having shown the complete independence of strategic power from the good epistemological power, de Man has also erected baffles that divide the space in which the battle supposedly rages. The absence of a relation between what is bipolarly paired not only makes battle between them dubious—the adversaries not even having a chance to meet—but affiliation is likewise disrupted, and even more radically than if the battle had been able to get underway. Rather than an example of the desired alliance between epistemology and rhetoric, Nietzsche's sentence will thus have proven that there is only discontinuity, a division so deep that nothing relates to anything so that even the possibility of battle, like that of peace, becomes disabled.

This completes de Man's reading of Nietzsche's sentence. It is a reading driven by the inner constraints of reading and as rigorous as the reading of the title of Keats's poem. From a formal point of view, the operations that make up these readings are identical. The question as to whether de Man's reading encounters the text it reads must therefore be posed again. Does what it constructs in its reading, which demonstrates the workings of language, affect the language of Nietzsche's sentence at all? Can one say that the reading adds anything to Nietzsche's text, an insight, for example, that might allow one to come to an understanding with

Nietzsche? Even though de Man's reading does not actively interpret Nietzsche's text, unlike Derrida's reading of Plato, it would be presumptuous to conclude no relation between Nietzsche's sentence and its de Manean reading. To denounce such a reading as only arbitrarily relating to the text or merely plundering it for purposes foreign to the text would be equally misleading. The way de Man's readings relate to texts can hardly be conceptualized in the usual ways in which one thinks of such relations, one reason being that *text* is no longer understood in its conventional sense. Before any evaluation of what reading does or does not do to the texts it reads, *text* has first and foremost to be thought in de Man's own terms. In other words, the relation in question must be seen as a disjunction. Indeed, the exposition in de Man's reading of the intricate web of relations that invalidates all possible claims of Nietzsche's judgment and that shows language at work not only takes off from Nietzsche's sentence but relates to it by being entirely in excess of it. It relates to it by not encountering it. The heterogeneity between them is first that of the general and the singular, of the general concept of language expounded in the reading and Nietzsche's singular sentence. Yet this in no way suggests that the reading of Nietzsche's sentence is simply a case subsumed under a general conception of language. From the perspective of a reading bent on enacting and reenacting language, language's singular occurrences are as many instances of language's deconstructive power. Following de Man's imagery, one could say that the particular linguistic events keep on falling. They are cases *of* language, not in the sense of exemplars but in the sense that they quicken the falling of language. In falling, they demonstrate that language is a general falling, a falling in which not even this generality is to be spared. It too falls headlong. Would this then mean that questions as to reading's pertinence are ill conceived? Have they become null and void?

A systematic comparison of de Man's readings of "Correspondances" and "Obsession" with these poems "themselves" and their scholarship would undoubtedly bring us closer to understanding the precise import of a rhetorical reading. Reasons of economy, however, prohibit such an exercise. I will thus limit myself to a further analysis of the immanent "logic" of de Man's reading itself. By calling "Correspondances" a "canonical and programmatic sonnet," de Man makes clear the stakes of his reading. It is a poem, he notes, that has provoked innumerable commentaries. Moreover, its oracular nature has made it the object of all sorts of questions that it "has never failed to answer to the satisfaction of the questioner" (*RR*, p. 244). One can assume that the programmatic status the poem enjoys has to do with its declarative nature: "Not a simple negation, interrogation, or exclamation, not a single verb that is not in the present indicative, nothing but straightforward affirmation," de Man contends. It is throughly objective, "all assurance and all answer." Indeed, given that the poem can pretend to have accomplished its program—bringing together and harmonizing "corps" and "esprit" (*RR*, p. 245)—no question haunts or disturbs its smooth surface. Why choose then a poem as serene, as seamless, as "'Correspondances' to explicate the quandaries of language as truth, as name, and as power" (*RR*, p. 243)?

But de Man has not yet finished describing the smoothness of the poem. In terms of both form and content, it is a sheer success. Of its form de Man writes:

> The serenity of the diction celebrates the powers of tropes or "symboles" that can reduce any conceivable difference to a set of polarities and combine them in an endless play of substitution and amalgamation, extending from the level of signification to that of the signifier. Here, as in Nietzsche's text, the telos of the substitutions is the unified system "esprit/sens" . . . the seamless articulation, by ways of language, of sensory and aesthetic experience with the intellectual assurance of affirmation. Both echo each other in the controlled compression of a brief and highly formalized sonnet.   (*RR*, p. 244)

"Correspondances" is thus a formal masterpiece that controls difference on all relevant levels through a bipolar and symmetrical pairing that prevents any of the poles from becoming independent and hence a threat to the inner unity and the harmonious exchange of the signifiers within the poem. And it is the power of the tropes (or symbols) that achieves such a feat. Baudelaire's formal polishing of the endless play of linguistic substitution and amalgamation in the poem makes it successful in solving what de Man had called "the major crux of all critical philosophies and 'Romantic' literatures," namely, at securing "the continuity of aesthetic with rational judgement" (*RR*, p. 239). "Correspondances" is a poem in which the linguistic tropes have seamlessly interwoven the sensual with the intellectual faculties. Hence the poem's assertive nature and its ability to provide answers without end. In this poem epistemology and rhetoric are of a piece.

On the thematic level, "Correspondances" is successful at juxtaposing, with no hint of paradox, themes of incompatible meanings: the vastness of the night—which de Man deems to mean "sensory diffuseness"—fuses with the vastness of light interpreted as the intellect's power of analytical precision in a dialectic bent at producing cognitive judgments. The thematic success is such that even the verb chosen for the fusion of the spirit and the senses condenses, in its semantic ambiguity, the modes of gathering characteristic to both the spirit and the senses: The verb "se confondent," de Man notes, "can designate the bad infinity of [sensory] confusion as well as the fusion of opposites into synthetic judgments" (*RR*, p. 245).

Finally, on its discursive level the poem is no less accomplished. The "the text's entire program" of bringing together and harmonizing "corps" and "esprit" is manifest on this last level in the "self-consciously verbal" way in which the senses and the mind are shown to embrace one another. Not only is the poem aware of the fundamental mediating role that language plays in the production of the harmony of the senses and the intellect, the poem is also intensely aware of the fact that the division to be overcome traverses language itself.[15] It is through a dramatization of events of discourse (like "the couple 'se confondent/se répondent'"), and anagrammatic condensation (such as in the title "Correspondances" in which "corps' and "esprit" are tied together by means the *ance* of assonance that reverberates through the tercets), that the poem manages to bridge the disjunction on the level of language itself between sensory confusion and intellectual differentiation.

Unlike Nietzsche's sentence—which de Man deconstructed in no time—Baudelaire's sonnet, which, to all appearances, succeeds on all levels in bringing about a synthesis of aesthetic and rational judgment, and even seems to neutralize the disjunctive power of language, promises to become a real challenge for deconstruction. The formidable achievement of the sonnet is no doubt indicative of a certain superiority of literature over the philosophy of even a classical philologist. As it would seem, (Romantic) literature has at its disposal more powerful means than philosophy to achieve solutions to the dilemma of (critical) philosophy, that is, to link epistemology with rhetoric. A deconstructive reading of "Correspondances" is therefore highly charged. In light of the poem's extraordinary linguistic feat, any rhetorical reading capable of coming to grips with it should be able to exhibit the disruptive power of language in ways significantly more refined and more perverse than is the case with texts of philosophy. Such a reading would also dispense not only with critical (and Idealist) philosophy but with literature under its Romantic appearances.[16] Later in the text de Man brashly calls the reconciliation of aesthetic and rational judgment a "philosophical phantasm" (*RR*, p. 258). Romantic literature, according de Man, pursues the same philosophical delusion but with seemingly greater success. A reading capable of deconstructing Baudelaire's poem and its program would thus dispense not only with philosophy but with Romantic literature as well, and this in the name of neither philosophy nor literature but rather, I would say, in the name of (a "philosophy" of) language.

When discussing the formal level of "Correspondances," de Man had accented Nietzsche's and Baudelaire's common goal of realizing a harmony of the spirit and the senses. He had further emphasized that this common goal could be achieved only by means of the substituting power of the tropes. Following elaborations on the discursive level of the poem, de Man remarks that "the assertion, or representation, of verbality" on this precise level of the sonnet "also coincides, as in Nietzsche's text, with the passage from tropes—here the substitution of one sense experience by another—to anthropomorphism." To support this contention, de Man notes the fact that the various sense experiences are said to "se répondent" and that the living pillars of the temple of nature produce "de confuses *paroles*" (*RR*, p. 245). Might the tropological substitition on which the whole program of the poem rests be put at odds, in a way similar to that within Nietzsche's sentence, by an arresting anthropomorphization that creeps into the poem at the precise moment it seeks to control the role that language plays in the sought for synthesis? Does what looks like a reference to human verbality disrupt from within and scatter the intended unity of the spirit and the senses beyond all recuperation? In contrast to the dominant tradition of interpretation of this poem, which stresses in what de Man calls "a perhaps overhasty reading" (*RR*, p. 245) the anthropomorphic aspects of nature in the poem, de Man will cast doubt on such an interpretation. In other words, de Man's strategy would seem to make Baudelaire's poem even more triumphant in securing the unity of the senses and spirit. It would have achieved what Nietzsche's sentence couldn't, namely, warding off the disrupting effect of anthropomorphism on the tropological chain. Differently put, "Correspondances" would then be the flawless completion of the aesthetic project, a bulwark, as it were, against any critique or challenge. But is it so simple? Let me first establish how, in what amounts to a critique of the assertion of anthropomorphism, de Man takes the poem's side against the leading trend in Baudelaire scholarhip without, however, rejecting the possibility of anthropomorphism out of hand.

de Man admits that the sonnet's "opening lines allow but certainly do not impose such a [anthropomorphizing] reading" (*RR*, p. 246). What suggests that an anthropomorphic interpretation is not entirely aberrant is that a purely tropological interpretation of the beginning of the poem might encounter difficulties. What they are have as yet to be explained. de Man hints only at a supposedly enigmatic nature of the first line. "'La Nature est un temple' is enigmatic enough to constitute the burden of any attempt at understanding and cannot simply be reduced to a pattern of binary substitution" (*RR*, p. 246). But the difficulties of understanding the opening line tropologically should not suggest that an anthropomorphic reading of the poem—on the occasion of "vivant pilliers," for example—might be any less problematic. While in itself "vivant pilliers" intimates the human being's erect stature, in the poem the anthropomorphic essence of nature and of its woods of living pillars is suggested only by "des *forêts* de symboles." But, de Man remarks, since the forest is one of "symboles" (that is, tropes), such a reading "is by no means compelling." Further, it is not at all certain that Baudelaire's "forest" belongs to nature. Indeed, if with Baudelaire one may never have left the world of the humans, the city, and its crowds in which he had a persistent and dominating interest, it is always possible that nature, in the text's figuration, may have no relation to the "sylvan world." And if there might be nothing to anthropomorphize in the first place, it could be entirely irrelevant to speak of anthropomorphism at all, de Man argues. He concludes: "Perhaps we are not in the country at all but have never left the city . . . 'Symboles' in 'des forêts de symboles' could then designate the verbal, the rhetorical dimension within which we constantly dwell . . . That the possibility of this reading seems farfetched and, in my experience, never fails to elicit resistance, or that the forest/temple cliché should have forced itself so emphatically upon the attention of the commentators is one of the cruxes of 'Correspondances'" (*RR*, pp. 246–247). Even though de Man has thrown the traditional anthropomorphizing reading (on the basis of the "forest/temple cliché") into doubt, he will not simply declare in favor of his alternative, farfetched reading that would treat the poem right away as a poem on language to be read tropologically. At this point de Man wishes only to emphasize that this uncertainty is one of the difficulties and unresolved questions of the poem itself. The crux consists not in a difficulty of deciding one way or the other, but in that the poem itself both forces an anthropomorphic reading upon its commentators and elicits their resistance against reading it rhetorically. This conundrum is so pronounced that it has even forced an anthropomorphic reading of itself on its first reader, Baudelaire, de Man explains, gesturing toward the poem "Obsession" to which he will turn later. What, then, so forcefully provokes a reading of this sonnet for which there is, it seems, no real textual evidence and hence no compelling reason? Nonetheless, let us bear in mind de Man's suggestion that notwithstanding the lack of good reason, the poem certainly allows for an anthropomorphic reading: "The possibility of anthropomorphic (mis)reading is part of the text and part of what is at stake in it. Anthropomorphism seems to be the illusionary resuscitation of the natural breath of language, frozen into stone by the semantic power of the trope. It is a figural affirmation that claims to overcome the deadly negative power invested in the figure" (*RR*, p. 247). In short, an anthropormorphic (mis)reading does not violate the text. The text makes it possible, invites it, and is part of what is at stake in it. What is the status of this possibility? Given the unquestioned success of the poem in manifesting by means of purely tropological ways the conjunction of body and spirit, where, why, and how does this possibility (that after all is not truly a necessity) arise? The definition of *anthropomorphism* given in the context of these questions might provide us with a clue. Anthropomorphism, de Man claims, seems to be an attempt to reclaim language for the human. In the text the semantic power of the trope and its ability to infinitely engender substitutes have been so effective that, to pick up de Man's imagery, language's suspendedness from the human breath in *parole* and from the meanings that the human beings have bestowed on it has been cut off, frozen into stone. This is an image for the autonomous potential of language, for the mechanical unfolding of tropological substition. The temple in "Correspondances," a mere construct of stone, de Man holds, is "the icon of this central trope" of "the deadly negative power" of language in which the natural breath of language is dehumanized. Anthropomorphism then would be an inevitable but also desperate attempt to bring language back to life, to restore its human breath, to make it again a *parole,* by rendering it intelligible and meaningful once again. It is now clear whence the possibility of anthropomorphism arises. It is the tropological success of the poem that invites such a reading to counter the deadly, negative power of its purely tropological substitution. It represents the effort to save the striven for unity of spirit and sense from turning into a senseless construct of stone with no link to human concerns. In a strange way, anthropomorphism could be a necessary ingredient of the project itself, notwithstanding its interruption of the tropological chain on which the latter is based. But de Man does not choose to pursue this avenue.[17] For de Man anthropomorphism is more a reaction from the outside, as it were, against the disquieting success of tropological substitution and the threat of language becoming independent, a reaction that leaves that power of language essentially intact. But let us remember that de Man, at the beginning of the essay, had stated his lack of interest in the critical schemes themselves that put certainty into question only to better reaffirm it. It is to the pattern that disrupts the surreptitious reappropriation of certitude that de Man shall rather devote his further analyses. The balance of the discussion of "Correspondances" is given over to a close examination of the icon of the temple in the poem. For the temple represents the context in which the disruption in question will be shown to occur. de Man begins this examination by saying:

> This verbal building, which has to celebrate at the same time funeral and rebirth, is built by the infinite multiplication of numbers raising each other to ever higher arithmetic power. The property which privileges "parfums" as the sensory analogon for the joint powers of mind and body . . . is its ability to grow from the infinitely small to endless expansion . . . The religious connotation of "temple" and "encens" suggests . . . a transcendental circulation, as ascent or descent, between the spirit and the senses, a borderline between two distinct realms that can be crossed.   (*RR*, p. 247)

de Man thus interprets the temple in "La Nature est un temple" as the image—the verbal building—for the unity of the senses and the spirit that is to be brought about in the poem. Even though reference to numbers and infinite multiplication might suggest how this building takes shape, the text does not support such language.[18] By contrast, the scents of the perfumes—"the sensory analogon for the joint powers of mind and body," at least as far as ambre and incense are concerned—suggest expanses and elevation in space as they spread from the infinitely small to the infinitely large. The temple is thus the verbal construct in which the lower and the higher realms come together in a movement of constant exchange. "Yet this movement is not unambiguously sustained by all the articulations of the text," de Man contends. Indeed, the unbroken and unending passage from lower to higher and ever higher levels (and vice versa) encounters some textual obstacles. A hiatus exists, de Man intimates, between the striven for transcendental circulation and the text itself.

The first in the series of increasing obstacles to the sought for transparency and continuous passage between the spirit and the senses is the ambiguity of the expression "passer à travers." It can be read to mean to exit what has been crossed but also its opposite, to wander around within the confines of an enclosure. Even though the latter meaning would suit the represented scene better than the first, it is, de Man claims, "incompatible with the transcendental claims usually made for the sonnet" (*RR*, p. 248). A passing through without crossing a threshold would block the declared intention of the poem to link the sensory to the spiritual and to move "from simile to symbol and to a higher order of truth" (*RR*, p. 248). Closing his examination of this first textual articulation that blurs the continuous movement of exchange between the senses and the spirit, de Man writes: "Ambivalences such as those noted in 'passer à travers'. . . complicate this expectation [of "transcendental circulation"] perhaps more forcefully than its outright negation" (*RR*, p. 248). Considering de Man's discussion of the grammatical reaffirmation of certitude in even its most radical negation, it is safe to assume that the ambivalences in question rank among those patterns that supposedly disrupt negation's reappropriative effects.[19] The linguistic ambiguity of "passer à travers"—supposing it is indeed one *in* the text of the sonnet, and not merely a general semantic possibility—would thus have a force, more powerful than outright negation, to destabilize the poem's program. "The complication is forceful enough to contaminate the key word that carries out the substitutions which constitute the main structure of the text: the word 'comme'" (*RR*, p. 248), de Man continues. The linguistic ambiguity of "passer à travers" that makes it doubtful whether any passage to an another, higher order in fact occurs propagates through the text imbuing with equal, increased, uncertainty the very operator of the substitutions by which the passage in question is managed. It is able to contaminate the metaphoric *comme* in such a way as to make it duplicitous, hence, incapable of achieving totality and a higher order of truth, by being the textual manifestation of the order of language itself, of it autonomous potential and its independence with respect to intentionality and meaning. Once the signifier "itself" has made an act of presence in the text, its contaminating effects can no longer be checked.

After a first example in which the *comme* "does its work properly and and clearly" duly raising "the process to the desired higher power," de Man stops at another occurrence of "the preposition of resemblance" in which the comparison already "makes less sense" (*RR*, p. 248), conceding at the same time that "all this is [still] playing at metaphor according to the rules of the game. But the same is not true of the final 'comme' in the poem" (*RR*, p. 249). The last *comme* in the text of the sonnet is unlike the others. "It does not cross from one sense experience to another . . . or from the sensory to the intellectual realm" (*RR*, p. 249). Whereas "in each of . . . [the previous] cases, the 'comme' is what avoids tautology by linking the subject to a predicate that is not the same," the final *comme* in the tercets of the sonnet—"*comme* l'ambre, le musc, le benjoin et l'encens"—does not (simply) do so. This last *comme* relates to its subject, the subject "parfums," "in two different ways or, rather, it has two distinct subjects" both of which are grammatically acceptable. If related to "l'expansion des choses infinies," this final "comme" still functions "like the other 'commes,' as a comparative simile: a common property ("l'expansion") links the finite senses to an experience of infinity. But 'comme' also relates to 'parfums' . . . 'Comme' then means as much as 'such as, for example' and enumerates scents . . . This working out by exemplification is quite different from the analogical function assigned to the other uses of the 'comme'" (*RR*, p. 249). While it is easy to agree to this conclusion, why, one wonders, is this duplicity more than just another ambiguity? Why does it, in particular, sound the knell of everything the poem sought to achieve?

The explanation is this: "Considered from the perspective of the 'thesis' or of the symbolist ideology of the text, such a use of 'comme' is aberrant" (*RR*, pp. 249–250). "Correspondances," de Man had asserted, was a programmatic text, its entire program intended to bring together and harmonize "corps" (the sensory and asthetic) and "esprit" (rational judgment, or espistemology) in a totalizing interconnection of the two so different realms, with the (rhetorical) help of the "presupposition of resemblance" that is the "comme." de Man not only takes at face value the aim of "Correspondances" to harmonize the body and the spirit, he also takes it for granted that this aim includes the demand for a total and absolute submission of language to the ideological project. Only on the assumption that the project of a reconciliation of the sensory and the spiritual demands an absolute transparency of the language and rhetoric required to mediate between the two realms is it possible to understand the "comme" of enumeration to have such an apocalytic effect. Only from the perspective of what the symbolist ideology at work in the poem supposedly sets up as a norm is it possible to construe the ambiguity of "passer à travers" (one of its meanings having been "to wander and err") and especially of the tautological "comme," as deviating, and straying, from the right path, as an aberration, in short.

Having stressed that "the burden of totalizing expansion" rests on the particular scents enumerated by the last "comme," de Man remarks that rather than helping to move beyond themselves, this "comme" restrains and confines them to repetitive tautology. No comparative "comme" transfigures and raises these perfumes to a higher level, in spite of the fact that at least some of them are symbols for the psychic thread between the individual and the cosmic soul (amber) or of the association of the human being and divinity (incense).[20] This final grammatical function of the "comme" in the poem leaves only, according to de Man, senseless enumeration. Not only senseless but evil repetition as well. Even though "l'ambre, le musc, le benjoin et l'encens" are said to be corrupt, rich, and triumphant, and thus contrast with the scents of innocence, this quali-fication is bestowed upon them only by virtue of their having "l'expan-sion des choses infinies." In the poem itself nothing permits any associa-tion with Turkish baths or black masses, amber and incense having, moreover, clearly spiritual meanings. The invocation of evil on their occasion is above all a rhetorical means to further vilify the power of the enumerative "comme" to corrupt the symbolist project. de Man writes: "For what could be more perverse or corruptive for a metaphor aspiring to transcendental totality than remaining stuck in an enumeration that never goes anywhere? . . . Enumerative repetition disrupts the chain of tropological substitutions at the crucial moment when the poem prom-ises, by way of these very substitutions, to reconcile the pleasures of the mind with those of the senses and to unite aesthetics with epistemology" (*RR*, p. 250). This enumerative and tautological "comme" that not only irrupts into and disrupts the hereto successful tropological substitution but appears at the very moment the poem promises to make good on its promise is where, for de Man, the autonomy of language manifests itself with a vengeance. In the "comme" of repetition and enumeration, language reveals itself in what I had called its (self-)immanence, its lack of transcendence. It demonstrates that, as the power not to relate, it thwarts any dream of linking the aesthetic and the intellectual. Emphatically exorbitant, yet at the same time in a bipolar relation of subversion to the transcendental unity, the "comme" of substitution seeks to fashion, it emphatically refuses to lend itself as rhetoric to the projects of epistemology. Later in the essay, when returning to this last "comme," de Man characterizes it in terms of "the stutter, the *piétinement* of aimless enumeration" (*RR*, p. 254). Running in place, language stagnates, it does not go anywhere. de Man closes his elaboration on the disruptive "comme" with the following: "That the very word on which these substitutions depend would just then [namely, at the crucial moment of keeping its word] lose its syntactical and semantic univocity is too striking a coincidence not to be, like pure chance, beyond the control of author and reader" (*RR*, p. 250). With this remark de Man makes it amply clear that the function of language that reveals itself in the irruption of the enumerative "comme" stands in an adverse relation to the entire program of the poem and, more generally, to any attempt to conciliate incommensurable opposites in a unity or totality. Further, he makes the point that what happens to the ideological project of reconciling the senses and the spirit by way of language can happen only against its will, unwittingly. What manifests itself through the enumerative "comme" is something entirely beyond this project's control. The aberration of the "comme" is thus that of a language entirely autonomous.

The encroachment of the "comme" of senseless enumeration on the analogizing "comme" also allows "for a sobering literalization of the word 'transport' in the final line 'Qui chantent les transports de l'esprit et des sens'" (*RR*, p. 250), de Man remarks. Given the repetitive "comme"'s obstruction of an analogizing step-beyond, the celebrated ecstatic transports of the senses and the spirit, "in a common transcendental realm," begin to ring in a much more prosaic mode. Measured against the tension felt by "the attentive readers of Baudelaire" (*RR*, p. 251) between two incompatible kinds of transports—ecstatic self-loss, on the one hand, and on the other, a cold cerebral exaltation, if not calculation—de

Man's sobering up of "transports" is considerably more drastic. We must first keep in mind that the radical force of de Man's interpretation does not lie in his assimilation of "transports" to public transportation or the movement of goods. When de Man insists—following Derrida, no doubt, who, in "The *Retrait* of Metaphor," had noted that means of transportation are called *metaphorikos* even in modern Greece[21]—on recognizing "the spatial displacement implied by the verbal ending of meta-*phorein*" in Baudelaire's "transports," he wants to emphasize that such a displacement is still very much in line with the cerebral transports that in Baudelaire so often negate sensual abandon. This is why he can maintain that a prosaic interpretation of the "transports de l'esprit et des sens" "is entirely in the spirit of Baudelaire and not by itself disruptive with regard to the claim for transcendental unity" (*RR*, p. 251). This sober interpretation of transport serves a cold intellectual mode of transport only to reassert the possibility of transport in general by expanding its notion and by thus securing the desired transcendental unity. What de Man is after is rather a sobering that disrupts even the prosaic literalization's reaffirmation of a more comprehensive idea of transport.

The reason that the sobering reading of "transports" as public transportation does not, in de Man's analysis, fundamentally upset the poem's program seems to be that its interpretation as spatial displacement complements, rather than disrupts, the transports of metaphor or analogy. de Man argues that "the transfer indeed merges two different displacements into one single system of motion and circulation, with corresponding economic and metaphysical profits. The problem is not so much centered on *phorein* as on *meta* (trans . . .), for does 'beyond' here mean a movement beyond some particular place or does it mean a state that is beyond movement entirely? And how can 'beyond,' which posits and names movement, ever take us away from what it posits?" (*RR*, p. 251). For de Man, the problem that threatens Baudelaire's sobering expansion of the notion of transport to a more comprehensive one lies in the fact that in such a notion two heterogeneous, incompatible meanings of *meta*, or of the whereto of transporation, become mixed. In the one single system of motion and circulation in which prosaic and metaphysical transports are reconciled, it not only becomes impossible to decide whether "trans" or "beyond" signifies the passage to another place or a passage to the far side of passage entirely, that is, to a state beyond movement. Moreover, "beyond," being indicative of movement, the idea of a place beyond "beyond," seems to catch the unified concept of transport in an inextricable contradiction. And de Man pronounces that this undecidable question "haunt[s] the text in all its ambiguities, be it 'passer à travers' or the discrepancy between the 'comme' of homogeneity and the 'comme' of enumeration" (*RR*, p. 251). Even though the word "beyond" is not part of the text itself but one to which the focus on the "trans" of transports leads, the uncertainty that it raises—whether the generalized transport is merely a transfer to another empirical place or to a place beyond transportation, a metaphysical place—is the matricial uncertainty for all the uncertainties encountered hitherto. Retrospectively, the question regarding the possibility of a beyond appears to have been the question at stake in all the previous questions about whether the "comme" effectuates an analogical transition to a higher order or just to stands still, as well as the question as to whether, in crossing, one exits at the other end or continues to err within the confines of the (un)crossed compound. The matricial question relative to the beyond, the pattern of undecidability that it bestows on the nature of transport, concerns the possibility of transport in general. It boils down to knowing whether or not there can be passage, that is, any relation at all. This question is the key to de Man's reading of "Correspondances."

It is certainly appropriate to briefly pause to wonder why transport becomes such a problem for de Man. If, according to de Man, the ambiguity of the "beyond" entirely foils the program of the poem to link the senses and the spirit, two heterogeneous realms, in one higher unity, what might this tell us in turn about how de Man understands "transport" (and for that matter, "passage," "relation," etc.) itself. Unable to decide where it is going, the transport must undoubtedly run in place. But why does undecidability become such an issue in the first place? Is it not because of the fundamental difference between a passage merely to another place and one that passes to a place beyond all transferring movement? Is it not because de Man distinguishes between a prosaic and an emphatic concept of the beyond? And this emphatic beyond, beyond all movement, cannot, de Man emphasizes, be on the far side of movement. Qua beyond, it can never take us away from the movement it posits. But if these linguistic difficulties can play such an important role, is it not fundamentally because a highly emphatic concept of "transport" is at work in the first place? By taking the idea of transport to imply being carried away to an entirely heterogeneous realm (even beyond the senses and the spirit), de Man has obviously adopted a formal and abstract concept of transport. Philosophers and Romantic writers no doubt have celebrated such transports but never without presupposing a mediation—at least, of sorts—between one side of the process and the other. Without a minimal trace in the self of the absolute Other to which it is to be related, whatever the mode of such a relation, the notion of transport makes no sense whatsoever. For de Man, however, such a trace is the virus of aesthetic ideology.

In the remaining and rather obscure part of his reading of the poem, de Man adds an additional ambiguity between the poem itself, as it were, and its reading. Invoking the "apparent rest and tranquility" of the poem within the corpus of *Les Fleurs du Mal,* he characterizes it as lying "indeed beyond tension and motion." "Correspondances," de Man suggests, enjoys a state of inner motionlessness similar to the one aimed at by the transports it celebrates. It has the look of a beyond that has been able successfully to overcome what the beyond posits. But unlike the beyond to which language with its tropological substitutions is supposed to take us, the sonnet's tranquility owes to language's (self-)immanence and indifference to transcendence. To make this argument, de Man claims that between what the sonnet says about nature as a temple and about human transports there is no relation or communication. He writes:

> If Nature is truly a temple, it is not a means of transportation . . . Nature in this poem is not a road toward a temple, a sequence of motions that take us there . . . And if man (l'homme) is at home among "regards familiers" within that Nature, then his language of tropes and analogies is of little use to them. In this realm, transfer tickets are of no avail. Within the confines of a system of transportation—or of language as a system of communication—one can transfer from one vehicle to another, but one cannot transfer from being like a vehicle to being like a temple, or a ground. (*RR,* pp. 251–252)

I here recall de Man's mystifying contention that the opening line of the poem was enigmatic. de Man now explains that, as a temple, nature prohibits all travel to, all communication with, it. A language of tropes and analogies, a language (in short) always on the way, never attains the stony silence of nature shaped as a temple.[22] Such a nature goes nowhere—hence its tranquility and rest—and no path can be cut toward it. But recalling de Man's previous assimilation of the autonomous potential of language to the architectural icon of the temple, nature as a temple must now be interpreted as language in its pristine state. Nothing can be said about it, and it never leads beyond itself. Between it and a language of communication no transfer is possible. Between language and itself only an abyss obtains. In short, then, facing itself "as such," more precisely as a linguistic event, language as a system of transports and communication stagnates and fails to reach and read itself. In its epistemological, aesthetic, poetic function, it runs in place, incapable of pinpointing and coinciding with itself. Before itself, language becomes superfluous. All "Correspondances" break down at that point. And this is precisely what the poem states, de Man contends. "Like the perfumes enumerated by 'comme,' [the language of transports] remains condemned to the repetition of its superfluidity," de Man asserts (*RR*, p. 252).

It is to be remembered that for de Man, the cruxes of "Correspondances" made Baudelaire generate another sonnet, the poem "Obsession." While "Correspondances" states the failure of its language to achieve a unity with itself and "offers no explicit alternative to this language" of failure, "Obsession" states nothing of the kind. On the other hand, "little clarity can be gained from 'Correspondances' except for the knowledge that disavows its deeper affinity with 'Obsession'." In proposing a language other than the tropological language of "Correspondances," "Obsession" becomes "its 'echo' as it were" (*RR*, p. 252). Further, by denying all relation to "Obsession," "Correspondances" only proves, to the point of confusion, its proximity to it. But it is the peculiar relation of "Obsession" to "Correspondances" that will primarily concern de Man in the last part of "Anthropomorphism and Trope in the Lyric." "Obsession" "can be called a *reading* of the earlier text, with all the complications that are inherent in this term. The relationship between the two poems can indeed be seen as the construction and the undoing of the mirrorlike, specular structure that is always involved in a reading" (*RR*, p. 252).[23] I note first, particularly in light of the preceding remarks about the (non-)relation between the two poems, that a relation of reading prevails in the absence of any positively stated relation, or rather where such relations are negated in oblique ways. In any case, as a result of what I had called the "compulsion to binarize," de Man's reading of "Correspondances" needs to come up with a second poem that undoes what the first poem purported to construct. Reading the reading that "Obsession" performs of "Correspondances" completes de Man's own reading. But further it is of interest to note that "Obsession" *itself* is said to read "Correspondances." While we have been told that "Correspondances" forced Baudelaire to generate "Obsession," it is this poem itself that reads the first sonnet in what is an objective event, as it were, one that takes place among and between texts. Considering that "Correspondances" is all affirmation (even if it had to affirm the failure of its language), "Obsession" must be a mirrorlike negation of what the first had both positively and negatively established. de Man continues: "On both the thematic and the rhetorical level, the reverted symmetries between the two texts establish their correspondance along a positive/negative axis. Here again our problem is centered on the possibility of reinscribing into the system elements, in either text, that do not belong to this pattern" (*RR*, p. 252). If the two poems stand in a relation of correspondence, it is because in one everything (content and form) is positive while in the other everything is negative. They relate despite the lack of all relation between them. All reading, de Man emphasizes, presupposes a specular construction and undoing of the constructed. But this is not the whole truth of reading. As de Man has repeatedly pointed out, reading requires finding those patterns that disrupt the certainty that the critical schemes reestablish despite their radical putting into question of certainty. de Man strengthens this notion of reading when he states that the problem of reading is to find elements that do not belong to the pattern of symmetrical reversal between texts. Reading, consequently, is intent on questioning the possibility of specular correspondence between texts, if not of all relation, and hence the certainty that such reflection would still provide. What we can already begin to make out is that while the binary pressure predominates in de Man's reading, this reading also consists in finding those elements or patterns that prevent binarism from turning reflexive or specular, in short, from yielding a totalizing system of identity. A reading is not rounded off until the specularity and reflexivity with which it has been involved have been thoroughly undercut. It is thus to be expected that with the analysis of how "Obsession" reads "Correspondances" and how it fits into de Man's reading, we will be able to substantially complete our understanding of the concept and practice of de Manean reading.

This question concerning what disrupts the reassuring symmetric reflection between texts can also "be asked in historical or in generic terms but, in so doing, the significance of this terminology risks being unsettled," de Man writes (pp. 252–253). If I briefly mention this aspect, it is primarily in view of the question previously raised as to how mere reading relates to the specificity of its object. For historical and especially generic distinctions are the traditional means for determining the precise nature of a piece of literature or poetry. Let me briefly review de Man's argument concerning the possibility of a generic difference between the poems.[24] Is it possible to describe their difference in generic terms, if, as de Man contends, all such attempts stumble over "the uncertain status of the lyric as a term for poetic discourse in general" (*RR*, p. 254)? If it is not even certain that these two poems are poems, distinguishing them one from the other in generic terms becomes a problem. Undoubtedly, "Correspondances" claims to sing, and hence to be lyric. "Obsession," in contrast, despite the clear presence of a personal voice, does not pretend to sing—it howls. Yet, recalling his reading of "Correspondances," de Man notes the stutter and the possibility of running in place by which the claim to sing is at all times threatened in this poem. If the claim to lyricism depends on "this eventuality, inherent in the structure of the tropes" (*RR*, p. 254) that constitute it, "Correspondances," despite its claim, can, even less than the howling "Obsession," pretend to be a lyrical poem. In conclusion, it must thus be said that mere reading does away with any specificity based on the generic differences of the texts it reads. It becomes impossible to attribute a text to a specific genre, even when that text itself lays claim to such a genre. It is also impossible, therefore, to make any distinction between texts that, at first glance, seem to belong to a particular genre. Specificity, for mere reading, is a meaning stated of texts that is oblivious to the disabling nature of the linguistic tropes on which such a statement depends. Any effort by a text to set itself apart, to mark its difference from another text, any such effort, at least when it rests on generic distinction, is bound to fail. From the perspective of mere reading, specificity is illusive and illusory. The tropological textuality of the text undermines any such claim, revealing them to be illusions of aesthetic ideology. Whether the text, as de Man understands it, can in addition to being read for the general linguistic operations at work in all texts also be read for what is singular (to avoid the term "specificity") about it is an open question. In what terms could mere reading account for such singularity? In view of the uncomparable uniqueness presupposed of language by mere reading, could every text as a manifestion of language be construed as inevitably unique? But uniqueness is not yet singularity. Would mere reading not be forced by its own rigor to state the illusory quality of singularity, even that of texts?[25]

"No lyric can be read lyrically nor can the object of a lyrical reading be itself a lyric—which implies least of all that it is epical or dramatic" (*RR*, p. 254), de Man concludes. In a complete reversal of the Romantic precept that of poetry one can only speak poetically,[26] mere reading shows poetry to undermine its own aspiration to be song. Lyric is not of a piece and hence erodes its possibility of being read lyrically. But why can the object of a lyrical reading not be a lyrical object? If Baudelaire read "Correspondances" lyrically, "Correspondances" could not have been a lyric. But "Baudelaire's own lyrical reading of 'Correspondances' produced at least a text, the sonnet entitled 'Obsession'" (*RR*, p. 254), de Man continues. This text, one must assume, is a lyrical reading of "Correspondances." Let me then try to tease out from de Man's extremely dense discussion of this poem—dense to the point of obscurity—the major articulations of what "Obsession" supposedly achieves with respect to the first sonnet.

The very first quatrain of "Obsession" naturalizes what in "Correspondances" allowed the anthropomorphic reading that forced itself on most of its commentators to the point of shaping the entire tradition of Baudelaire erudition. From the outset, the living columns are taken to represent "a sylvan scene," and their "surreal speech" becomes "the frightening, but natural, roar of the wind among the trees" (*RR*, p. 254). de Man writes: "The benefits of naturalization—as we can call the reversal of anthropomorphism—are at once apparent. None of the uncertainties that obscure the opening lines of 'Correspondances' are maintained. No 'comme' could be more orthodox than the two 'commes' in these two lines. The analogism is so perfect that the implied anthropomorphism becomes fully motivated" (*RR*, p. 255). As it inverts all of the first sonnet's anthropomorphic effects into natural effects, "Obsession" eliminates all of "Correspondances"'s uncertainties making this poem readable—in short, intelligible. The comparisons effected by the "commes" are perfect examples of tropological substitution, and where there is an implication of anthropomorphism, it is fully motivated in that it is just one more substitution. In short, a naturalizing reading of the first sonnet provides a considerable advantage. Unlike the relatively ineffective anthropomorphism of "Correspondances" that failed to render its tropes intelligible by arresting them in one ultimate signifier, naturalization avoids that difficulty and makes the sonnet's meaning crystal clear.[27]

As he had done for "Correspondances," de Man stresses the perfection of "Obsession" on all its levels. But with the latter poem, the perfection is even greater. Lacking the uncertainties of anthropomorphism that after all haunt "Correspondances," "Obsession" is a complete success. On the thematic and formal level, the unification is of a piece. "The adjustment of the elements involved . . . is perfectly self-enclosed, since all the pieces in the structure fit each other . . . Everything can be substituted for everything else without distorting the most natural experience" (*RR*, p. 255). The "power of the analogy" is so effective in this poem that it even brings off a naturalization of what at first sight seemed to except itself from the poem's tropological analogism: the attribution of speech to the woods. The anthropomorphism of lyric address "appears so natural that it takes an effort to notice that anthropomorphism is involved" at all (*RR*, p. 256), de Man argues. This naturalization of verbality that secures the poem's unity on its discursive level is achieved by "the omnipresent metaphor of interiorization" in the poem (*RR*, p. 256). Unlike "Correspondances" in which the reflection on the mediating role of language took place in mutiple ways ranging from assonance to anagrammatical inscription, here it operates "initially by ways of the ear alone" (*RR*, p. 256). And yet, the dramatization of language in the later poem is so much more cogent.

In distinction from "Correspondances," "Obsession" is not restricted to a knowledge of the vastness of expanse (and elevation). Instead, as the *De profundis* of the forests that resonate echolike in our hearts—"et dans nos coeurs maudits . . . Répondent les échos de vos *De profundis*"—suggest, this last poem also and especially knows depth. It is "the explicit theme of the poem," de Man claims. Having flawlessly naturalized verbality, this poem succeeds in tropologically substituting—though not without pain and with the pathos of "much represented agony"—for the depth of the forests that of "the enclosed space" of interiority. The "analogy between outer event and inner feeling" is one between the depth of the forest's penitential prayer and "the subject's presence to itself as a spatial enclosure, room, tomb, or crypt in which the voice echoes as in a cave" (*RR*, p. 256). In an ostentatious display of the powers of tropological substitution whose possible anthropomorphic leftovers have been corrected by naturalization and which has thus been cleansed of all residue that could obstruct its meaning, the poem, by dint of an exchange between outside and inside, engenders nothing less than "the metaphor of the lyrical voice as subject." By producing in such an analogical exchange the subject as a metaphor of the outer depths of the forests and their naturalized verbality, "'Obsession' asserts its right to say 'I' with full authority," de Man concludes. It reads "Correspondances" in a lyrical voice.

In sum, "Obsession" exemplifies the rigor of tropological substitution as well as what such substitution can engender, especially under the aegis of naturalization. But, according to de Man, substitutive troping was to serve as a means to reconcile aesthetic and rational judgment, the senses and the spirit. Can the considerably more perfect tropological language of "Obsession," a language whose analogizing function is not hampered by any unorthodox "commes," achieve what "Correspondances" failed? In pointing out that the inside/outside pattern of the exchange that founds the metaphor of the lyrical voice harbors an additional possibility, de Man seems to address this question. "In a parallel movement, reading interiorizes the meaning of the text by its understanding. The union of aesthetic with epistemological properties is carried out by the mediation of the metaphor of the self as conscious of itself, which implies its negation" (*RR*, p. 256). Inasmuch as "Obsession" reads and understands the meaning of the earlier sonnet, this meaning, previously outside, is now interiorized within "Obsession." What happens here is presumably an impeccable reconciliation of outside and inside, of the aesthetic and epistemological. For a reading that understands, everything becomes meaningful within the interiority of a self conscious of itself. Here everything outside, and of the order of the senses, is imbued with intelligibility. However, this ideal union of outside and inside brought about by the mediating metaphor, or totalizing figure of the self as a self-conscious self, while internally flawless, is said, quite surprisingly, and with no elaboration, to imply its own negation. Is this to say that in reading "Correspondances," "Obsession" would also negate the union of the aesthetic and the epistemological central to that sonnet? And if so, does "Obsession" negate only the particular way in which the first poem achieves the union, or does it negate the union of the senses and the spirit in general? But, first, why does the union brought about by the metaphor of the self-conscious self imply a negation of "Correspondances"'s rather successful interweaving of both the aesthetic and the epistemological? The following passage perhaps provides an answer: "The specular symmetry of the two texts is such that any instance one wishes to select at once involves the entire system with flawless consistency . . . The law of this figural and chiastic transformation is negation. 'Obsession' self-consciously denies and rejects the sensory wealth of 'Correspondances'" (*RR*, pp. 256–257). Earlier de Man had stated that, as a reading of "Correspondances," "Obsession" constructs an inverted replica of the first poem that is to be undone again within that same reading. Insofar as the reading constructs an inverted version of the text read, it does so in a systematic manner. If the opposite of one element in the first poem becomes a feature of the second poem, all the elements interlinked with it are specularly inverted as well. Now, such mirrorlike inversion amounts to a negation of what is inverted, de Man insists. If "Obsession"'s lyrical reading claims the authority of the "I," it is in order to negate the impersonality of "Correspondances." All the elements interwoven with the "I" negate in turn all those connected to the third-person discourse of the earlier poem. In addition, and most importantly, the self-conscious mode in which the union of the sensory and the spiritual is achieved in the later poem negates "the sensory wealth" of the earlier poem, and, one can confidently say, its synaesthetic mode of synthesis. Such negation is apparent not only in "Obsession"'s desire for emptiness, it pervades the entire text of the poem, "be it in terms of affects, moods, or grammar" (*RR*, p. 257). Yet, this relationship of negation that prevails in reading is

> a figure of chiasmus, for the positive and negative valorizations can be distributed on both sides. We read "Obsession" thematically as an interiorization of "Correspondances," and as a negation of the positivity of an outside reality. But it is just as plausible to consider "Obsession" as the making manifest, as the exteriorization of the subject that remains hidden in "Correspondances." Naturalization, which appears to be a movement from inside to outside, allows for affective verisimilitude which moves in the opposite direction. In terms of figuration also, it can be said that "Correspondances" is the negation of "Obsession": the figural stability of "Obsession" is denied in "Correspondances."   (*RR*, p. 257)

The distinctive relationship of constructing and undoing in reading is thus truly specular. Straddled by the rhetorical figure of the chiasmus, this relationship permits negative valorizations to be substituted for positive ones, and vice versa. Consequently, in addition to its negative sweep and its interiorizing rejection of exteriority, "Obsession" can be said to make a positive contribution to the earlier sonnet by bringing out the interiority of a subject in the impersonal poem "Correspondances." Naturalizing the earlier poem, "Obsession" gives the affects of "Correspondances" the appearance of truth, suggesting that these affects make the presence of a subject manifest in that text. But from the position of a negated entity, "Correspondances" also rises up to negate "Obsession." This happens, de Man's writes rather elliptically, in terms of figuration. The earlier poem denies the later poem's "figural stability." "Correspondances" puts the figure into question by means of which "Obsession" has fixed the meaning of the first poem into place. Because the two texts entertain a specular relation, "Obsession"'s reading must be undone by "Correspondances." Not only are the valorizations that "Obsession," in its reading, bestows on "Correspondances" reversible, but the earlier poem in its turn reverses these reversed valorizations as it relates to "Obsession" in the figure of chiasmus. But although this is a necessary consequence of the "specular structure that is always involved in a reading," the earlier poem's negation of the latter is not to be understood in terms of reading. Whatever the ambiguities are, and they are numerous, it must be said that only "Obsession" reads, and it consists of making the earlier poem intelligible to begin with. The first poem, by contrast, undoes what the latter reads, and this is what de Man's reading—mere reading—of the specular interplay between the two poems shows. But rather than lingering on "Correspondances"'s undoing of "Obsession"'s reading, de Man chooses to pursue "the recuperative power of the subject metaphor in 'Obsession'" (*RR*, p. 257).

Taking up the interiorizing and cognitive power of metaphor in the tercets, he writes:

> As soon as the sounds of words are allowed, as in the opening stanza, to enter into analogical combinations with the sounds of nature, they necessarily turn into the light imagery of representation and of knowledge. If the sounds of nature are akin to those of speech, then nature also speaks by ways of light, the light of the senses as well as of the mind. The philosophical phantasm that has concerned us throughout this reading, the reconciliation of knowledge with phenomenal, aesthetic experience, is summarized in the figure of speaking light which,

as is to be expected in the dialectical mode of negation, is both denied and asserted.   (*RR*, pp. 257–258)

The recuperative power of the metaphor of the subject in "Obsession" is found in its rejection of the union of the spirit and the senses that also reinstates it all the more powerfully on its own more sophisticated level. Certainly, it is not at all obvious why the analogical combination of the sounds of words and the sounds of nature must turn "necessarily" into "the light imagery of representation and of knowledge." It is also far from clear why this combination distinguishes the metaphor of the subject. But, granted that speaking sheds the illuminating light of the senses and the spirit on what is, combining the sounds of nature with those of speech—the figure of speaking light, a figure that unites the senses and the spirit—reinstates their union denied to "Correspondances."[28] In an extremely rapid succession of assertions, and with reference to an early fragment of the poem in which the "toiles" of darkness are canvasses on which one paints, de Man suggests that light implies space, which in turn implies spatial differentiation, which implies the possibility of pictorial "foreground-background juxtaposition," hence, "the aesthetics of painting." Painting, in turn, is a representation of previous perceptions, but, as so often happens in hallucination and dream, it is the "recollection and . . . re-cognition, as the recovery, to the senses" of what is beyond experience. Now, in view of the last tercet of the sonnet where Baudelaire writes:

> Mais les ténèbres sont elles-mêmes des toiles
> Où vivent, jaillissant de mon oeil par milliers,
> Des êtres disparus aux regards familiers,

de Man holds that these three lines establish the definite loss of sensory plenitude while at the same time reaffirming its recollective representability, hence the possibility of knowing it. For de Man, this tercet is where "Obsession" recovers the union of the senses and the spirit that it denied to "Correspondances." He writes: "The possibility of representation asserts itself at its most efficacious at the moment when the sensory plenitude of 'Correspondances' is most forcefully denied. The lyric depends entirely for its existence on the denial of phenomenality as the surest means to recover what it denies" (*RR*, pp. 258–259). If I understand correctly, the reinstitution of denied phenomenality takes place as remembered and represented phenomenality, that is to say, as phenomenality interiorized, hence made intelligible by the subject, or lyrical voice. It is the recuperation of the sensory that comes with the interiorizing and negating powers of a structure, or metaphor, such as the subject, independently, de Man adds, of its good or bad faith.

In reading "Correspondances," "Obsession" not only renders the union of the senses and the spirit that it first denied to the early poem, intelligible by interiorizing it, it does the same to all the elements of the text and, indeed, to the text of "Correspondances" itself. "'Obsession' translates 'Correspondances' into intelligibility, the least one can hope for in a successful reading," one is told. The "esoteric *correspondances*" by which the union of the senses and the spirit is achieved in the early poem, becomes, when read lyrically, enlighteningly intelligible (*RR*, p. 259). Let me here recall the specular structure of the two poems. Indeed, the gist of the preceding elaborations consists in stressing the symmetry of all the chiasmic potentialities between the two texts. The operations of negation and affirmation traveling from one text to the other are equally plausible, de Man had stated. Deriving from the latin *plausibilis*, deserving applause, praiseworthy, acceptable, pleasing, the word would seem to suggest that the specular symmetry achieved by the two texts pleases the eye and the mind. As de Man has made it quite clear on other occasions, specularity, self-referentiality, and self-reflection are phenomenal, that is, world-oriented, conceptions.[29] The formal structure of symmetry is beautiful and, at the same time, immediately intelligible and, in this capacity, an ultimate refuge for what de Man had called the "philosophical phantasm." From everything we have seen, the logic immanent to mere reading requires that the phantasm be dispelled; especially when disguised as formalism, it hides in mere reading itself. After all, such aesthetic formalism traps mere reading into rendering intelligible what it reads. In conformity with the major movements of de Man's readings in "Anthropomorphism and Trope in the Lyric," the disruption of the mirrorlike reflection of the two texts mutually reading themselves is to be found in a pattern that disrupts the recuperative power of the subject metaphor in the later poem.

In light of the perfect symmetry that we have discerned between the two texts and their readings of each other, it comes as a surprise that de Man could say that this pair of texts is "a model for the uneasy combination of funeral monumentality with paranoid fear that characterizes the hermeneutics and the pedagogy of lyric poetry." Indeed, given the previous analyses, what could possible make one uneasy? Could it be that this distress is just the symmetrical reverse of the beautiful symmetry that prevails between these two texts on the union of the senses and the spirit that relate themselves to each other as objectivity and subjectivity, phenomenality and understanding? The unease would then be rooted simply in the plausibility of the possible reversals between the two poems. It is an uneasiness that does not threaten the stabilized harmony between the two poems. But what about the poem's very title "Obsession"? Is it not, de Man asks, the locus where "the far-reaching symmetry between the two texts" is threatened? "For the temporal pattern of obsessive thought is directly reminiscent of the tautological, enumerative stutter we encountered in the double semantic function of 'comme,' which disrupted the totalizing claim of metaphor in 'Correspondances.' It suggests a psychological and therefore intelligible equivalent of what there appeared as a purely grammatical distinction" (*RR*, p. 259). The movement of besetment, or domination by a recurring feeling, idea, or the like expressed by "Obsession" would thus represent the pattern that undermines the unifying effort of the lyrical voice. But, if it is indeed the perfect equivalent of the disrupting stutter of "Correspondances," it achieves nothing but a further cementing of the aesthetic symmetry between the two texts. If the patterns of disruption of the certitude inherent in negation that are to be found in each poem stand in a relation of inverse symmetry, the specularity between them is even more powerful. As we know, de Man *must* be able to show how this symmetry is effectively disrupted. This after all is what mere reading is all about. As previously noted, the steps of a mere reading are rigorously predictable, while it is impossible to predict the exact textual support for that reading's various moves. The argument on which de Man rests his case against the specularity of the two sonnets is the finest example of a mere reading's surprise effects.

Aesthetic ideology, the philosophical phantasm of a union of sensory experience and rational knowledge, is pervasive to the point of modeling the mirrorlike symmetry between the two poems and their respective readings. This symmetry is the form of the totalization toward which philosophical reconciliation strives. But it is successful only if its specu-

larity is absolute, de Man insinuates. The mirroring reversals must operate at all times, on all levels, between all elements, for the symmetry to
claim truth. It is with this totalizing exigency in mind that he writes:

> Yet, if the symmetry between the two texts is to be truly recuperative, it
> is essential that the disarticulation that threatens the first text should
> find its counterpart in the second: mere naturalization of a grammatical
> structure, which is how the relationship between enumeration and ob-
> session can be understood, will not suffice, since it is precisely the
> tension between an experienced and a purely linguistic disruption that
> is at issue. There ought to be a place, in "Obsession," where a similar
> contrast between infinite totalization and endless repetition of the same
> could be pointed out. No such place exists. (*RR*, pp. 259–260)

In other words, precisely because it is an intelligible counterpart of the
linguistic stutter in "Correspondances," the merely psychological mode
of compulsive repetition cannot interrupt the intelligibilizing potential
of the subject metaphor. Only a linguistic counterpart of the verbal
standing about of the "comme" could fulfill this task. Since "Obsession"
proves not to be obsessive enough to effect a disruption of the affirmative
twist of negation, the striven for symmetry breaks down. By the same
token, the reconciliation between the senses and the spirit reveals itself
as deluded not only in the sense of being deceitful but in the sense of
having been thwarted by the cunning play of language. As if language
itself had, at the most crucial moment, withheld the means necessary to
complete the aesthetic program, the cunning of reason is outsmarted.

"At the precise moment where one would expect" to find a contrast
between infinite totalization and endless repetition" in "Obsession,"
namely, "at the moment when obsession is stressed in terms of number
[the reference is to "par milliers" in the last tercet], 'Obsession' resorts to
synthesis by loosing itself in the vagueness of the infinite" (*RR*, p. 260).
This lack of precision thus appears to be the exact place where the
heretofore rigorous symmetry between the two poems breaks down. Instead of being a disruptive enumeration, such lack of precision is a
"reassuring indeterminacy," de Man contends. Aware of the burden thus
imposed on the role of "par milliers" in the poem, de Man has to find a
way to convincingly argue the reassuring quality of these infinite thou-
sands. This he achieves by contrasting it with the "genuine terror" of
numerical precision in "Les sept vieillards," a poem that, as he is quick to

admit, "can however in no respect be called a reading of 'Correspon-dances,' to which it in no way corresponds" (*RR*, p. 260). Apart from the "decisive contrast" constructed for the occasion, there is no relation between "Obsession" and "Les sept vieillards." Yet, the presumed con-trast between their ways of handling numbers has nevertheless given a cast to "Obsession"'s lack of numerical precision that brings to a close a reading that could not stop before having made the last move that its own logic rigorously prescribes.

de Man's concluding remarks are principal statements that concern the nature of texts and the status of reading in general. These statements will in turn allow me to answer at least some of the questions raised in reading de Man's readings. However, before pursuing this opportunity, some clarification is required. Throughout the exposition of the relation-ship between the two sonnets, de Man has emphasized a process of reading that takes place between the two sonnets themselves. But the re-flections that follow in the final portion of his essay concern the reading itself that reads those two texts, one of which—"Obsession"—reads the other—"Correspondances"—which in turn undoes this reading. Failing to heed this shift in the notion of reading, indeed, makes some of the claims in this final section of de Man's essay seem to contradict state-ments made earlier in his reading of "Correspondances" and statements relative to "Obsession"'s reading of the earlier sonnet. Attention to the shift in question is further important in that it explains why de Man now devotes his main attention to "lyrical reading." It is in contradistinction to lyrical reading—a reading bent on understanding what it reads—that mere reading will be highlighted. In addition, we need to note that the general remarks of this last part also serve to counter the objection that de Man's opposition of "Obsession" to "Correspondances" was no mere whim. In retrospect it appears that the pairing was not de Man's but, rather, that these two poems always already called upon one another.

Alluding to the reading that takes place between Baudelaire's two son-nets, de Man defines it as "a process of translation or 'transport' that incessantly circulates between the texts" (*RR*, p. 260). Reading in this sense is, as we have seen, an "objective," intratextual process, something that happens between two texts but that remains within the boundaries of the texts. As de Man intimates in a response to Riffaterre, reading is a necessary, or "structural part of the form" of texts (*RT*, p. 31). To the ex-tent that readings must circulate, "there always are at least two texts, regardless of whether they are actually written out or not; the relationship between the two sonnets . . . is an inherent characteristic of any text. Any text, as text, compels reading as its understanding" (*RR*, pp. 260–261). The presence of two texts is thus fundamental. Equally fundamental is the exigency that these two texts mirror each other, as did Baudelaire's two poems. But, interestingly enough, the second text does not have to be written out. It "exists" anyway regardless. One text being given, the other text must be present, at least in some fashion. But it is no mere virtual possibility but rather an actual virtuality. Since reading is understanding, understanding is likewise an "objective," intratextual occurring. There are always two texts, one needing the other to be read and understood. The reader of a text is thus another text, its specular and inverse other. One text makes the other intelligible. But, let us recall, reading is not limited to conferring intelligibility on a text's specular counterpart. But first this: "What we call the lyric, the instance of the represented voice, conveniently spells out the rhetorical and thematic characteristics that make it the paradigm of a complementary relationship between grammar, trope, and theme" (*RR*, p. 261). The choice of two poems to exhibit the objective process of reading was no accident. Nor were the poems selected because of any commitment to the lyrical in all its specificity. On the contrary, expediency alone motivates the choice of lyrical examples. The set of characteristics paradigmatic to the relationship between grammar, trope, and theme—from the mirrorlike symmetry and its reversals along a positive/negative axis to the transformation of trope into anthropomorphism—conveniently spells out an intra- and intertextual relationship valid for all texts and the relations between them. But if the lyric, rather than being a generic term, is one name among others to designate the intertextual relation of understanding, to call it "lyric" also emphasizes that understanding on this intertextual level is no welcoming openness to the other text. This is what I understand de Man to mean in the following statement: "The lyric is not a genre, but one name among several to designate the defensive motion of understanding, the possibility of future hermeneutics. From this point of view, there is no significant difference between one generic term and another" (*RR*, p. 261). Indeed, the interiorizing reading through which "Obsession" renders "Correspondances" intelligible proceeds via negation and reverting transformations. In this sense, compelling a reading from another text, inasmuch as this reading is to be an understanding, forces the text in question into a defensive mode. Reading as intelligibilization—and the lyric demonstrates this most economically—puts the reading text on the defense against what it reads. The reading text resists the sheer incomprehensibility of the first text, understanding being a buffer, or baffle, against incomprehensibility. On the other hand, it is the first text itself that compels the other into this defensive motion. Reading a text thus also shields that text from the text that reads it. This is why readings are so baffling. They leave the texts they read unread, retrenched in unreadability. Readings prevent the two texts involved in all readings from encountering one another. The specular mirror play of reversals between two texts also keeps them apart.[30]

But as de Man emphasizes, a reading by one text bent on understanding another is only one way of reading. He writes:

> We all perfectly and quickly understand "Obsession," and better still the motion that takes us from the earlier to the later text. But no symmetrical reversal of this lyrical reading-motion is conceivable . . . "Obsession" derives from "Correspondances" but the reverse is not the case. Neither does it account for it as its origin or cause. "Correspondances" implies and explains "Obsession" but "Obsession" leaves "Correspondances" as thoroughly incomprehensible as it always was. In the paraphernalia of literary terminology, there is no term available to tell us what "Correspondances" might be.   (*RR*, p. 261)

What de Man claims here is that, in spite of all symmetries that we have encountered, a lyrical reading, that is, an understanding-reading by "Correspondances" of "Obsession" is not possible. "All we know is that it is, emphatically, *not* a lyric," de Man states. As a lyrical reading of the early sonnet, "Obsession" can be said to derive from it. But "Correspondances" does not derive in any possible mode from the later poem. It is a first text. By this I do not mean that it was written before "Obsession." de Man makes it quite clear that even if Baudelaire had "written, in empirical time, 'Correspondances' after 'Obsession,' this would change nothing" (*RR*, p. 261). Rather, it is a first text in that it is nothing but text, nothing but a textual event, inexplicable in the punctuality of its being there. As such a first text, "Correspondances" both implies "Obsession" and explains why there is such a poem in the first place. Of "Correspondances," de Man writes that "it, and it alone, implies, produces, generates, permits (or whatever aberrant verbal metaphor one wishes to

choose) the entire possibility of the lyric" (*RR,* pp. 261–262). "Obsession," by contrast, although it reads in a lyrical voice and renders "Correspondances" intelligible, leaves this text untouched, unread, unreadable.
While it is the first poem's incomprehensibility that incites the second,
the second in its turn shields and protects this very incomprehensibility.
No second text, no hermeneutical effort at all, can ever hope to come to
grips with the sheer unintelligibility of the first text to which the later
text, and, by implication, all hermeneutics as well, owes their existence.
Total unintelligibility, or unreadability, is the correlate of all understanding. Whereas understanding honors this unintelligibility that has made
its existence possible, by preserving the text through its defensive motion. de Man goes on:

> Whenever we encounter a text such as "Obsession"—that is, whenever
> we read—there always is an infra-text, a hypogram like "Correspon-
> dances" underneath. Stating this relationship, as we just did, in phe-
> nomenal, spatial terms or in phenomenal, temporal terms—"Obses-
> sion," a text of recollection and elegiac mourning, *adds* [the italics
> are de Man's] remembrance to the flat surface of time in "Correspon-
> dances"—produces at once a hermeneutic, fallacious lyrical reading of
> the unintelligible. The power that takes one from one text to the other
> is not just a power of displacement, be it understood as recollection or
> interiorization or any other "transport," but the sheer blind violence
> that Nietzsche, concerned with the same enigma, domesticated by call-
> ing it, metaphorically, an "*army* of tropes."   (*RR,* p. 262)

To the infratext, that is, to the matricial senseless text, the hypogram to
which all reading, as understanding, must respond—"Obsession" being
a case in point—reading can add only deception and error. "Whenever
we read," this is the case. When subjects read, the reading is lyrical.
When such a reading occurs, it means that its subject has been compelled by an infratext. The subject is lured into producing an illuminating interpretation of the infratext that is in truth nothing but a fallacious
addition. Subjective reading, thus, is not subjective. It not only obeys an
injunction to read but is deluded into thinking that it has made the
unintelligble intelligible. The addition that subjective reading makes to
the first text, an addition inevitably duped into believing that it comes to
an understanding with that text, never reaches that text. Its thread becomes never woven into the fabric of the infratext. Even though etymol-

ogy does not warrant the wordplay, the addendum's fallaciousness makes it fall away from the text it sought to illuminate. It is, moreover, violent in the full sense of the term, yet not for the banal reason that it forces an interpretation on a virgin text or betrays the essential unintelligibility of its object but because reading, being the result of a coercion by the first text, partakes in the sheer violence of that first text, entirely unintelligible in its firstness. Lyrical reading, a reading obsessed with understanding, is not in the least subjective, if "subjective" implies freedom and discernment. It rather manifests the violence of the incomprehensible positing power of language, or as de Man writes in the concluding lines, of "the materiality of actual history" (*RR*, p. 262).

Lyrical reading has now been put in its place and told its limits by a reading that reads what is always involved in a reading. "Obsession," for one, is deluded in its lyrical response to "Correspondances." Not only are generic terms such as *lyric* "always terms of resistance and nostalgia," but lyrical reading, even though a textual function, is a defense against the first text's incomprehensibility and hence likewise nostalgic of meaning. The remembrance and mourning that it adds to "Correspondances" betrays a "desired consciousness of eternity and temporal harmony as voice and song." By contrast, true "mourning" is less deluded. The most *it* can do is to allow for noncomprehension and enumerate nonanthropomorphic, nonelegiac, noncelebratory, nonlyrical, nonpoetic, that is to say, prosaic, or, better, *historical* modes of language power (*RR*, p. 262). One can confidently assume that this true "mourning" is mere reading, a reading that reads what happens in reading. In distinction from lyrical reading, this is nonlyrical. Without voicing an "I," such a reading is entirely impersonal. Rather than being on the defensive, that is, rather than seeking to understand, this reading that reads the Ur-text's coercion of lyrical reading into delusion allows for noncomprehension. It truly mourns in that it ruminates on the text alone. It is, therefore, a "pure" reading, of sorts.[31] In contradistinction to lyrical reading, mere reading adds nothing either to the unintelligible first text or to what the latter necessarily engenders. Consequently, unlike lyrical reading, it is never mystified. Rather than adding, mere reading repeats like the senseless "comme" of enumeration. It is, in de Man's words, a prosaic reading, one that repeats nothing less than language's arbitrary positing power. It becomes itself, thus as inexplicable and unaccountable as the Ur-text. Ascetically limited to reactivating the irreducibly incomprehensible event of the first text, or what de Man alludes to as "language's *materialist historicality*," mere reading successfully escapes all the illusions coextensive with all efforts to come to an understanding.[32]

"Anthropomorphism and Trope in the Lyric," as if a critical response to Derrida's conception of reading in "Plato's Pharmacy," strikes even the attempt to read understandingly with the uncompromising verdict of nostalgia and ideology. Even though the text manifests "itself" only through the distortions mere reading shows it to inflict on all the efforts to render it intelligible, the only thing mere reading strives at is to reactivate the text in its "purity," that is, before all obfuscating meaning sedimentation that renders the text's pristine unintelligibility unintelligible. Is there anything left to add to this conception of reading and the linguistic, or textual ontology, on which it rests? There is certainly nothing left to add to it if reading is thought to have done away with addition for good. But has mere reading indeed accounted for the delusive nature of all questions? Even granted that it has succeeded in bracketing all presuppositions proceeding with total sobriety and without illusion, what about its singular, if not idiosyncratic, kind of unconditionality? Is it not rooted in presuppositions and assumptions that it cannot neutralize, lest it jeopardize its own existence?

Most of the questions raised at the beginning of this chapter have now found an answer. But these questions presupposed others that I touched upon before and can now reformulate, or at least articulate. Let me, therefore, recall that one of the purposes of de Man's reading of the two Baudelaire poems was to suggest that the failure of literature, equipped as it is with comparatively superior rhetorical means, to fashion a union between the realm of aesthetic and cognitive judgment, or, respectively, between epistemology and rhetoric in general, compromises this project even more thoroughly than philosophical texts. The question regarding this union is undoubtedly a venerable issue. But if one factors into this equation that de Man's terms merely restate the old problem of being and thinking, a problem concommitant with philosophy, one sees that the stakes in demonstrating that the "crux of all critical philosophies and 'Romantic' literatures" (*RR*, p. 239) is hopelessly unsolvable are indeed quite high. de Man's concern with Cratylism, for one, clearly indicates his full awareness of the far-reaching consequences of such a philosophical debacle. Indeed, without a fundamental union on some level of being and thinking, theoretical and practical reason—to use Kantian terminology—stand no chance. Now, Romantic aesthetic ideology is, no doubt, one of the many faces that the union of being and thinking has taken in the history of Western philosophy. But this is precisely the problem. However, it must first be acknowledged that de Man's focus on the role that language and rhetoric play in making this union possible certainly opens new avenues in assessing the difficulties into which the necessary assumption of a fundamental unity of thought and being has consistently run. Yet, asserting that the historically specific formulation that shapes the problem of such a union in Romanticism, a problem that de Man's term "aesthetic ideology" aptly catches, is representative of the problem in general—of the shape such a union takes in Kant, for instance—is entirely misleading. Without wishing in any way to assert that no trace of aesthetic ideology exists in the history of philosophy, it is essential to distinguish, and hold separate, the levels on which it is thought necessary to posit the union in question. de Man, however, collapses things as different as the union of an ultimate (transcendental) condition of possibility of theoretical and practical judgments and the ideological or utopic dream of achieving the identity of being and thinking in the shape of a total harmony of the lived experiences of an aesthetically educated individual with the world or state. Only on condition that the union in question implies totality and demands inclusion of all possible levels of reality and ideality can immaculate transparency, absolute coinciding, perfect fitting, unbreachable identity, etc., become the problems that they are for de Man. Is it not precisely because of such a generalization of the norm of transparency, and a secret adherence to a form/content identity, that the question of rhetoric arises in the first place? If de Man did not assume that a poem, or a philosophical text, must stand as a linguistic artifact and on all its imaginable strata and in all parts of its syntax in a one-to-one relation of total transparency to what it announces, the question of language's disruption of the union of the signifier and the signified, form and content, would simply not pose itself. If the enunciative program is faulted by what occurs on the level of enunciation, it is because their total symmetry has been made the criterion of the truth of the enunciated.

Yet if the way meaning is conferred is in a position to interrupt in totality meaning itself, that is, the possibility of meaning defined as it has been, namely, as resting in a union of the aesthetic and the epistemological, an additional presupposition of mere reading comes into view. It concerns the ontological status of language and meaning. Indeed, for language to at all be able to disrupt the union supposedly aspired for in meaning, and with this, meaning itself, it must not only be irreducibly singular, it must also as such participate in what it disjoins. Brutally put, language must be meaningful itself, or meaning itself must be exclusively linguistic. If language, by virtue of the materiality of the signifier, or the "the *historical* modes of language power," is to stand a chance of exposing meaning as ideological in totality—and, mind you, reading is not intent on demonstrating that this or that seme is ideological, but that meaning is false consciousness *in toto*—the materiality of the signifier, or the unique event character of language, must have a certain ideality. They must, as I have suggested before, operate in the shape of a (general) conception of language. The other possibility for the way meaning is conferred to intervene in a disruptive mode in meaning itself requires that meaning has been beforehand stripped of all aesthetic, cognitive, or practical implications. It must have been reduced to what Friedrich Schiller, responding to a brand of skepticist criticism of his time not unrelated to mere reading, called its "crude element."[33] If one finds in de Man's work those two possibilities, is it not because the answer to the (transcendental) question of the possibility of disruption has been left pending?

I recall that for de Man, language wrecks the union between the senses and the spirit, the aesthetic and the epistemological, because it refuses to enter their equation. It draws baffles between the poles to be unified leaving them unable to cross to one another. With such total disjunction of what was to be united, the mediation and union in question are defeated for good. The very idea of mediation and union is ideological. The verdict reminds one of what the logical positivists called "pseudo-problems *(Scheinprobleme)*." de Man's critical debunking of all attempts to unify, or gather, though considerably more intransigent, is not unrelated to the Vienna School's critique of metaphysics, in that it proposes a categorical abandonment of all traditional philosophical issues.[34] Whereas the logical positivists relinquished many traditional philosophical problems as meaningless because no empirical (or rather material) truth criteria could be provided to verify them, de Man abandons them in their entirety because the criteria for there to be truth have been expanded to such a degree as to definitely foil all possibility of judgment. The criterion being the total transparency and absolute coinciding of the way meaning is conferred and meaning itself, all one is left with is hopeless juxtaposition, disjunction, contradition, and so forth. There is no way out of such impasse. *Aporia* is certainly not, as it is with Derrida, the very condition for (ethical) decision, invention, or interpretation. The traditional opposition's unsolvability voids them as legitimate problems in de Man's eyes. Notwithstanding the heightened sensibility to contradiction, a sensibility that itself is a function of an emphatic conception of identity or transparency, the underlying unthought of de Man's approach is a secret adherence to a formalist ideal of logical non-contradiction.

Since it is language itself, its autonomous positing power, that disrupts any attempt to bring about the union of the senses and the spirit, and hence any possibility to know, language itself, in its material historicality becomes the object *par excellence* of reading. Everything besides language is of the order of phantasm, and it, therefore, must enjoy the unconditional interest of the reader. Its injunction is to be repeated, to be infinitely reenacted in the randomness, uniqueness, and incomprehensibility of its occurring. Yet what is it that makes this resolute ascetism an inevitable necessity for mere reading? An additional hidden presupposition of mere reading resides in this: Given that everything a text seeks to achieve is of the order of false consciousness, the uniqueness of a text becomes necessarily divorced from its purpose, project, message, intentionality, meaning, etc. A text is no longer unique as the particular response that it provides to a question or as the particular way that it formally solves it but in its quality alone as a linguistic event as such. This presupposition forces mere reading into running in place and into the monotonous repetition that language (is) language (is) language (is) . . . Undoubtedly, the uniqueness beyond comparison makes reading a monotonous, mechanical, mindless operation. Yet, by way of this repetition, language in its irreducible randomness and meaninglessness, doubles itself and becomes ideal—in fact, ideality itself. Paradoxically, then, through reading, through its stubborn repetition of the mindless and blind materiality of the signifier, meaning returns. Reading achieves this unlikely task of transforming the meaningless into what alone is "universally" meaningful.

Appendix: On the Edges

After the liberation of Belgium, the editors and journalists of the collaborationist *Le Soir* were summoned to appear before the *Auditeur Général* to be interrogated about their activities. Paul de Man, who between 1940 and 1942 had contributed some 170 pieces of cultural and literary criticism to the newspaper in question, was among them. Yet, unlike Raymond de Becker, editor-in-chief until September 1943, and most of the other editors, de Man was not judged guilty, much less sentenced by this public institution initiated by the new Belgian government, whose verdicts are known for their severity. In 1955 Renato Poggioli, at that time director of the Harvard Society of Fellows, called on de Man to respond to anonymous accusations of collaborationist activities during the war, and he acknowledged, though quite evasively, having contributed literary articles to *Le Soir* and explained that he ended his work for the newspaper after the introduction of preventive censorship for the literary and cultural columns. The discovery in 1988 of de Man's wartime journalism by Ortwin de Graef made all of de Man's contributions publicly available and could have set the stage for a judicious and judicial appraisal of these early texts, some of which are indeed troublesome, and some, revolting. It could have been an occasion to question not merely why so many European intellectuals between the wars, and even during the war, could have been lured into collaborating with the occupier but why both the most staunch defenders of the humanist heritage as well as intellectuals with leftist leanings could, whatever the ambiguities were, and were it only for short periods, settle with the most reprehensible ideology in modern times. It could, in particular, have been an opportunity to ask what in the humanist tradition itself made such collaboration possible or, at least, did not prevent it, and thus to ask the question concerning the temptations for which, insofar as we continue to claim that heritage, we ourselves might fall. But, unfortunately, this was not to

235

be so, and an opportunity has thus been missed. The judgments by the press and some in academia that have been pronounced on Paul de Man since the issue of his wartime journalism has resurfaced share the common particularity that with few exceptions, they exempt themselves from observing what judgment qua judgment requires, namely, doing justice in judging. In their rush to judgment, they sacrifice justice itself. Indeed, as Geoffrey H. Hartman aptly remarks in "Judging Paul de Man," the "issue of judgment . . . is at the heart of the matter."[1]

One cannot but be struck by the haste with which in most cases the accusations have been made and the eagerness with which hearsay, rather than diligent documentation, has been used as evidence.[2] Indeed, as the at times even explicit dismissal of any need to read the articles of *Le Soir* demonstrates, de Man's judges thought themselves exempt from the obligation to proceed on the basis of publicly available historical facts. They made their case against de Man without reading, without analyzing, the texts in question. By refusing to read these texts, refusing even to try to understand them in their historical context, rhetoric, and their themes, did not the critics demonstrate that reading itself was one of their principal targets? Reading de Man's journalism, it was felt, would excuse, relativize, minimize the charges to be brought against him. It would also have meant an unacceptable delay in a verdict that had already been made in advance. In fact, for the most part, the charges had little to do with de Man's early deeds or errors in judgment.[3] It would thus have been a waste of time to give them the attention they would have required. From the beginnning the texts of the early "collaborationist" were only a side issue, a pretext for denouncing and silencing what the mature de Man stood for, a discipline of reading, in short, what he practiced and understood as deconstruction. Construing reading (and attention to language) as devious and destructive of the moral and humanist values of literary works,[4] the self-righteous critics of the allegedly nihilistic writings of the later de Man themselves dispensed with reading. This lack of probity is not a mere accident in the belated trial of de Man's later work in light of his early journalism. As Werner Hamacher has argued, the whole vocabulary in which the indictments are made and in which the sentence is pronounced as well as the position from which they are formulated show the prosecutors to simultaneously assume the role of judge and executioner, and thus to suspend "the principle of the separation of powers, one of the basic institutions of non-totalitarian societies."[5] The fear of reading is, of course, not unjustified. Reading the early texts would have exposed the critics in question to public scrutiny from which they sought to escape by presenting themselves as the "public" itself. It would also have made it more difficult for these critics to uphold their moral and humanist high ground in that such reading would have forced them to frontally face the fact that humanist values easily go hand in hand with the worst totalitarian ideologies and practices that humanity has known. Indeed, in the majority of cases, and for all the reasons seen, de Man's "public" trial in the aftermath of the revelation of his collaboration with the Nazi-controlled Belgian newspaper, a trial short of being a show trial, had only one objective: to discredit an uncomfortable scholar and teacher, to intimidate his followers, in the hope of initiating an academic purge.

While the above assessment of de Man's judgment does not amount to a wholesale acquittal, or even a search for mitigating circumstances, it does point out that this judgment is without justice. Indeed, it is not a judgment at all. The "public" outcry, lacking all the constitutive aspects of what a judgment implies, more often than not has taken the form of plain slander. And the recourse to the pettiest anecdotes of de Man's life demonstrates the intent to have been overkill.[6] Does not the discursive violence done to de Man in the denunciations and indictments in question border sometimes on what Primo Levi has called "unneccessary violence?"[7] The question imposes itself since many of the verdicts on de Man have been testimony to something other than judgment, something quite frightening. Judgment is indeed at issue in the de Man affair: de Man's own judgment or, rather misjudgment, between 1940 and 1942, that of his contemporary "judges" but also "our" ability to judge his misjudgments to begin with. This is not, I reiterate, a question of avoiding, suspending, or even delaying judgment. Nor is it to suggest that in this case all moral indignation is out of place, or that those who publicly made their indignation known are necessarily naive, or, at the very worst, malicious. I judge indeed de Man's collaboration with *Le Soir,* whatever the mitigating reasons, to have been inexcusable. In spite of the fact that he was probably pressured, even threatened with dismissal and forced labor, to write "Les Juifs dans la littérature actuelle,"[8] I judge the however convoluted anti-Semitism of that article to have been inadmissible support for an ideology that at that time had already become a murderous reality. But to judge and condemn is not enough, if the judgment is to be just. It does, undoubtedly, fulfill the duty to preserve the memory of one of the most horrendous events in history, what Hartman refers to as the judgment's aim "to change history into memory; to make a case for what should be remembered, and how it should be remembered."[9] Yet the uncompromising demand of judgment never to forget is not sufficient. As Nancy has remarked, "condemnation keeps at a distance, along with the condemned, the question of what it is that made their guilt possible." Judgment must, therefore, interrogate ideology, it must interrogate all the values, moral, humanist, and intellectual, that either made racism and the extermination camps possible, or did nothing to oppose to them.[10] Only by taking a deconstructive responsibility for the history of ideology—the ideology of values and their system at the heart of modern representations of the world—can judgment hope to be adequate to its task. In addition to demanding remembrance, judgment must reflect on what it is that made racist ideology and the Holocaust possible—or at least what did not prevent it—and what is today virtually capable of it. Only in this case can the judgment be a judgment, that is, a just judgment, a judgment with the least violence.

What became manifest in the "public" anger at de Man's wartime writings and in the subsequent denunciations is the tenacity of certain patterns of thinking and practices in dealing with the Nazi era and with its appeal to many intellectuals of the time. Although these patterns are not *per se* fascist, they lend themselves to fascist appropriation. How the de Man affair has been handled by the press has been a clear reminder of the potential threat to justice and democracy that these patterns represent. At best, they are unable to resist fascist appropriation. To respond to a case such as de Man's, it is imperative to confront the danger in question by inquiring into the duplicity of the vocabulary, conceptuality, and rhetorical and argumentative practices that have been mobilized in such an event. The first step must be the careful and patient reading of de Man's wartime essays themselves! One of the goals of such a reading would be to demonstrate that the ideas and ideologies that lead to fascism, or that don't oppose it, are still the same today. Undoubtedly, some of these ideas and ideologies are still very much alive. More importantly, by seeking to understand what it is in these early texts that made the "collaboration" in question possible, the goal of such a reading is to develop the critical skills requisite to responsibly resist the becoming ideological of our judgmental categories. Analyses by Werner Hamacher,

Samuel Weber, and Jean-Luc Nancy of de Man's early texts are exemplary
in this regard. Weber's outline of the evolutionist concept of history at
work in the young journalist's writings,[11] Nancy's underscoring of the
ideology of the intellectual, national-populist revolution, and of artistic
nationalism that animates and informs de Man's wartime texts,[12] and
Hamacher's insistence on the crucial ideology of realism in de Man's
thinking at the time are *incontournable* in this respect. They achieve at
least three things. They explain which totalitarian ideas and ideologemes—far from being exceptional for their time, broadly shared as they
were almost throughout the entire political spectrum—while not fascist
in a strict sense, made collaboration with the Nazi occupiers a possibility.
They also account for the fact that in the case of de Man these totalitarian ideas and ideologemes could (and even had to) be turned against
official Nazi doctrine—thanks to what Hamacher calls the "ambidexter-
ity" of these ideologemes[13]—in relentlessly defending a Belgicist position
against the occupiers. But what these analyses also do is to draw attention to the fact that neither self-righteous condemnation of de Man's
wartime activities nor honest and well-intended indignation about his
past face the issue. Without addressing the ideological reasons that made
collaboration a possibility—and here dialectical vigilence and determinate negation are equally insufficient—without taking responsibility for
them inasmuch as they are, as Nancy has put it, "our" history, judgments
about de Man's past remain hypocritical, to say the very least. By not
engaging the ideologemes in question critically (or deconstructively)—
the continuity and meaningfulness of history, the possibility of reactivating this meaning in totality at every and all moments, the spirituality of
the West, of nationalism, to name a few—all rebuttals continue to share
the responsibility for the disaster. For it is on the grounds of these ideas
and ideologemes that others, such as racism, could flourish. For racism
can not only coexist with them, while they, for their part, and there is
ample historical evidence of this, can put up with it, they can even, on
occasion, turn it to good account.

As I have already noted, the "public" trial of de Man for having written
for *Le Soir* served primarily to target deconstruction—with which the
name of de Man has been associated. Right from the start, the issue has
been one of continuity. That de Man could, possibly, have changed his
ideas since 1942 was not even taken into consideration. By surrepti-
tiously suggesting that, because de Man had sympathized with a detest-

able ideology in the forties, he must still hold the same ideas, his critics have denied him the right to difference, to having become different from what he had been at one time. Such change, moreover, is too much, too complex, too complicated, for the simple and straightforward mentality of the prosecutor, a threat to it, indeed, from which he or she must wash him or herself clean. In any case, the genetic, organic, or biologist fallacy at the heart of this reasoning that serves to cover up the self-righteousness of the "judges'" implicit claim to moral purity, simplicity, and integrity prefigures the outcome of the argument: de Man, and his work, are to be silenced. Since deconstruction is the real defendant in the trial in question, one cannot but observe that using de Man's work for the collaborationist Belgian newspaper to discredit and vilify it amounts to a most revolting and terrifying simplification of fascism. On trial for its incomprehensibility, obscurity, negativism, nihilism, antihumanism, general unwholesomeness, and whatever you wish, the fascism to which deconstruction is said to belong is not only recast in these same banal terms, but it is turned in the most irresponsible manner into a commodity. The denunciation of deconstruction's complexities and difficulties as fascist make use of "fascism" as a deterrent to impose, or reimpose, straightforward thinking and moral purity. These critics, evidently, do not know what they are talking about.

The whole de Man affair being conducted from the outset with the intent to disgrace de Man's later work, his self-styled judges have cast the question of how his early work may relate to the later work in a predictable manner. First, it must be noted that the way the link is made presupposes an organicist concept of the author and his work. Hartman writes: "By linking up not only the early and the later writings, but both of these bodies of work with a totalizing figure that claims to unify everything (his life, his writings, his writings with his life), we exhibit the very drive that led Adorno to the Aphorism: 'The whole is the untrue'."[14] Further, those judges that claim that the later writings are either a more sophisticated version of the abominable ideology at work in the essays of *Le Soir* or a clever cover-up of that ignominious past reveal themselves to be functionaries of the same ideologemes that informed de Man's early work and that, as has been said, either made collaboration with fascism a possibility or did not prevent it. The ideologemes that structure these judges' conceptual gestures declare that the meaning of history, or of an entire life, remains intact—whatever turns it might have taken (the turns being only variations of an invariable substrate)—and available in full at all moments, notwithstanding possible eclipses (such as in the fascist era). Do these critics, in particular, not know what they are doing? In what amounts to irresponsibility itself, they not only refuse the accused the promise of a future, they have always already deprived the defendant of that chance, and hence of what constitutes the other as other. The question of how the early work relates, or how it "relates" if it does not relate (that is, in a mode of continuity or discontinuity), is, of course, to be addressed. But the question of this relation must be taken up in a way that does not anticipate an answer. A just appraisal of the relation between the journalist writings and the mature work must make room from the start for the possibility that the "meaning" of that relation is still outstanding. Without allowing for surprise, without granting the chance of any future determination, no justice can prevail. Among the several axioms spelled out by Derrida for reading, and rereading, de Man and, in particular, for articulating the early with the later writings, I retain his injunction not to fall prey to two symmetrical errors, the first consisting of disclaiming all relation between the wartime writings and the work to come, the other, in asserting their complete identity.[15] Hartman has sought to address the links between the two segments of de Man's work by establishing symmetries (rather than identities) between them, but emphasizing above all what he calls, their "asymmetry."[16] He is not alone in suggesting that the later writings of de Man are infinitely distanced from his earlier positions. Needless to say, for anyone who has any (be it the most rudimentary) knowledge of the thrust of his later writings, nothing could be more evident. de Man's mature production is indeed an inexorable and devastating critique (uncomfortably severe for his critics, in that it draws the ground out from underneath of them) of precisely some of those concepts, ideas, categories, and ideologemes that allowed him to compromise with a disastrous ideology. de Man's relentless and uncompromising attempt to track down totalizing gestures is an attempt so radical as not even to spare its own totalizing temptation. With this, the later work is considered to relate to the earlier in a negative fashion— as its complete negation. The later work, while not heterogeneous to the early work, would derive its meaning from the negation *in toto* of everything that characterized the war writings. But construing the thrust of de Man's mature work in this way does not do him justice. Take, for instance, an issue that occupies de Man in his latest texts: materiality. In these texts, materiality comes to address the totalizing tendencies of language itself. Now, pitched against phenomenalism, materiality can (and must) be read, as Hamacher has suggested, as "an elaboration of the early theme of realism." But, even more than this, if de Man's thought on materiality forms a "system" with the notion of arbitrariness, punctuality, absence of relation, that is, with what I have highlighted under the term of absolute "singularity," then one must consider the possibility that "materiality" is a recast concept of the immediate. And the immediate is, as Hamacher has so convincingly shown, the desired effect of realism in de Man's wartime journalism.[17] At the very least, the early themes of immediacy, directness, and actual experience do reverberate in the notion of materiality. In this context, I would like to call attention briefly to Cathy Caruth's intriguing demonstration of a paradox present in de Man's deconstruction of reference. In her very dense essay "The Claims of Reference," she argues that de Man's insistence that language resists perceptual analogies and that "reference emerges not in its accessibility to perception," de Man allows for a "referential significance of his own theory," one "in which the impact of reference is felt, not in the search for an external referent, but in the necessity, and failure, of theory."[18] This referential significance beyond (perceptual, intuitive) reference—which has led Jürgen Fohrmann to invoke a "new unambiguity"[19]—suggests a mode of referring and signifying that is not mediated by theory and that is actualized in, or as, the failure of theory itself. With "materiality," then, we find an aspect of de Man's later work that is neither simply identical with the theme of immediacy in the earlier writings nor simply different from it. It is something else, something other, something that cannot be grasped entirely from the earlier work— in so far as it stands in a relation of negation to the wartime writings— but neither can it be understood merely from the perspective of the later works insofar as it replays the earlier. What materiality is can be got at only by resisting the alternatives of a heterogeneity or a complete identity of the two bodies of writings. Understanding the notion of materiality, understanding de Man's thought more generally, does indeed call for interpretation, on a different time, a future time. If we are to judge this thought, and to judge it justly—that is, acknowledging that it is ultimately impossible to go give the other his due justice—we must concede the possibility of its being understandable only from interpretations still to come.

Judgment is at the heart of the de Man matter. I recall Primo Levi's analyses of the "grey zone" of the *Lager,* that is, of the *Sonderkommandos* made up by certain prisoners who had collaborated with the Nazis. Before we judge the errors and weaknesses of these prisoners, we must, Levi argues, take into account that corrupting prisoners by tempting them with power was the most diabolical crime of national-socialism, and only those "who found themselves in similar circumstances and had the opportunity to test for themselves what it means to act in a state of coercion" can judge them.[20] While no comparison can obtain between these prisoners forced into collaboration and Paul de Man,[21] can one, even in his case, judge without questioning, at least, the grounds of self-certainty implied in the act of such judgment, without wondering if one would have resisted, would have shown the civil courage to say no, even at the threat of deportation and death? Judge we must, but we must judge justly, responsibly, that is, in full awareness of the impossibility of doing justice to the Other. Such a judgment must therefore step away from the certainty and the self-congratulation that thinks itself immune to the corruption by power. Such a judgment must be willing to question both the ideas and ideologemes of fascism itself, and those ideas and ideologemes that can, and in secret, tolerate a tendency in that direction.

The text that follows was written in 1988. It responds to the disclosure of de Man's wartime writings. This response bears the traces both of the singularly painful discovery and the not less revolting, and irresponsible, reaction by the media. Despite its shortcomings—in particular, the too benign criticism of de Man's traditionalist and conservative views in most of his essays on literary and cultural issues, and of the potentially fascistic tendencies of his nationalism and Europeanism (even when turned against the political ambitions of Nazi Germany), and of the naiveté with which he expected an intellectual and artistic revolution to meet the problems of the day—it appears here unchanged.

Undoubtedly, the discovery of de Man's early journalistic writings represents a formidable legacy for his friends and foes alike. The bequest consists of coming to grips, in an intellectually and ethically responsible fashion, with the shocking fact that during a brief period, the young de Man wrote a literary chronicle for *Le Soir,* a newspaper whose political columns were at that time under strong German control. Responsible examination, however, requires detailed and in-depth documentation of the historical, cultural and political situation of Belgium between 1939 and 1942, so that the truly incriminating facts can be established with the necessary precision, and no confusion remains as to what under the given circumstances can and cannot be laid to de Man's charge. Responsible examination also requires that such inquiry be conducted in the spirit of respect that both friend and foe, as Others, demand. Yet, from the precipitation with which de Man's case has been taken up by the academic community and the newspapers, from the ludicrous and delirious charges leveled against him, as well as from the hatred that is evident in so many of the accounts, it is more than clear that the challenge of determining exactly what de Man's wartime activities amount to and what they mean has not been met. Or rather, since most of the discussions that have taken place have deliberately dismissed the most elementary rules of documentation (in this case, reading for instance, the incriminating material) as well as all other standards of philological honesty and integrity, not to mention the basic ethical guidelines for any debate, the minimal conditions for discussion have simply not been met. One cannot but be deeply terrified by the silliness, stupidity and maliciousness of the accounts in question, especially if one keeps in mind that the primary goal of the rage in question is a settling of accounts with "deconstruction." Indeed, one must assume that such trampling of all rules intellectual and ethical in the rampage against de Man and "deconstruction" is supposed to set future standards for the academic community. Disregard of history, disrespect for textual evidence, wild analogization, subjective elucubration, irrational outburst, are among the stupefying exemplars raised to the status of precepts for the learning community.

If we are then to take account of de Man's war-time writings,[22] and if we may, indeed, be compelled to consider them irresponsible and unpardonable, let us at least establish as precisely as possible what it is that we may have to judge as inadmissible. Intellectual probity and moral integrity require that we do so.

de Man's collaboration with a Nazi-controlled newspaper was obviously utterly irresponsible. But if this is not to be an abstract judgment (and thus a misjudgment) the irresponsibility has to be set into its proper context: the desire on the part of the young de Man to write on literature, perhaps at any price (a desire which becomes understandable if one recalls that his education did not permit him to study literature at any

Belgian university), his economic situation, the publication opportunities in Belgium at that time, or the fact that he stopped writing for the
literary column of *Le Soir* when that column was censured as well, etc.
Fully irresponsible also is one article of the approximately 290 articles
and reviews that he wrote between 1939 and 1943—"Les Juifs dans
la Littérature Actuelle" (*Le Soir,* March 4, 1941)—that uses undeniably
anti-Semitic language, and perhaps two others which are much more
ambiguous, as we will see in a moment, and which, respectively, hold
Jews responsible for decadence in art and seem to celebrate Hitlerianism
as the essence of the German soul. But these two last essays—"A View
on Contemporary German Fiction" (*Het Vlaamsche Land,* August 20,
1942) and "*Voir La Figure,* de Jacques Chardonne" (*Le Soir,* October 28,
1941)—definitely fall in a different category from the article on the Jews
in literature. As I will argue, these two articles, in different ways, give in,
more clearly than the others, to some Nazi stereotypes which they are
naive enough to believe that they can circumvent and undo by textual
maneuvers. To have given in to making use of these stereotypes, however
ambiguously, to have perhaps believed that they could be subverted by
other articles de Man wrote at that time, is perhaps a sign not necessarily
of irresponsibility, but certainly of naiveté and confusion. But let me
come back to "Les Juifs dans la Littérature Actuelle." It is the one truly
incriminatory piece. Although the essay is undoubtedly rather complex,
and is, as Derrida has pointed out—not in what Richard Bernstein calls
"a bravura act of deconstruction," but merely in an act of attentive reading of what this text unmistakingly tells us—motivated by a desire to
criticize vulgar anti-Semitism (and through it perhaps all anti-Semitism),[23] it also speaks of Jews as foreign, or alien powers, of having
meddled in all aspects of European life (except literature), and finally
refers in a quite equivocal manner to the possibility of solving the Jewish
problem by creating a Jewish colony isolated from Europe. Obviously,
these statement are a far cry from the official anti-Semitism of the day,
but they are nonetheless objectionable and unpardonable. If one can
trust testimony by relatives and close friends (Jewish and non-Jewish) of
the young Paul de Man, he had not the least strain of anti-Semitism. But
that in order to be able to write in these journals he gave in to the
language of Nazi ideology, that he did not resist anti-Semitic stereotypes
on several occasions, these are the facts with which we must charge de
Man. They speak to his confusion at the time, to a certain blindness and

opportunism on his part. These facts are bad enough, but, making due allowances, one must also admit that, however awful, they are rather harmless. The *Auditeur Général* who examined Paul de Man after the war decided not to pursue his case—in contrast to other journalists of *Le Soir.* This amounts to clearing de Man of the charge of collaboration and is thus evidence of the political and historical insignificance of his wrongdoings. In short, his wrongdoings must be seen in their proper perspective. To disregard the exact nature of his "crime," as it has been called, is to bear witness to an inexcusable injustice resulting either from stupidity or maliciousness. But it is not only an injustice regarding de Man himself—as when Jon Wiener calls him "something of an academic Waldheim"[24]—it is also more importantly, more atrociously, an inexcusable injustice with respect to the Jewish people. To put Waldheim and de Man on the same plane is to show a staggering lack of historical discrimination which implies a shameless belittling of Nazi atrocities and the suffering of the Jewish people during World War II. Indeed, from many of the articles published on the de Man issue, it is rather obvious that their authors, or some of those quoted for statements, are less concerned with historical accuracy than with the attempt to settle accounts, even if this takes place at the price of all justice and decency. The de Man affair, although it has found its way into major newspapers, is a strictly academic affair. It makes sense only with respect to a debate that divides academics around something called "deconstruction." To score a hit against this spectre of perversion as its critics see it, they are willing, as one could witness over the last several months, to trash all standards of intellectual and ethical integrity. What is thus truly at stake in this debate is, as mentioned above, nothing less than the minimal criteria and rules of professional ethics and intellectual probity.

Naturally one understands the groundless assertions and authoritarian presumptions leveled against de Man, without difficulty. Nothing is easier to fathom than their riskless pretensions that are of the order of irrational outbursts and settling of accounts. In traditional terms, they belong to the immediacy of nature, or what Benjamin calls the "mythical." Riskless, these assertions fall behind as they fail to make the leap without which no thinking gets off the ground. Many may share them, and yet they do not hold, to adapt Kantian terminology, before a tribunal that assures to reason its lawful claims. But, one understands them just as easily for their complete lack of all objectivity and universality.

If, consequently, one article that contains decidedly anti-Semitic statements, two that in spite of their ambiguity still seem to tilt in the direction of anti-Semitic ideology or of an uncritical acceptance of Hitlerianism, and finally the fact that most of these articles were written for a newspaper that followed (as far as its political content was concerned) a Nazi line, are the incriminating charges to be held against the young journalist as clearly disastrous evidence that allows for no attenuation, what then is the status of the remaining articles—288 to be precise? What happens if we read them?

To read, here, means to attentively seek to understand the sense of the writings in question which also implies situating them in their proper context, a skill normally to be expected from educated persons, but nowadays often associated with deconstruction, especially if the sense of the written does not fit preconceived notions. For anyone who is cognizant of the issues debated by both the left and the right between the wars, as well as of the style of those debates, these are not collaborationist or pro-Nazi writing as they have been labeled on numerous occasions. One cannot even say that they express a clear sympathy for German culture and literature.[25] They certainly do not advocate any of the themes of German cultural politics. Still, since the bulk of these articles is far from being unambiguous, and I more often than not feel quite ill at ease with what I read in them, I choose to approach them through the two articles that I have singled out as being on the borderline between anti-Semitism and the inefficient subversion of its premises. Indeed, all the articles written during the occupation that are not just simple reviews have such a double face, owing to de Man's sometimes successful, sometimes unsuccessful, maneuvers between ideological positions. Sometimes the stakes are high as is the case with the two articles in question—"A View on Contemporary German Fiction" and the Chardonne review—most of the time, the issues debated are of secondary interest. But from the start let us emphasize that such maneuvering is not characteristic of Nazi writings. Although one would have liked to see de Man opt unambiguously for one of the positions in question, and in spite of the fact that these articles convey at times a shocking violence, one must have the honesty to admit that in tone and style they are quite different from any of the collaborationist writings of the period. To show this, let me then focus, first on "A View on Contemporary German Fiction." In this article, de Man, seemingly in conformity with the Nazi defamatory evaluation of modern art, classifies expressionism as "aberrant" and "degenerate." In addition, he claims "that it was mainly non-Germans, and specifically Jews who went in this direction" (p. 325).[26] It is undoubtedly difficult to remain aloof when encountering such a statement, in particular, since it echoes the accusation made by the Nazis that this art is "subversive," and "un-German" (*undeutsch*). De Man, indeed, demarcates the "strongly cerebral disposition, founded upon some abstract principles and very remote from all naturalness" of the expressionist group, from another group at work in Germany that "remained true to the proper norms of the country." Nothing, ultimately, will make one's discomfort go away regarding these painful utterances by the young de Man. Yet, such distress does not exempt us from the obligation to examine these quotations in their proper context—the content of the article itself, as well as the whole production over the three years in question. Because I am profoundly upset by what I read I am not acquitted from the responsibility of reading the texts in which these statements occur and of properly situating them. Intellectual probity requires that I acknowledge the following: First, expressionism as a whole is not condemned, but only a certain group that uses "the though very remarkable in themselves theses of expressionism" in an aberrant fashion.[27] In no way identical to the Nazi condemnation of expressionism which include those "very remarkable theses" as well, and which made no distinction between groups within this movement, de Man's elaborations are also extremely elusive as to the identity of the group he is talking about. Second, the "good" German literature pitted against this limited group of expressionist writers is not characterized in terms that would emphasize their Germanic qualities (*deutsch,* or *völkisch*) but in terms that stress this literature's "assimilation of foreign norms which are transformed and reduced to a number of specific and constant values, the own spiritual property of the nation." Small wonder, then, if among the writers thus celebrated de Man not only lists Carossa and Stehr whose mysticism and ethical concerns are indeed more specifically German according to de Man's classification, but also, and especially, Jünger and Alverdes whose susceptibility to French sensibility and psychological analysis is underlined as a characteristic of the status of their work as "world literature." This characterization of "good" German literature is not in conformity with the premises of Nazi cultural politics geared toward the elimination of all literature not only of bolshevist but also of cosmopolitan signature. Third, the cerebral quality of expressionism, that sets it over and against the other type of German literature, is an attribute associated throughout all the articles not only with Jewish thinking but with French culture in particular. As we have seen, at least one group of the German writers that de Man celebrates in his essay is influenced by a cerebrality which in their case is even raised "to the realm of crystal clear beauty." And finally, the qualification 'degenerate' is, at least, complicated by the fact that de Man seeks to keep French artistic production clear from such accusations. Taken as a whole, French literature is said to be engaged in experiments that show "such sharp aberrations" that they cannot be classified. Yet, he goes on, it would be "a dangerous artificial simplification" to apply the criterion "degenerate" to French art. In an article from the same journal (dated May 17–18, 1942, entitled "Contemporary Trends in French Literature") he notes that "almost monstrous hair-splitting" and a "style which has used up all of its vital force" (to be found on English and Dutch rather than on French soil) is not without "indisputable merit" if one thinks of Joyce, Woolf, or Vestdijk. As he points out here, "decadence and inferiority are not necessarily synonymous" (p. 305). Considering this positive valorization of the notion of decadence, a valorization based precisely on some of the dominant features of Nazi characterizations of decadence, one cannot but wonder what this notion can still mean when applied to a group of expressionist writers. The fact remains, of course, that de Man depicts this group as "decadent," and that he writes that "mainly non-Germans and specifically Jews" contributed to the production of the group in question. But after what we have seen, what precisely can the semantic value of the term "decadent" be? From the article, one gathers that this term designates cheap showmanship, artificiality, "aimed at easy effects," "forced, caricatured representation of reality" (which, by the way, is not, as we will see later, the strength of German literary writing, according to de Man), "cheap successes by using imported formulas" (p. 325). "Decadent" thus means nothing less and nothing more than lousy, artless art, perhaps also vulgar art in the sense that de Man gives this term on several occasions. "Decadent" also means the inability to assimilate foreign norms—apparently a strength of German literature—and thus the failure to mediate imported values and the spiritual values of a nation. Such failure turns the imported into cheap effects in art, into artless artifice. The article, as we have seen, associates "mainly non-Germans and specifically Jews" with this failure. It is difficult, if not impossible, to know whom de Man is particularly thinking of here, especially since not all of expressionism is included in this condemnation. Moreover, such characterization of the group in question does not match very well with its "apparently strong cerebral disposition." It harmonizes even less with the brilliant cerebral qualities of the Jewish mind, to which he refers in the article on "Les Juifs dans la Littérature Actuelle." In the same way that the pejorative use of "decadent" merely means "cheap" and "artless," the reference to the Germans, non-Germans, and Jews responsible for decadent art seems to boil down to a reference to third-rate artists. Kafka, undoubtedly, does not fall into this category. In short, then, the distressing fact remains that de Man draws on some themes of Nazi ideology, and that he gives in to the denunciatory gestures of pointing at alien forces and influences. This fact remains, and in all its bewildering force. But what a more careful reading of a text such as the one just analyzed shows is that the terms and the gestures referred to, when not simply hollowed out as is the case with the notion of "decadence," are complicated to the point of confusion. No deconstruction is necessary to see this, just a simple attentive reading. What such a reading brings to light is the true dimension of what we must continue to be upset about—namely, to have given in to drawing on Nazi stereotypes and ideological themes, unaware of the danger that they represented, in the naive hope of containing them through textual manipulation. But once again, this sorry fact, for both historical as well as material reasons, is no excuse for calling de Man's early writings Nazi or collaborationist propaganda. Although the ambiguity of some of these texts remains intact, and although one's discomfort with some of their topics lingers on, one must also remain sensible to the strategies they display. One must, to do justice, patiently follow de Man's moves throughout these texts, in a war of displacements that could not be won.

In an article entitled "Que pensez-vous de la guerre?" (*Jeudi*, January 4, 1940), he writes: "In the same way that one has to eliminate the causes of the war in order to overcome the war, so one must prevent creating a terrain propitious to its development in order to overcome Hitlerianism" (p. 13). With this aim in view, he recommends a total reversal of European interior and exterior politics, a reversal that would serve to overcome the nationalist spirit of the European countries which is at the root of the problems that have led to the war. Although the bulk of the articles written for *Le Soir, Cahiers du Libre Examen,* and *Het Vlaamsche Land,* need a more careful and patient study than I can devote to them here, it can be said that with the German occupation of Belgium, with the German hegemony in Europe having become an indisputable fact, de Man turns away from the internationalism of his writings in *Jeudi,* and takes recourse to the themes of nationalism and cultural patrimony in order to resist German rule. This issue which is a decisive thread throughout most of the articles—the concern with national personality and difference, patriotic feeling, the protection if not creative development of the national patrimony, the insistence on the independence of nationalities—is incongruous with the dominant Nazi ideology. Now, it is certainly true that defense of national autonomy belonged, at first, to the type of opposition permitted (and even encouraged for a brief period) by the occupation forces. de Man's emphasis on nationalism would thus seem to be a part of what was tolerated by the Nazis, and to lack all connotations of resistance. But this initial liberalism on the part of the Nazis came to an end toward the beginning of 1943 when it was no longer permitted to publicly reflect on the destiny of Belgium in the new European order. It was not an abrupt end, however, to the extent that truly energetic defense of national independence had never been to the liking of the occupiers. But to evaluate de Man's stress on nationalism it is, indeed, necessary to realize that independently of the initial climate of tolerance that existed in Belgium, national politics could not, in principle, be compatible with the implicit and explicit aims of Nazi politics. According to Heinrich Himmler's directive for "the new European order," all development of national consciousness and culture was to be foiled, especially (or let's say, first), in the East. All national cultural and artistic life was to be destroyed, as has been demonstrated in the case of Poland.[28] de Man's continuous emphasis on the independence of nationalities, especially in his writing for the Nazi controlled *Le Soir,* is thus a paradox of sorts that needs to be investigated a little further.

From the outset, let me say that not everything in these articles is entirely consistent. Especially when it comes to evaluating the role of Germany in Europe, what Germany's annexational politics and hegemony mean for Europe as a whole, de Man wavers. In March 1942 ("A la recherche d'un nouveau mode d'expression"), he writes: "For him who like me finds himself immersed in the hurly-burly of facts and actions, it is difficult to acquire a sufficiently synthetic overview of things in order to be able to grasp the meaning and the direction of the evolution that one is going through" (p. 208). Yet, in spite of all these doubts, uncertainties, and ambiguities whose effects (to the extent that they produce occasionally one-sided valorizations) are of course not negligible, a quite coherent picture arises if one reads the totality of the articles. This picture provides, indeed, an answer to the question of how de Man understood the German hegemony in Europe, and what the occasional reference to "immediate collaboration" in his articles could have meant. In a review from October, 1941, of Jacques Chardonne's book, *Voir La Figure*—that is, in the second borderline article—de Man explains that "the future of Europe can only be anticipated within the frame of the possibilities and the needs of the German genius" (p. 158). The war, he notes, is the result of "the definitive emancipation of a people that finds itself, in its turn, called upon to exercise a hegemony in Europe," of a people in which the "Hitlerian soul" fuses with the "German soul" for reasons that lie with "elementary givens, that is, with the historical constants that give the German people its unity and specific character." Now, what this means for de Man, and it is clearly spelled out, is that this war has a "national character." However deceptive this conclusion may seem (and we will come back to this issue later), one cannot overlook its rather unorthodox implication: if the war is a symptom of Germany's coming into its own proper national identity, then the hegemony that it is supposed to play in Europe must, obviously, come to a halt precisely at the borders of the other national blocks that make up Europe as a whole. As for many other thinkers during the years before the war (but afterward as well: E. R. Curtius, for instance), for de Man "Europe," and "Western culture and civilization," are politico-cultural categories in the name of which all events become evaluated. But what distinguishes de Man's concept of "Europe" from that of a Europe under German rule, or of a Europe as a spiritual unity beyond all nationalities (Curtius), is his insistence on the constituting role of the various nationalities that make up Europe as a geographical unit. de Man's emphasis on a "European thinking" in which "national sentiments can freely come to expression and . . . (in which) every nation is fully conscious of its own worth" (*Het Vlaamsche Land*, March 29–30, 1942), has the practical aim of defending "Western culture against a decomposition from the inside or an overwhelming onrush by neighboring cultural norms" (p. 303). It goes without saying that this concern with warding off "the increasingly menacing interferences" that threaten the values of the West (*Le Soir,* March 12, 1942) can lend itself to all forms of xenophobia, anti-Semitism first and foremost (p. 204). "Les Juifs dans la Littérature Actuelle" is ample proof of this, as many of the present accounts of the de Man affair also exhibit a similar xenophobia of their own. Indeed, any discourse, then and now, that becomes set on defending a state of affairs, or values in the name of the proper, homogeneity, continuity, etc. *can* slip into fascist exorcism of the Other. The debate around the de Man affair and "deconstruction" is just another case in point. But, apart from some occasional ambiguities, de Man's insistence on a nationalism whose conception is "miles apart from sentimental patriotism" (*Het Vlaamsche Land,* March 29–30, 1942), serves to counter nationalistic isolation and hardening, and to keep interference by one nation in the affairs of another in check (p. 303). Indeed, "the disappearance of one of those original centers [the individual nations, R.G.], as a result of political arbitrariness or economic injustice," has to be avoided at all cost since it would mean "an impoverishment for the whole of Europe," de Man writes (ib.). Paradoxically, the idea of a "European parallelism" (ib.), that is of a nationalism that is "the exact opposite of being exclusive," is said to have been developed primarily in Germany (*Le Soir,* March 31, 1942), thus, by that nation which, at the time de Man is writing, has occupied most of Europe (p. 217). Of this present nationalism, de Man says that it is "complementary. Its object is to discover the national virtues, to cultivate and to honor them, but also to adapt them to those of neighboring peoples in order to achieve, through such summation of the particular gifts, a real unification of Western culture" (*Le Soir,* April 28, 1942) (p. 226). This is the point, then, where the references to the question of collaboration can be discussed. It is raised by de Man precisely in the *Le Soir* article on Chardonne (October 28, 1941) in which he argues that the German hegemony and the ensuing war are profoundly nationalistic in character. Yet he notes that the arguments that plead for immediate collaboration please only those who are already of such an opinion while they fail to convince anyone who is not. Similarly, in an article from October 14, 1941, after having claimed that the need for action under the form of immediate collaboration "is a compelling reality to any objective mind," he claims that it is too early to "become disheartened by the universal incomprehension [regarding this necessity, R.G.] and to withdraw into one's ivory tower," because in any case such "activity cannot take on a direct and material form" (p. 154). The context for these statements is a review of Daniel Halévy's *Trois Epreuves* in which de Man insists that

France can only be saved if it returns to its past in order to "discover among the laws, customs, and aspirations that constitute the patrimony of the nation, those that need to be eliminated or favored for the regeneration to take place" (p. 153). From this context, it becomes clear that "immediate collaboration," a necessity that arises from the need of a nation under German rule to choose between death and life, in no way means collaboration with the Nazi oppressor in the sense of denationalization and assimilation into the *Reich*. This is clearly spelled out in "Le destin de la Flandre" (*Le Soir,* September 1, 1941), where such temptation is called catastrophic. "Immediate collaboration" is said to be indirect and nonmaterial because all it can consist of is a furthering of national identity and independence (thus exactly the opposite of what the Germans demanded of the subjected countries) (p. 140). It is thus not a collaboration with the occupier that de Man is advocating here, but collaboration at creating a Europe where "a free contact between peoples that know themselves as different and insist on difference, but also hold each other mutually in high esteem, secures political peace and stability" (*Le Soir,* April 28, 1942) (p. 227). It is a collaboration, thus, that seeks to contain the assimilation threat by working at creating a Europe in which each nation, although it tries at first to be itself, also respects the character of other nations, "and does not dream for one moment to impose its own views" (p. 226). The question that remains undecided is whether such European parallelism is to be achieved under German rule ("We can only be dignified members of a German state in so far as that state allows us to be dignified Dutchmen"), or in a Europe in which the German cultural bloc is contained by an equally powerful French cultural bloc ("'To be dignified Dutchmen' amounts to maintaining between the two cultural blocs that are France and Germany that center [*noyau*] that was able to give humanity admirable products of an independent genius"). This uncertainty traverses all the articles, and in particular "Le destin de la Flandre" (September 1, 1941), from which I drew the preceding citations (p. 140). Yet the sympathy of the young journalist is clearly with a Europe in which a confederation of nationalities evens out the strengths and weaknesses of any particular nation. This is manifest especially in the decisive role that de Man implores the French to play with respect to German culture within a unitary Europe. The fact that de Man is at times critical of French cerebrality, and has some good things to say about German novels, has led a number of hasty interpreters to conclude that his sympathies were unequivocally with German culture. Nothing could be more wrong, as a patient reading of the articles in their totality reveals.[29] Indeed, de Man's pessimistic account of French thought between the wars, and above all since the armistice, has all the qualities of a call to action. In his eyes, only French genius can in the long run contain German mysticism and obscurantism. Let me develop this point in some greater detail.

In a review of Friedrich Sieburg's "Dieu est-il français?" (*Le Soir,* April 28, 1942), de Man defines the collapse of France as "signifying infinitely more than just another episode in the present war. It is the destruction," he writes, "of a spirit, a system of values, of an entire *Weltanschauung,* which marks a decisive date in the history of civilization." What has made this collapse possible, and forecloses any "optimism as to the future possibilities of French culture," is the French's stubborn entrenchment in a mentality of individualism (p. 226). It is a mentality, de Man remarks in an article on *Notre Avant-Guerre* by Robert Brasillach (*Le Soir,* August 12, 1941), profoundly unpolitical and involved with aesthetic and poetic pleasure. What de Man terms on several occasions "the present revolution," however, is, he writes, political, and corresponds as an "inevitable necessity" to "the peoples who have a very developed notion of the collective, and who have spontaneously turned to modes of life that are less individualistic" (p. 131). The French, by contrast, lack political sense. Their individualism prevents them from understanding the true causes of the collapse of France. It is interesting to note here that it is especially French writers who are right-wing sympathizers that de Man accuses of lacking this sense of the political. Brasillach is a case in point. As proof of this inability on the part of writers to understand what is happening in Germany, de Man writes—in a sentence whose violence remains astounding in spite of the point that it tries to make: "The reaction of Brasillach before a spectacle such as that of the Nazi party congress at Nurnberg on the occasion of which he shows terror about the 'strange' nature of that demonstration, is that of someone for whom this sudden importance of the political in the life of a people represents an inexplicable phenomenon." This discovery of the political by the German people not only translates as an effervescence of grandeur and a sense of the infinite, it also takes on an aura of mysticism. "We enter a mystical era, a period of faith and belief . . .," de Man writes in his review of Sieburg's book (p. 227). It is an era that resembles in many ways that of the Middle Ages. Yet, in an article on Drieu la Rochelle's *Notes pour comprendre le siècle"* (*Le Soir,* December 9, 1941), de Man shows himself very critical of such an ideal, and the antirationalism associated with it ("theories that show a contempt close to hatred for cerebrality and that turn more toward the animal virtues that exist in man") (p. 170). In the Sieburg review, however, he seems at first to endorse the ideal in question to the extent that the norms that constitute the present political situation, and that "several authors" have compared to those of the Middle Ages, are said to possess today "the superiority of an extremely perfected technical and political organization" and to be permeated with "the lesson of an entire humanist past that protects against all obscurantism" (p. 227). But de Man does not seem to be too confident as to this last point, since it is on this occasion, precisely, that he appeals to the virtues of clarity, logic, and harmony that characterize French spirit. In the same way as he had already praised rationalism against Drieu la Rochelle, here again de Man takes recourse to "a certain form of French reason that seeks to fix the limits everywhere and to establish moderation." Indeed, the role of French cerebrality is essential to contain the obscurantism that pervades the political as it articulates itself in Germany. de Man writes: "The maintenance of the continuity of the French spirit is an inherent condition of the grandeur of Europe. Especially if the general orientation goes towards the deep, obscure, natural forces, the French mission that consists of moderating excesses, of maintaining the indispensable links with the past, of equilibrating the erratic drives, is of utmost importance." (And when right after this statement he calls upon the French "to freely open themselves to the foreign influences," it is precisely to ask them to play a moderating role by assuming the position of a cultural bloc that would hold at bay the nationalist excesses of Nazi Germany.) But this role of French intellectual culture is not merely limited to serving as a force of restraint vis-à-vis German extremism—such a role would, indeed, characterize French cerebrality as secondary and supplementary compared to German political culture—the French analytical and moderating spirit is expected to play a role equal to that of German profundity and mystical fervor. This becomes particularly clear in the article on "Le destin de la Flandre."

In this article, nationality is determined as an art that is specific to a people of a geographical area (and not in terms of culture which is defined as transnational), and de Man sets out to determine the irreducibly particular nature of Flemish art, and thus of that which profoundly distinguishes the Flemish nation from any other. Flemish art is subsequently determined according to categories that mark it off from those constitutive of the art and national spirit of other countries, more precisely from the art constitutive of what de Man calls here the two cultural blocs of Germany and France. Flemish art, he claims, is first and foremost, pictorial (even in literary writing) and realist. It is consequently different from French art, which is dominated by its abstract content (psychological analysis); but because it is realist, it is also opposed to German art, which "surrounds everything with a dreamlike mist." Indeed, it "remains realist in the sense that it tries to evoke nature in its rough state (*état brut*) without trying to catch its mystery by means of symbols"—the hallmark of German art (pp. 139–140). But symbolism which for de Man constitutes the essence of German artistic expression is also Romantic. Yet, in the same way that Flemish art must defend itself against French influences that risk hampering the Flemish creative élan, it must also be on guard against the German paradigm. As de Man puts it, "the romantic periods are not very favorable to the brilliant vitality of the Flemish artistic temperament which is oriented in an opposite direction" (p. 140). What is more, to become dissolved in a Germanic community would lead to the catastrophic state of effacing what constitutes, precisely, the profound originality of the Flemish genius. Under no circumstances must the political forces crush this creative potential, de Man notes, because it is bound to play a decisive role between the two cultural blocs of France and Germany, which are thus staged as independent, equally important nationalities and art styles. de Man's emphasis on the irreducible specificity of the Flemish genius thus seems to promote a plurality of independent nationalities that cohabit in one transnational unit—"Europe"—and in which none imposes its will on the others, although each becomes limited by the others, thus preventing the isolation and hardening of its own specificity. But his stress on the realist character of Flemish aesthetic sense could still have a further implication, namely, that of being capable of mediating between the two opposite blocs, France and Germany. Indeed, whereas French genius proceeds to a cerebral analysis of phenomena, German symbolic art "does not teach us anything concrete and does not enrich our knowledge." All it does is to produce "that thrill (*frisson*) that emanates from great art," de Man writes (*Le Soir,* March 1, 1942) (p. 216). The Flemish spirit is thus capable of a mediating role between highly abstract knowledge and a powerful emotional apprehending of things. Since Flemish art (and thinking) "attempts to reproduce reality without hiding any of its aspects even most fleeting and most ignored," its artistic discipline is not only capable of indisputable grandeur, as de Man remarks in the article on Flanders, but perhaps of a knowledge more objective and more balanced than French abstraction and German feeling (p. 140). de Man's insistence on the role that the Flemish are to play in Europe, "not as imitators of a neighbor whose state of mind is dissimilar," but as creators according to their own impetus, emphasizes the potential of this people for a less prejudiced understanding and realist accounting of what is happening in Europe.

Let me pause here for a moment. After having read as carefully as the present context permits some of the articles written for *Le Soir* and *Het Vlaamsche Land,* it should be evident that in spite of a variety of uncertainties and ambiguities that they contain, these articles cannot be called Nazi writings. They are not even sympathetic to the Nazi cause. They are, primarily, interested in protecting Flanders' independence. It must, however, be said that de Man's analytical vocabulary—his typology of nationalities and artforms, the binary oppositions of the aesthetic and the political, the abstract and the emotional, the spiritual and the social, the individual and the collective, rural and urban values, etc., as well as his emphasis on the spiritual unity of Europe (including Western civilization), and on what the individual nations are to contribute to it—has a strong traditionalist and conservative bent. Yet only someone who is ignorant of the intellectual climate between the wars, both on the left and the right, could mistake this analytical apparatus, and its use in de Man's journalistic writings, for rightist or collaborationist ideology. But to stress the traditionalist origin of de Man's categorial apparatus, as well as of his moves, is also to say that these articles are not very original and in themselves not especially interesting except perhaps for his emphasis on the specific character of the Flemish nation and the idiosyncratic implications of this valorization. Had he not become a well-known scholar at Yale, and were he not seen as a proponent of "deconstruction," these articles would have continued to go unnoticed. Although not particularly original, the articles are, however, intelligent, especially as far as their organization and their argumentative strategies are concerned. de Man's admiration for Valéry (and the rationalist spirit) is clearly expressed in several of the articles. On January 10–11, 1942, he writes: "This continuous need to reverify, to question *(mettre en doute)*, to express reservations, is an inevitable characteristic of any thinking that wishes to be rigorous" (p. 182). And he continues by saying that such "intellectual probity" manifests itself in a concern for exactitude and precision. Although de Man's categorial apparatus is very traditionalist, it is used with an analytical intent, and serves to get a hold on the events of the time by trying to circumscribe their meaning as precisely as possible. de Man's intellectual probity in the bulk of his journalistic writings—a probity, by contrast, blatantly absent from many of the recent articles published on his wartime productions—can be beheld in these essays' constant requestioning and delimiting of all the subjects broached. The typological vocabulary, as well as the set of binary oppositions, here serves to determine with as much accuracy as possible the contemporary situation, political and artistic, and not to polarize and to obscure it as would have been the case if the aim of the essays had been to commend Nazi ideology. This point being made, it must, however, also be acknowledged, that the essays of *Het Vlaamsche Land* and *Le Soir* do not show de Man to have sensed the catastrophic danger that Nazi Germany represented not only with respect to the Jewish people, but to the whole of Europe and the celebrated values of Western civilization as well. This is rather difficult to understand today, after the fact. But if de Man did not come to grips with the horror that was in the offing, it was *among other things* because his analytical apparatus did not provide the means to capture the viciousness and aberration of the Nazi endeavor *on all fronts.* Like so many other contemporary thinkers on the left and the right, the only categories that de Man had at his disposal to conceptualize his inevitable experience of the darker sides of Nazi ideology and the occupation were those of obscurantism, historical and cultural regression, extremist polarization, etc. In spite of what I believe to have been a truly passionate attempt on de Man's part to understand as precisely as possible the reality he was facing, his intellectual instruments (like those of most of his contemporaries, and of many present intellectuals as well) prevented him from doing so. Faced with what was already visible in 1941 and 1942, confronted with the implications of Nazi ideology, and in front of what was to come (the Holocaust), humanistic language, traditional modes of thinking, and the type of understanding that it permits, had to fail miserably. It was left to the later de Man to systematically put into question all those blinding schemes, categories, and concepts by means of which he had, in his journalistic writings, unsuccessfully tried to gain insight into the political situation in Belgium in the early forties.

Undoubtedly, it is the relation, the absence of relation, or something other than a relation (as I will suggest) between the early journalism and de Man's mature work that represents the most interesting problem in the debate triggered by the discovery of the early texts. All hasty assessments of this relation will necessarily take place at the price of intellectual accuracy and moral honesty. The number and complexity of the questions that have to be resolved before anything can be firmly established about this relation are enormous. The manner in which this relation has been described in several journals is clear evidence of the fact that none of these questions has been addressed, and that the linkage is being made in a prejudiced fashion—no analysis of what is to be related, of the *sort of relation that is possible, in the first place, between the relata*, seems to have been undertaken. In any case, the "critics" knew already in advance what they were going to say. The fact that it is seen as a relation between anti-Semitic and collaborationist texts and deconstructive texts is already testimony of such a prejudice, not to speak of the assessment of the relation between the two as either a covering up or as a secret continuation of the alleged pro-Nazism of the early texts.[30] Do the "critics" in question know what "deconstruction" is, and especially in its complex de Manean version that may—considering de Man's explicit reservations regarding deconstruction—share only the name with this brand of thinking? The answer, obviously, is no. Have they read the texts that they call pro-Nazi writings—read in the minimal sense defined above? Of course not, since that would considerably complicate their agenda. As for the relation that they establish between the two types of texts, anything goes as long as it can serve to deal a blow, preferably a violent one, to what most of these critics know by hearsay only or simply do not understand and that they call "deconstructionism," "deconstructivism," "deconstructionalism," "deconstruction," or the like.

I will not venture presently into a discussion of the complicated relation of de Man's mature work to deconstruction. I will refer only to what I consider the thrust of that later work by de Man, and to what sort of relation, hypothetically, one could perhaps consider worth discussing between that thrust and some of the issues in the earlier work. But in order to do so, I must return to the writings of the journalistic period.

Although, in these early articles, de Man claims that literature is "an independent domain that has a life, laws, and obligations that belong to it alone, and that in no way depend on the philosophical and ethical contingencies that take place on its margins" (*Le Soir,* December 2, 1941), the inquiry characteristic of the bulk of all these essays written between 1939 and 1943 is historical, sociological, and pursues issues that are of immediate practical concern (p. 168). The early de Man shares, indeed, with those "critics" who, at the present moment, want to turn this early work against his later writings, a similar, if not the same method and aim of interpretation, and to a large extent the same values (humanistic, Western, etc.) with respect to which interpretation of literary works is to occur. This is, of course, one of the ironies of the present debate, and a clear sign of the rush and furor with which it is conducted. But let me do justice here to the early de Man, whose interesting understanding of history and its relation to literature may become clouded through such a comparison with contemporary advocates of historical and sociological approaches to literature. The de Man of the forties was not a close reader of literary works (another trait he has in common with his enemies). In "Sur les possibilités de la critique" (*Le Soir,* December 2, 1941), he writes that "the analysis of works is not the ultimate aim of it [literary criticism, R.G.], but constitutes only a secondary and sometimes superfluous part of the examination." But although de Man did not consider analysis of individual works the main goal of literary criticism, he had a very clear sense of the specificity of the literary work, of the criteria that govern artistic values and that are not to be confounded with extraliterary values such as Good and Evil. The history that de Man is interested in concerns precisely these criteria that account for the specificity of artistic values. If de Man delves into the laws of genres, into their past origins, he does so not because of some aestheticist ideology that contemporary "critics" like to blame on anyone who respects the specificity of the domain of literature, but precisely for what he also considers the task of literary criticism to be, namely, "a guide for the critical investigation of existing conditions" ("Criticism and Literary History," *Het Vlaamsche Land,* June 7–8, 1942) (p. 313). It is on the basis of such an historical investigation into the particular laws of the novel that de Man can refute arguments made on moral prejudices, on extraliterary inclinations—that is, on much the same ground on which the enemies of textual analysis, or of what they view as deconstructive readings, object to contemporary trends—and which at the time de Man is writing served right-wing thinkers and Nazi ideologues to broadcast their indignation about the development of literature since the end of World War One (and to accuse the Jews of being responsible for this decadence). The historical study of the immanent laws of the genres permits de Man to argue for a necessary continuity between nineteenth century developments in the novel and what takes place in the writings of Proust, D. H. Lawrence, Gide, Kafka, and Hemingway. It represents the basis of his argument against vulgar anti-Semitism (in the article "Les Juifs dans la Littérature Actuelle") which made the Jews responsible for the alleged decadence since the end of the war. de Man's point here is that since the developments in twentieth century literature are the result of a continuous evolution of the realist agenda of the novel as a genre, there is no Jewish problem (at least as far as literature is concerned). Hence deporting the Jews to some colony isolated from Europe would not only have no deplorable consequences for the literary life of the Occident, but nothing would be won since literature would continue to evolve anyway according to its own laws as it always has. de Man's emphasis on history, his claim, in "Sur les possibilités . . .," that "before being a critic, one must first be the historian of that branch of human activity that is literature," thus has two functions: to secure respect for that domain, and to serve as a tool to "pass judgment on what is happening around us *now*" (p. 168). Then and now, "critics" by resorting to extraliterary criteria have repressed the history proper to genres and modes of thinking. Yet, as de Man notes in *"Notes pour comprendre le siècle,* par Drieu la Rochelle" (*Le Soir,* December 9, 1941), "from the moment that one does not consider literature from the angle of art, but that one seeks to look at it as the unfolding of an ethical evolution, one can make use of it for just anything" (p. 171). Without trying in the least to exonerate the disconcerting aspects of these early texts, one cannot but remark that the "critics" have not been able to avoid the pitfalls pointed out by the young de Man. They have made his texts say just anything whether in the name of good intentions or just out of pure hatred. Ironically, they confirm a law formulated by the later de Man, that the meaning attributed to a text is always the result of a violent and arbitrary imposition.

I have returned to de Man's articles of the forties once again in order for anyone familiar with his later work to realize how different they are in tone and intent. They are sharp, undoubtedly, and yet of a sharpness that traditional forms of literary criticism at times possess.[31] But considering what the later de Man was to develop, the writings during the war cannot be called de Man's mature work, which, by the way, is one of the reasons why all comparison between Heidegger and de Man is impossible. Heidegger's collaboration, a collaboration that is much less equivocal than that blamed on de Man, took place when his thinking had already matured. de Man's early writings, however, are a far cry from what he was later to become involved in, and thus it is no small task to demonstrate any *significant* relations between the two corpuses, that is, relations that are not based on analogical inference, or that are not simply pure inventions. If the later work is called "deconstructive," then there is no relation whatsoever between the early essays and the later work, because the antecedents of deconstruction lie with phenomenology. No trace of phenomenology can be detected in de Man's wartime publications. The difficulty in making a connection, however, has more profound, even essential reasons.

Although de Man has declared himself not to be a philosopher, his later work, say from *Allegories of Reading* to the project on aesthetics and ideology, indisputedly has a philosophical thrust. Even if it is the case that his later writings are not philosophical in a technical sense, if they make their argument in an unconventional manner, and do not even lead to the kind of tangible insights one would expect from philosophy, they presuppose and operate on a level of thinking comparable to that of philosophy, which demarcates them from other (empirical, regional) discourses such as literary criticism, for instance. Yet since such elevation to thinking does not go without what one variously calls abstraction, reduction, bracketing, or even stepping back, *simple* linkage of what has thus been transcended to the order of thinking is no longer possible. All coupling, especially if it mobilizes types of relation that are themselves of empirical origin (cause/effect, reflection, metaphor, analogy, etc.), necessarily presupposes a disregard, a lack of awareness of the difference that thinking makes. In short, to decree a relation of thinking (according to models of relation that thinking transgresses) to doxa, ordinary consciousness, the natural attitude, is to do so out of ignorance of the specificity of philosophical thinking. When such connections are not made out of sheer ignorance of the difference of thinking, they are the result of a resentment against thinking.

In other words, if the later work of de Man has an undeniable philosophical bent, then it is impossible to make it derive from the writings of the journalistic period whether such derivation is conceived of either as a direct consequence, covering up, or as analogical reference. To bring the early work to bear on de Man's later work is a sign of disrespect for the realm of thinking to which his later texts have raised themselves. Now, this does not mean that these later texts could not contain explicit or implicit references to the writings of the war years. However, to hunt these references down without attention to their particular status in the thinking enterprise of the later de Man, that is, without taking into account what they serve to perform on the level of philosophical argumentation (a performance that is possible only if what these references point to has been transformed to a certain level of generality), is an exercise in futility, if not merely an act of revenge.

But to demarcate as radically as I have done here the realm of thinking from that of ordinary experience—a difference that presupposes a bracketing of common modes of thought and concerns in order to achieve the realm of ideality characteristic of thinking as such—does not mean that no trace of what could be said to have been put to death, or actively forgotten, remains within thought itself. But if thinking is what it is, then such a trace to the past, the natural, the empirical, etc., cannot be a singular, concrete event, a particular past. What remains encrypted in the pure ideality of thinking as a trace of the abstraction and idealization process must also be ideal in some sense. In short, since the universality inherent in thought presupposes that it is intelligible to any one, the trace of what has been bracketed by thinking to reach its specific domain cannot be something individual, singular. To put it differently, if it can be shown that the philosophical discourse mourns what it has put to death, then this must be a mourning that all of us can share and can become involved in to the extent that we are thinking beings. If de Man's later texts are as I contend, philosophical in thrust, then the trace to a past and the mourning of what has been left behind, cannot ever be simply an autobiographical past or the particular expression of grief by a concrete individual. They must be assumable by others.[32] We must, therefore, out of respect for the order of thought that constitutes de Man's mature work, seek the relations that may exist between it and the writings from the journalistic period on a level appropriate to his thinking.

I mentioned already that by paying attention to the singular thrust of de Man's mature writings one could, perhaps, risk a hypothesis regarding possible links between it and the early writings. If one has already in advance decided on de Man's work as being "deconstructionist," this thrust cannot come into view, however, and one has, even before reading the work, lost the possibility of being challenged by it. To determine the particular verve of de Man's strong thinking I shall focus not on the whole of his work, but only on a particular important thread within it. This thread corresponds to what I have analyzed elsewhere in greater detail, as the attempt to conceive of, and to enact on a level pertinent to thinking, the absolute and irreducibly singular. Before concentrating on this issue, let me emphasize something that must be said of de Man's later work as a whole: It is a consistent and relentless attempt at debunking totalities, totalizing gestures, and ideologies in danger of turning totalitarian (even where his own work is concerned, including its "theoretical" direction). The thinking of irreducible singularity is one aspect of this critical journey. From what we have established with regard to the journalistic articles, it should be clear that de Man's concern with national peculiarity represented for him at that time the major critical tool for resisting the occupation forces and Nazi ideology. A continuity, on the basis of such a concern with singularity, could thus be affirmed between the two corpuses. But such a judgment would indeed miss the essential, namely, the difference between the two types of resistance against totalizing practices and gestures. Indeed, national particularity for de Man in the forties, although clearly braced against the notion of a *Reich,* is conceived of as a part of a whole—the spiritual unity of Europe. In addition, such national peculiarity, as has been seen, is determined in a differential manner (according to criteria such as symbolic, abstract, realist, for instance) which stresses the complementarity and mutual limitation of the various nationalities. Finally, de Man's mobilization of the notion of nationality takes place in the name of property and originality (the national patrimony), and is at the service of ideals such as continuity, unity, permanence, inner bond ("lien profond," says the article on "Le destin de la Flandre"), and so forth (p. 139). Yet de Man's later work extends its criticism of totalizing gestures to precisely the categories that conditioned his early attempts to conceptualize singularity and its subversive function. Throughout his mature work, de Man consistently points to the totalizing function of categories such as continuity, organicism, bondage, etc. On this basis alone it is already imprudent to establish a continuity between the later and the earlier texts. But the rupture is, indeed, much more incisive if one considers that the interest in singularity has become a *philosophical* issue with the later de Man. With this I do not mean, of course, that his early attempts to grope with this issue are negligible. The later essays, however, have raised it to a level of thought, and to a type of treatment, unparalleled in the earlier reflections on national singularity. But as we will see in a moment that is not yet the whole difference.

First, let me briefly circumscribe what such an endeavor of thinking the absolutely singular involves. The activity of thinking consists, according to Hegel (but Hegel's definition is not particular to Hegel alone since he determines thinking in line with the tradition), of elevating (sublating) all limitation and particular singularity to the level of, and into, the universal. Such elevation by thinking is possible because a singularity, although a pointlike and entirely exterior moment, is never a purpose in itself. *As* a singularity (that is, according to its logical status), it refers not only to other singularities, but to its opposite, its Other, the universal, the whole thing *(die ganze Sache),* as Hegel puts it.[33] Because the singular and the contingent *relate to,* and thus *exit from themselves,* they are determined and destined from within to pass into the universal. Hegel expresses this necessary determination of the singular in a most succinct manner when he notes that the truth of the singular is the universal. To think the absolutely singular thus implies the thinking of a singularity that has no relation to, and thus withstands the dialectic of universalization. Absolved of all relation such a singular escapes thinking as the act through which the universal as such is taken possession of. Ultimately, such a singularity free of all reference (that is of reference to Other, but *to self as well*) does not fit any of the classical philosophical definitions of philosophy. From a standpoint of thinking it is a thoroughly idiosyncratic notion that resists the universalizing bent of thought. The elaboration of such a notion is a prime thrust of de Man's rhetorical readings. What they seek to articulate by analyzing the literal, *material* properties of language, the *mechanical* rules of grammar, and the *historical* occurrence of linguistic acts is nothing less than the entirely arbitrary (that is, void of all meaning, because entertaining no relation to), atomistic individualities (of language), each one of which is its own species (if one can still make use of this terminology), stripped of all generality or universality.

I have spoken before of the mourning constitutive of philosophy as universal discourse, of the grief without which no thinking as elevation to the universal can take place, and have insisted on the fact that such grief cannot be the personal, singular grief of a singular individual. It must be a general grief, intelligible to anybody. If de Man's decisive writings are to be philosophical, or to have a philosophical inclination, then they must, in some way or another, take this structure of universalization and mourning into account. de Man's investigation of absolute singularity, as an enterprise of thinking, cannot but pursue this problem in a fashion that yields to the universalist standards of intelligibility, and in doing so mourn, in ways that all of us can assume, that which is forgotten, left behind, put to death by this very operation. Yet, precisely because of what thinking sets out to think in this case—absolute singularity—thinking steps back from the realm of universality, and risks becoming unintelligible, purely idiosyncratic. Indeed, the attempt to conceive of what is entirely without relations is that which cannot be thought, and any attempt to do so sacrifices the claim to universality inherent in thinking. Yet what makes thinking fail as thinking, in this case, is nothing less than thinking itself. In attempting to conceive the absolute limit of the relationless, it encounters its own limit of universalizing. It encounters encrypted in itself the irreducible contingency of itself, the singularity of its universalist claims. To "think" the absolutely contingent and singular, the irreducibly arbitrary, corresponds, indeed, to a mourning of another past that had to be forgotten for thinking to come into its own. And this mourning of the singularity of the universalist gesture of thinking, of the lack of generality of the act that gives rise to thinking, of its solitary happening forever cut loose from the particular philosophy it gives rise to, is a mourning of a past, an absolute past, which is not simply personal either. We can, *in general,* assume that grief as well. Yet such mournful thinking of an absolute, and hence meaningless past of thinking—an attempt that renounces all claim to universality, and that thus risks its existence as thinking and remains utterly singular—also borders on the unintelligible, on what is so singular that we cannot assume it in general. Beyond the irreducible finitude at the heart of all thinking, a finitude owing to the singularity of its occurrence, de Man's decisive texts also speak (of) something unspeakable, something so utterly contingent and unmotivated, that we cannot share it.

I said before that by calling attention to the singular thrust characteristic of de Man's work, a possible link between the later work and his early writings could perhaps be envisioned. This link is the concern with singularity, and with its disruptive function with regard to totalization, and as we have now seen, universalization. It is a concern with an issue that appears as disruptive of thinking and that forces thinking to abandon all authority and its claims to universality. But with this continuity of de Man's intellectual concerns we also encounter a profound rupture in his writings. Should I venture to say that the sacrifice of universal claims that de Man's later elaborations on the absolutely singular entail, is a sort of atonement or expiation of the earlier claims made? It would be presumptuous to do so. It would, indeed, imply that I have been able to read and understand the purely idiosyncratic in de Man's texts which beyond the finitude at the heart of all thinking hints at another unspeakable past. I do not penetrate its darkness and I must refrain from imposing any meaning on it. To do so would represent a violent imposition and disrespect of the Other, of a thinker in particular, who as Other and as thinker demands that I also assume my inability to understand the unspeakable to which his texts point us. For the same reason I shall abstain from categorizing the link that may exist between the early journalistic work and the thinking enterprise of the later writings. To call this link either a continuation or a covering up of the undeniably unpardonable aspects of some of the earlier texts is to miss the leap and the rupture that de Man's critical and philosophical writings have undertaken.

Precipitation in labeling this link is evidence of an unconsciousness with respect to what thinking means or simply disdain of thought. But above all, it is a contemptuous dismissal of what in thinking in general remains Other, other to the point of demanding that where thinking enters on its borders, a toll is inevitably taken of understanding.

Notes

Introduction

1. One paradoxical result of the de Man affair has been that it has made his work known in several European countries that had never heard of him before. Thus while the discovery that in his early twenties he had been a regular contributor to the literary column of *Le Soir,* a journal whose political sections were then under Nazi surveillance, served many in North American academia as a pretext for no longer having to cope with his difficult work, the publicity surrounding his past led many European students and scholars to discover de Man's mature writings. Even though at times the European intellectuals are not familiar with the specific methodological and philosophical traditions against which de Man has defined his position, their work on de Man is often interesting if not stimulating. Since it has taken over the stalled debate in this country, on de Man's later writings, I have sought to take some of this body of new criticism into account, especially in the last chapters of this book. Among the notable exceptions to the general dreariness of the more recent de Man studies in North America that need to be mentioned right at the outset of this book is the lengthy chapter on de Manean deconstruction by John Guillory in *Cultural Capital: The Problem of Literary Canon Formation* (Chicago: University of Chicago Press, 1993). Going on the assumption not only that deconstruction is on the decline (and with it theoretical studies as a whole) but that its end coincides also with the completion of its project (if not of "rhetoricism," "the epistemic feature of literary theory" [p. 180] in general), Guillory, in the course of an analysis in which rhetorical reading is seen as one example of the now defunct trend of theory in literary studies, has a distanced, and ideology-free, look at the phenomenon as a whole. Not only that, taking a long, and even "longer view of the moment of theory" (p. 259), deconstruction appears in Guillory's account at best as just one, perhaps extreme, but in no way unique, form among all the failed attempts to come up with a rationale for the literary curriculum since the transformation of "the university into the institution designed to produce a new

269

class of technical/managerial specialists" (p. 261). The discovery of de Man's wartime writings, in other words, the "relatively trivial question of 'de Man's politics'," has served to deflect from the task of analyzing deconstruction in this perspective and has "disabled any genuine ideology-critique of deconstruction" (p. 240), Guillory claims. *Cultural Capital*, by contrast, takes on this assignment. After centering on deconstruction's ideological role in the specifically American institutional academic apparatus, and the context of discipleship, it culminates in the conclusion that the "de Manian oeuvre . . . [is] a *symptomatic* discourse, a discourse that registers at the heart of its terminology the historical moment of the fusion of the university teacher's autonomous 'professional activity' with the technobureaucratic organization of intellectual labor." Yet, if, for Guillory, "rhetorical reading has the important symptomatic function of figuring a rapprochement with the institutional conditions of criticism, by acknowledging the loss of intellectual autonomy as a theory of linguistic determinism—at the same time that autonomy is continually reinvested in the figure of the master theorist" (p. 259), this is not at all specific to deconstruction. If deconstruction shares its ideology with all the other failed attempts to establish a rationale for the literary curriculum under the new conditions, it lends itself better—because of the charisma of de Man and the discipleship he generated (but the latter, he says, is not even anomalous)—than the other discourses on literature to exhibiting the ideology in question. Undoubtedly, Guillory's analysis of deconstruction in its institutional context provides a number of interesting, not to say intriguing, insights. But the specific way in which the author proceeds in this unquestionably important and necessary analysis leads him to systematically disregard everything that could be specific, singular, or even original about de Man's work. In other words, Guillory does not engage de Man's oeuvre itself and only rarely confronts the issues it raises. The symptomatic reading that he proposes of deconstruction, or rhetorical reading, not only presupposes that no such singularity or originality exists in the first place, it even serves to systematically void deconstruction of all possible distinction, hence, to preempt the possibility of it making any claims of its own. De Manean arguments are not to be taken "at face value," Guillory asserts (p. 197). No doubt, but would it not have been appropriate to first probe their inner logicity before reading them as symptomatic and thus displacing and replacing their meaning with "the *meaning* of . . . [these arguments] in their institutional context" (p. 258)? Is Guillory's denial that certain arguments of de Man on the nature of texts, or language are "ontological," that, by contrast, "the truth of . . . [his] statements is *historical*," not a plain sign of a strategy intent on depriving de Man's oeuvre of any specificity of its own? Finally, by "deemphasizing the idiosyncrasy of . . . [de Man's] materialism, and arguing for the symptomatic generality of theoretical notions such as the 'materiality of the letter'" (p. 374), Guillory explicitly sacrifices, in the name of generality, the possibility that de Man's conception may be unique, or singular, and which, as I will argue in this book, demands, therefore, to be taken seriously in itself, and on its own terms.

2. Frederic Jameson, *Postmodernism, or, The Cultural Logic of Late Capitalism* (Durham: Duke University Press, 1991), p. 238.

3. If *to think* means to rethink because, as Paul Valéry has said somewhere, that which has already been thought has not been sufficiently thought, the evolution of my assessment of de Man's work over a period of more than ten years should surprise no one. If, in this book, the fluctuations in my evaluation of his writings have not been corrected, it is primarily to emphasize that the questioning approach that de Man's singular work invites is a "process" in which thinking must remain open to the need to rethink that work again and again.

4. See Jochen Hörisch, *Die Wut des Verstehens: Zur Kritik der Hermeneutik* (Frankfurt/Main: Suhrkamp, 1988), pp. 50–52, 103.

5. John Guillory also acknowledges the singularity of de Man's rigor when he writes: "The rigor of rhetorical reading is thus more rigor than a science requires." But, claiming to investigate the institutional context of the term *rigor* in de Man's teachings, Guillory questions "the rigorousness of rigor" (p. 235) and is quick to suggest that "it is the rigor of a prescience, a foreknowledge" (p. 232). More precisely, the point the author of *Cultural Capital* seeks to make is that a de Manean argument is not rigorous because of its "unassailable logic" but because of an "effect of pathos" in the trajectory of the argument (p. 235). Undoubtedly, de Man's texts, more often than not, indulge in the pathos of rigor, to a point, indeed, where one could easily be tempted to read it as a strategy of compensation. But such pathos does not exempt the reader from having to analyze whether the claim to rigor is earned or not. Guillory concludes his account of de Manean rigor by holding that, in truth—that is to say, in the context of the technocratic bureaucratization of intellectual labor in the university—the rigor of rhetorical reading is the rigor of routinized labor in the bureaucratic sphere (p. 257). It is hardly necessary to underline that such a conclusion could be reached only because the arguments of rhetorical reading have not been faced in their inner logic to begin with.

6. Friedrich Schlegel, *Literarische Notizen 1797–1801*, ed. H. Eichner (Frankfurt/Main: Ullstein, 1980), p. 116.

7. Émile Benveniste, *Le Vocabulaire des institutions indo-européennes* (Paris: Minuit, 1969), vol. I, pp. 321–333.

8. Silvia Bovenschen, "Über-Empfindlichkeit: Versuch über den Begriff Idio-synkrasie," *Neue Rundschau,* vol. 105 (1994), pp. 2, 133–134.

9. Most of the information on wild cards has been compiled from John Scarne, *Scarne on Cards: How to Win* (New York: Crown Publishers, 1974), and John Scarne, *Scarne's New Complete Guide to Gambling* (New York: Simon and Schuster, 1974).

10. As Frances Ferguson aptly puts it, language, as understood by de Man, "might well be defined as prelinguistic than linguistic" (Frances Ferguson, *Solitude and the Sublime: Romanticism and the Aesthetics of Individuation,* [New York: Routledge, 1992], p. 154).

11. Wlad Godzich, *The Culture of Literacy* (Cambridge: Harvard University Press, 1994), p. 134. Jameson characterizes de Man's work as one that "begins from zero in the realm of thinking," and explains "the very crude-ness of its [*Allegories of Reading*] emergent philosophical generalizations" from the clumsiness congenial with newly forged thought (Jameson, *Post-modernism,* p. 220).

1. "Setzung" and "Übersetzung"

1. John R. Searle, "The Logical Status of Fictional Discourse," *New Literary History,* vol. VI, no. 2 (1975), p. 322.

2. J. L. Austin, *How to Do Things with Words* (Cambridge: Harvard University Press, 1975), p. 22.

3. Ibid., p. 21.

4. Jacques Derrida, *Limited Inc* (Evanston, Ill.: Northwestern University Press, 1988), pp. 47ff.

5. Austin, *How to Do Things with Words,* p. 3.

6. Ibid., p. 148.

7. Ibid., p. 61.

8. Ibid., p. 63.

9. Ibid., p. 71.

10. Ibid., p. 72.

11. Ibid., p. 70.

12. Ibid., pp. 72–73.

13. Ibid., p. 73.

14. Ibid., p. 17.

15. Ibid., p. 103.

16. Ibid., p. 112.

17. What is here being hailed as revolutionary, the rediscovery of the act-char-acter of language, is a view that the eighteenth century was very familiar with. One may think of Condillac's *langage d'action* or of Rousseau's *langage*

des passions. Besides Nietzsche's insight into the active nature of language (to which Austin seems to be secretly indebted), one cannot avoid mentioning Heidegger's analysis of *Zuhandenheit* in *Being and Time* (1927) of which Austin apparently was not aware. When Searle in *Speech Acts: An Essay in the Philosophy of Language* (Cambridge: Cambridge University Press, 1976) speaks somewhere of "the *classical* period of analytical philosophy" (emphasis by me), or when he writes that "reference has a long history of treatment by philosophers, going back at least as far back as Frege (and really as far back as Plato's *Theaetetus,* if not earlier)" (p. 77), one cannot but wonder, precisely because of the parentheses, in what ways this obvious absence of a sense of philosophical tradition affects the very project of speech acts.

18. Émile Benveniste, *Problèmes de linguistique générale* (Paris: Gallimard, 1966), vol. I, pp. 273–274.

19. Ibid., p. 274.

20. Jean Récanati, *La Transparence et l'énonciation: Pour introduire à la pragmatique* (Paris: Seuil, 1979), p. 21.

21. Austin, *How to do Things with Words,* p. 149.

22. In response to a suggestion of mine in "Deconstruction as Criticism" (now republished in *Inventions of Difference: On Jacques Derrida* [Cambridge: Harvard University Press, 1994], according to which the de Man of *Allegories of Reading* abandons the notion of self-reflexivity that in *Blindness and Insight* is still considered to be a dominating characteristic of literariness, Suzanne Gearhart has argued that no such break exists. Gearhart rests her argument on de Man's contention in the earlier work that language and literature is essentially metaphorical. Since metaphoricity, as she recalls, implies nonreferentiality for de Man, it is understood to escape the logocentric fallacy in that it closes language off from the logical and the epistemological, equated by de Man with metaphysics. Being metaphorical, language is then also self-reflexive. I certainly agree with this description of the constitutive role that metaphor plays in *Blindness and Insight* for de Man's understanding of language and literature. But, as I have argued in *"Setzung" and "Übersetzung,"* this is no longer the case in *Allegories of Reading* because metaphor here is seen to be a mode of reflective reappropriation and totalization of the figural constitutive of literary language, to be deconstructed along with all other such totalizing modes, as is, for instance, the self. In her account of the chapter "Metaphor" in *Allegories of Reading,* Gearhart distinguishes a "dédoublement" in the use of *metaphor* in the later essay. Citing de Man's sentence, "Metaphor is error because it believes or feigns to be believe in its own referential meaning" (*AR,* p. 151), she takes this sentence to condemn a use of metaphor in complicity with

metaphysics and to approve of another sense of the term in which *metaphor* would only feign "to believe in its own referential meaning" (Suzanne Gearhart, "Philosophy *before* Literature: Deconstruction, Historicity and the Work of Paul de Man," *Diacritics,* 4 [1983], pp. 79–80). But does de Man's sentence not accuse *both* of erring? Or, more precisely, is the feigning to believe in its own referential meaning, that is, the fiction of the reality of what it refers to, not constitutive of metaphor itself? Such fictionality, however, is erroneous. de Man writes: "Metaphor overlooks the fictional, textual element in the nature of the entity it connotes. It assumes a world in which intra- and extra-textual events, literal and figural forms of language, can be distinguished, a world in which the literal and the figural are properties that can be isolated and, consequently, exchanged and substituted for each other. This is an error, although it can be said that no language would be possible without this error" (*AR,* pp. 151–152). Pitching de Man's devalorization of history against the "historical" nature of Derridean deconstruction, the point Gearhart makes is that in spite of all the rapprochements and changes, de Man, in *Allegories of Reading,* remains as critical of Derrida, and opposed to him, as he had been in the essay on *Of Grammatology.* Yet, in seeking to demonstrate that he abandons a conception of the literary as based on self-reflection in the later work, I never meant to say that with this deconstruction in de Man's sense and in Derrida's sense would already have become the same. Nor did I wish to imply that the specific nature of the critique leveled against reflection in *Allegories of Reading,* but in later work as well, escapes at all times, to quote Frederic Jameson, the danger of being "fatally menaced at every point by a resurgence of some notion of self-consciousness that its language vigilantly attempts to ward off" (Frederic Jameson, *Postmodernism, or, The Cultural Logic of Late Capitalism* [Durham: Duke University Press, 1991], p. 245).

23. Metaphor, then, is no longer the tropological concept known from classical rhetoric. As Jameson has remarked, metaphor acquires in *Allegories of Reading* a "mediatory function" as a consequence of which tropology is allowed "to become attached terminologically to a range of other objects and materials (political, philosophical, literary, psychological, autobiographical) where a certain account of the tropes and their movement then becomes autonomous. Metaphor is thus the crucial locus of what we have called transcoding in de Man" (Jameson, *Postmodernism,* p. 238).

24. Johann Gottlieb Fichte, *Science of Knowledge,* trans. P. Heath and J. Lachs (New York: Meredith, 1970), p. 226.

25. Ibid., p. 241.

26. Ibid., p. 244.

27. Ibid., pp. 231–232.

28. Ibid., p. 39.

29. Ibid., p. 17.

30. Ibid., p. 34.

31. For this relation between positing and reflection, see Walter Benjamin, "Der Begriff der Kunstkritik in der deutschen Romantik," *Gesammelte Werke* (Frankfurt/Main: Suhrkamp, 1974), vol. I, no. 1, pp. 22–25.

32. For a nonconventional interpretation of Fichte's principle, as well as for the transformation of his philosophy into the philosophy of the early Romantics, see the remarkable article by Werner Hamacher, "Der Satz der Gattung: Friedrich Schlegels poetologische Umsetzung von Fichtes unbedingtem Grundsatz," *MLN*, 95 (1980), pp. 1155–1180.

33. Martin Heidegger, *On the Way to Language,* trans. P. D. Hertz (New York: Harper and Row, 1971), p. 118.

34. Fichte, *Science of Knowledge,* p. 153.

35. Friedrich Daniel Ernst Schleiermacher, *Hermeneutik und Kritik,* ed. M. Frank (Frankfurt/Main: Suhrkamp, 1977), p. 327.

36. Georg Wilhelm Friedrich Hegel, *The Difference between Fichte's and Schelling's System of Philosophy,* trans. W. Cerf and H. S. Harris (Albany: SUNY Press, 1977).

37. Martin Heidegger, *Poetry, Language, Thought,* trans. A. Hofstadter (New York: Harper and Row, 1971), pp. 82–83.

38. Martin Heidegger, *Wegmarken* (Frankfurt/Main: Klostermann, 1967), p. 269.

39. Ibid., pp. 267–268.

40. Schleiermacher, *Hermeneutik,* p. 139.

2. In-Difference to Philosophy

1. Heinrich Niehues-Pröbsting, "Die 'Episode' im 'Theaitetos': Verschärfung der Begriffe von Rhetorik und Philosophie," *Archiv für Begriffsgeschichte* (Bonn: Bouvier, 1982), vol. 24, no. 1, pp. 16–23.

2. Gottfried Wilhelm Friedrich Hegel, *Aesthetics: Lectures on Fine Art,* trans. T. M. Knox (Oxford: Clarendon Press, 1975), vol. 1, p. 315.

3. Josef König, "Das spezifische Können der Philosophie als *eu legein*," *Blätter für deutsche Philosophie* 10, (1937), p. 134.

4. Ernst Cassirer, *Kant's Life and Thought,* trans. J. Haden (New Haven: Yale University Press, 1981), pp. 326–327.

5. Peter Szondi, "Hegels Lehre von der Dichtung," *Poetik und Geschichtsphilosophie* (Frankfurt/Main: Suhrkamp, 1974), vol. II, pp. 366–367.

6. Hegel, *Aesthetics,* pp. 494–496.

7. Gottfried Wilhelm Friedrich Hegel, *Enzyklopädie der Philosophischen Wis-*

senschaften, vol. II (*Werke in zwanzig Bänden,* vol. 10) (Frankfurt/Main: Suhrkamp, 1970), pp. 267, 269.

8. Hegel, *Aesthetics,* pp. 312–313.

9. Hegel, *Aesthetics,* p. 304.

10. Hegel, *Enzyklopädie,* p. 270.

11. Gérard Genette, *Figures of Literary Discourse,* trans. M.-R. Logan (New York: Columbia University Press, 1982), p. 120. In a manner very similar to Genette, de Man objects to the ideology of Cratylism on the basis that it dreams of language as motivated, i.e., as being in essence symbolic and, thus, as being (or having primitively been) a medium in which speech *is what it says.* Like Genette, all differences respected, de Man also objects to the possibility of textual self-reflexivity, contending that it is a major form of sign-motivation, ideologically oblivious to the founding arbitrariness of the linguistic signifier and act and, thus, tributary to the dominating understanding of art as involved in a nostalgic misunderstanding of language as essentially symbolic.

12. de Man refers to the work of Sarah Kofman and Philippe Lacoue-Labarthe.

13. Reflecting on how the formal reveals itself for de Man as material, Frances Ferguson concludes: "Materiality . . . is, then (or would be), formality without idealism, the stuff of language before it is appropriated to perception, to meaning" (Frances Ferguson, *Solitude and the Sublime: Romanticism and the Aesthetics of Individuation* [New York: Routledge, 1992], p. 158).

14. Friedrich Schlegel, "On Incomprehensibility," *Lucinde and the Fragments,* trans. P. Firchow (Minneapolis: University of Minnesota Press, 1971), p. 268.

15. Immanuel Kant, *Critique of Judgement,* trans. J. H. Bernard (New York: Hafner Press, 1951), p. 110.

16. Apart from de Man's cursory reference to Kant's *Logic,* the *Critique of Judgement* carries the main brunt for his argument regarding a purely material, that is, mindless, vision. Undoubtedly, in the section about the analytic of the beautiful, Kant speaks repeatedly of "mere observation," or the "mere *consideration* of the object" (pp. 38, 79), the "mere representation of the object" (p. 39), and the "mere intuition (by the measurement of the eye)" of magnitude. In the section on the sublime, he also refers to "the mere apprehension" of what causes in us a feeling of the sublime (p. 83). But as one can easily demonstrate, such mere observation, or intuition, is not blind. Nor is it mindless. Certainly it is a beholding without *determinate* concepts, but, as Kant emphasizes, such mere beholding or representation takes place in reference to what he calls "cognition," or "concept" in general. Indeed, as I shall demonstrate elsewhere, in mere intuition one beholds something that is, in principle, cognizable, insofar as it has the mere form of an object. What is thus judged to have the mere form of an object

(without any further determination) is judged beautiful. By contrast, where the imagination fails to gather the manifold into the form of a mere object but still is capable of judging that the formless, or inordinately large, has magnitude, the judgment is sublime.

17. For a detailed discussion of the interrelatedness of the faculties in the judgment upon the beautiful, see my "Transcendentality, in Play," *Kant's Aesthetic,* ed. H. Parret (Berlin: de Gruyter, 1996).

18. Kant, *Critique of Judgement,* p. 107.

19. Ibid., p. 108.

20. For a detailed discussion of Kant's understanding of hypotyposis, see "Some Reflections on the Notion of Hypotyposis in Kant," *Argumentation,* 4 (1990), pp. 85–100.

21. Kant, *Critique of Judgement,* p. 115.

22. Alexander Gottlieb Baumgarten, *Aesthetica* (Hildesheim: Olms, 1961), p. 13.

23. Kant, *Critique of Judgement,* pp. 109–110.

24. Ibid., p. 111.

25. de Man's evocation of a stony gaze echoes, no doubt, Derrida's question, in "Plato's Pharmacy," concerning the resemblances that underlie Socrates' statements, in *Phaedrus,* or *Republic,* that painting and writing are homologous: "From out of what horizon arise their common silence, their stubborn muteness, their mask of solemn, forbidding majesty that so poorly hides an incurable aphasia, a stone deafness, a closedness irremediably inadequate to the demand of *logos?*" (*D,* p. 136). While the stony deafness of writing is, for Derrida, a judgment upon writing from the perspective of *logos,* hence, a metaphysical appraisal of it, the "stony gaze" de Man refers to, is a positive given, an objective datum, in Kant's text that can be taken for granted. The difference between de Man's and Derrida's use of *stony* could well serve to construe the difference between their respective enterprises. de Man's inference that *Augenschein* is a stony glance hinges entirely on Kant's reference to the heaven as a vault. What are the theoretical underpinnings, one would like to ask, that permit de Man to take words that denote architectural constructions and that supposedly are made of stone, for stones in the text? Or to rephrase the question in view of the analysis in Chapter 6 of "Anthropomorphism and Trope in Lyric," on what basis can de Man take words that express violence to be violent themselves, and, furthermore, to reveal, better than other words, the workings of language?

3. Apathetic Formalism

1. Ernst Robert Curtius, *European Literature and the Latin Middle Ages,* trans. W. R. Trask (Princeton: Princeton University Press 1978), p. 241.

2. Ibid., p. 241.

3. Ibid., pp. 20, 28–29.

4. Ibid., pp. 36–37.

5. Ibid., p. 36.

6. Ibid., p. 14.

7. Ibid., p. 77.

8. Ibid., p. 65.

9. Ibid., p. 70.

10. Ibid., p. 67.

11. Ibid., p. 390.

12. Ibid., p. 391.

13. Ibid., p. 394.

14. Ibid., pp. 70, 79.

15. "Kant's Materialism" is a paper that Paul de Man read on a panel on "Kant and the Problem of the Aesthetic" organized by Jonathan Culler during the 1981 meeting of the Modern Language Association. It is a piece that he had not the time to revise for publication. It has been published in Paul de Man, *Aesthetic Ideology,* ed. Andrzej Warminski (Minneapolis: University of Minnesota Press, 1996), pp. 119–128. All page references in this chapter are to this edition.

16. For instance, see Heinrich Lausberg, *Elemente der literarischen Rhetorik* (Munich: Max Hueber, 1967), p. 154.

17. It must be noted here that all the translations of Kant in de Man's essay are his own translations. In the German original, Kant writes that a pure aesthetic judgment *ascribes* sublimity to something (*die ein reines aesthetisches Urteil diesem Gegenstande beilegt*). If one can speak at all of sources in this case, it is the aesthetic judgment, and not the sublime, that represents a source. The full passage in which the sentence occurs will be quoted in full in the following from Immanuel Kant, *Critique of Judgement,* trans. J. H. Bernard (New York: Hafner, 1951), pp. 110–118.

18. Since it rests entirely on the materiality of the prefixes *Ver-* and *Be-,* this is an altogether arbitrary distinction for de Man. There is no way in which one could conclude that this linguistic distinction would refer to a corresponding distinction in the subject matter. de Man's special attention to such linguistic differentiation can be set clearly against a similar interest of Derrida's for the differentiating power of the linguistic. It can indeed serve to demarcate both thinkers from each other. Whereas for de Man, the Kantean recourse to the prefixes in question is a sign if not of the impossibility of making a distinction in the thing itself, that is, the emotions in question, then at least of Kant's embarrassment; such differentiations, for Derrida—and *Glas,* would be an excellent point in case—in no way render

the distinctions that they refer to obsolete but show them to rest on a law that comprehends in itself heterogeneous linguistics traits.

19. Kant, *Critique of Judgement,* p. 113.
20. Ibid., p. 91.
21. Ibid., pp. 110–111.
22. This is also the point where one can begin to understand what de Man means by 'form', 'formal', etc. As in Hegel, it seems to connote isolation, abstraction, immediacy. Yet, whereas these connotations of the merely formal situate it as the *first* moment of a process of development that culminates in the concrete universal, the 'formal' for de Man remains entrenched in the separation and isolation that it insinuates.
23. Jean-Luc Marion, *Dieu sans l'être* (Paris: Fayard, 1982), pp. 166–171.
24. What de Man conceptualizes under the expression "positional power of language" is thus language's constitutive ability (and it is language's distinctive trait) to produce absolutely unrelated and isolated, i.e., random, events.
25. Hermann Diels, *Die Fragmente der Vorssokratiker* (Berlin: Weidmannsche Buchhandlung, 1952), vol. II, p. 97 (I thank James I. Porter for having directed me to this passage). In *On the Natural Faculties,* Galen remarks that all substance or faculty peculiar either to Nature or the Soul "result from the way in which primary corpuscles, which are unaffected by change *(apathon),* come together" (trans. A. J. Brock [Cambridge: Harvard University Press, 1979], pp. 44–45).
26. With one exception, of course, namely, the sense of wonder *(thaumazein),* which, according to Socrates in *Theaetetus,* is the philosophical pathos *par excellence.* He says to Theaetetus: "This sense of wonder is the mark of the philosopher. Philosophy indeed has no other origin, and he was a good genealogist who made Iris the daughter of Thaumas" (Plato, *The Collected Dialogues,* ed. E. Hamilton and H. Cairns [Princeton: Princeton University Press, 1980], p. 860). On the pathos of wonder, see Martin Heidegger, *Was ist das—die Philosophie?* (Pfullingen: Neske, 1966), pp. 24–26. See also John Llewelyn, "On the Saying That Philosophy Begins in *Thaumazein,*" *Post-Structuralist Classics,* ed. A. Benjamin (London/New York: Routledge, 1988), pp. 173–191.
27. The notion of apathetic rhetoric evokes as well the stoic or religious idea of a purer, more spiritual, if not even miraculated, cognition.
28. Aristotle, *Rhetorica,* trans. W. R. Roberts, *The Works of Aristotle,* ed. W. D. Ross, vol. XI, 1355a, pp. 25–30.
29. Ibid., 1355b, pp. 25–27.
30. Ibid., 1356a, pp. 13–16.
31. Ibid., 1378a, p. 20.

32. This is also what allows Heidegger, in *Being and Time,* to claim that the second book of *Rhetoric* "must be taken as the first systematic hermeneutic of the everydayness of Being with one another," rather than that sort of thing that according to the traditional orientation "we 'learn in school'." The extent to which this second book has been decisive for the development of *Being and Time* will become fully clear only with the publication of Heidegger's lectures from 1924 on Aristotle's *Rhetoric* (Martin Heidegger, *Being and Time,* trans. J. Macquarrie and E. Robinson [New York: Harper and Row, 1962], p. 178.

33. Roland Barthes, *L'Aventure semiologique* (Paris: Seuil, 1985), pp. 146–147.

34. It is perhaps not inappropriate to mention here that Schiller did not consider tragedy an entirely free art, precisely for the reason that arts of emotion "are enlisted in the service of a particular aim (that of pathos)." Perfection in art is, therefore, a function of the work's "respect (for) the freedom of the spirit" (*On the Aesthetic Education of Man in a Series of Letters* [New York: Ungar, 1988], p. 106). Pathos is thus thought to be linked to particular aims and thus forfeits any generality, be it aesthetic or philosophical.

35. Plato, *The Collected Dialogues,* 493*a–b.*

36. Ibid., 491*e.*

37. Ibid., 492*a–b,* 491*e.*

38. Ibid., 491*b–c.*

39. Ibid., 493*a–d.*

40. Ibid., 495*b–c.*

41. But even Derrida's reflections on singularity continue this tradition in that a singularity is shown to require universally intelligible constitutive traits, and were it only for it to be able to be identified as a singularity. See my *Inventions of Difference: On Jacques Derrida* (Cambridge: Harvard University Press, 1994), pp. 2–16.

42. Adriaan Th. Peperzak, *Philosophy and Politics: A Commentary on the Preface to Hegel's Philosophy of Right* (Dordrecht: Martinus Nijhoff, 1987), p. 9.

43. Ibid.

44. Reiner Wiehl, "La Rationalité du Singulier," trans. E. Poulain, *Critique,* 493–494 (1988), pp. 531–533.

45. I can point here only to the inevitable question of whether such a singularity could still be dealt with in language at all, that is, within the general structure of determined verbal utterance based on the general form of the proposition and the judgment. Klossovski in a remarkable essay on the theme of apathy in de Sade—an essay that is, so to speak, an invitation to read together de Sade and de Man on singularity—poses the question in the following terms: Can one *in speaking* "demonstrate in *the name of generality* that *there is no* generality and that norms of the species have no real existence?" (Pierre Klossovski, "Le Philosophie Scélérat," *Sade mon prochain*

[Paris: Seuil, 1967], p. 35). See also in this context Jean-Francois Lyotard, "Apathie dans la théorie," *Rudiments paiens* (Paris: Union Générale d'Editions, 1977), in particular, pp. 24–27. Since what is to be thought here is to escape universality altogether, including all *tension* toward universality, the treatment to which language has to be subjected in order to bring the apathetic linguistic atoms, structures, or acts into view must necessarily differ substantially from the calculated language games that Derrida engages in in order to think, say, the nonnecessary, nonunitary "origins" of reason.

46. Considering how scarce references to the notion of the idiosyncratic are to come by, I should at least point to the quite idiosyncratic use that Theodor W. Adorno makes of the notion of idiosyncrasy in *In Search of Wagner,* and later in *Dialectic of Enlightenment,* to conceptualize anti-Semitic reaction. Adorno writes: "The old answer of all the anti-Semites is an appeal to idiosyncrasy . . . idiosyncrasy inheres in the particular. The general, that which fits into the functional context of society, is considered to be natural. But nature which has not been transformed through the channels of conceptual order into something purposeful, the grating sound of a stylus moving over a slate, the *haut goût* which recalls filth and decomposition, the sweat which appears on the brow of the busy man—everything which has failed to keep up, or which infringes the commandments which are sedimented progress of the centuries—has a penetrating effect; it arouses disgust" (Max Horkheimer and Theodor W. Adorno, *Dialectic of Enlightenment,* trans. J. Cumming [New York: Herder and Herder, 1972], p. 180). However, anti-Semitism's rationalized idiosyncrasy becomes mobilized, Adorno holds, against the presence in civilization of remnants of an archaic, or first-order, idiosyncrasy that consists in a mimetic petrification in order to be able to survive in face of exterior threats. Anti-Semitism's idiosyncrasy is a gut's reaction against what the universalizing civilizatory process ought to have wiped out, Adorno holds—"archaic schemata of the urge to survive" (p. 180), and hence, the desire for freedom—and that notwithstanding the fact that it is repelled by such idiosyncrasy, is mimetically reproduced by the latter as a second-order idiosyncrasy. In short, the hypersensitive reaction of anti-Semitism is one against "infectious gestures of direct contacts suppressed by civilization" (p. 182) and against "freedom (that) still shines out irresistably as the thwarted destiny of matter" (p. 183). (For an excellent discussion of the complex web of relations in which Adorno situates idiosyncrasy, and especially, for his double concept of idiosyncrasy, see Silvia Bovenschen, "Über-Empfindlichkeit: Versuch über den Begriff Idiosynkrasie," *Neue Rundschau,* 105 [1994], 2, pp. 137f.; see also Alexander Garcia Düttmann, *Das Gedächtnis des Denkens: Versuch über Heidegger und Adorno* [Frankfurt/Main: Suhrkamp, 1991], pp. 117–

120). Idiosyncrasy, then, is rooted for Adorno, in the "biological prehistory" of human beings (p. 180). As such, it can become the *sociopsychological mode of reaction* characteristic of anti-Semitism as analyzed in *Dialectic of Enlightenment*. The "idiosyncratic" as I have used it to conceptualize absolute singularity, however, is not a sociopsychological or biological mode of behavior or allergic reaction. It serves to think *absence of reaction,* more generally, *of relation,* and is thus a "logical" and "ontological" concept. Ultimately, it refers to what escapes *all* relation (logical, emotional, instinctive, etc.), the relation to self included—in other words, to a nonidentical that is no longer to be thought in contradistinction from (and thus in relation to) the identical.

47. What is true of the concept of apathetic rhetoric is true as well of de Manean expressions such as "formal materialism" or "stony gaze." Rather than evoking a union of values, through conjoining antithetic terms (as oxymorons do in general, unless they serve to convey a sense of self-contradiction), expressions such as those mentioned above represent for de Man self-canceling *conceptions.* They ensure that what is *thought* in each of these instances is not raised to the status of a (universal) concept.

48. One could, of course, argue that apathy is still a pathos and that apathy cannot entirely avoid being 'pathetic'. This is certainly the case as far as the tone and the language itself of de Man's writings are concerned. The question, however, is whether this pathos of apathy that derives from the historical and psychological conditions under which de Man's texts have been written can be brought to bear on the philosophical attempt of *conceiving* of apathy not only as an absence of all emotions and feelings but also as having no emotional relation to itself anymore. If the apathetic in de Man's sense is to preclude all (emotional) relations, it can no longer have the identity of an emotion.

49. In this context I also would like to refer the reader to the excellent pages that Werner Hamacher has devoted to the figure of pathos as the "figure of immediate communication," "pure understanding," "sheer intentionality," and to de Man's suspicion of this figure as a function of texts "destined to disavow their own contingency" (Werner Hamacher, "Lectio: De Man's Imperative," *Reading de Man Reading,* ed. W. Godzich and L. Waters [Minneapolis: University of Minnesota Press, 1989], pp. 180–181).

4. The Fallout of Reading

1. Gottfried Wilhelm Friedrich Hegel, *Aesthetics: Lectures on Fine Art,* vol. II, trans. T. M. Knox (Oxford: Clarendon Press, 1975), pp. 1036–1037.

2. Jacques Derrida, *Of Grammatology,* trans. G. C. Spivak (Baltimore: The Johns Hopkins University Press, 1974), p. 160.

3. This observation, however, is only the prelude for an inquiry into the paradigm of musical reception that, according to Hart Nibbrig, underlies de Man's theory and practice of reading and that effects a return of the aesthetics that this theory sought to evacuate in order to forgo ideological reaestheticization. See Christiaan L. Hart Nibbrig, "Musik der Theorie oder: Was heisst darstellen? Zur Dekonstruktion Paul de Mans," *Was heisst 'Darstellen'?*, ed. Christiaan L. Hart Nibbrig (Frankfurt/Main: Suhrkamp, 1994), pp. 431, 433f.

4. Derrida, *Of Grammatology,* p. 160.

5. Jesper Svenbro, *Phrasikleia: Anthropologie de la Lecture en Grèce Ancienne* (Paris: Éditions de la Découverte, 1988), p. 73.

6. Ibid., pp. 6, 20, 72.

7. Ibid., p. 30.

8. Massimo Cacciari, *Gewalt und Harmonie: Geo-Philosophie Europas,* trans. G. Memmert (Munich: Carl Hanser, 1995), p. 98.

9. Svenbro, *Phrasikleia,* p. 183.

10. Jacques Derrida, *Dissemination,* trans. B. Johnson (Chicago: University of Chicago Press, 1981), p. 153.

11. Svenbro, *Phrasikleia,* pp. 222–226.

12. Ibid., p. 233.

13. Ibid., p. 182f.

14. Maria Tasinato, *L'Oeil du Silence: Éloge de la Lecture* (Lagrasse: Éditions Verdier, 1989), p. 23.

15. Ibid., p. 29.

16. Ibid., p. 35.

17. Ibid., p. 27.

18. Ibid., pp. 28, 33.

19. Ibid., pp. 66, 90.

20. de Man adds: "Hegel's somewhat cryptic reference to Plato in the *Aesthetics,* may well be interpreted in this sense" (*RT,* pp. 9–10). Although it may be difficult to see what is cryptic about the at least twelve passages in the *Aesthetics* in which Hegel refers to Plato, especially since not one of them is a reference to the *Cratylus,* once Hegel's aesthetics has been defined as the complete unfolding of a model of language according to which a natural link exists between the referential quality of the sign and what is designated as its reference and of which the Cratylian conception of language is a version, the presence of the name Plato in the corpus of the *Aesthetics* is the figure manifest in the text by which its underlying Cratylist assumptions are betrayed. For a more detailed discussion of these questions, and in particular de Man's contention that Hegel's conception of art is symbolic, see Chapter 2.

21. de Man acknowledges that the affinity between structural linguistics and

literary texts "is not as obvious as . . . it now may seem." Indeed, one had to wait for philologists and literary critics to discover what he terms "the natural attraction of literature to a theory of linguistic signs" (*RT,* p. 8). But literary critics steeped in linguistics, and who have become aware of what de Man will call the "autonous potential of language," face another danger, the danger of emphasizing the "material, phenomenal aspects of the signifier." Drawing them into the foreground "creates a strong illusion of aesthetic seduction" (*RT,* p. 10), he holds. Linguistically oriented approaches to literature are thus seduced into the illusion of formalism and formalistic methods, the last aesthetic stronghold, as it were, before the event of the resolutely antiaesthetic discipline of mere reading.

22. Even though "de Man consistently described himself as a materialist," more precisely, "an eighteenth-century mechanical materialist," his views on language, Frederic Jameson argues, reveal him to be not only a nominalist but to have adopted a dominant ideology in contemporary thought, that is to say, "the nominalist imperative in contemporary times: the tendency toward immanence, the flight from transcendence," etc. (pp. 246, 250) The thrust of Jameson's chapter on de Man in *Postmodernism* is to show that "de Man's intensely postcontemporary system" (p. 245) is, if not contradictory, *uneven* in its development. It combines potentially promising strands of thought, such as certain aspects of de Man's rhetorical account that are "fully compatible" with Marxian analyses or his materialism—although the fact that de Man did not live long enough "to explore and articulate the encounter with Marxism that he promised us in his last years" (p. 230) restricted his rhetorical analyses to being only "a late form of eighteenth-century rationalism" (pp. 228, 246) and his materialism, a form of eighteenth-century mechanical materialism—with contemporary metaphysical or ideological conceptions (as is obvious from his nominalist understanding of language) as well as "very old-fashioned" values "more characteristic of a pre-World War II European intelligentsia" (p. 256), and which can be made out in the "peculiar survival (in his writings) of an older conceptuality" (compared to the conceptuality to be found in Derrida) (p. 245), the concept of irony, for one, or, negatively, by what it is that his work seeks to undo or liquidate. Undoubtedly, Jameson's account points suggestively at the idiosyncrasy of de Man's work. But is it as uneven or contradictory as he seems to hold? de Man's materialism is after all a linguistic materialism and, as such, not at all in contradiction with his nominalist, immanentist conception of language. Finally, if the values that this materialist conception of language seeks to undo appear strangely obsolete, is it not because they represent inappropriate expectations to which no philosophy, or poetics, for that matter, could seriously lay claim?

23. For a detailed discussion of Heidegger's claim that the original meaning of *phenomenology* implies a thinking that is tautological, see Jean-François Courtine, "Phenomenology and/or Tautology," in *Reading Heidegger: Commemorations,* ed. J. Sallis (Bloomington: Indiana University Press, 1993), pp. 240–257.

24. de Man distinguishes thus two sets of entirely heterogeneous principles, one for language, the other for the phenomenal world. Knowledge, strictly speaking, is possible only of the world, and it is nonlinguistic. Language does not tell us anything about it. Of language we have only the certainty, and it is an *a priori* certainty for de Man, that it "is a reliable source of information about . . . its own language" (*RT,* p. 11). Consequently, there is a kind of knowledge by language about language. But it is "a negative knowledge," de Man insists, one about language's lack of relating to anything but its own elements.

25. In the preface to a volume of essays by de Man in German translation and in which Christoph Menke elaborates in some detail on de Man's contention that literature and the theory of literature are a significant tool in the unmasking of ideological mystifications, in order to demarcate de Man's conception from Marxist forms of ideology critique, Menke remarks that without surrendering the possibility of criticism, de Man renounces the expectation that opposites can be reconciled. He writes: "The criticism of *one* side that has ideologically been rendered absolute develops a dialectic between what has been separated, and which recalls the existence of the *other* side, without ever being able to bring both sides together. Indeed, the articulation of each side is subject to the law of an inevitable dissimulation: both sides of the divide cannot be thought at once and together, because to think one is to necessarily dissimulate the other. Yet not for the trivial reason that both cannot be thought simultaneously, but because they cannot be thought *together.*" Menke sees the ideology critical thrust of de Man's position in this refusal of all integration (Christoph Menke, "'Unglückliches Bewusstsein,' Literatur und Kritik bei Paul de Man," in Paul de Man, *Die Ideologie des Ästhetischen,* ed. C. Menke [Frankfurt/ Main: Suhrkamp, 1993], p. 289).

26. As Jameson has noted, "de Man's work is unique among that of modern critics and theorists in its ascetic repudiation of pleasure, desire, and the intoxication of the sensory," which he extends to the question of artistic *Schein,* assigning it "the negative status of aesthetic ideology and falsehood or bad faith" (Jameson, *Postmodernism,* pp. 254–255).

27. Here a redoubtable question arises: Indeed, if language bears no substantial relationship to the mundane world and if such relations are merely of the making of language itself, on what basis and according to what criteria can

one know that language and the world remain separate? If cognition is limited to the phenomenal world and proceeds as well only by dint of equally phenomenal abilities, on the one hand, and, on the other, the epistemological thrust of language is merely negative, what kind of knowledge is it that permits the recognition of the difference?

28. It must, however, be noted that "arbitrary" and "conventional" are not necessarily identical terms for de Man. In the critical discussion of Speech Act Theory, toward the end of the essay "The Resistance to Theory," de Man, after having claimed that "the characterization of the performative as sheer convention reduces it in effect to a grammatical code among others," writes: "The performative power of language can be called positional, which differs considerably from conventional" (*RT,* p. 19). Even though speech act theorists speak of "convention" to describe the perfomative function of language in terms that are "not only not dependent on any form of phenomenalism but on any form of cognition as well" (*RT,* p. 18), "convention," which implies consensus, agreement, solidarity, etc., is still profoundly ideological for de Man. Calling the performative power of language "positional," he stresses its power to disrupt conventions, and thus valorizes the performative power of language's arbitrariness.

29. In all fairness to Aristotle, it must be noted that if, in *Rhetoric,* analogy is the metaphor *par excellence,* the analogical displacement that characterizes it is itself only an effect of mimesis. Mimesis itself, however, is not a rhetorical category.

30. Indeed, if a potentiality would immediately, and always, turn into action, it could not be distinguished from the act to begin with. See Aristotle, *Metaphysics,* in *The Complete Works of Aristotle,* ed J. Barnes (Princeton: Princeton University Press, 1984), vol. II (1652), 1046*a,* p. 32. See also in this context, Giorgio Agamben who in *Bartleby ou la création* (Saulxures: Circé, 1995), pp. 15f., situates Bartleby's repeated statements, "I would prefer not to," within the context of Aristotle's doctrine on potentiality and its prolongation by his Islamic disciples, thus interpreting the scrivener's replies to all requests as the "*restitutio in integrum* of possibility, one that maintains it in equilibrium between occurring and non-occuring, between the power to be and the power not to be" (p. 74).

31. de Man writes: "As most philosophers well know, the very concept of certainty, which is the basis of all concepts, comes into being only in relation to sensory experience be it, as in Hegel, as unmediated assurance, or, as in Descartes, as reflected delusion" (*RT,* p. 48).

32. Michel Foucault, *The Order of Things: An Archeology of the Human Sciences* (New York: Vintage Books, 1973), pp. 240–241.

33. As Lutz Ellrich and Nikolaus Wegmann have argued, by breaking with the

habitual reference quantities, such as the idea that an interpretation has to pinpoint a universal truth or that the subjective intention of the author or reader sets the standards for interpretation, the truth claims of de Man's readings must inevitably be based on the internal coherence and necessity of reading ("Theorie als Verteidigung der Literatur? Eine Fallgeschichte: Paul de Man," *Deutsche Vierteljahresschrift für Literaturwissenschaft und Geistesgeschichte,* vol. 64, no. 3, [1990], p. 475).

34. For their discussion of parts of this chapter at the DFG sponsored symposium in 1995, "Poststrukturalismus: Herausforderung an die Literaturwissenschaft," in Steinheim (Germany), I would like to mention David Wellbery and Lutz Ellrich and take the opportunity to thank them here for their interventions. Wellbery compressed the main arguments of this chapter into three theses: (1) that de Man accuses philosophical and literary aesthetics of giving in to a naturalist (or Cratylian) semantics; (2) that, for de Man, linguistic reference is exclusively intralinguistic and therefore unable ever to refer to anything other than itself; and (3) that de Man's theory rests on a presumed dualism between language and the empirical (cognizable) world. These three central points of de Manean thought, Wellbery argued, are critical points: (1) since to attribute a Cratylian ideology to aesthetics is to measure philosophy up to inappropriate expectations, a position that no philosopher has ever seriously upheld; (2) since reference is not simply a linguistic function and since such an assumption leads, moreover, to absurd epistemological consequences; and (3) in that de Man cannot provide any criterion for the presumed radical distinction between language and reality. After having recognized that these three theses are, indeed, intimately interlinked, Ellrich argues that were they acknowledged and understood as theoretical propositions or (even worse) as philosophical statements, the theses in question would make de Man's position a thoroughly untenable one. In order to ward off such a disastrous consequence, Ellrich suggested that one might interpret the three theses in a different way; not understand them as theoretical assertions but rather translate them into strategical instructions for reading. Thus translated and confined to mere directions for reading, the three theses would read as follows: First, the Cratylian elements within the intricate weave of the text's meaning-formation—which occurs by way of (metonymic) meaning-displacement—could be defined as those (purely) literal elements that are to be looked for in reading and that, because of their manifest identification of sign and meaning, resist text-contextualization and hence interrupt the metonymical chain of meaning-formation. Second, rather than holding that linguistic reference is in general intralinguistic, thesis 2 instructs the reader of texts to consider all (intra-) textual reference to an outside of the text (its theme)

as exclusively a means for the text to thematize itself—its own structure and its own status as text—and not as the generation of any particular meaning about specific things or events outside the text. Finally, as a strategy for reading texts, the Manichaean assumption of a divide between language and a prelinguistic world could possibly be translated into an imperative to clearly differentiate, within texts, between the always self-deconstructing linguistic meaning-formation and the overdetermination of meaning (intent on blackening out meaning's self-destruction) by way of a recourse to sensible evidence that remains inaccessible to language. Ellrich's suggestive retranslation of the main assumptions and presuppositions that I take to inform de Man's thinking deserves a lengthy and meticulous discussion that, in the present context, I cannot even hope to begin. A few remarks, signposts for a future debate, must therefore suffice. When they are restricted to strategies for reading, the three theses indeed lose much of their outrageousness. Nor do they any longer threaten to render suspect the very mode of argumentation that produces such claims. But, I would ask, since strategies are functions of desired goals, what is the telos of such a reading? Is the goal set by the three instructions for reading compatible with what de Man explicitly demands of reading? Does it aim at something other, or does it, in the end, not rejoin the untenable claims de Man makes about reading? As to Ellrich's retranslation of the three theses, I limit myself to the following remarks. The goal of reading in de Man is to show that what interrupts texts are instances in which it is, precisely, the Cratylian suture of sign and meaning that fails. Cratylian elements, according to de Man, are not elements of subversion in the weave of a text but rather make up the texts that philosophical aesthetics seeks to weave and are thus what a reading is supposed to subvert. Undoubtedly, de Man often refers to the text (and language) in the terms of an entity that knows itself and offers only knowledge about itself. But I hope I have shown in this chapter that the implications of a purely intralinguistic nature of all reference are not only that language, and for that matter texts, do not tell us anything about the world but that they also prevent us from *knowing* anything about them. Finally, I would ask: Can de Man's assumption of an unbridgeable gap between language and world be reduced to an effect of the meaning-formation of a text? Hardly, I would think, since de Man's point is not so much, as Ellrich seems to suggest, that linguistic meaning requires the nonlinguistic to cover over the deconstruction by which it is always structurally threatened, but that, ultimately, to say it plainly, meaning is not linguistic at all and that the linguistic is deconstructive of meaning only to the extent that it is expected to stand in its service in the first place. The gap that yawns between language and meaning is precisely the gap existing between language and the world.

35. Needless to say, such radical immanence of language's reference also means that it is hardly relational within itself anymore.

36. Even though admitting that "a perplexing development regarding the issue of the empirical may indeed have taken place in de Man's theoretical thinking" (p. 104), compared to his earlier, more phenomenological approach and in which he separated language and literature from empirical reality, Outi Pasanen has taken issue with my attempt to demarcate de Man and Derrida along the empirical-transcendental divide. (See Outi Pasanen, "Gasché on de Man and Derrida: Forgetting the Moment of Crisis," *Afterwords*, ed. N. Royle [Tampere, Finland: Outside Books, 1992]). Pasanen writes that the issue of the empirical "could be regarded [in my readings of how de Man and Derrida understand deconstruction] as the matrix which generates a polarization of the Derridean and the de Manian deconstructions into something more or less resembling philosophical-general and empirical-singular positions" (p. 96). Indeed, I hold that the distinction between the empirical and the transcendental can serve to account for the difference between the two approaches, however, on condition that both concepts are rethought in accordance with the works whose thrust they are to characterize. From what we have seen, de Man's critique of phenomenalism implies, of course, also a rejection of empiricism in its usual philosophical sense. If de Man himself speaks of the inevitably empirical, or pragmatic, aspect of reading, for instance, it is certainly not because he would privilege sense data as the source of knowledge. Indeed, as will become clear hereafter, the empirical, as understood by de Man, does not come without a certain generality, or ideality. Further, as the prefix *quasi*-affixed to *transcendental* insinuates, Derrida's concern with structures of ideality is not transcendentalist in any of the common understandings of that approach. The *quid juris* thematics of Derridean deconstruction is, indeed, intimately bound up with questions of singularity, occasionality, etc. Although I have emphasized this aspect of the infrastructures more forcefully in more recent work, it is already evident from the way infrastructures are shown to be crafted in *The Tain of the Mirror* (Cambridge: Harvard University Press, 1986).

37. Needless to say, this claim that language, at its most elementary, is rhetorical, rests, as Anselm Haverkamp has argued, "on one of the most radical revisions that the concept of rhetoric has undergone in this century." This revision, Haverkamp continues, is linked to de Man's reading of Nietzsche ("Figura Cryptica: Paul de Man und die Poetik nach Nietzsche," *Nietzsche oder 'Die Sprache ist Rhetorik'*, ed. J. Kopperschmidt and H. Schanze [Munich: Fink, 1994], pp. 241f.)

38. Apart from the fact that it is hard to see in what way the *trivium* could be characterized as the most general of all linguistic models or for whom it is

so familiar, scholars will find de Man's contention truly shocking, namely, that this specifically medieval conception of language and its arts, prevalent from the fifth to the fifteenth centuries, would continue to dominate not only during the sixteenth and seventeenth centuries on whose epistemology he draws to determine, for instance, the meaning of logic in the *trivium*—which, as the art of disputation, has very little in common with seventeenth century logic—but even contemporary semiotic and linguistic aproaches to literature (one example being Greimas). If one takes de Man to make a historical statement (and to some extent he does), the disregard for historical facts is truly upsetting. But what interests de Man in the *trivium* is restricted to something so general that, indeed, it is not specific to this historic conception at all and can easily be found everywhere. Basically, the only thing he retains of the *trivium,* in which, he holds, logic dominates grammar and rhetoric—which is, by the way, according to Roland Barthes, only the case from the eleventh to the fifteenth centuries (see *L'Aventure Sémiologique* [Paris: Seuil, 1985], p. 106)—is its opposition to the *quadrivium.* This allows him to assert that the model in question not only prioritizes the logical over the grammatical and the rhetorical functions of language but that it also ties the whole of language to the world and the natural sciences. Undoubtedly, such a conception of language is a most general one and familiar to the point of being trivial.

39. It is not correct to conflate geometry and the sciences of the world. It is primarily a science of ideal shapes, a purely formal discipline, which can, as the success of the natural sciences in the seventeenth century demonstrates, be applied to nature. In principle, geometry cannot, therefore, serve to demonstrate a connection between the science of language and the sciences of the world. But this does not simply mean that de Man's argument collapses altogether. Some verisimilitude can be restored to it if one recalls Husserl's elaborations in *The Crisis of European Sciences and Transcendental Phenomenology* on the ideality of geometry and formal mathematics. Geometry's ideality, Husserl argues, originates in the life-world. Only by becoming oblivious to its roots in the concerns of humanity could it be misconstrued as a purely abstract discipline. Its origins in the life-world must, he claims, be reactivated in order to return geometry to the sciences of the phenomenal world to which it belongs.

40. Is it necessary to point out that the difficulties de Man pinpoints among the disciplines that make up the *trivium* arise only if logic in the *trivium* is not understood in the singular medieval sense as *disputatio* whose object is not the world but logical conundrums such as the *insolubilia, impossibilia,* and *sophisamata,* but in the modern sense? But even then the questions remains in what sense dialectic and logic are to be understood. Indeed, if grammar

is said to be an isotope of logic or dialectic, it is quite decisive to specify how one is to take the latter. In addition to the obvious reference to Nietzsche's contention that grammar is metaphysics for the people, de Man's identification of logos and grammar seems also to echo the following statement from Heidegger (but not Heidegger's constructive attempt to free grammmar from Aristotelean logic): "The Greeks had no word for 'language'; they understood this phenomenon 'in the first instance' as discourse. But because the *logos* came into their philosophical ken primarily as assertion, *this* was the kind of *logos* which they took as their clue for working out the basic structures of the forms of discourse and its components. Grammar sought its foundations in the 'logic' of this *logos*. But this logic was based upon the ontology of the present-at-hand. The basic stock of 'categories of signification', which passed over into the subsequent science of language, and which in principle is still accepted as the standard today, is oriented towards discourse as assertion" (Martin Heidegger, *Being and Time*, trans. J. Macquarrie and E. Robinson [London: SCM, 1962], p. 209).

41. Ancient rhetoric distinguished quite clearly not only between tropes and figures (it is the oldest rhetorical distinction) but also between grammatical and rhetorical figures on the one hand, and, on the other, grammatical and rhetorical tropes. (For the distinctive criteria, see, for instance, Barthes, *L'Aventure Sémiologique,* p. 158). If there has been uncertainty, it concerned decisions about the rubric in which specific figures or tropes were to be classified.

42. Rather than an expedient to conclude an argument about the *trivium* with nondiscursive means, as I argue here (since de Man seems to find it difficult to argumentatively demonstrate an actual presence of the tension between grammar and rhetoric in the *trivium* itself), Cathy Caruth, in "The Claims of Reference," claims that de Man's reading of the title of Keats's poem "The Fall of Hyperion" at this precise point of his discussion of the *trivium* might be explained by the fact that toward the end of the seventeenth century the Newtonian discovery of the force of gravity put an end to the successful description by geometrical language of a phenomenal world thought to be governed entirely by motion. She writes: "For the world of simple motion was ended, once and for all, with the discovery, by Newton, of gravitational force, or the revolutionay notion . . . that objects fall toward each other . . . It could be said indeed, that with this assertion, the world of motion became, quite literally, a world of falling" (*Critical Encounters. Reference and Responsibility in Deconstructive Writing,* ed. C. Caruth and D. Esch [New Brunswick, N.J.: Rutgers University Press, 1995], p. 93).

43. See, for example, Roman Jakobson, "Linguistics and Poetics," in *The Struc-*

turalists from Marx to Lévi-Strauss, ed. R. and F. DeGeorge (Garden City, N.Y.: Doubleday, 1972), pp. 89f.

44. "Since the poetic (as distinguished from aesthetic) structure has to do with the necessity of deciding whether a statement in a text is to be taken as a figure or *à la lettre,* it pertains to rhetoric" (*RT,* p. 67).

45. For a more detailed discussion of de Man's understanding of chiasm, see my "Reading Chiasms: An Introduction," in Andrzej Warminski, *Readings in Interpretation* (Minneapolis: University of Minnesota Press, 1987), pp. XVIII–XIX.

46. The relation between grammatical and rhetorical reading here sketched out, corresponds, of course, to the way de Man conceives of the relationship of hermeneutical and poetico-rhetorical reading. He writes: "One has to have 'read' a text in terms of poetics to arrive at a hermeneutic conclusion . . . But one also has to read it hermeneutically to 'understand' it as poetics." "Hermeneutics and poetics, different and distinct as they are, have a way of becoming entangled" (*RT,* p. 56). Yet such complementarity does not imply symmetry. For a good discussion of this "theorem of the asymmetrical complementarity" of hermeneutics and rhetorics, at the heart of de Manean deconstruction, see Harro Müller, "Hermeneutik oder Dekonstruktion? Zum Widerstreit zweier Interpretationsweisen," in *Ästhetik und Rhetorik:Lektüren zu Paul de Man,* ed. K. H. Bohrer (Frankfurt/Main: Suhrkamp, 1993), pp. 105–110.

47. For Husserl's reference to the "Faktum der Sprachen" (to "existent languages," as it has been translated), see *Logical Investigations,* trans. J. N. Findlay (New Jersey: Humanities Press, 1970), vol. I, p. 266. See also Derrida's comments on this issue at the beginning of *Speech and Phenomena: And Other Essays on Husserl's Theory of Signs,* trans. D. B. Allison (Evanston: Northwestern University Press, 1973), p. 4.

48. Edmund Husserl, *The Crisis of European Sciences and Transcendental Phenomenology,* trans. D. Carr (Evanston: Northwestern University Press, 1970), p. 143.

5. Giving to Read

1. Richard Klein, "The Blindness of Hyperboles: The Ellipses of Insight," *Diacritics,* 3 (1973), p. 34.

2. One such attempt has been made by Lutz Ellrich and Nikolaus Wegmann. Although quite penetrating, as far as de Man is concerned, their comparison, inevitably, takes place to Derrida's disavantage. Indeed, despite the authors' reservations regarding Habermas's reception of Derrida, the authors—who present Derrida's work as divided between a (positive)

philosophical part, characterized as a theory of the *aporia* of signification, and a playful and artistic part, intent on translating the philosophical theory into an immediate experience with language, which instead of enhancing the theoretical insights, undercuts them in self-deconstruction—remain indebted to Habermas's (and Rorty's) reductive appraisal of Derrida's thought ("Theorie als Verteidigung der Literatur? Eine Fallgeschichte: Paul de Man," *Deutsche Vierteljahrsschrift für Literaturwissenschaft und Geistesgeschichte,* vol. 64, no. 3 [1990]. See, in particular, pp. 495–499).

3. Klein, "The Blindness of Hyperboles," pp. 39–42.

4. Jacques Derrida, *Dissemination,* trans. B. Johnson (Chicago: University of Chicago Press, 1981), pp. 61–171.

5. Jesper Svenbro, *Phrasikleia: Anthropologie de la Lecture en Grèce Ancienne* (Paris: Éditions de la Découverte, 1988), pp. 72–73, 223.

6. This understanding of reading is neither unique in Derrida's thought nor limited to his earlier work. In *Aporias,* to take this more recent text, his reading of Heidegger's elaborations on death consist of "filtering into" *(filtrer dans),* or "weaving into [as T. Dutoit translates] the existential analysis death" the concept of *possibility* as guided by the rule of the "title and what accompanies it (*Aporias,* Dying—awaiting (one another at) 'the limits of truth' [*S'attendre aux "limites de la vérité"*])." In short, the semantic possibilities of the French idiomatic expression "s'attendre à" serve to bring out, and render intelligible, a number of implications in the concept of possibility that is at the heart of Heidegger's thinking about death (Jacques Derrida, *Aporias,* trans. T. Dutoit [Stanford: Stanford University Press, 1993], p. 62).

7. Edmund Husserl, *The Crisis of European Sciences and Transcendental Phenomenology,* trans. D. Carr (Evanston: Northwestern University Press, 1970), p. 105.

8. Derrida, *Of Grammatology,* p. 158.

9. Ibid., pp. 163–164. In a shrewd attempt to elicit the precise point at which de Man, in "The Rhetoric of Blindness: Jacques Derrida's Reading of Rousseau" *(BI,* pp. 102–141), disagrees with Derrida's conception of reading, Wlad Godzich has shown that the point of contention concerns not so much Derrida's claim that Rousseau is blind to his own textuality but rather what de Man is silent about, namely, "the guiding principle of Derrida's meditation upon reading: production" (pp. 182–183). Whereas such production by which the blind spot of a text becomes accessible to knowledge is for Derrida the sole condition under which deconstruction can have a bearing on logocentrism, for de Man it is "to still hold out for a possibility of undeceived language" (p. 188). The price de Man pays for his own radicality, Godzich suggests, is that his understanding risks reproducing

what Derrida calls "the gesture of self criticism in philosophy in its internal tradition" ("Ja, ou le faux-bond," *Digraphe*, 11 [1977], p. 117). It must remain content to operate on texts alone. In addition, de Man's selective silence about production and, consequently, the interventionist thrust of deconstruction allow him to advance "ironically a reading of Derrida to which Derrida can only assent" (p. 182). This, however, Godzich argues, amounts to nothing less than a taming of Derrida. ("The Domestication of Derrida, in Wlad Godzich, *The Culture of Literacy* [Cambridge: Harvard University Press, 1994]). For additional aspects of de Man's debate with Derrida in "The Rhetoric of Blindness," see also Suzanne Gearhart, "Philosophy *before* Literature: Deconstruction, Historicity, and the Work of Paul de Man," *Diacritics*, 4 (1983), pp. 74–79.

10. Even though Derrida sustains his claim that the *logos* is an inverted, good *pharmakon,* an antidote, through references to the *Critias* and *Charmides,* some philologists have objected to this on the basis that it "does not deal with Plato's actual direct meaning." See, for instance, Jacqueline de Romilly, "Plato and Conjuring," in *Plato: True and Sophistic Rhetoric,* ed K. V. Erickson (Amsterdam: Rodopi, 1979), p. 162.

11. Needless to say, one could have here discussed how philosophy relates to sophistry, to mythology, to the nonphilosophical in general, distinctions that are all intraphilosophical.

12. "Language can also be compared to a sheet of paper: thought is the front and the sound the back; one cannot cut the front without cutting the back at the same time" (Ferdinand de Saussure, *Course in General Linguistics,* trans. W. Baskin [New York: McGraw-Hill, 1966], p. 113).

13. "How can we set off in search of a different guard, if the pharmaceutical 'system' contains not only, in a single stranglehold, the scene in the *Phaedrus,* the scene in the *Republic,* the scene in the *Sophist,* and the dialectic, logic, and mythology of Plato, but also, it seems, certain non-Greek structures of mythology? And if it is not certain that there are such things as non-Greek 'mythologies'—the opposition *mythos/logos* being only authorized *following* Plato—into what general, unnamable necessity are we thrown? In other words, what does Platonism signify as repetition?" (*D,* pp. 167–168).

6. Adding Oddities

1. For a succinct formulation (based on a discusion of de Man's essay "Semiology and Rhetoric" in *Allegories of Reading*) of the principle of mere reading, see Andrzej Warminski, "Ending Up/Taking Back," in *Critical Encounters: Reference and Responsibility in Deconstructive Writing,* ed. C. Caruth and D. Esch (New Brunswick, N.J.: Rutgers University Press, 1995), pp. 18–19.

2. I am responding here to Wlad Godzich's suggestion that "rhetoric, as a mode of language, accommodates itself to the human finitude" (Wlad Godzich, *The Culture of Literacy* [Cambridge: Harvard University Press, 1995], p. 157).

3. In distinction from Werner Hamacher, who in his introduction to the German translation of *Allegories of Reading*, characterizes the language of allegory as the rhetoric of an ontology of finite being, and irony, in which even the negative knowledge of allegory is dismantled, as "the most radical linguistic form of finitude and of the impossibility of underwriting the subject," I do not believe it still to be possible to conceive of de Man's notion of language of terms of finitude, unless "finitude" is entirely rethought (Werner Hamacher, "Unlesbarkeit," in Paul de Man, *Allegorien des Lesens* [Frankfurt/Main: Suhrkamp, 1988], pp. 11–12).

4. Paul de Man, "Forward," to Carol Jacobs, *The Dissimulating Harmony* (Baltimore: The Johns Hopkins University Press, 1978), p. xi.

5. Jacques Derrida, *Of Grammatology,* trans. G. C. Spivak (Baltimore: The Johns Hopkins University Press, 1976), p. 162.

6. For a fine discussion of the question of the specificity of literature, see David Martyn, "Die Autorität des Unlesbaren. Zum Stellenwert des Kanon in der Philologie Paul de Mans," in *Ästhetik und Rhetorik: Lektüren zu Paul de Man,* ed. K. H. Bohrer (Frankfurt/Main: Suhrkamp, 1993), pp. 20f.

7. Friedrich Nietzsche, "On Truth and Falsity in their Ultramoral Sense," *The Complete Works of Friedrich Nietzsche,* vol. II, ed. O. Levy (New York: Russell and Russell, 1964), p. 180.

8. Ibid., p. 180.

9. Ibid., p. 183.

10. In this context, also see de Man's statement that only in the hands of philologists (such as Roman Jakobson and Roland Barthes) was structural linguistics transformed into a theory of literature, in other words, into a rigorous theory of language (*RT,* pp. 8–9).

11. Is anthropomorphism a figure after all that assumes something prior to language? And thus grounds the continuity of word and thing that grammar and logic presuppose?

12. If I wish to refer the reader here to John Guillory's very convincing discussion in *Cultural Capital: The Problem of Literary Canon Formation* (Chicago: University of Chicago Press, 1993) of de Man's assimilation in *Allegories of Reading* of synecdoche and metaphor, it is because the thematism on which Guillory shows this operation to rest not only explains why "the names of the tropes are in de Man's reading [so very detached] from their conventional significations in rhetoric" (p. 226) but especially because, as I believe, this implicit thematism accounts for the so very abstractness of the de Manean tropes. As Guillory demonstrates, it is only because "the concepts

of identity, totality, and necessity have already been imputed to metaphor as its defining attributes," even though these concepts "do not describe in any general way the properties of metaphor" (p. 225)—in other words, it is because *metaphor* had been reduced to a theme and has been made to *mean* necessity that de Man can at all proceed to the interpolation in question. Guillory concludes: "What de Man called the 'metafigural' level of the text was never anything other than a preexistent thematic, now superimposed upon the figural language of the text" (p. 227).

13. It may seem a bit surprising that de Man excludes the possibility that the reference to *army* could mean that Nietzsche conceived of the tropes as troops in a battle against error. Truth, de Man holds (in what is rather a debatable opinion), stands neither in critical philosophy nor in Nietzsche (since the latter's text has already been termed a "late Kantian text") in a relation of opposition to error. "No such dichotomy exists in any critical philosophy, let alone Nietzsche's . . . Whatever truth may be fighting, it is not error but stupidity," he writes (*RR*, p. 242). Could de Man here refer to the following passage in Kant: "Deficiency in judgment is just what is ordinarily called stupidity, and for such a failing there is no remedy. An obtuse or narrowminded person to whom nothing is wanting save a proper degree of understanding and the concepts appropriate thereto, may indeed be trained through study, even to the extent of becoming learned. But as such people are commonly still lacking in judgment . . ., it is not unusual to meet learned men who in the application of their scientific knowledge betray that original want, which can never be made good" (Immanuel Kant, *Critique of Pure Reason*, trans. N. Kemp Smith [New York: St. Martin's Press, 1965], p. 178)? If yes, it must, however, be remarked that stupity does not stand in a relation to truth but to correct judgment.

14. See *Webster's New Collegiate Dictionary*.

15. de Man writes: "As in 'confuses paroles' and 'symboles' in the opening lines, the stress on language as the stage of disjunction is unmistakable" (*RR*, p. 245).

16. For a fine discussion of de Man's (ambivalent) relation to Romanticism, see Cynthia Chase, "Literary Theory As the Criticism of Aesthetics: De Man, Blanchot, and Romantic 'Allegories of Cognition,'" in *Critical Encounters: Reference and Responsibility in Deconstructive Writing*, eds. C. Caruth and D. Esch (New Brunswick, N.J.: Rutgers University Press, 1995), pp. 44f.

17. Indeed, could it not be that the anthropomorphic reading is made possible and necessary by an inherent flaw in tropological substitution that gives anthropomorphism a constitutive role to play in the poem's effort to bring about a unity of spirit and body? Or could it not be that, even though it interrupts the chain of substitutions which hereto seemed to guarantee the

sonnet's unequivocal success, anthropomorphic figuration is required at one particular point to complete the project?

18. Needless to say, the analogy with the infinite multiplication of numbers is a reference to Paul de Man's essay "Pascal's Allegory of Persuasion" in *Allegory and Representation,* ed. S. J. Greenblatt (Baltimore: The Johns Hopkins University Press, 1981), pp. 1–25.

19. It is useful to recall here de Man's definition of *rupture* in the Pascal essay: "A rupture or a disjunction, is not to be thought of as a negation, however tragic it may be. Negation . . . is always susceptible of being reinscribed in a system of intelligibility. Nor can we hope to map it out as one *topos* among *topoi,* as would be the case with regular tropes of substitution. It is possible to find, in the terminology of rhetoric, terms that come close to designating such disruptions (e.g., *parabasis* or *anacoluthon*), which designate the interruption of a semantic continuum in a manner that lies beyond the power of reintegration" ("Pascal's Allegory of Persuasion," *Allegory and Representation,* ed. S. J. Greenblatt [Baltimore: The Johns Hopkins University Press, 1981], p. 12).

20. See Jean Chevalier and Alain Gheerbrant, *Dictionnaire des Symboles* (Paris: Robert Laffont/Jupiter, 1982), pp. 29 and 403.

21. Jacques Derrida, "The *Retrait* of Metaphor," trans. F. Gasdner et al., *Enclitic,* vol. 2, no. 2 (Fall 1978), pp. 5–6.

22. As in his analysis of the opening line of Shelley's *Triumph of Life,* in *Shelley Disfigured,* de Man presupposes here that the whole linguistic exercise of "Correspondances" consists in the failed attempt to recuperate what happens in the positing event of the opening statement read as a manifestation of the autonomous positing power of language. It is in this sense that the following sentence is to be read: "The epistemological, aesthetic, and poetic language of transports or of tropes, which is the theme though not singly the rhetoric of this poem, can never say nor, for that matter, sing or understand the opening statement: 'La Nature est un temple'" (*RR,* p. 252).

23. Is it farfetched at all to suggest that this reciprocal reading of two sonnets by Baudelaire resembles in some regards what Derrida has undertaken in *Glas,* namely, to confront a philosophical and a literary text? Among the many differences, on which a patient comparison between de Man's essay and Derrida's work would have to linger, I mention only the significant fact that the confrontation serves de Man to argue for the undoing of philosophy under the form of Romantic literature at the hands of language and to show such undoing to take place within literature itself. If the comparison is meaningful, and holds up, it would be a way to demonstrate that notwithstanding numerous rapprochements, de Man's objections to Derrida are in this late text still the same as in "The Rhetoric of Blindness."

24. To explain the difference between the two poems in terms of historical periods is "more convenient than legitimate" (*RR*, p. 254), de Man holds, because "such a historicizing pattern, a commonplace of aesthetic theory, is a function of the aesthetic ideologization of linguistic structures rather than an empirical historical event" (*RR*, p. 253). de Man's argument is this: The classification of "Correspondances" as a Parnassian, neoclassical poem and "Obsession" as a specimen of nineteenth-century lyric Romanticism brings to light an underlying complementarity between the two poems. Because of its "symbolic 'depth'" that makes up for "Correspondances"'s loss of "personal expressiveness" as a classical poem, it has been viewed as a forerunner of symbolism. Although a classical poem, it is intrinsically symbolic. The poem "Obsession," by contrast, as a modern poem, is totally self-conscious, and it is romantic. But even though symbolist art is only a variety of Romanticism, Romantic art is symbolic to the core. This implicit symbolism of (neo-)classical art, and of symbolist Romantic art as well, is indicative, for de Man, of an understanding of art as symbolic in general. This conception of art, which de Man associates with Hegel (for a more detailed discussion of this identification, see Chapter 2, "In-difference to Philosophy"), is itself rooted in the linguistic structure of symbolism particular to poetic language in general. In conclusion, to distinguish the two poems in terms of the classical and the romantic is to conceive of their relationship itself as a symbol: "The two sonnets complement each other like the two halves of a *symbolon*" (*RR*, pp. 253–254).

25. And, if the same is true for all historical distinction as well, as de Man intimates in his discussion of situating the difference between the two poems in historical terms (see Note 24), one can only wonder whether mere reading has any means at all to assess the singularity of texts.

26. Friedrich Schlegel, *Dialogue on Poetry and Literary Aphorisms*, ed. E. Behler and R. Struc (University Park: Pennsylvania State University Press, 1968), p. 54.

27. Returning to his analysis of the two Baudelaire poems in "Aesthetic Formalization: Kleist's *Über das Marionettentheater*," de Man notes that "the processes of anthropomorphism and naturalization . . . guarantee the intelligibility of tropes" (*RR*, p. 266).

28. The metaphoricity of light has indeed dominated the Western conception of knowledge, but is that reason enough to invoke this conception each time one encounters light imagery? In evoking a light that speaks a known language, Baudelaire states only this language's intelligibility, and not that it itself produces knowledge.

29. In "Reading and History," for example, de Man speaks at one point of the "specular (that is to say solar and phenomenal) conception of a 'poetry of

poetry,' the self-referential text that thematizes its own invention, prefigures its own reception, and achieves, as aesthetic cognition and pleasure, the recovery from the most extreme alienations" (*RT*, p. 69).

30. Paradoxically, understanding itself might thus be the surest mode of undermining the union of the aesthetic and the epistemological.

31. Ruminants are classified among the pure animals. See *Leviticus*, 11, 3, and *Deuteronomy*, 14, 6.

32. de Man's talk of history in this context (but on other occasions as well) is rather elliptical. As the evocation of a "materiality of actual history," or of the "*historical* modes of language power," shows, history here is especially a name for the sudden emergence of linguistic events, but also for the actual historical event understood as *stigme,* the emphasis lying on the irreducibly unintelligible and punctual nature of what happens. In order to appreciate what is specific about this concept of history and what its import is, it would be necessary to first distinguish it in all rigor from Heideggerian *Geschichtlichkeit* (of *Dasein,* in particular, of *Ereignis*), and Derrida's notion of a future-to-come (*à-venir*), and the openness to the always possible that it implies.

33. For a more detailed discussion of the nature of the criticism in question, its affinity to what de Man calls "mere reading," and Friedrich Schiller's and the Schlegel brothers' response to it, see my essay "Under the Heading of Theory," *Institutions in Cultures: Theory and Practice,* ed. R. Lumsden and R. Patke (Amsterdam: Rodopi, 1996), pp. 118ff.

34. Taking up de Man's characterization of science, John Guillory notes that this characterization "marks rhetorical reading as the latest development of *anti*rhetorical epistemology firmly grounded in the discourses of early modernism, where a polemic against tropes was indeed a programmatic feature of scientific discourse formation" (*Cultural Capital,* p. 220). If indeed, rhetorical reading can be said to continue in a certain way the positivist agenda of a critique of metaphysics, it is because the rhetorical reading concept of rhetoric and trope is no longer that of the tradition.

Appendix: On the Edges

1. Geoffry H. Hartman, *Minor Prophecies: The Literary Essay in the Culture Wars* (Cambridge: Harvard University Press, 1991), p. 125.

2. Is it not remarkable that *Le Soir,* in an article of December 3, 1987, had to call upon the *The New York Times,* in which the first article on de Man's wartime journalism appeared on December 1, 1987, to get its facts straight? But not only is the initial reporting on the de Man affair in question, based as it was on at best a good dozen of the usually very short pieces

that he wrote in the early forties. At issue is the whole media coverage of
the case not only in North America but elsewhere as well, including countries where the name of Paul de Man was not known at all. In the first
article of *The New York Times,* de Man came under scrutiny by virtue of the
fact that he had published in the collaborationist *Le Soir* between 1940 and
1942 and for a single piece—"Les juifs dans la littérature actuelle"—of that
publication and one single sentence of that piece. That first reporting, its
limited documentation (close to zero), and the judgment to which it led,
provided (perhaps unwittingly) the stereotype for all subsequent reports,
and judgments of the case in the process of the extraordinary internation-
alization of the affair whose critical history still needs to be written. Although journalists, to name only Jon Wiener (*The Nation*), David Lehman
(*Newsweek*), Walter Kendrick (*The Village Voice Literary Supplement*),
Frank Schirrmacher (*Frankfurter Allgemeine Zeitung*) went one better than
The New York Times, their articles only raised the tone and the stakes set in
The New York Times, without feeling the slightest need to refine the docu-
mention. Finally, do the reviews of David Lehman's *Signs of the Times:
Deconstruction and the Fall of Paul de Man* in a number of newspapers not
clearly establish that in the de Man case, anyone who wanted to jump into
the fray had merely to read others who had pretended to have read de Man?
What can explain the ease with which the critics excused themselves from
the task of reading the texts themselves (and of informing themselves about
the situation in Belgium during the war years)? Why do they show no signs
of any ethical stress? Does the nature of the accusation (collaboration with
the Nazis, anti-Semitism) *per se* absolve the critics, whether journalists or
academics, from any obligation to verify the facts, that is, from reading the
incriminating material itself, and in its entirety? Or is it the label "deconstruction" associated with the name of de Man sufficient to justify such
negligence? In any event, the judgments made have been made on the basis
of what others claimed to have read, that is, resting on mere summaries of
the content of one article, or a few rudimentary quotes. Some of these
judgments even repeated the errors present in their sources.

3. "Is it a surprise that the really incriminating evidence against de Man—
   signing on to Hitler's Europe—was left unanalyzed while the journalists
   talked about what really exercized them—the incomprehensibility of deconstruction and the nihilism of de Man's views of literature? Certainly
   Lehman's long book devotes very few pages to Nazism; it became a side
   issue, a mere mote in the eyes of the attacking journalists and the many
   humanists who joined them, compared to the offensive beam in the eye
   that was the teaching of Chairman Paul" (Lindsay Waters, "Professah de
   Man—he dead," *American Literary History* [1995], p. 295).

4. See Samuel Weber's analysis in "The Monument Disfigured," *Responses: On Paul de Man's Wartime Journalism,* ed. W. Hamacher et al. (Lincoln: University of Nebraska Press, 1989), p. 405, of Walter Kendrick's article on the de Man affair in the *Village Voice Literary Supplement.*

5. Werner Hamacher, "Journals, Politics: Notes on Paul de Man's Wartime Journalism," *Responses: On Paul de Man's Wartime Journalism,* ed. W. Hamacher et al. (Lincoln: University of Nebraska Press, 1989), p. 463.

6. David Lehman's front cover essay in *The New York Times Book Review,* May 24, 1992, entitled "Paul de Man: The Plot Thickens," is a case in point: de Man, at one point, had been a bad tenant. For some other examples of overkill, see Waters, "Professah de Man—he dead," p. 294.

7. Primo Levi has termed "unnecessary violence" a violence that degrades its victim to the point that his or her prosecutor/judge/executioner (or murderer, in the *Lager*) can pretend to ignore the outrage of his or her own action (Primo Levi, *The Drowned and the Saved,* trans. R. Rosenthal [New York: Summit, 1988], pp. 125–126).

8. According to de Man's first wife. See Hamacher, "Journals, Politics," p. 461.

9. Hartman, *Minor Prophecies,* p. 148.

10. Jean-Luc Nancy, "Our History," *Diacritics,* Fall 1990, pp. 106, 110f.

11. Weber, "The Monument Disfigured," pp. 408f.

12. Nancy, "Our History," pp. 98–100.

13. Hamacher, "Journals, Politics," p. 440.

14. Hartman, *Minor Prophecies,* p. 140.

15. Jacques Derrida, "Like the Sound of the Sea Deep within a Shell: Paul de Man's War," trans. P. Kamuf, *Critical Inquiry,* 14 (Spring 1988), p. 640.

16. Hartman, *Minor Prophecies,* pp. 138–141.

17. Hamacher, "Journals, Politics," pp. 451–453.

18. Cathy Caruth, "The Claims of Reference," *Critical Encounters: Reference and Responsibility in Deconstructive Writing,* ed. C. Caruth and D. Esch (New Brunswick, N.J.: Rutgers University Press, 1995), p. 103.

19. Jürgen Fohrmann, "Misreadings Revisited. Eine Kritik de Konzepts von Paul de Man," *Ästhetik und Rhetorik: Lektüren zu Paul de Man,* ed. K. H. Bohrer (Frankfurt/Main: Suhrkamp, 1993), pp. 86–87.

20. Levi, *The Drowned and the Saved,* p. 44.

21. With the exception of the article from March 4, 1941, "Les juifs dans la littérature actuelle" (written shortly before leaving *Le Soir*), de Man does not seem to have been coerced into collaboration, nor does he seem even to have been tempted by Nazi ideology itself. But his own Belgicist agenda could certainly tolerate it to a certain point. In the end, I believe de Man's collaboration to have been motivated more by opportunism and careerism.

22. All references to these writings are to Paul de Man, *Wartime Journalism:*

1939–1943, eds. W. Hamacher et al. (Lincoln: University of Nebraska Press, 1988).

23. Jacques Derrida, "Like the Sound of the Sea Deep Within a Shell: Paul de Man's War," *Critical Inquiry,* vol. 14, no. 3 (Spring 1988), pp. 621ff.; Richard Bernstein, "Critics Attempt to Reinterpret a Colleague's Disturbing Past," *The New York Times,* July 17, 1988, E6.

24. Jon Wiener, "Deconstructing de Man," *The Nation,* vol. 246, no. 1 (January 9, 1988), pp. 22–24.

25. On this point I disagree with Geoffrey Hartman's otherwise lucid article "Blindness and Insight," *The New Republic,* March 7, 1988, pp. 26–31.

26. The page references that appear throughout the rest of the Appendix refer to Paul de Man, *Wartime Journalism: 1939–1943,* and extend to all the quotes that follow until a new page reference is given.

27. On two other occasions at least, de Man speaks positively of German expressionism. In light of what I am developing here regarding "A View on Contemporary German Fiction," from August 20, 1942, it is in particular the article "Un Roman allemand, *Loups parmi les Loups,* de Hans Fallada" (*Le Soir,* September 16, 1941), that must be mentioned. In this article, in which de Man demarcates expressionism as a whole from "the truly German way" of writing (characteristic of writers whom he criticizes rather sharply in other reviews), he justifies expressionism's excesses and deformations, monstrosities and hypertrophies, as resulting, according to "the imperious law of evolution," from the attempt to rejuvenate a concept of reality "around which more than half a century of artistic life was centered." Expressionism, he claims, "illustrates the end of a development that has exhausted its last resources." But although it "constitutes a true theoretization of this decadence," and although its works of art "are more remarkable as phenomena than as artistic achievements properly speaking" (which implies that its artistic "production was not of the first order"), such "degeneracy" is *not* to be considered pejorative. The law according to which it takes place is imperative as seen, and "one has seen masterpieces originating in such moments." And he concludes that "to belong to such a generation cannot serve as a pretext for passing a definite sentence on an artist." But the other text, "André Lhote, *Peinture d'abord,*" *Bibliographie Dechenne,* August 1942, p. 20, is remarkable as well, and I will quote it almost in its entirety: "He, André Lhote, has made himself the protagonist of a tendency that is fully opposed to the traditions of conventional realism. At the basis of his ideas you find the following condition that 'in order for a painting to reach truth, it can express it only with the help of particular, that is to say, deforming means.' This apparent paradox is constitutive of the whole originality and importance of the expressionists. By bringing this

question up again for discussion, a particularly authoritative and intelligent voice has come to express its support in favor of a theory whose present eclipse is perhaps infinitely less advantageous *(heureuse)* than some seem to believe."

28. Hildegard Brenner, *Die Kunstpolitik des Nationalsozialismus* (Hamburg: Rowohlt, 1963), pp. 131ff.

29. His interests seem to go rather toward British literature, D. H. Lawrence and Charles Morgan, for instance, to whom, significantly enough, he compares Ernst Jünger at one point, who of the German writers he reviewed, is the only one he admired (see *Le Soir,* March 1, 1942).

30. See in this respect Jeffrey Mehlman's statement in David Lehman, "Deconstructing de Man's Life," *Newsweek,* February 15, 1988, pp. 63–64.

31. Let me mention here that one of de Man's favorite literary critics is Marcel Raymond (see *Het Vlaamsche Land,* June 7–8, 1942).

32. See Jacques Derrida, *Memoires for Paul de Man* (New York: Columbia University Press, 1986).

33. G. W. F. Hegel, *Grundlinien der Philosophie des Rechts, Werke in Zwanzig Banden,* vol. 7 (Frankfurt/Main: Suhrkamp Verlag, 1970), p. 127.

Index

305